GLOBAL MIXED RACE

D1431756

Global Mixed Race

Edited by
Rebecca C. King-O'Riain, Stephen Small, Minelle Mahtani,
Miri Song, and Paul Spickard

NEW YORK UNIVERSITY PRESS
New York and London

NEW YORK UNIVERSITY PRESS
New York and London
www.nyupress.org

© 2014 by New York University
All rights reserved

References to Internet websites (URLs) were accurate at the time of writing.
Neither the author nor New York University Press is responsible for URLs that
may have expired or changed since the manuscript was prepared.

Library of Congress Cataloging-in-Publication Data
Global mixed race / edited by Rebecca Chiyoko King-O'Riain and others.
pages cm
Includes bibliographical references and index.
ISBN 978-0-8147-7073-3 (hardback) — ISBN 978-0-8147-8915-5 (paper)
1. Racially mixed people—Case studies. I. King-O'Riain, Rebecca Chiyoko.
HT1523.G65   2014
305.8'05—dc23   2013039339

New York University Press books are printed on acid-free paper, and their binding materials
are chosen for strength and durability. We strive to use environmentally responsible
suppliers and materials to the greatest extent possible in publishing our books.

Manufactured in the United States of America
c 10 9 8 7 6 5 4 3 2 1
p 10 9 8 7 6 5 4 3 2 1

Also available as an ebook

ACC LIBRARY SERVICES AUSTIN, TX

CONTENTS

Global Mixed Race

An Introduction

STEPHEN SMALL AND REBECCA C. KING-O'RIAIN

US President Barack Obama is an international figure with a widely recognized multiracial and multinational history. He is also seen as perhaps the single most powerful "mixed-race" individual in the world.[1] However, his work as a community activist, his religious and social affiliations and his cultural activities, are clearly focused primarily on African Americans and Obama defines himself as African American—publicly, politically, and perhaps personally. At the same time, Obama talks openly about the fact that his father is Black and from Kenya and that his mother is White and from Kansas but that his mixed origins are not the most important component of his identity. So to what extent are Barack Obama's mixed origins of social significance if he doesn't identify himself as such? If people of mixed origins mobilize to highlight his mixed origins, should he be expected to respond? He is not the only person to downplay their mixed origins. Besides, historically, isn't everyone mixed? If so, then what is the big deal?

What is "mixed race" anyway? We use the term "mixed" in this book for people who feel they are descended from and attached to two or more socially significant groups. The term should be read with assumed scare quotes around it, to signify recognition of its socially bound nature. For simplicity's sake we do not use actual scare quotes throughout the text. We have capitalized *Black* and *White* throughout the book where the terms are applied to racialized groups, but have left them in lowercase when used as nonracial adjectives.

Global Mixed Race presents new, empirical data collected from around the world primarily from outside of the US. We use the North

American experiences and histories as a backdrop to assess the ways people of mixed descent identify, speak, defy, and bolster identities in other countries. We pay particular attention to the ways that these experiences help us think through how we see and engage with social differences such as the relationship between physical appearance and ethnicity (in Mexico), gender (in Trinidad and Tobago), or religious identity (in Kazakhstan). Do critical and comparative explorations of the experience of mixing undo meanings of race and challenge standard modernist categories of identity? Not always.

But should all people of mixed descent (usually defined as immediately descended from two racialized discrete and identifiable groups) be expected to identify as being mixed? Besides, what is the difference between mixed ethnicity and mixed race? How do tradition and power fit into the equation? We find answers from many different nations while keeping in mind the tragic and bloody colonial encounters across national boundaries (for example, transatlantic slavery) that have formed the foundations on which we have come to understand the multiracial experience in some places.

In *Global Mixed Race* we compare the status and identity of mixed people within a global framework in order to better understand how race, ethnicity, culture, class, and gender work in local and national contexts within a global world. We unpack how some of the concepts just mentioned get constructed, used, or thwarted in different contexts. In each chapter we ask: How has globalization and the role of the state (among other things) affected the mixed experience in each country or context and what are the similarities/differences across countries?

Mixed people have always existed, but what is new, we argue, is the expanding populations of mixed people, as well as the increasing recognition and visibility of mixed people and identities within contemporary societies. In particular, we highlight how mixed people have been used as emblems of multiculturalism—as "chic" and "new" and how those ideas are commodified (particularly on mixed-race bodies) within global capitalism while at the same time being seen as suspect because they are considered not pure or "inauthentic."[2]

While President Obama may not embrace or publicize his mixed origins, there are many other individuals and groups today that do. In South Africa, for example, people of mixed origins were able to carve for themselves a distinctive social and economic position in society, with privileges over people without mixed origins presumed to be "pure" Blacks. With vigorous endorsement by the dominant White power structure, mixed people became a buffer group between a small number of elite and powerful Whites, and a large number of exploited and oppressed Blacks.

People of mixed African and European origins across Brazil and the Caribbean also highlighted their mixed origins from the early days of colonial conquest. Evidence from surveys in the US and the UK indicate that, increasingly, people with mixed origins are far more likely to reject a monoracial identity and embrace a mixed identity.[3] There is similar evidence that this is true as well for people of mixed origins in Germany, the Netherlands, and France. In Asia, *haafu* celebrity actors, athletes, and musicians, like traditional *enka* singer *Jero* in Japan, also highlight their mixed origins.

However, many individuals of mixed origins hide their mixed background due to shame, guilt, or fear of persecution in Japan, Vietnam, and Malaysia. Why do some groups highlight their origins and others do not? What are the key factors that shape both individual and group identities of mixed origins? Some individuals and groups may see it as an advantage, often providing status, privilege, and resources, including legal rights. Others may see it as a disadvantage, having confronted stigma, discrimination, hostility, and persecution. Yet for others being mixed is neither a meaningful nor significant identity. But what drives these differences?

Mixing across the Globe or Global Mixed Race?

The nature and responses of mixing racialized and/or ethnic identities have varied tremendously in different parts of the world and within specific social contexts over time. In the US, interracial dating and marriage were once illegal and socially disdained by Whites, but at the same time, widely practiced clandestinely by White men; as a result, a population of mixed origins with distinct and prominent communities emerged across the southern US. Dramatic changes have resulted from the Civil Rights Movement, Black Power, and the Women's Movement.[4] Since the last laws against interracial marriage ended in 1967, patterns of residential and educational segregation changed significantly, and the social acceptance of people of mixed origins has increased dramatically across the nation.[5]

In Brazil, mixed-race people have been a major demographic group in the national identity for centuries.[6] Throughout the twentieth century, people of mixed descent most frequently distanced themselves from Brazil's Black population. And yet in recent decades, there is evidence that many of them are increasingly rejecting a mixed identity and embracing a Black identity. Much of this trend, we are told, has been shaped by significant influences on these groups from the United States, most notably the Black Power movement. Across other areas of Latin America—as well as in the Caribbean—populations of mixed origins have long occupied an intermediate position, with relative power of various kinds.[7]

In East Asia, where patterns have been different, people of mixed origins have often been rejected.[8] People of mixed descent who are products of the long Western military presence in Japan and Okinawa, or the presence of other ethnic groups such as Koreans in Japan, are often seen as problematic in Japanese society, which is based on a strong ideology of racial purity.[9] For many years, people of mixed descent in Japan were denied public recognition, since they did not have 100 percent Japanese ancestry or at times even Japanese family names and therefore could not attain Japanese citizenship.[10] With increased globalization, these patterns are changing.

Clearly then, racial, ethnic, religious, linguistic, and national mixing has been around for centuries.[11] It reflects patterns of power, migration, conquest, and colonization. In several key nations where significant numbers of people of mixed origins developed out of these interactions they have been studied for some time.[12] So if mixing has been around so long, what is new about it? And what does a book like this have to add to the analysis and debates?

A study of people of mixed origins across nations raises fascinating questions about the changing social construction of race, the changing social significance attached to mixed origins, and the changing relevance of biology and genetics. It raises questions about the role of individuals and the role of communities and institutions, and the ways in which social context (including laws, politics, and social acceptance) works to shape attitudes and behavior. This book places these processes in the context of the dramatic changes in nations across the world that have been created by the dizzying pace of international migration and globalization.

Why Globalization?

But what has been the impact of global forces on people of mixed descent? Is there a global mixed race? Globalization involves highly complex political, economic, and cultural dimensions. The movement of populations and the movement of ideas have deep racial and cultural dimensions including increased sexual contact; dating and marriages across racial, ethnic, and national boundaries; and far greater social acceptance and social circulation of ideas about mixing.

What are some of the dimensions of globalization that directly shape the experiences and expressed identities of people of mixed racial descent? One tenet of globalization is that alongside deterritorialization the processes described broadly as hybridity (seen as cultural, ethnic, and racial blending) are increasingly a defining characteristic of globalization.[13] With increasing hybridity, there has been an increasing social acceptance of mixed cultural identities (both individual and collective) across the world. This acceptance is far more common and far more widespread than in the past. Thus, the idea of having multiple allegiances to multiple racial or ethnic groups is more socially accepted, if unevenly expressed across national boundaries. We explore the contours, the social texture, and the cultural fabric of these patterns.

There has been massive population movement since the end of the Second World War. Large numbers of people have moved in search of work, others as students, still others as refugees. Thousands of workers are involved in foreign nations for humanitarian projects. Substantial numbers of men and women travel abroad for the far more dubious purposes of sex tourism. Many women migrate and settle in other nations to carry out care work or sex work.[14] International dating and marriage add another significant dimension to this mix. Gender shapes all these movements and relationships, as do racial and gender stereotypes such as the image of submissive, passionate, erotic Asian women, highly sexualized Brazilian or Caribbean women and powerful, independent, economically successful White men.[15]

Some people move long distances and stay permanently; others move short distances and commute back and forth. Whichever pattern prevails, new sexual, emotional, and marital relationships, including same sex relationships, have developed. Some of these movements have added new ethnic, national, and religious mixes to long-established populations. Other movements have introduced entirely new mixed populations to nations and contexts that typically represented themselves as monoracial.

In addition to the facts of migration, the social significance of being mixed is also affected more and more by the flow of racial ideas across the world. The frequency of interracial dating and marriage, the size and visibility of people of mixed racial origins, including celebrities, and the greater tendency to express pride in mixed-heritage backgrounds have all become far more visible—for example, in media (movies, television, music, magazines, and literature), online and web communications, censuses, conferences, and a wide range of academic studies. While most images in the past were created by people who are not of mixed origins, today more and more people of mixed origins are at the forefront of the production and dissemination of such images. For example, there are increasing numbers of images of race mixing in popular culture and we see relationships and people of mixed racial descent prominently normalized in movies and on television. There is also a growing interest in novels, poems, and memoirs written by people of mixed race[16] and many international beauty pageants are becoming dominated by women of mixed origins. The allure of mixed race has become chic and the marketing of "*Generation E.A.: Ethnically Ambiguous*" has become big money.[17] How are these images used to sell products and ideas premised on unrealistic ideas of multiculturalism? To what extent have mixed bodies been used to further neoliberal ideologies of choice and multiculturalism without tackling the lived experiences of marginalization and discrimination that people of mixed descent may encounter?

In online and web communications, issues of mixed-descent identity, experiences, and expressions are more and more common. Men seek women (sometimes of color) online to have sex, date, or enter into long-term relationships. Websites have been set up to celebrate mixed-race identity. Other websites increase contact across cities, regions, and nations and the use of webcam technology such as Skype has brought mixed families across the globe into closer communication with one another.[18] In all these areas of popular culture, ideas about mixedness are circulating internationally and globally and may become embedded in nation-state apparatuses through censuses, government policies, ideas, and ideologies about race that have traveled the globe.[19]

Another goal of *Global Mixed Race* is to raise the level of discussion about the interaction between long-established patterns of mixed-race interactions and identities, for example, in the context of conquest and colonization, and about new patterns of migration in an age of national independence, quotidian international jet travel, and the global network of media and communications now available. Globalization has expanded and speeded up processes of recognizing mixedness that were already well under way. Old and new patterns are clearly not identical, linear, or developmental. The forced contact and unrecognized social status for mixed people in places that experienced colonialism in the past are very different from newer patterns that involve far more voluntary, cosmopolitan, and socially accepted or even valorized patterns of mixing. But several things are distinctly new including the far greater contemporary flow of racial ideas and the growing tolerance and choice to identify as mixed. There is a unique mixed experience coming out of these patterns as state borders become more porous and people and ideas move around more quickly. One notable development is the way in which people of mixed origins are working together across national borders to organize social support, rights movements, and increasing media exposure to push back against state institutions that try to make them chose just one identity on passports, in racial/ethnic record keeping in schools, and for census enumeration.

Getting Out of the Box

Historically most research on mixed-race people has taken place in the United States. Secondary sites in terms of the volume of the literature include Latin America, the Caribbean, and the United Kingdom. We address the latter three areas, but we have left the United States out of our analysis because such a heavy preponderance of study has taken place there. Instead we take our inquiry to other parts of Europe, including Germany, to Canada,to Japan, and to Africa and Central Asia using the United States as a backdrop and comparator.

We examine nations with long-established, large, socially distinct, and visible populations of mixed origins, for example, in nations like Zambia, Brazil, Mexico, Trinidad and Tobago, and Kazakhstan. We also investigate countries where socially recognized and publicly visible distinctive populations of mixed origins are of relatively recent origin, like Great Britain, Germany, Canada, and Japan. We recognize and accept that from a historical perspective many, even most, nations, have involved significant patterns of racial, ethnic, and national mixing. But we believe it's clear that these nations reveal different and even divergent patterns of the circumstances in which mixing happened (colonization, conquest, military occupation, economic migration) and the social significance attached to such mixing (for example, the introduction of laws to forbid mixing or the celebration of ethnic chic). On the other hand, there has been a range of responses by and on behalf of populations of mixed origins. Therefore, this book analyzes some of the ways in which these variations have occurred and assesses their significance in a globalizing world, identifying the various ways in which forces of globalization have disrupted, changed, or expanded historically entrenched patterns.

We explore the dynamics of mixed-descent issues in these places, and do so in a way that highlights common as well as diverging issues across various parts of the world today. We identify the racial and ethnic definitions of these groups, including externally imposed definitions (by academics, politicians, policy makers, and media commentators) and self-definitions; we consider some of the unique issues that currently affect these groups in specific nations; and we consider common issues and themes pertaining to these populations across the various social, geographical, and national contexts.

The impact of global forces on these groups is a central theme in this book. This includes a focus on the wide range of population movements in the last fifty years, and many of the ways in which changing nation boundaries, (for example, the end of the Soviet Union) have had an impact on people of mixed origins. What do these local or national idiosyncrasies tell us about mixed-origin issues in the global order? And how are the increased dynamics of globalization affecting the lives and social placements of people of mixed descent?

The Contribution of Globalizing Mixed Race

The analyses in this book proceed along four areas of inquiry: a consideration of the historical growth of mixed populations in a range of nations in all their unique trajectories; a consideration of the nature and dynamics of each context in the present period; a comparison of important experiences and issues attendant upon mixed-origin groups in a variety of social and political contexts around the globe; and a consideration of the impact of the key dynamics of globalization on people of mixed descent and the meaning of racial mixedness in particular.

The analysis across chapters is undertaken on two overlapping levels. One is the popular level of on-the-ground experiences, activities, issues, discussions, and groups. That is, authors seek to explain who the people of mixed racial descent are in each context, what they are doing and saying, how they are experiencing their racial mixedness, and how issues of mixed identity are being discussed and debated in the public sphere of media and politics. In particular, we seek to ascertain whether mixedness has gone global and how the debates and experiences are being influenced by global trends.

The second level of analysis is academically oriented. Authors seek to identify and evaluate analysts of the mixed phenomenon in various contexts. What are their arguments and issues? What are the concepts that they use and how do analysts of experiences of mixed descent in these various places position themselves regarding the concept of race? That is, do they reify race? Are they opposed to using the concept of race? Do they position themselves as post-race? In each context, what are the main disciplines being brought to bear on the analysis of mixed-descent issues?

Overview of the Contents of the Book

Global Mixed Race begins with an overall comparison of 141 countries in terms of their racial and ethnic categorization. In chapter 1, "Multiraciality and Census Classification in Global Perspective," Ann Morning compares the racial or ethnic categorization of mixed people and examines how mixed-race people are classified and recognized in censuses in countries across the globe. Morning demonstrates that most countries permit some form of mixed identification. They do so in two different ways: (1) self-identification through open-ended response formats or (2) an indication of mixed background by selecting either multiple choices, a generic mixed option, or specific combinations of racial background. Terms that enumerate ethnicity and race include *ethnicity*, *nationality, race, indigenous group, ancestry*, and *cultural group*. Morning argues that such approaches to racial classification have repercussions for how mixed-race people identify themselves, and they reflect the political and social processes that inform them.

We proceed then to look more specifically at social contexts where there has been a recognized history of mixing: Zambia, Trinidad and Tobago, Kazakhstan, Brazil, Australia, and Mexico. We then turn to societies with newer populations of mixedness: Japan/Okinawa, Germany, the UK, and Canada.

Juliette Milner-Thornton, in chapter 2, "'Rider of Two Horses': Eurafricans in Zambia," explains the historical and contemporary processes of identity formation in Zambia (formerly Northern Rhodesia) of the mixed-descent colored community. She finds that so-called Coloureds accused of *riding two horses,* claiming to be African or European depending on social and political goals, were criticized for incorporating not their African, but their European lineages in their cultural practices. *Eurafrican* (recognizing the parentage of British fathers and African mothers) was not a label available to many of mixed descent and the official recognition of British paternity and citizenship was not bestowed upon them. Using an autoethnographic and historical approach, Milner-Thornton demonstrates the enduring legacies of imperial ideologies of race, gender, class, and categorization in the postcolonial context by exploring coloredness in Zambia through tracing Eurafricans' progressive adoption of *Coloured* in their political campaigns to the local British administration and its current application as an ethnic categorization in Zambia.

In chapter 3, "'Split Me in Two': Gender, Identity, and 'Race Mixing' in the Trinidad and Tobago Nation," Rhoda Reddock demonstrates that the number of those identifying as mixed in the national census is growing. The term *mixed* has shifted from those of African European, *creole* descent to also mean those of African Indian (South Asian) descent, known as *douglas.* Looking at race mixing in the popular imagination (culture, music, and discourse), Reddock shows how race mixing has permeated the national discourse of Trinidad and Tobago as a mixed nation and how this contributes to continued notions of colorism and gendered sexual competition.

In chapter 4, "In the Laboratory of Peoples' Friendship: Mixed People in Kazakhstan from the Soviet Era to the Present," Saule Ualiyeva and Adrienne Edgar focus on the former Soviet Republic. Independent since 1991, modern-day Kazakhstan promotes itself as a global blend of East and West and a stable economy within the central Asian region, with mixedness promoted as one source of its success. This rise in the appreciation of mixing has coexisted alongside a resurgence of Kazakh consciousness, particularly in terms of pride in the Kazakh language. Religion also continues to be a salient issue in marriage decisions. Kazakhstan provides a fascinating counterexample of mixing in a non-Western context unlike ones that are the focus of so many accounts; here former Soviet notions of ethnicity and nationality prevail but race does not.

Brazil has long been recognized as a multiracial nation and, in fact, much of the narrative about the nation is premised on the mixing of racial and ethnic groups. However, G. Reginald Daniel and Andrew Michael Lee find in chapter 5, "Competing Narratives: Race and Multiraciality in the Brazilian Racial Order," that since the 1970s, the Black movement has articulated a binary racial project that combines Black and multiracial individuals into a single African Brazilian category distinct from Whites to heighten awareness of and mobilize opposition to the racial discrimination that exists in Brazil. In the early twenty-first century, various individuals, along with Brazil's Multiracial Movement, countered with a narrative supporting Brazil's ternary racial order. The goal has been to defend and reassert the historical process of racial blending that has characterized the Brazilian people as well as to affirm the right of individuals and the nation by extension to identify as multiracial. The chapter ends by analyzing Brazilian racial formation and national identity, particularly as they relate to ongoing formations of Blackness and Whiteness.

We next move to Australia and New Zealand, both settler societies, where a conversation about personal biography and "whom we think we are" involves, as always, a mixed dimension. Through an examination of testimonies from "light-skinned" Aboriginal people and Australians of color, Farida Fozdar and Maureen Perkins argue in chapter 6, "Antipodean Mixed Race: Australia and New Zealand," that both race and mixed race are important categories for thinking about the lives of Australians and New Zealanders. They focus on how globalization has produced a need for authenticity among indigenous populations with mixed heritages despite Australia's thirty-year history as an officially multicultural society. They also find that, in a global context, mixed-race individuals may have more of a cosmopolitan orientation than those who are monoracial.

In chapter 7, "Negotiating Identity Narratives among Mexico's Cosmic Race," Christina Sue examines how Mexican *mestizos* of varying colors construct their identities within the context of a national ideology of race mixture. She shows how "light-skinned" *mestizos* claim mixed-race status as a strategy to wed themselves to the nation at little to no social cost, while simultaneously reaping the social benefits of their "light skin." Darker-skinned *mestizos,* on the other hand, stress a mixed-race identity, but as a means of highlighting their European origins. Both of these groups are far less aware of the specifics of their non-European ancestors. Consequently, individuals turn to another information source—Mexico's national ideology that centralizes the Indigenous root of the Mexican mixture—to inform their understandings of their own mixed-race backgrounds. As such, this chapter presents a concrete case of how and when national citizens use official ideology to inform their understandings of their own identities.

From these older mixed-race societies, we move to societies that some might not think about in terms of mixing. In chapter 8, "Multiraciality and Migration: Mixed-Race American Okinawans, 1945–1972," Lily Anne Yumi Welty bases her research on interviews with people of mixed descent in Okinawa, a militarized doubly postcolonial context (having been occupied both by the US military and Japan) in the Pacific. She finds that for mixed-race Okinawans immigration is not one-way but rather back and forth, and that these individuals have transnational lives, which contributes to their transnational, multiracial, and multicultural identities.

In chapter 9, "The Curious Career of the One-Drop Rule: Multiraciality and Membership in Germany Today," Miriam Nandi and Paul

Spickard find that the specifics of German history culturally predispose Germany to reject explicit discussion of race, while the country has nonetheless adopted a one-drop rule, defining as German people who have only the smallest shred of actual German ancestry, language, or culture. However, the same cannot be said for mixed people whose non-German ancestry comes from darker, more pigment-rich places, even when they were born and raised in Germany and perform German culture perfectly. They remain racialized Others within German society. The chapter examines the position of Black Germans historically and at present, and the racialization of people of mixed German and Turkish, German and Arab, German and Mexican, and German and South Asian ancestry. It contrasts their situations to those of other interviewees, who mix German parentage with Irish or Dutch. The former group are all racialized as foreigners; it is to the latter only that the one-drop rule of German ancestry works. Not surprisingly, the difference is race. And most ethnic Germans really don't want to talk about it.

In Chapter 10, "Capturing 'Mixed Race' in the Decennial UK Censuses: Are Current Approaches Sustainable in the Age of Globalization and Superdiversity?" Peter Aspinall and Miri Song present data from the UK at the crossroads of official state-level racial categorizations and individual personal categorizations by people of mixed descent. They find that *official* British conceptualizations are increasingly challenged by the preferred descriptors used by mixed-race people and also by the growing diversity of the population. Their chapter focuses on how different types of mixed people understand and articulate their identifications. They question the salience of race, more generally, as a marker of difference in relation to the lived experiences of many mixed people in Britain today. They tackle the disjuncture between official categories (as used in the census) and the ethnic and racial terms and understandings used by young mixed people themselves.

In chapter 11, "Exporting the Mixed-Race Nation: Mixed-Race Identities in the Canadian Context," Minelle Mahtani, Dani Kwan-Lafond, and Leanne Taylor show how Canada's multiculturalism, enshrined in its constitution, actually plays out in mixed unions with the population of mixed descent on the rise. This chapter asks how mixed-race people in Canada understand multiculturalism and a series of related questions: How multicultural policy facilitates celebratory readings of mixed-race identities, while simultaneously reinforcing discourses of race and ethnicity that maintain traditional understandings of monoraciality? How is continued social inequality understood in a multicultural Canada? And what is the particular experience of the Métis people, that is, individuals who identify as being of both First Nations and French ancestry?

We conclude in chapter 12 with an examination of social-identity categories and the processes both of *identity declaration* and *identity differentiation and categorization* by tracing how racial ideas travel from place to place. We analyze mixed experiences at different levels of social analysis such as at the national level in Mexico and Brazil, in terms of governmentality in Kazakhstan, in terms of citizenship and national identity in Zambia, in terms of racial/ethnic categorization in the UK, and transnationally across countries such as linkages between the US and Okinawa.

There is evidence that many mixed people across the globe still must choose one and only one identity even where there is state valorization of mixedness. The experiences vary, but there are still racial hierarchies that are unequal along racial lines and in some cases mixed people lose out. Sometimes mixed people embrace multiple identities, but often they identify themselves monoracially out of necessity. Does this make a global mixed-race community or collective identity across the globe? Not necessarily, but there are issues of global discrimination, commodification, and commercialization that have rallied and united mixed people on certain issues and experiences through the global flow of racial ideas.

We also find that, despite predictions that the role of nation-states would decline, in many places the role of the state is still strong. However, even nation-states that say they are multicultural and mixed still struggle to make good on this claim—to be mixed in fact, not in name only. So what is it like to be mixed in the increasingly global world in which we live? Let's find out.

NOTES

1. We wish to acknowledge the generous support of a grant in aid of publication from the National University of Ireland.

2. Matthews, "Eurasian Persuasions: Mixed Race, Peformativity and Cosmopolitanism"; Haritaworn, "Caucasian and Thai Make a Good Mix."

3. Ali, *Mixed-Race, Post-Race:Gender, New Ethnicities and Cultural Practices;* Parker and Song, *Rethinking "Mixed Race."*

4. Wilson, *The Declining Significance of Race;* Collins, *Black Sexual Politics: African Americans, Gender and the New Racism.*

5. DaCosta, *Making Multiracials: State, Family and Market in the Redrawing of the Color Line.*

6. Degler, *Neither Black Nor White: Slavery and Race Relations in Brazil and the United States;* Daniel, *Race and Multiraciality in Brazil and the United States: Converging Paths?*; Loveman, "The Race to Progress: Census-Taking and Nation-Making in Brazil 1870–1920."

7. Whitten and Torres, *Blackness in Latin America and the Caribbean, Vol. II: Eastern South America and the Caribbean;* Reddock, "Jahaji Bhai: The Emergence of a Dougla Poetics in Trinidad and Tobago"; Premdas, *Identity, Ethnicity and Culture in the Caribbean.*

8. Spickard, *Mixed Blood: Intermarriage and Ethnic Identity in Twentieth Century America.*

9. Lie, *Multiethnic Japan.*

10. Armstrong, "Racialisation and Nationalist Ideology: The Japanese Case."

11. Elam, *The Souls of Mixed Folk: Race, Politics, and Aesthetics in the New Millennium.*

12. Spickard. *Mixed Blood: Intermarriage and Ethnic Identity in the Twentieth Century America;* Spickard and Daniel, *Racial Thinking in the United States: Uncompleted Independence.*

13. Appadurai, *Modernity at Large: Cultural Dimensions of Globalization;* Tomlinson, *Globalization and Culture.*

14. Kempadoo, *Sun, Sex, and Gold: Tourism and Sex Work in the Caribbean;* Cabezas, *Economies of Desire: Sex and Tourism in Cuba and the Dominican Republic.*

15. Padilla et. al., *Love and Globalization: Transformations of Intimacy in the Contemporary World;* Constable, *Cross-Border Marriages: Gender and Mobility in Transnational Asia;* Childs, *Fade to Black and White: Interracial Images in Popular Culture.*

16. Fulbeck, *Part Asian, 100% Hapa;* Marchetti, *Romance and the "Yellow Peril": Race, Sex, and Discursive Strategies in Hollywood Fiction;* Childs, *Fade to Black and White: Interracial Images in Popular Culture;* Hugel - Marshall, *Invisible Woman: Growing up Black in Germany.*

17. La Ferla, "Generation E.A.: Ethnically Ambiguous"; Spencer, "Mixed-Race Chic."

18. King-O'Riain, "Globalization, Emotional Ties, and Digital Technology: Skyping and the Intimate Transnational Practices of International Couples and Families."
19. Nobles, *Shades of Citizenship: Race and the Census in Modern Politics;* Morning, "Ethnic Classification in Global Perspective: A Cross-National Survey of the 2000 Census Round."

PART I

Societies with Established Populations of Mixed Descent

1

Multiraciality and Census Classification in Global Perspective

ANN MORNING

What Maria Root called "the multiracial experience"[1] has rarely been studied from a comparative perspective.[2] Although scholars of race and ethnicity have long recognized the importance of placing diverse national contexts side by side in order to glean insights about both their similarities and their particularities, mixed-race people have too often slipped through the cracks. To be sure, international comparison has often dwelled on the tendencies of some countries and not others to recognize racial mixture in their populations; notable examples include Nobles on Brazil and the United States, and Marx on the same nations as well as South Africa.[3] But in these works, multiracial people are of interest as components of larger systems of racial structure and ideology; it is not their experience in particular that is at the heart of comparative inquiry.

Why this failure to consider multiraciality as a social identity that transcends state borders? I suggest three reasons. First is simply that "mixed-race studies" in general are fairly new as a subfield of social scientific research. Although multiracial people are hardly new as topics of scientific inquiry (Park's "marginal man," for example, dates back to 1928), a solid body of research that focuses on them is a recent

phenomenon.[4] Second, most investigations of multiracial people's identity or classification explore how they are forged by local or national
contexts and institutions.[5] In other words, such studies have privileged
close examination of specific cultures in order to trace the development of local notions of "who" or "what" racially mixed people are.
Such findings, however, are rarely juxtaposed with similar observations
from many different cultural settings. Finally—and in a related vein—I
would argue that scholars have envisioned multiracial people as forming a series of small, unconnected, nation-specific communities—such
as Métis in Canada or Eurasians in Vietnam—rather than as a transnational community whose members share the socially meaningful experience of being considered racially mixed. Perhaps a diasporic model
that conceives of far-flung groups as being part of a larger whole—such
as Indian-origin communities in Africa, Asia, Europe, North America,
the Caribbean, and the Pacific—would be a useful model for understanding multiraciality in global perspective.

But perhaps not. The bottom line is that scholars have not seriously
asked, in an empirical manner, what we might gain from international
exploration of the multiracial experience. As a result, it is hard to say
whether a transnational model of multiraciality—which might presume
for example a widespread consciousness of being members of a global
population—has any utility at present. Regardless of the answer to this
question, however, cross-national comparative research would nonetheless benefit current scholarship on mixed-race people for at least
two reasons. First, it would entail exposure to diverse systems of racial
ideology that would help us better identify the meaningful characteristics of any single one in particular. Second, it would help us analyze
the causes and consequences of different approaches to conceptualizing
mixed identity.

In this chapter, I take a comparative look at the classification of multiethnic people worldwide by studying how they were enumerated on
nearly 140 censuses over the 1995–2004 period. As I explain below, I
will use the word *ethnic* as an umbrella term to capture the wide range
of descent-related concepts that censuses use, including *race*, *tribe*,
ancestry, and others. Multiraciality then is just one form of multiethnicity (or "mixedness") that censuses measure. My aim is to identify the
strategies that national governments take with respect to mixed people

and investigate how these strategies vary by world region. In short, this project contributes to a map of what might be called "the geography of mixedness." Finally, I draw on this mapping to demonstrate how understandings of multiraciality are shaped—indeed constrained—by local (or national) concepts of race.

Studying Census Classification Worldwide

Why use censuses as a window onto how mixed people are understood and classified around the world? After all, state classification schemes are not the same as everyday folk categories. In the United States, for example, official terminology like "non-Hispanic Whites" or the "Asian alone or in combination population" are probably not used very often outside the halls of the Census Bureau. Yet official classification systems do reflect—and shape—those everyday discussions. More importantly for the purposes of this chapter, they offer a clear measure with which to make comparisons across a large number of countries at once.

The research described below is based on a collection of 138 national census questionnaires that were fielded during from 1995 to 2004—that is, during the period demographers call "the 2000 census round."[6] As large as this sample is, however, it covers only 69 percent of the nation-states that fielded a census from the mid-1990s to the mid-2000s. More-over, this coverage is geographically biased. Europe is best represented, with 100 percent of its censuses included, and Asia (which includes the Middle East), Oceania, and South America are all well covered, with 79 to 80 percent of the 2000-round censuses of each region included.[7] In contrast, only 51 percent of the censuses fielded in North America (including Central America and the Caribbean) and 42 percent of those conducted in Africa during the 2000 round were located for this sample. As a result, African, Central American, and Caribbean countries' experience with multiethnic enumeration is not adequately reflected below. This is worth keeping in mind since the Caribbean in particular may be a region where censuses acknowledge racial mixture more frequently than elsewhere.

Until this point, I have referred to the experience of multiraciality. However, the term *race* is so often confounded with *ethnicity* (in scholarly, political, media, and everyday discourse) that when studying census enumeration, I cast a wide net and look at questions about "ethnicity," "race," "nationality" (when clearly distinguished from citizenship), "indigenous group" or "tribe," "ancestry"/"descent"/"origin," "cultural group," "community"/"population," "caste," and "color" or "phenotype." In short, I aim to analyze census classification of groups that are understood to be "communities of descent,"[8] and I use the term *ethnicity* as an umbrella label to include these varied formulations of the basic notion of a descent-based community. Indeed, Weber's definition of "ethnic groups" conveys a sense of the variety of conceptual forms these may take:

> We shall call "ethnic groups" those human groups that entertain a subjective belief in their common descent because of similarities of physical type or of customs or of both, or because of memories of colonization and migration; this belief must be important for the propagation of group formation; conversely, it does not matter whether or not an objective blood relationship exists.[9]

In other words, some ethnic identities may place greater weight on similarity of physical type (which is central to the race concept) or customs (e.g., "cultural group") or descent (e.g., "ancestry"). The importance accorded to appearance or traditions or historical memories may lead to different conceptions of shared descent. But whether "caste" or "tribe" or "race" is in play, they are all instances of a broader phenomenon of meaning-making around common descent, and it is that range of notions of communities that I sought to investigate on national censuses, and that I refer to using the term *ethnicity* for shorthand.

This means that the study I conducted was really one of multiethnic rather than strictly multiracial census enumeration. Or rather, it is an exploration of the official recognition of "mixedness" regardless of the terms in which groups are locally conceived (for example, as castes, or tribes, or races). Yet the overarching theme of this chapter is multiraciality, that is, mixedness in its specifically racial framing. Because race has a specific set of connotations, multiraciality also carries its own associations, distinct from being multiethnic or multicultural or multinational. Race hinges above all on beliefs about essential biological characteristics and thus has specific implications for understandings of multiraciality—ideas, as we will see below, of how individuals acquire their racial characteristics and identities. Hence I distinguish multiraciality from the broader range of types of multiethnicity as a particular theoretical concept. However, when referring to the analysis of censuses I will use the terms *multiethnic* or simply *mixed* people to denote the wide array of labels that official questionnaires employ.

One last comment on the data analyzed below. I did not approach the census questionnaires with a preconceived list of qualifying terms; instead, I worked inductively to include within the project's scope any question that referred to subdivisions in a national population that implied group cohesiveness born of shared ancestry. I did decide from the outset, however, to exclude question items on language, religion, and legal citizenship. Although these could certainly be considered reflections of ethnic affiliation, I judge them to be relatively indirect references to ancestry. (Consider for example how poor an indicator of ethnicity "Native English Speaker" status would be in a multicultural society like the United States.) As a result, the treatment of census enumeration below is based on a particular approach to defining "ethnic" classification, one that yields different results than would a study that incorporated census items on language or religion.

How Do Censuses Count by Ethnicity?

Using the method described above, I determined that of the 138 national census questionnaires analyzed, 87 countries or 63 percent employed some form of ethnic classification. North America (including Central America and the Caribbean), South America, and Oceania were the regions with the greatest propensity to include ethnicity on their censuses; 82 to 84 percent of the 2000-round censuses fielded in each of those regions counted their populations by ethnicity. While Asia's tendency to enumerate by ethnicity was close to the sample average, both Europe and Africa were much less likely to do so; in both regions, 44 percent of census questionnaires included ethnicity items. This relatively low rate of ethnic enumeration may stem from government concerns that such categorization would be detrimental to projects of national unity.[10]

Regions varied too in the terminology used on their census questionnaires, depending on their histories of colonialism, slavery, migration, and political boundary shifts. Overall, references to "ethnicity," "nationality" (as distinct from legal citizenship), indigenous status, and "race" predominated; together, these four terms accounted for 90 percent of the descent items on the censuses sampled. The modal term of ethnicity was most frequent in Oceania, where it appeared on 81 percent of the censuses sample, and least prevalent in South America, where it appeared on only 33 percent.

In contrast, references to "indigenous status" or "tribe" reached their peak in South America (appearing on 67 percent of censuses there), but were absent on European and Asian censuses. Thus indigeneity seemed particularly salient in societies where European colonialism resulted either in considerable *mestizaje* that became the norm against which the indigenous were marked (as in Latin America), or in a European-dominated population in which indigenous people were equally marginalized (e.g., the United States, Canada, Australia and New Zealand).

Conversely, "nationality" appeared on none of the American censuses (South or North), but figured on more than half of the European censuses. This was particularly true of Eastern Europe, where historical and often war-related movements of political borders and peoples have frequently left groups with allegiances to past or neighboring governments situated in new or different states.[11] Moreover, the former Soviet Union's practice of identifying distinct nationalities within its borders extended the equation of nationality with ethnic membership that is still seen in post-USSR states such as Tajikistan, Turkmenistan, and Uzbekistan.[12]

Finally, "race" is not found on European or Asian censuses, but appears on almost half of those used in North/Central America and the Caribbean. In fact, race as a census item is used virtually exclusively by either New World former slave societies (United States, Anguilla, Bermuda, Brazil, Jamaica, Saint Lucia) and/or their territories (United States Virgin Islands, Puerto Rico, American Samoa, Guam, Northern Mariana Islands). This marked geographic concentration of race terminology may be another reason that multiraciality has not often been researched from an international perspective. The term *race* seems to have less purchase outside the Americas, and thus less immediate salience as the basis for a wide-ranging cross-national comparison.

Census questionnaires also varied notably in the response formats they provided for ethnicity questions. These formats were fairly evenly divided across three types:

1. Closed-ended responses (e.g., category checkboxes or code lists)
2. Closed-ended with open-ended "Other" option (i.e., permitting the respondent to write in a group name that is not included on the list presented)
3. Open-ended (i.e., write-in blanks)

The ways in which respondents are permitted to report their ethnic affiliation is of central importance to the question of how censuses recognize and record mixedness. As the typology above suggests, different response formats offer respondents different amounts of latitude as well as different frameworks for reporting a mixed identity.

Counting Mixed People

Among the census questionnaires I studied, five approaches to enumerating mixed people emerged:

1. *Nonrecognition.* On some censuses with a closed response set (e.g., checkboxes), registering a mixed identity was simply not an option. This was a rare occurrence, occurring on only six questionnaires (Zambia, Cyprus, Hungary, Costa Rica, Mexico, and New Caledonia). For example, the Mexican census *pertenencia etnica* question asked only whether the respondent belonged to an indigenous group, offering simply "yes/no" response options. In such a framework, registering a multiethnic identity is not possible.

2. *Combination of predetermined categories.* Other censuses with a closed-response set permitted individuals to combine predetermined ethnic options. For example, New Zealand's census asked, "Which ethnic group do you belong to? Mark the space *or spaces* which apply to you" (emphasis added). Canada and the United States used the same approach. In these cases, the number and kinds of mixed identities that one can report are limited by the menu of ethnic categories that is offered from which to select. I discuss these limits further below.

3. *"Mixed" category.* Still other censuses with a closed response set included a generic "mixed" category among their options. Examples include the "mixed" category on the censuses of Zimbabwe, Trinidad and Tobago, and Jamaica, and the *"Mestizo"* option in Belize and Peru.

4. *Predetermined combinations.* Yet other closed-response census items included among their checkboxes categories that specified particular group combinations (or groups whose label denoted a specific combination). For example, Bermuda's census included "Black and White" and "Black and Other," the Cook Islands specified "Part Cook Island Maori" as a response option, Singapore included "Eurasian" as a response, and Sri Lanka's census enumerated "Burghers."

5. *Unconstrained recognition.* In contrast to censuses that used closed-ended response formats to enumerate ethnicity, questionnaires that permitted open-ended (i.e., write-in) responses offered total latitude in indicating a mixed identity. These censuses provide the bulk of the opportunity for individuals to report mixed affiliations. Examples of this open-ended approach can be found in the censuses of Mauritius, Senegal, Armenia, China, Iraq, Vietnam, and Russia.[13]

To determine which of these five strategies were most common, and in which regions, I looked at the subset of countries that did not use code lists, because they were not always available. From the resulting subset of 74 countries, or 85 percent of all those I had found to enumerate by ethnicity, I calculated that only a few—six, or 8 percent—actually fell in the first category where mixed identification was impossible (see table 1.1). In other words, in the overwhelming majority of cases of census ethnic enumeration I observed—92 percent—it was possible to register a mixed identity (although not necessarily the specific group or nomenclature one might prefer). The most common route to such self-identification was through write-in responding: 38 of the ethnicity-enumerating countries, or 51 percent, allowed this approach. However, a sizable share of nations—30, or 41 percent—explicitly provided for mixed identification, usually by offering multi-ethnic response options (i.e., types 3 and 4 above, as opposed to type 2, letting people "mark one or more").

Table 1.1 orders world regions according to their likelihood of explicitly permitting mixed reporting (see the row labelled "Allow Mixed Identification"). Explicit provisions for multiethnic identification were most frequent in South America, North America, and Oceania, and were rare in Europe and Asia.

Table 1.1. Multiple-Identity Classification by Region

Census approach to enumerating mixed individuals:	South America	North America	Oceania	Africa	Europe	Asia	TOTAL	
	%	%	%	%	%	%	%	N
No Recognition	0	17	6	17	6	5	8	6
Open-Ended	20	8	31	33	81	84	51	38
Allow Mixed Identification	80	75	63	50	13	11	41	30
Regional N	5	12	16	6	16	19	–	74

Accounting for this geographic distribution of mixed-identity report-ing is unfortunately beyond the scope of the present chapter. However, its strong association with the Western hemisphere brings at least two factors to mind. One is the role that relatively recent histories of migration play in producing not just intergroup mixture but also official recognition of such mixture. Second is the role that the framing of group differences as "racial" may play. As discussed previously, the term *race* appears almost exclusively on the censuses of former New World slave societies. These are the same societies that nurtured an often-elaborate calculus of racial difference according to fractions of blood quantum; the *casta* paintings of the Spanish colonial world and even English-language terminology like "quadroon" or "half-blood" speak to this.[14] As a result, the greater tendency to permit contemporary citizens to identify with mixed affiliations may be a legacy of the Americas' racialized understanding of group membership, one where descent is inherited in mathematical fractions of biological essences.

Multiracial Classification in Cultural Context

The widespread opportunity to identify as mixed on censuses that request ethnic information may come as a (welcome) surprise to multi-racial people. Yet it is important to be aware that opportunities for mul-tiple-race identification come with constraints. In particular, they are limited by the broader cultural systems of racial conceptualization and classification in which they are embedded. In the comments to follow, I will illustrate these conventions by drawing on the official practices of racial classification in the United States.

Three constraints are of particular importance. First and most fundamentally, the notion of who is multiracial hinges on which groups are perceived to be races in the first place. We might call these "primary" races, like the so-called "primary colors" whose mixture is understood to give rise to the rest of the spectrum.[15] This relationship between multiraciality and racial classification in general is clear when we stop to define what we mean by mixed-race persons. I define multiracial individuals as descendants of two or more groups currently believed to constitute distinct races. In other words, belief about which groups constitute distinct primary races is central for any designation as multiracial. For example, according to the United States' official racial classification standards, Hispanics do not make up a race; they are considered instead to be an ethnic group.[16] As a result, a person of, say, Irish and Mexican ancestry is not necessarily a multiracial person, because in this view, Mexican origin does not denote any particular racial membership and so it does not translate to a racial identity distinct from that of (now-)White Irish descendants. If however the 2020 census comes to include "Hispanic or Latino" among its race categories, then a person who checks off both White and Hispanic as her races will be a mixed-race person from the government's standpoint. Hence the importance of "current belief" in defining multiraciality: being mixed race is not the same in 2010 as it was in 1910, or perhaps as it will be in 2110.

To be more precise, notions of which primary races exist in the world should be understood as one facet of our broader concepts of what race is. Our beliefs about the nature of race—for example, how many races there are and how they are distinct from each other—form complexes that can be labeled *concepts of race*.[17] And although I have emphasized the role that our ideas about which primary races exist play in our recognition of multiraciality, other understandings of how race works matter too. One example is our model for how racial membership is transmitted across generations. In the United States, the "one-drop rule" dictates that any amount of African ancestry renders an individual racially Black (like President Barack Obama), making it difficult to recognize a part-Black person as multiracial.[18] American discussions of multiracial people also tend to rule out individuals with genealogically distant mixed ancestry, excluding African Americans with European ancestry stemming from 19th-century intermixture, or Latinos with longstanding European and indigenous roots. In short, culturally specific ideas about how race is inherited (in this case via a one-drop rule) and which mixtures are salient (those stemming from recent, voluntary unions as opposed to older, coerced unions in the context of slavery and imperialism) also constrain common thinking about who can or should identify as mixed.

A second major constraint for multiracial reporting, even on censuses that allow it in some way, is that not all types of mixed ancestry have recognized labels or widespread social salience. For example, late 19th- and early 20th-century US censuses included categories for Black/ White mixture: mulatto, quadroon, and octoroon. They did not, however, provide categories for White/American Indian mixture or Black/ Indian mixture.[19] It seems fair to say that while the term "mulatto" was widely familiar, names for Black/Indian mixture like "mustee" had less currency and prominence. For historical social and political reasons, certain groups come not only to be understood and therefore labeled as groups (e.g., mulattoes), but also to be subject to interest that encourages broad awareness of their existence. Mulattoes in the 19th-century United States straddled the all-important Black-White color line and thus were subjects of intense interest in a century during which the placement and the meaning of that line was hotly debated. People of Black and American Indian ancestry on the other hand received much less attention, as their mixture crossed a boundary line of much less significance for the White majority. Thus official designation as "mulatto" was possible whereas recognition as "mustee" was not.

This historical example is closely related to a third major constraint shaping mixed identification on censuses: nation-states make certain identities but not others available for selection on censuses. To return to a contemporary census, the United Kingdom provides for the recognition of certain kinds of racial mixture but not others. The 2001 England and Wales Census enumerates "White and Black Caribbean" people, "White and Black African" respondents, and "White and Asian" inhabitants, but it does not inquire about "Asian and Black Caribbean" people, or "White and Chinese," for example (although it provides a write-in blank). In other words, state interests single out certain kinds of mixed descent for scrutiny, and ignore others. While the relative size of specific mixed groups may partly account for state recognition of

specific "mixtures," it is likely to be only one among various considerations. As a result, only some kinds of mixedness can be registered in
official contexts.

The statistic that most ethnicity-enumerating censuses allow for
some kind of multidescent reporting is perhaps misleading. It does not
mean that in all such instances an individual has free rein to identify
with the multiracial community of their choice. Add to this governmental restraint the underpinning social concepts according to which
some kinds of ancestry are perceived as mixed and others are not, and
it is clear that our notions and recognition of multiraciality are everywhere embedded in broader and deeper beliefs about racial difference.

One of the significant results of our culturally constructed systems
for identifying racial mixture is that the statistics that censuses produce
inevitably give us just one slant among many other possible ones on the
numbers of people who are mixed race. As Harris and Sim noted of the
2000 U.S. census, "it was a count of *a* multiracial population, not *the*
multiracial population."[20] In the case of the United States, only a frac-
tion of the people who could be considered mixed race are actually designated as such on the decennial census. The 2000 census estimated the
multiple-race population at just over 2 percent; this, to put it mildly, is
just the tip of the iceberg.[21] If we considered the U.S. multiracial population to consist not only of the 2 to 3 percent who identified as such on
the 2000 census, but also Latinos and African Americans—three-quarters of whom were already considered by census officials to be mixed
race a century ago—as well as Whites who report having some American Indian ancestry (or the 20 percent that some scholars argue have
non-European ancestry), we would probably put the share of mixed-
race people between 30 and 50 percent of the total U.S. population.[22]

Conclusion: Multiraciality as Global Phenomenon

The panorama of censuses conducted around the world suggests that the
notion of ethnic mixedness is a widespread one. Opportunities to identify with multiple origins however are not unlimited or unconstrained.
Local and regional concepts of group difference shape the categories
that are socially and officially available, and state interests lead some
but not others to be included on census questionnaires. These beliefs

and policies are underpinned by broader systems of cultural meaning and social structure. As a consequence, it is clear that we cannot study multiracial people in a vacuum, just as we cannot examine any racially classified group in isolation. To fully understand their experience and circumstances, the larger complex of racial ideology and categorization that is at work in a given society must be taken into account.

Just as comparative research helps identify important features of racial systems in general, it also offers a great deal to the study of multiraciality in particular. First, as the research outlined here shows, comparison draws attention to social or official conventions that are rare or otherwise distinctive. For example, few census questionnaires let respondents express a multiracial identity by combining any primary races they wish; instead, nations generally channel the expression of a mixed identity into a few predetermined categories. Second, this highlighting of particular practices also helps us generate hypotheses about why such approaches have formed, and about the effects they ultimately have. We might ask, for example, what nations that offer "mixed" categories have in common. I have already suggested that the high frequency of explicit multiple-origin options on census questionnaires in the Americas might be related to that hemisphere's relatively high use of "race" as a central ethnic concept. A different kind of inquiry would be to explore the role that the recognition of mixed people might have (or not) in defusing national ethnic tensions.

In closing, I will return to the question I posed at the outset: Should we think of mixed-race people as constituting a global community of sorts, or rather as a dispersed collection of separate, more or less nation-bound groups? The emphasis I have placed on the culture-specific nature of multiracial classification may suggest that mixed people form local rather than transnational communities. Moreover, there is little evidence to date of a shared consciousness of multiraciality that transcends state borders. Yet it is also clear that, as censuses demonstrate, the social and political awareness of mixedness is fairly widespread throughout the globe. This leaves open a starting point for comparative research on multiraciality, and it signals a potential body of data with which to do it—namely, the demographic information that censuses ultimately collect. These statistics have the potential to reveal how mixed-race populations are changing over time, in terms of both size and other characteristics. If multiracial people come to make up increasing shares of national populations (as seems likely), and acknowledgment of multiraciality grows apace, in the context of an ever more global world we may well witness the future emergence of a transnational consciousness of mixedness.

NOTES

1. Root, *Multiracial Experience*.
2. The author wishes to thank Alondra Nelson and Wendy Roth for their helpful comments. This chapter is reprinted with permission from: Rosalind Edwards, Suki Ali, Chamion Caballero, and Miri Song (eds.). 2012. *International Perspectives on Racial and Ethnic Mixedness and Mixing*. Abingdon, Oxon., and New York: Routledge.
3. Marx, *Making Race and Nation*; Nobles, *Shades of Citizenship*.
4. Thompson, "A New Take."
5. Brunsma, *Mixed Messages*; DaCosta, *Making Multiracials*; Gross, "'Of Portuguese Origin'"; Saada, "Race and Sociological Reason."
6. Readers who would like greater detail about the data, methodology, and results of this study are encouraged to consult Morning, "Ethnic Classification in Global Perspective."
7. Regional groupings are taken from the United Nations Statistical Division, which provided the bulk of the questionnaires in the sample.
8. Hollinger, "National Culture."
9. Weber, *Economy and Society*, 389.
10. See Rallu, Piché, and Simon, "Démographie et Ethnicité," for a series of hypotheses regarding country approaches to ethnic classification.
11. Eberhardt, *Ethnic Groups and Population Changes*.
12. Blum and Gousseff, "Statistiques Ethniques et Nationales."
13. It is worth noting however that in nations where ethnic affiliations are linked or assigned to individuals through other administrative means (e.g., identity cards, passports), the apparently unconstrained choice offered by the census may in reality be no more than a rehearsal of official categories that individuals are expected to report on multiple occasions.
14. Katzew, *Casta Painting*; Moreno Navarro, Los *"Cuadros del Mestizaje Americano"*; Wilson, "Blood Quantum."
15. And as Pastoureau has shown in *Noir*, our notions of which colors are primary are just as historically contingent as our beliefs about principal races.
16. Office of Management and Budget, "Revisions to the Standards."

17. Morning, *Nature of Race.*
18. Khanna, "If You're Half Black"; Rockquemore and Brunsma, *Beyond Black.*
19. They did however furnish enumerators with instructions for such classification; see Morning, "New Faces, Old Faces." Note I use the term *American Indian* to refer to the indigenous peoples of North America (and not to Americans of Asian Indian descent).
20. Harris and Sim, "Who Is Multiracial?", 625.
21. Grieco and Cassidy, "Overview of Race and Hispanic Origin."
22. Morning, "Who Is Multiracial?"; Stuckert, "'Race' Mixture"; US Census Bureau, "Negro Population."

2

"Rider of Two Horses"

Eurafricans in Zambia

JULIETTE BRIDGETTE MILNER-THORNTON

Four generations of my mixed-descent Eurafrican family have experienced Colouredness in Zambia, the former British colony of Northern Rhodesia. In this chapter, I chart the shifting production and construction of "Colouredness" from its initial racial categorization to its current application as an ethnic and cultural identity in modern-day Zambia.

In this chapter, I use the terms "Eurafrican" and "Coloured" despite their historically controversial nature. Both terms are of historical and contemporary significance in Zambia. The term "Eurafrican" defines my community and family genetically, culturally, and historically—it is a cultural expression that effectively chronicles and historicizes our origins in Northern Rhodesia and Great Britain/Europe, British/European and African ancestry, integrated cross-cultural practices, contemporary return migration to Great Britain, and middle-class upbringing in Zambia and schooling in England. In the 1970s and early 1980s a large number of middle-class black Zambian, European, and Eurafrican families (including my own) sent their children to British educational institutions. We went to school in Britain to avoid compulsory Zambian military conscription and symbolize our parents' newly acquired postcolonial middle-class status. We were not alone in our ambitions as evidenced by my fellow middle-class West African, South American, Caribbean, and Southeast Asian students in my boarding school in Sussex.

Nonetheless, in contemporary Zambia the Eurafrican community is known as "Coloured." This concurs with the current application of "Coloured" as an ethnic identity and cultural classification characterized by Eurafricans' and so-called Indo-Africans' historical experiences of marginalization and alienation in colonial Zambia. The "illicit born half-caste child of a white father and native mother" was of particular interest to British administrators, beginning in 1928 with Northern Rhodesian governor Sir James Crawford Maxwell's (1927–31) biological assimilative efforts to breed Eurafricans into the predominant African community.[1] Indo-Africans were not considered a threat because there were not many and more importantly their Indian fathers were not part of the colonial elite in Northern Rhodesia. On the other hand, "the colony of half-castes" whose "tendency is European-wards" were viewed as a particular menace to White hegemony as they did not conform to the administration's "ideal . . . that half-castes should identify with and be absorbed in the native population."[2] White officials discovered that "in effect this was not likely to happen in all cases"—particularly in the Eastern Province of Northern Rhodesia, where the largest number of Eurafricans resided with their British fathers and African mothers.[3] Consequently, Eurafricans were governed as contagions that needed to be constrained to empire and denied admission to the metropole. In contemporary Zambia many Eurafricans and Indo-Africans have married, and their familial connections can now be traced back to British/ European pioneers.

Consequently, British lineages are a fundamental characteristic of Colouredness in Zambia. The majority of Zambian Coloureds are the descendants of British men who for the most part were pioneers and the colonial elite in Northern Rhodesia. Similarly, to a large degree Eurafrican mothers were of noble birth, the daughters of various African rulers. Consequently, in Zambia the creation of a mixed-descent Coloured community and identity cannot be separated from the larger issues of gender, race, class, and sex in the British Empire.

White officials in both colonial Zambia and London were particularly concerned about Eurafricans' British paternity mainly because of its capacity to qualify Eurafricans for British nationality and citizenship in the metropole. Beginning with Maxwell in 1928, several generations of British officials prevented this from happening, first by discrediting Eurafricans as rightful descendants of British men and second by advancing Eurafricans' biological assimilation into Northern Rhodesian African society. Paradoxically, in the contemporary context, the historical questions concerning Eurafricans' British genealogies, legitimacy, and nationality exclude Eurafricans/Coloureds as a separate category in Zambia's national census and facilitate their return migration to Great Britain.

The 1980 census was the last time "Eurafrican" was officially included as a separate category by the Zambian government.[4] In 1964, newly independent Zambia became a racially integrated nation—at least in the public sphere—segregated schools, housing and hospitals were memories of the colonial past. Kenneth Kaunda, the first president of Zambia, through his catchphrase "One Zambia, One Nation" promoted a common national identity among the nation's disparate ethnic and cultural groups. Eurafricans, like the wider Zambian community, were proud of our new independent nation and announced themselves "Zambian." Yet despite Kaunda's political advancements both the Zambian people and government in official documents continue to define Zambian people in accordance with their ethnic affiliations.[5]

The Zambian government's elimination of "Eurafrican" as an official category in 1980 implies Eurafricans/Coloureds vanished from Zambia's social landscape, a memory of Zambia's colonial past. Ironically, in 1981 Britain changed its immigration laws to incorporate sanguineous clauses. This was a significant change in British immigration policy. Prior to 1981, British citizenship was awarded to the legitimate children of British men. The British Nationality Act 1948 introduced a legitimacy clause wherein only children born in legitimate marriages of their British fathers were entitled to British citizenship.[6] The British Nationality Act 1981 revoked Eurafricans' transgenerational humiliation and stigmatization of illegitimacy; providing they could prove they were consanguineous descendants of a specific British person (regardless of their ancestor's marital status), they could apply for "the right of abode" in Great Britain and subsequently apply for British citizenship.[7] Zambian Coloureds seized this opportunity and claimed what historically had been denied them—British citizenship.

In this chapter, I distance my gaze to read official historical papers and handwritten remarks in the margins and footnotes of official papers—in Laura Anne Stoler's words, to read the "granular hues" within a larger national and transnational framework.[8] Handwritten notes in official documents reveal White officials' "unofficial" opinions about and intense opposition to Eurafricans' assertion of their British nationality and citizenship. I also write and present firsthand auto-ethnographic accounts to reflect upon Eurafricans' marginalization and alienation in colonial Zambia, and their desire to be recognized as the legitimate descendants of British men, as well as to explore the ongoing legacies of these historical proceedings in Zambian Coloured people's contemporary political experiences and cultural practices. To better understand Zambian Coloured people's contemporary exclusion from Zambia's national census and appreciate their return migration to Britain, we need to examine British imperial procedures in colonial Zambia.

Cultural Estrangement or Integration?

In his revolutionary book *Black Skin, White Masks,* Franz Fanon suggests that "any idiom is a way of thinking. . . . And the fact that the newly returned Martinican adopts a language different from that of the community in which he was born is evidence of a shift and split."[9] Although Fanon applies the concept of cultural "estrangement and dislocation" to returnee Martinicans, his characterization is equally applicable to Eurafricans. By identifying as "Eurafrican," mixed-descent Northern Rhodesians were seen to "shift and split" from their Northern Rhodesian African families and heritage. Africans understood Eurafricans' identification as a denigration and devaluation of their African origins. Similarly, British authorities were unnerved by Eurafricans' self-assertion to be both British and African for several reasons: first, it confirmed a relationship between Europeans and Africans; second, it revealed European men's racial and sexual indiscretions with African women; and finally, it exposed the fragility of European identity and authority.

Racial anxieties were not restricted to colonial Zambia. In other British imperial sites, similar anxieties were expressed by White officials and settlers about interracial sexuality and the production of mixed-descent people. From the late eighteenth century, alongside Europeans' fascination and "scientification" of race, the color line progressively became more pronounced.[10] Across the British Empire, cultural groups—usually on the margins of White identity—sought and acquired recognition that they were White.[11] Whiteness was championed in conflict to indigenous people and indigenous culture; it was a racial marker distinguishing the colonizers from the colonized, and so-called half-castes compromised these distinctions. Eurafricans, in common with other mixed-descent communities, were commonly regarded as "outcasts," and as a "tragedy and danger" to European settler society.[12] In Zambia, White officials were especially hostile to the Eurafrican child. They refused to recognize Eurafricans' British paternity and from 1928 subsequent Northern Rhodesian administrators refused to establish separate schools for so-called half-caste children because it would "simply create difficulties in the future by creating a small class despised by whites and looked on contempt by the native."[13] The main anxiety in recognizing Eurafrican children's educational needs was that their paternity would have to be taken into account, and this in turn would bring into question the status and citizenship of their British fathers and White settlers' sovereignty. Consequently, the British government sidestepped the question of Eurafricans' British nationality for over fifty years.

In contemporary Britain, persons of mixed descent born in unregistered marriages are not subjected to Eurafricans' historical public stigma of illegitimacy and exclusion from British citizenship. In chapter 9, Peter Aspinall and Miri Song point out that mixed people are one of the fastest-growing groups in British society. In the 1990s, the British government recognized this trend and incorporated a "mixed" category in its national census. Aspinall and Song note that this initial "mixed" categorization had limitations because it did not fully incorporate the cultural and ethnic diversities of mixed descent persons and therefore fully gauge the cultural diversity of contemporary British society.

Nonetheless, ethnic and cultural identities are social constructs. Stephen Cornell and Douglas Hartmann rightly point out that "races, like ethnic groups, are not established by some set of natural forces, but are products of human perception and classification."[14] In colonial Zambia, Eurafricans were seen to be *purely* African by both settler and African society, with no room to incorporate Eurafricans' ancestry or cultural practices. On the other hand, Eurafricans saw themselves as being both African and European, as they shared a comparable genetic, historical, and cultural connection to both Europe and Africa. Paraphrasing Cornell and Hartmann, "there are two axes of variation in ethnic and racial identities . . . 'more assigned' and 'more asserted' identities." By combining these two axes, "one traces the degree to which an ethnic or racial identity organizes the social life of a people, and the other traces the relative importance of external and internal forces in the making and maintaining of both boundary and identity."[15] Historically, "Coloured" *is* a racial identity that *has* progressed to an ethnic identity in the contemporary context. Eurafricans were initially assigned Coloured identity by colonial society. On the other hand, Eurafricans asserted their European and African lineages as being markers of their ethnic identity. Spickard writes, "[W]e ought to pay attention to the things that characterize groups and hold them together, to the content of group identity and activity, to patterns and means of inclusiveness and belonging."[16] By identifying as Eurafricans, mixed-descent Northern Rhodesians characterized their African and European genealogies, historical origins, and integrated cultural practices as being of equal importance to their group identity. However, Northern Rhodesian Africans, Europeans, and even Cape Coloureds criticized Eurafricans for defining themselves in this way. Their condemnation was not an uncommon reaction in the early part of the twentieth century. Spickard points out that "before the last third of the twentieth century, multiracial individuals did not generally have the opportunity to choose identities for themselves."[17]

Even in the twenty-first century, mixed-descent individuals are not given the opportunity to choose identities for themselves. This has been the experience of my teenage sons, Cameron and Dion, in present-day Brisbane, Australia, where my family lives. My sons are generally thrust into a specific category. They are not given the opportunity to embrace the White Australianness of their father, Bob, and my mixed Eurafrican Zambian identity. Cameron and Dion are generally defined as ethnic, meaning they are neither Indigenous Australians nor White Aussies. My Black African heritage is thrust upon them by the wider Australian community even though in our home we incorporate and perform Australian, South Pacific,[18] and Zambian cultural practices and celebrate our diverse origins.

In chapter 6, Fozdar and Perkins correctly point out that despite categories of difference playing a significant role in contemporary Australian society, official recognition of the population's cultural diversity is "a multiplicity of hyphenations." For example, I am described by the wider Australian community (and now describe myself) as an African-Australian.[19] My hyphenated categorization emphasizes my African heritage and Australian citizenship, and not my multiple cultural heritages. Fozdar and Perkins further note "there are two main categories of mixed race populations in Australia, those with mixed Aboriginal/non-Aboriginal ancestries, and those with mixed white and other ancestries." They point out that the "life chances and identities of the two differ significantly" and that "Aboriginality is associated with social disadvantage and marginality in Australia."[20] Indigenous Australians' marginality is an outcome of Australia's historical racialized narrative.[21] Racism has been institutionalized in Australia through various historical government policies and practices—namely the "White Australia Policy" and state government interventions to biologically "breed out" Indigenous Australians and Indigenous culture into mainstream White Australian society.[22] Consequently, Black Africans—like their fellow Black Indigenous Australian counterparts—"find they are racialized in their interactions with other Australians who are deracialized because they are white."[23] In 1940s colonial Zambia, my community met intense resistance from both Africans and White settlers. For example, in 1947 a group of Eurafricans went to a local cinema in Lusaka and the European cinema manager refused to sell them cinema tickets. The manager claimed it was a 'European cinema and not for Coloured people." A Eurafrican man wrote a letter of protest to a local newspaper. He stated in the past they had bought cinema tickets at the same price as European customers; however Eurafricans had to sit away from European patrons at the back of the cinema. The Eurafrican stated there was no sign on the cinema designating it a "whites only" space. He described his hurt and public humiliation 'it is not our fault that we are Eurafricans, but the fault of our fathers, who were themselves Europeans'.[24]

Eurafricans were also subjected to African hostility. Some Africans accused "Eurafricans of despising their mothers and their African relatives" and claiming "they were white men, and not black men."[25] In 1947, an African man identified as Mr. Mabulyato wrote a letter to the second Coloured Persons Committee (a committee commissioned by the Northern Rhodesia government to investigate the status and welfare of Coloureds in the territory) in which he accused "the Coloured people in this country [of] creating an unnecessary problem," claiming "it is obvious that they wish to be Europeans and Africans at the same time because they do not know their proper status in the country."[26] He claimed that the Northern Rhodesian Coloured community was disunited because "some of them call themselves Cape Coloureds and others Eur-Africans."[27] Mabulyato ridiculed Eurafricans, saying "they have even braced themselves with a meaningless name of the 'Eur-Africans.'" He overlooked the fact that Eurafricans' Northern Rhodesian origins and British and African cultural practices were unlike those of the Cape Coloured community, and it was due to these cultural and historical differences that Eurafricans resisted being categorized as Coloured— which essentially was a South African categorization. He accused Eurafricans of not knowing their rightful place in Northern Rhode sia, and stated that "such a rider of two horses does not help them in the long run nor does it help the Government and other races in this country." Mabulyato demeaned Eurafricans, claiming that they were backward and even went so far as to claim Eurafricans' African mothers were prostitutes and a disgrace to African society.[28] In demeaning and devaluing Eurafricans' African mothers and cultural practices, Mabulyato worked to devalue African culture and traditions—he essentially derided and devalued *himself*.

Frantz Fanon's insightful comment about colonized people's ambivalent position is applicable to the predicament of non-White Northern Rhodesians:

> All colonized people—in other words, people whom an inferiority complex has taken root, whose local cultural originality has been committed to the grave—position themselves in relation to the civilizing language: i.e., the metropolitan culture. The more the colonized has assimilated the cultural values of the metropolis, the more he will have escaped the bush. The more he rejects his blackness and the bush, the whiter he will become.[29]

Northern Rhodesian White settler society propagated a sense of abject inadequacy and inferiority in the minds of African people; this was especially so for African men, whom they infantilized portraying them as unmanly.[30] Africans viewed themselves through the lens of their White colonial masters, and thus perceived their Blackness as inferior to Whiteness. In order for Europeans to govern and control the immeasurable numbers of colonized people globally, Whiteness had to reign supreme. Catherine Hall points out that "making" new subjects was part of the colonial project in the British Empire: "the colonized were only to know themselves through the eye of the colonizer."[31] Eurafricans were the biological children of European men; despite this, the Northern Rhodesian administration categorically classified them as British Protected Persons, a term that materialized in the nineteenth century but was only quantified in the British Nationality Act 1948 legislation. Eurafricans acquired their African mothers' social and political "native" colonized status rather than their European fathers' White "governing" status. British Protected Persons were granted "imperial 'political' protection in places *outside* the Crown's dominions" rather than British citizenship or nationality.[32] Eurafricans aspired to Whiteness by emphasizing their European genealogies and British cultural practices. Homi Bhabha theorizes Europeans' indoctrination and conditioning of Whiteness as "the ambivalent figure of 'mimicry'—a reformed recognizable Other, *as a subject of difference that is almost the same, but not quite.*"[33] Globally, colonized peoples mimicked European ideologies and cultural practices.

In the next section, I turn my gaze to British imperial legislation and colonial governance in Northern Rhodesia. I pay particular attention to an address by W. H. Gardner to the minister of the colonies in Northern Rhodesia in 1952. In Gardner's presentation, he expresses Eurafricans' concerns about their status in the proposed Central African Federation, and their intense frustration with the *British Nationality Act 1948*. This act was of grave concern not only to Eurafricans but also to other colonized subjects in Britain's dependencies as far afield as the New Hebrides (present-day Vanuatu) in the South Pacific and the Persian Gulf (the present-day United Arab Emirates).[34] Although the act introduced British citizenship by naturalization, it also effectively dispossessed the bulk of colonized people of British citizenship, including Eurafricans.

Northern Rhodesia: British Imperial
Legislation and Colonial Governance

On August 11, 1952, in the Eastern Province of Northern Rhodesia, W. H. Gardner, the president of the National Association of Northern Rhodesia, addressed Henry Hopkinson, minister of the colonies. In the opening paragraphs of his presentation, Gardner introduces Northern Rhodesian Eurafricans as "persons of European and African parentage, origin and descent who form part and parcel of this Territory."[35] Throughout his representation, Gardner emphasizes Eurafricans' British and noble African parentage, and utilizes the language of his British colonizers by drawing class distinctions between Eurafricans and the African population.

In his address, Gardner voices Eurafricans' anxieties about their exclusion from the British government's proposed plans for the Central African Federation of Northern and Southern Rhodesia and Nyasaland: "We as a community in Northern Rhodesia are in a state of uncertainty and frustration. . . . There are no definite and progressive plans to deal effectively with the problems of the community." Gardner informs the minister that "the *British Nationality Act 1948* has deprived us of our British Status and as a result members of our community who were on the voters' roll have been removed." He claims that this is "viewed as a policy in keeping with the Union of South Africa." Gardner sought recognition of Eurafricans:

> as an established fact that . . . the community were British subjects by birth, until just recently we have come to realize that the position was reversed and we are to be known as British Protected Persons, and we are required to Naturalize if we wish to attain the Status of British Subject and to have the Franchise.[36]

With grave disappointment, Gardner states that "today as a result of the *British Nationality Act 1948* not one Eurafrican born in Northern Rhodesia has the Franchise or Status of our Father the European." He reminds the minister that "it cannot be denied that the majority of us are Sons and Daughters of the early Noble Pioneers who opened up these Territories." Gardner further informed the minister that

[British men] . . . came with out [sic] wives and how else could you expect them not to take upon themselves African [sic] women. . . . [T]hey did so for various reasons . . . 1./ economical; 2./ health; 3./ the country was wild and danger lurked everywhere; 4./ the present comfort and conveniences were not exisetant [sic]. [37]

He ends by noting, "I should like at this stage to record for all time that these early pioneers took upon themselves African woman of noble birth or of noble standing in the Tribe."[38] Gardner distinguished Eurafricans' parents as being of the African noble class and the British middle class. A large number of British officials and administrators in British Central Africa and the wider British Empire were middle-class graduates of Britain's finest public schools and universities, including Cambridge and Oxford.[39]

A note dated September 8, 1952, addressed to Mr. Williams, is appended to Gardner's typed presentation to the minister. The writer states that "at the Minister's meeting in Fort Jameson with the coloured community (which you know is strong there, and of a very high quality), their leader, Mr. Gardner, made a particular point . . . which I have marked in red."[40] The British official identified Eastern Province Eurafricans as "strong and of a high quality" because the majority were the descendants of colonial officials and pioneers, including His Majesty's Consul to British Central Africa Sir Alfred Sharpe, H. S. "Dongolosi" Thornicroft, E. H. Lane-Poole, and Captain Frank Robertson.

The points marked in red on Gardner's presentation were the claims he made about the *British Nationality Act 1948* dispossessing Eurafricans from British citizenship and disfranchisement in Northern Rhodesia; he also raised a further point about the propriety and legality of European and African women's marriages in accordance with African customary marriage practices, which he argued legitimized Eurafricans—thus qualifying them as British nationals and citizens with a franchise. A handwritten remark in the margins of a draft of an official paper in response to Gardner's assertions cautions, "NO whatever we do, we cannot assimilate monogamous systems with a polygamous system."[41] White officials were concerned European marriage practices threatened the sanctity of English Christian marriage traditions.

Gardner's evaluation of the *British Nationality Act 1948* was correct. Although the Act did in fact introduce the option of British citizenship by naturalization for the first time, it also firmly established *jus sanguinis* clauses whereby British citizenship by descent could be inherited only by the legitimate children of British men.[42] Northern Rhodesian officials did not recognize European men and African women's traditional African marriages as legitimate because they were not sanctioned under the statutes of the *Northern Rhodesian Marriage Ordinances 1918*.[43] Interestingly, Northern Rhodesian marriage legislation implied but did not stipulate that European men and African women could not marry each other across color and class lines, and this gravely concerned British officials in London, who did not want to be accused of instituting racialized policies. It appears that Northern Rhodesian officials safeguarded themselves from white settler condemnation for condoning miscegenation by not officially recognizing European men and African women's interracial marriages as legitimate thus guaranteeing Eurafricans' illegitimacy.[44] Consequently, illegitimacy is one of the painful legacies in Zambian Coloured families.

However, as my following autoethnographic representation demonstrates, British bloodlines are not the only historical legacy that continues to overshadow Colouredness in modern-day Zambia. Nineteenth-century European racialized ideas simplify Colouredness to a racial classification, thus dismissing it as a cultural and ethnic identity.

Complexities and Entanglements of Colouredness in a Global Context

In 1990, my nine-year-old son Courtney and I returned to my family home in Chingola, Zambia. One afternoon, Courtney returned home from school and told me about meeting a Coloured boy from Australia named Greg. Courtney and his friends were amused that Greg got upset when they called him Coloured. In a small mining town like Chingola, word soon got around that there was a mixed-descent kid who was having an identity crisis. Greg was constantly teased when he defined himself as an Australian—which he essentially is. In 1990s Chingola, as in the rest of Zambia, you were either categorized as European (meaning White), African/Zambian (meaning Black),

Indian, Chinese, or Coloured (of mixed descent). Eleven-year-old Greg refused to be pigeonholed into any one of these racial categories. Soon I befriended Greg, and explained the racial dynamics in Zambia to him. I told him that since his father, Bob, was a White Australian and his late mother, Margaret, had been a Pacific Islander, this essentially meant Greg was categorized as Coloured in Zambia. Thereafter, when asked what he was, Greg would promptly reply "Coloured" and the teasing stopped.

In 1994, I migrated to Australia with my Australian family. In 1999, we moved to live in Brisbane, Queensland, where I commenced my undergraduate studies. By this time, Greg's Australian father and I had been married for seven years and Courtney sadly had died under very tragic circumstances in Zambia. My studies at university caused a major shift in my thinking. I was especially interested in the painful legacies of mixed-descent Indigenous child separation and biological assimilative policies in Australia, which I found to be in many ways comparable to Eurafricans' historical experiences in Zambia and Zimbabwe. I also discovered that Indigenous Australians do not define themselves as Coloured. They consider this term a derogatory historical racial classification.[45] I realized *my* wrongdoing in inscribing Colouredness on Greg, who had not had any experience of either the racialized origins of Colouredness in the British Empire in Southern Africa or the discriminatory historical practices associated with Colouredness until he came to live in Zambia.

During Courtney's thirteen-year lifetime, he lived in a multicultural family in both Zambia and Australia and he never questioned his "Coloured" classification despite the fact that his paternal grandfather is Scottish and paternal grandmother is first-generation Northern Rhodesian/Zambian-born Eurafrican, of English and African descent; his maternal grandmother, my mother Nellie Milner, is second-generation Northern Rhodesian/Zambian-born Eurafrican, of English, Italian, and African descent; his maternal grandfather, my late father Japhet Milner, was first-generation Southern Rhodesian/Zimbabwean-born Eurafrican of Lithuanian Jewish and Zulu descent; and his adopted grandparents, my husband Bob's late mother, Alsa, and late father, Norm Thornton, were Australian-born of English and Scottish descent. Courtney's experiences are not unusual. Kwame Anthony

Appiah describes sharing with his siblings a similar experience of being "children of two worlds" and "seeing the world as a network of points of affinity."[46]

Historicizing Colouredness: Zambia

Courtney and Greg's story reveals the resilience of imperial racialized ideologies in Zambia, where there is a predisposition (and in this regard I implicate my *former* self) for Colouredness to continue to be used as a racial categorization to describe persons of mixed African and European heritage. Interestingly, from the 1930s to the 1960s, the Northern Rhodesian government could not agree on who could or should be categorized as Coloured.[47] Each time questions surrounding Eurafricans' social, political, and economic circumstances were raised, the issue of Eurafricans' paternity inevitably was broached—accompanied by highly emotional discussions about their citizenship and belonging. These external forces played a key role in Eurafricans' conceptions of their community and greatly assisted in Eurafricans' progressive adoption of Coloured to its current application as a cultural and ethnic identity in Zambia. Eurafricans' British paternity was an especially contentious issue in Northern Rhodesia.

In April 1953, officials in the British Colonial Office discussed Gardner's presentation to the minister of the colonies.[48] In various drafts of official correspondence, which seemingly circulated between five particular bureaucrats in the Colonial Office, two issues were singled out as being of particular importance to Northern Rhodesian Eurafricans. These were Eurafricans' housing and paternity. Of these, Eurafricans' British paternity was of special interest to British officials, as it brought into question their legitimacy and thus official status in the British Empire. The issue of Eurafricans' legitimacy and status in the British Empire quietly simmered beneath the surface of British colonial politics, occasionally bubbling over into the center of imperial politics in the periphery and the epicenter of empire in London.[49]

The questions about Eurafricans' legitimacy and status centered on the legality of the marriages between Eurafricans' European fathers and African mothers; this is disclosed in a British Colonial Office minute dated April 1, 1953, written by G. L. Gobling:

The chances of the necessary proof of these facts [European men and African women's marriages] being forthcoming now are, to say the least of it, remote. But if these three points could be proved the children of the union would be legitimate and therefore take up [their] father's nationality. If the change of domicile—a matter of intention evidenced by the facts—could not be proved the marriage would be invalid and the children illegitimate and they could not take their father's nationality.[50]

In a handwritten note on the bottom of the minute, Mr. D. W. Williams in the Colonial Office responds to Gobling's remarks, noting that "during his visit last year the Minister, like Mr Griffiths before him, was deeply impressed by the Coloureds and promised to look into their grievances." Eurafricans' grievances were their housing and status. In reference to housing, Williams agrees that it is almost nonexistent and the standard of what is available is deplorable, but he notes that this could easily be resolved. On the other hand, "the question of [Coloureds'] status . . . this (alas!) is a question of almost Byzantine complexity. It boils down to the simple question! 'Are first generation Coloureds born in N. Rhodesia all illegitimate?'"[51]

The Northern Rhodesian marriage legislation did not condone, but neither did it prohibit, European men and African women marrying; however, condemnation from White officials and settler society was enough of a deterrent for the large majority of white men to choose a double life: they lived in the privacy of their homes with their African wives and Eurafrican children, but in the public sphere portrayed themselves as bachelors in order to be accepted by White settler society and enjoy the privileges of Whiteness.[52] In addition, when European men married European women it was not uncommon for them to neglect their Eurafrican children. This was the case for Rosemary Innes: "her father . . . a European planter now married to a European woman . . . formerly took care of his two daughters but since his marriage they have been neglected."[53]

Biological Assimilative Advancements

In January 1928, shortly after undertaking his appointment as governor, Maxwell advanced the biological absorption of Eurafricans into the predominant African community in Northern Rhodesia. Maxwell's biological assimilative scheme was prompted by debates centering on the inadequate—or, more accurately, nonexistent—educational facilities for Eurafrican children in Northern Rhodesia. In 1927, local missionaries questioned the Northern Rhodesian Education Department's indifference to half-caste children's inadequate educational services in the territory.[54] The government constructed and financially supported schools for African and European children, but no schools for Eurafrican children. The missionaries appealed to the Northern Rhodesian government for financial assistance to build missionary schools specifically for Eurafricans. The Northern Rhodesian Native Education Advisory Board supported the missionaries' recommendation. Maxwell was troubled by their standpoint.

In January 1928, Maxwell wrote a letter to Mr. L. S. Amery, the secretary of state in London, expressing his displeasure about and opposition to building separate schools for so-called half-caste children in Northern Rhodesia.[55] Maxwell cautioned Amery, "if separate schools were instituted and supported by the Government we are creating an entirely artificial class who, as stated at the Board, will not be regarded as either white or native." He further claimed, "[They] will continue to look to Government for the provisions of employment for the rest of their lives."[56] Maxwell prejudiced Whitehall and his own government's position on Eurafricans and predisposed successive Northern Rhodesian governments to a racialized standpoint about Eurafricans' education and status for the next three decades. Indeed, in 1958, the Eurafrican Society in Lusaka wrote to Roy Welensky, the prime minister of the Central African Federation. The society complained to Welensky that, prior to the Federation's establishment in 1954, "both the Northern Rhodesia and Nyasaland Governments gave our people the benefits of employment in their various Government departments." The society noted that it is "indeed a sorry state of affairs [that] since Federation no such practices have been established or carried out fully."[57]

Maxwell's letter and the correspondence it generated suggests that Maxwell's far graver anxiety was miscegenation and Eurafricans' ability to claim their British fathers' nationality and citizenship and thus gain a high economic and political status in Northern Rhodesia. Prior to his governorship in Northern Rhodesia, Maxwell had worked in Sierra

Leone and Ghana for over twenty years and observed "half-caste men and women [occupying] prominent positions," whom, he noted, identified "themselves as a rule with the interests of the African race from which they are partly descended."[58] Maxwell essentially argued Eurafricans should identify as Africans and not as Europeans or a distinct mixed-race population. In Western British Africa, Eurafricans married into and within the Western African Eurafrican commnity, which as a result was well educated, prosperous, and politically formidable. Seemingly, Eurafricans moved seamlessly between European and African society in Ghana and Sierra Leone.[59] In advancing Eurafricans' biological assimilation into the predominant African society Maxwell set out to prevent a similar scenario from occurring in Northern Rhodesia. He was particularly contemptuous of Eurafrican children because of the complications their British fathers' elite status represented for the local administration's efforts to safeguard the color and class distinctions in the territory.

In Northern Rhodesia, British fathers' identities were simultaneously closely guarded and an open secret. In 1950, the Kreft Committee (the third committee appointed by the Northern Rhodesian government to investigate Eurafricans' welfare in the territory) reported that although Eurafrican children's British paternity was almost entirely undocumented it was known to European contemporaries, the children's African mothers, and Eurafrican children themselves.[60]

Nevertheless, Maxwell was not the only settler to express reservations about advancing Africans' education in Northern Rhodesia. In 1931, Dr. Sidney Spencer "Kachalola" Broomfield, a transnational traveler, explorer, and pioneer of Australia and Northern Rhodesia, mournfully wrote about "[those] good old days of African travel and shooting." He lamented that "one never sees the likes of those days," and complained that "natives have got a taste of civilization and education. Add to that a little religion and you have an impossible native."[61] Broomfield disclosed White settlers' anxieties about educating Africans: they were apprehensive that educated Africans would encumber the economic, social, political, and intellectual privileges of Whiteness in Northern Rhodesia. Broomfield's attitude is especially disturbing because of its implications for his own children. Kachalola Broomfield was my English great-grandfather—my grandfather, Stephen Broomfield, was his Northern

Rhodesian–born Eurafrican son. Broomfield is literally drawn into the national histories of Zambia and Australia: in these two countries, he is on the periphery and at the center of historical events. In Zambia, Broomfield is celebrated for his hunting prowess, sexual role, and pioneering activities. In the Eastern Province of Zambia, a town is named Kachalola in honor of his pioneering and hunting. In Australia, he is distinguished as an author, pioneer, explorer, cartographer, and medical doctor.[62] Whereas Broomfield is celebrated in Australian and British imperial history, his Eurafrican descendants are referred to by Lord Foggin as "a great evil and . . . unfortunate addition" to the Empire.[63]

In the next section, I demonstrate that the questions surrounding Africans' education—and particularly Maxwell's contribution—represent crucial episodes in the engineering of a separate Coloured mixed-race community and ethnic identity in Northern Rhodesia.

Engendering a "Native" Mixed-Descent Status in the British Empire

In 1929, the debate about Eurafricans' status in Northern Rhodesia became an international one. Shortly after Maxwell outlined his assimilative agenda, a local court case in neighboring Nyasaland (present-day Malawi) was at center stage of British imperial politics. A local British judge determined that members of Nyasaland's so-called half-caste population were "nonnative"—meaning that they were British citizens. This judgment incited international deliberations between and among British men about the social, legal, and political standing of mixed-descent Africans in Britain's African dependencies and colonies. The Colonial Office was concerned particularly about the backlash created by the verdict. It set out to engender and sanction a single unifying category of "native" under the jurisdiction of individual administrative decrees in Britain's African territories as an alternative to the jurisdictions of British law, which in principle were color- and class-blind. However, as the Colonial Office soon discovered, defining and then enforcing "native" as a common legal category in its African colonies and dependencies was not a straightforward undertaking.[64]

In 1931, Maxwell responded to the half-caste status debate. He wrote to a representative of the Colonial Office recommending that a "mode of living standard" be applied to determine half-castes' "native" or "non-native" classification in Africa. Maxwell argued that a half-caste with European parentage on one side could be classified as either a European or African—their manner of living should determine their racial categorization.[65] In principle, this meant Eurafricans could change their status to European, but only if they lived like Europeans; on the other hand, if they lived as Africans they would be classified as "native." Seemingly, the foremost objective in Northern Rhodesian officials' minds—and particularly Maxwell's—was to discredit Eurafricans' legitimacy, and thus stop them claiming British nationality and citizenship. The official objective in Northern Rhodesia was to breed out Whiteness—more specifically, British bloodlines. In British officials' correspondence with one another, their choice of terminology reveals that their overall intention was to breed Eurafricans *into* African society and breed *out* White British bloodlines from Eurafrican genealogies. The status of Eurafricans in Northern Rhodesia and the wider British Empire remained a contentious issue throughout the period of British colonial rule, and subsequent Northern Rhodesian administrators continued to adopt Maxwell's assimilative initiatives for over thirty years.

Eurafricans' Legitimacy and Status in Northern Rhodesia

In June 1952, in the same year that the British Colonial Office was discussing Gardner's presentation to the minister, an official in the Colonial Office made observations about British men and African women's customary marriages in Northern Rhodesia. The official noted that "marriages between natives according to native law would be regarded as legal unions, and that the offspring of such marriages are not branded as illegitimate, nor are their rights (e.g. of inheritance in doubt)."[66] The official compassionately argued that "it is very easy to see, therefore, why Africans and Euro-Africans find it difficult to understand why the products of *mixed* marriages celebrated under native law and custom should be branded as illegitimate"[67]—particularly Eurafrican children who were born to interracial marriages sanctioned by traditional African customary practices with the payment of *lobola* (bride price). Nonetheless, the overriding argument of white officials in the Colonial Office was that "all Coloureds were held to be illegitimate [because]

Section 47 of the Marriage Ordinance (Cap. 132) excludes the possibility of legal marriages between a European and an African."[68]

Eurafricans' unpredictable status was also influenced by the segregated social institutions to which they were confined—socially, politically, and economically. For example, Coloureds were employed in segregated jobs, hospitalized in segregated wards, and lived in segregated housing estates known as the "Coloured quarters" (built by local councils) on the fringes of European society in the major industrial towns. Coloured children were railed out by train to Coloured missionary schools in neighboring Southern Rhodesia (present-day Zimbabwe) until 1955, when the government and Whitehall succumbed to Eurafrican and Coloured pressure and permitted the Dominican nuns to build Fatima Convent, a school specifically for Eurafrican and Coloured children on the outskirts of Ndola in the Copperbelt.[69]

The Northern Rhodesian government undertook such separatist measures under the instruction of the Colonial Office (and in compliance with Whitehall) and categorically refused to legitimize "Coloured" as a legal classification in Northern Rhodesia, because it would be seen by Coloureds—and particularly Eurafricans—as the first step towards recognition of their status as the blood descendants of British men. The Colonial Office was especially concerned by this state of affairs. It criticized the Kreft Committee for trying to create "namely . . . a 'new race' with a legal standing."[70]

The Kreft Committee suggested to the Northern Rhodesian government that one way to overcome Eurafricans' inconsistent status and nationality was to inform them about "the procedure to be followed to obtain naturalisation papers" in order to become British citizens.[71] Naturalization was not an agreeable option for Northern Rhodesian Eurafricans.[72] They pointed out that their fathers were "pukka Britishers," and as such this predetermined their entitlement to British citizenship.[73] In handwritten notes on an archival document, a British official noted his exasperation at Eurafricans' unwillingness to pay £5 to be naturalized as British subjects. He lamented that "the problem would be solved" if Eurafricans paid the £5 fee. He noted Eurafricans' strong resistance to and resentment about paying the fee: "on principle being deprived of status they once possessed . . . they can't be expected to sit down under the argument that the chap who gave them their 'British

Passports' had no right to do so."[74] Eurafricans strongly resisted paying such a fee to be naturalized because they simply could not afford it. The average monthly income for Eurafrican men in Lusaka was between £15 and £25; they could barely make ends meet each month—in fact, most lived on credit.[75]

In 1957, the British administration revisited the question about citizenship in Central Africa. In order to become a citizen of the Federation a person had to "accept British subject status" and to qualify for the electoral roll they had to earn an "income of £720 plus four years' secondary education."[76] These qualifications were beyond the means of most Eurafricans/Coloureds because of their meager pay and basic primary education, even though the Central Province Eurafrican Society implored Prime Minister Welensky to change his mind, saying that "we feel our people deserve better in view of our higher standards as compared to Africans."[77]

Eurafricans' aspirations to be recognized as the authentic descendants of British men and African women were dismissed as an "internalized" inferiority complex generally expressed by the community.[78] However, Eurafricans' social, economic, and political aspirations were no different from those of their fellow Black Northern Rhodesians: both sought relief from discriminatory policies and practices. The only way they could see to do so was by successfully claiming White identity.

Whiteness in Northern Rhodesia

Eurafricans' social aspirations were reasonable, as there were social, political, and economic advantages to being categorized as White in Northern Rhodesia. For example, so-called Europeanized Coloureds who lived in accordance with European standards were paid higher wages than Coloureds who lived like the native population.[79] Many light-skinned South African Coloureds used their immigration to Northern Rhodesia and Europeanized lifestyles as an opportunity to change their status and pass as White in the territory. "Play Whites" were people of African descent who identified themselves with European society because they lived in conformity with a European lifestyle. They were thus excluded from the Coloured categorization and the discriminatory policies associated with the classification.

In the 1930s and 1940s, at the same time that Eurafricans were clamoring for British nationality and citizenship, British identity was only just coming into being as an ethnic categorization. Chris A. Bayly reminds us that "Britishness was a recent fragile and contested ideology of power."[80] In the colonies, a common British identity had to be forged and established[81] and in Northern Rhodesia, the working class "adopted whiteness as a sense of self, nation and community."[82]

In Northern Rhodesia, Eurafricans were inside/outside, looking into/ looking out from African and European colonial society; they belonged to both but were incorporated in neither, and as a result realized that the only way to gain political and social advantage was to bond with other non-White groups that shared similar experiences of marginalization and alienation. From the late 1950s, Northern Rhodesian Eurafricans joined forces with immigrant Cape Coloureds' and Southern Rhodesian Eurafricans' political campaigns and progressively came to identify themselves as Coloured.

Colouredness in Contemporary Zambia: A Duplication or Legacy of Colonial Processes?

In the preceding sections we have seen the external and internal factors that helped to shape Coloured identity in colonial Zambia. It is from these historical origins that Coloured identity has evolved into its current ethnic and cultural identity in contemporary Zambia.

Nonetheless, Eurafrican Coloureds are still not officially recognized as a cultural and ethnic group in Zambia by the Zambian government. In spite of Eurafrican Coloureds' historical and genetic origins, the Zambian government excludes them from the country's national census—and has done so for the past thirty-two years:

> *Eurafrican (or EuroAfrican).* A word used to refer to people of mixed racial ancestry, the so-called "coloured" in *South Africa.* (The term "coloured" is disfavoured as derogatory.) Historically, some of their leaders once formed the *Northern Rhodesian Eurafrican Association.* The nearly 6,000 such people [i.e. Eurafricans]—mostly located in urban areas—in the 1980 census then constituted 0.1 percent of the Zambian population. Subsequent censuses did not include the category.[83]

According to this excerpt from the *Historical Dictionary of Zambia*, Eurafricans and thus Coloureds officially do not exist in Zambia. They have been erased from Zambia's cultural and historical landscape. The full results of Zambia's 2010 national census have not been collated and released to date. Nonetheless according to Zambia's 2000 census, "the Zambian population mostly constitutes of persons of African origin, 99.5 percent. The American, Asian, European and 'Other' ethnic groups make up the remaining 0.5 percent."[84] The report goes onto say that this "ethnic composition [is] dominated by Africans."[85] This implies that the Zambian population is homogenous. I suggest that Coloureds' exclusion from the census is a legacy of British imperial governance, wherein "Colouredness" was seen and administered as a racial anomaly rather than an ethnic and cultural identity.

Despite the historical and contemporary omission of government officials to differentiate Eurafrican Coloureds as a distinct culture and ethnicity in Zambia, Coloured people perceive themselves to be, and are seen by the wider Zambian community as, separate from the predominant African community. Coloureds constitute an ethnic and cultural group that has its historical origins in Zambia. Eurafricans emphasized their African and European historical connections and cross-cultural practices as a significant part of their community's cultural practices and were branded racist by the general African public, which accused Eurafricans of denying their African origins and heritage. These historical ideas are articulated in contemporary Zambia by some Zambian people who label Coloureds dangerous and chiefless, with no villages that they can claim within Zambia as their ancestral home. Coloured women are also stereotyped as "high-class prostitutes,"[86] just one of the many legacies of the British Empire.

British bloodlines in the contemporary context *seemingly* preclude Zambian Coloureds from being included as a separate ethnic identity and cultural classification in Zambia's national census, and facilitate their return to the United Kingdom and their reclamation of British citizenship. Admittedly, traumatic events did not prompt the return migration of Coloureds to Great Britain. Their dispersal from Zambia is the result of the complex circumstances of their cultural, historical, and geographical origins, as well as their economic predicament in Zambia.

The "return migration" of Zambian Coloureds to Britain suggests they are a part of both the British *and* African diasporas.[87] Return migration is confined not only to the British Empire. Other returnees assert their ancestral connections by returning to their ancestral homelands—for example, the Indo-Dutch from Indonesia to the Netherlands and Japanese Brazilians to Japan from Brazil.[88] Migration theorist Russell King points out the motivation to return is varied, complex, and individual, and often leads to difficulty integrating in the place of origin; upon arriving, the returnee finds that "there is no place back home."[89] In Britain, Zambian Coloureds find themselves looking on the outside into British society; this is particularly pronounced in Southampton, where the community is a tight-knit group of families who are interrelated by marriage. The Southampton Coloured community involves a large web of familial connections tracing back to British men and African women in colonial Zambia. King reminds us that although returnees return to their place of origin, the circle is incomplete as notions of home and abroad become blurred, as do the definitions of migration, return, mobility, travel, and so forth.[90] Zambia Coloureds' return migrations are a reflection of transnational communities in diaspora; they are both transgenerational and transnational, and mirror similar journeys undertaken by descendants of pioneers in the former British Empire.[91]

Conclusion

Colouredness in Zambia is an ethnic and cultural identity, with historical origins in the British Empire in Northern Rhodesia. It is characterized by a history of marginalization and alienation in Coloured missionary schools, the Coloured quarters, and racially segregated jobs simply because they were mixed race—and more importantly the progeny of the British colonial elite—and the contemporary transgenerational and transnational experience of diasporic journeys to Great Britain that encompass four to six successive generations of Eurafricans who continue to articulate and express their genealogy and historical origins through their integrated cross-cultural African and European traditional customary practices.

In contemporary Zambia, a Coloured person is recognized by the wider Coloured/Zambian community as someone who or whose family has experienced the historical processes of Coloured identity-formation I have described in this chapter, either first-hand or through various family members. This makes Colouredness an exclusive identity, one that does not incorporate those of mixed European and African ancestry who were born in independent Zambia after 1964. Nor does it incorporate mixed-descent persons who have lived in Zambia for short periods of time and who have not interacted with Zambian Coloureds and participated in Zambian Coloured cultural practices during their stay.

NOTES

1. NAZ SEC1/575, "Education of Coloured Children," Governor James Crawford Maxwell's letter to L. S. Amery M.P., dated January 16, 1928.
2. NAZ SEC1/575, "Education of Coloured Children," undated memorandum by the Government of Northern Rhodesia.
3. Ibid.
4. Simon, Pletcher, and Seigel, *Historical Dictionary of Zambia*, 111.
5. Milner-Thornton, *The Long Shadow of the British Empire*, 10; Republic of Zambia Statistics 2000 Housing and Population Main Zambia Census Report, vol. 10, chap. 3, "Population Composition and Size," 38. http://www.zamstats.gov.zm/media/chapter_3_population_comp._size_and_growth-_final.pdf, accessed April 20, 2012.
6. http://www.ukba.homeoffice.gov.uk/sitecontent/documents/policyandlaw/IDIs/idischapter1/section1/annexa.pdf?view=Binary.
7. Ibid., 2, 3.
8. Stoler, *Along the Archival Grain*, 8, 52.
9. Fanon, *Black Skin, White Masks*, 9.
10. Anderson, *The Cultivation of Whiteness*, 127; Lake and Reynolds, *Drawing the Global Colour Line*, Introduction; Smithers, *Science, Sexuality, and Race in the United States and Australia*, 5.
11. Roediger, *The Wages of Whiteness*; Brodkin, *How Jews Became White Folks*.
12. Caplan, *Children of Colonialism*; Reynolds, *Nowhere People*.
13. NAZA SEC1/575, "Education of Coloured Children," confidential letter to the director of European education from Chief Secretary of Northern Rhodesia D. M. Kennedy, dated January 22, 1931.
14. Cornell and Hartmann, *Ethnicity and Race*, 24.
15. Ibid., 85.

16. Spickard, "Illogic of American Racial Categories," 151.
17. Ibid.
18. Margaret, the mother of my children Lyle, Dianne, and Greg, was a Pacific Islander.
19. Milner-Thornton, *The Long Shadow of the British Empire*.
20. For Aboriginal history, see Broome, *Aboriginal Australians*; Haebich, *Broken Circles*.
21. See Moreton-Robinson, "Whiteness Matters."
22. White Australia Policy, Australian Government Department of Immigration and Citizenship. http://www.immi.gov.au/media/fact-sheets/08abolition.htm, accessed November 20, 2011.
23. See Windle, "The Racialisation of African Youth in Australia."
24. Milner-Thornton, *The Long Shadow of the British Empire*, 165.
25. NAZ SEC1/581, "Extract from Minutes of the 4th Meeting of the Northern Rhodesian Province (Western Areas) African Provincial Council Held at Kawambwa, on Monday and Tuesday April 28th and 29th 1947."
26. Welensky Papers, Bodleian Library, Rhodes House, Oxford, Box 5, Folder 5/1, "Mr. R. M. Mabulyato from the Training Institute Kafue Letter Addressed to the Coloured Persons Committee Dated 20th January 1948."
27. Ibid., 4.
28. Ibid.
29. Fanon, *Black Skin, White Masks*, 3.
30. Mrinalini, *Colonial Masculinity*; Woollacott, *Gender and Empire*, 8.
31. Hall, "William Knibb," 303.
32. United Kingdom Home Office, Part VI: British Protected Persons Clause 54.1.1 and 54.1.2.http://www.ukba.homeoffice.gov.uk/sitecontent/documents/policy-andlaw/nationalityinstructions/nichapter54/chapter54?view=Binary, accessed April 20, 2012.
33. Bhabha, *The Location of Culture*, 122.
34. British National Archive, CO126/8, *British Nationality Act 1948*, Treatment of British Protected Persons and British Registered Persons.
35. British National Archives, CO 1015/673, "The Status and Welfare of Coloured Persons in Northern Rhodesia."
36. Ibid.
37. Ibid.
38. Ibid.
39. Milner-Thornton, *The Long Shadow of the British Empire*.
40. PRO CO1015/673, April 1, 1953, "The Status and Welfare of Coloured Persons in Northern Rhodesia."
41. Ibid.
42. For British immigration law, see Dummett and Nicol, *Subjects, Citizens, Aliens and Others*.

43. CO795/170/14, *Report of the Committee to Inquire into the Status and Welfare of Coloured Persons in Northern Rhodesia 1951.*

44. CO1015/673. "The Status and Welfare of Coloureds in Northern Rhodesia 1952," memorandum addressed to Mr. Marnham, dated September 29, 1952.

45. Fozdar and Perkins, "Antipodean Mixed Race: Australia and New Zealand," in this volume.

46. Appiah, *In My Father's House*, vii.

47. Milner-Thornton, *The Long Shadow of the British Empire*, 85–866, 97, 212–13, 223.

48. PRO CO 1015/673, "The Status and Welfare of Coloured Persons in Northern Rhodesia."

49. Milner-Thornton, *The Long Shadow of the British Empire*, 79–91, 107–18, 133–226.

50. PRO CO1015/673, April 1, 1953, "The Status and Welfare of Coloured Persons in Northern Rhodesia."

51. Ibid.

52. Milner-Thornton, *The Long Shadow of the British Empire*, 166–70.

53. NAZ, letter addressed to the director of European education of Northern Rhodesia from A. H. Green, principal of Katapola School, Fort Jameson, Northern Rhodesia, dated May 4, 1954.

54. PRO CO795/23/12, "Education of Half-caste Children." For Coloured missionary schools in Southern Rhodesia, see Mandaza, *Race, Colour and Class in Southern Africa*, 195–225; Muzondidya, "Sitting on the Fence or Walking a Tightrope?"

55. Welensky Papers, Bodleian Library, Rhodes House, Oxford, Box 5, File 5/1, Governor Maxwell Letter to Mr. L. S. Amery, Colonial Office London, dated January 16, 1928.

56. Ibid.

57. Welensky Papers, Bodleian Library, Rhodes House, Oxford, Box 397, Folder 4 and Folder 2, letter to Prime Minister Roy Welensky from the Eurafrican Society, Lusaka, Central Province, Northern Rhodesia, dated May 20, 1958.

58. Welensky Papers, Bodleian Library, Rhodes House, Oxford, Box 5, File 5/1, Governor Maxwell's letter to Mr. L. S. Amery, Colonial Office, London, dated January 16, 1928.

59. Doortmont, *The Pen-Pictures of Modern Africans and African Celebrities by Charles Francis Hutchinson.*

60. Milner-Thornton, *The Long Shadow of the British Empire*, 209–11.

61. Broomfield, *Kachalola*, 132–33.

62. "Romantic Career," *Courier-Mail* (Brisbane), October 26, 1933.

63. Lord Foggin, chairman of the "1933 Southern Rhodesian Inquiry into the Questions Concerning the Education of Coloured and Half-Caste children in the Colony," in NAZ SEC1/576, the Committee to Inquire into Questions Concerning the Education of Coloured and Half-Caste Children in Southern Rhodesia, 1933, 26.

64. PRO CO822/36/16, "East Africa Status of Half-Castes 1931: Justice Haythorne Reed's Ruling dated 19th April 1929."

65. NAZ SEC1/575, "Northern Rhodesian Government Minute dated 21st January 1935."

66. PRO CO795/170/14, *Report of the Committee to Inquire into the Status and Welfare of Coloured Persons in Northern Rhodesia 1951.*

67. Ibid.

68. Ibid., 1.

69. Snelson, *Educational Development in Northern Rhodesia 1883–1945*, 182, 262–63.

70. PRO CO 795/170/14, *Report of the Committee to Inquire into the Status and Welfare of Coloured Persons in Northern Rhodesia 1951*, 1.

71. Leiden University, Africa Studies Centre 301.185.12–054.9/689.4, Northern Rhodesia, *Report of the Committee to Inquire into the Status and Welfare of Coloured Persons in Northern Rhodesia, 1950* (Lusaka: Government Printer), 47.

72. Welensky Papers, Bodleian Library, Rhodes House, Oxford, Box 5, File 5/1.

73. Ibid.

74. PRO CO1015/673, April 1, 1953, "The Status and Welfare of Coloured Persons in Northern Rhodesia."

75. *Report of the Committee to Inquire into the African and Eurafrican Housing Position in Lusaka, 1953* (Lusaka: Government Printer, 1953), 6.

76. Welensky Papers, Bodleian Library, Rhodes House, Oxford, Box 39/, Folder 4 and Folder 2 letter to Prime Minister Roy Welensky from the Eurafrican Society, Lusaka, Central Province, Northern Rhodesia, dated May 20, 1958.

77. Ibid.

78. Milner-Thornton, *The Long Shadow*, 147.

79. *Report of the Committee to Inquire into the African and Eurafrican Housing Position in Lusaka, 1953* (Lusaka: Government Printer, 1953), 6.

80. Bayly, "The British and Indigenous Peoples, 1760–1860," 19.

81. Ibid.

82. See Bonnet, "How the British Working Class Became White," 322.

83. Simon, Pletcher, and Seigel, *Historical Dictionary of Zambia*, 111.

84. Republic of Zambia Statistics 2000 Housing and Population Main Zambia Census Report, vol. 10, chap. 3, Population Composition and Size, 38. http://www.zamstats.gov.zm/media/chapter_3_population_comp._size_and_growth-_final.pdf, accessed April 20, 2012.

85. Ibid.

86. Ferguson, *Expectations of Modernity*, 289.

87. Cohen, "The Diaspora of a Diaspora"; Okpewho, Boyce Davies, and Mazuri, *The African Diaspora.*

88. Tsuda, "No Place to Call Home," 50.

89. King, "Generalizations from the History of Return Migration," 17, 19.

90. Ibid., 45.

91. For Anglo-Indian immigration, see Blunt, *Domicile and Diaspora*, 72–174; Caplan, *Children of Colonialism*, 129–56; Dutt, *In Search of a Homeland.* For return migration, see Ghosh, *Return Migration*; Sheffer, *Diaspora Politics at Home and Abroad.*

3

"Split Me in Two"

Gender, Identity, and "Race Mixing" in the Trinidad and Tobago Nation

RHODA REDDOCK

The Caribbean, an early locus of colonial capitalist export agriculture, is central to Robert Young's discussions of hybridity in *Colonial Desire* and it remains a site for much of the discussion of linguistic hybridity as well.[1] The term "hybrid," Young reminds us, has its origins in biological science, where it emerged to refer to a cross between two species such as the mule and the hinny,[2] which would be defective and barren and thus eventually become extinct.[3] Young refers to the contributions of Jamaican slave-owner Edward Long to the 18th-century debate on where Africans should be placed in the hierarchical scale of being. Should they be in the animal kingdom next to the ape or in the human species at the bottom of the "great chain of being"? Long argued in *The History of Jamaica* that for his part, "there were potent reasons for believing that the White and the Negro are two distinct species."[4] This had implications for biological hybridity, examples of which Long could no doubt observe all around him in 18th-century Jamaica. Despite arguments challenging this position—for example from the Anti-Slavery Society, which argued for a common humanity—Long concluded that although there had been fertile unions between Whites and Blacks in Jamaica, this fertility eventually declined through the generations.[5]

Today generations of Jamaicans and other "hybrid" populations have proved Long and similar thinkers wrong; however it is questionable how subversive such hybridity or any hybridity has been.

It is also interesting that the same Caribbean that Edward Long used to justify his argument for the nonviability of mixed race is today constructed as a hybrid, mixed, or *creole* space. The emergence of the concept of hybridity in the late 20th century, reflects many of the ideas already expressed by Caribbean scholars of creolization in the 1960s and 1970s. The terms *creole* and *creolization* have been used to refer to cultures and cultural processes, language and language development, as well as to peoples with origins elsewhere but born in the Caribbean region. More recently however it has come to refer to the "mixedness" that is supposed to characterize the region as reflected in the diverse combinations of language, cultures, and ancestry that inhabit that space. In many ways their use by postcolonial writers and scholars was a rehabilitation of a tainted term, tainted with the stigma of impurity. Of special significance here is the work of E. Kamau Brathwaite of Barbados—in particular his extended essay "Contradictory Omens, Cultural Diversity and Integration in the Caribbean"[6]—and more recently Edouard Glissant of Martinique and his concept of *Antillianté*,[7] which refers to the specific construction of Caribbean cultures as the coming together of disparate elements. In both instances the mixing of cultures was paramount but for the people of these countries, creoleness also related to the mixing of the people.

While Caribbean creoleness has been celebrated and become a central component of Caribbean identity, it has also been continuously contested. As Brathwaite stressed, the coming together of the dominant and dominated groups in the slave and postslave eras took place in a context of unequal power, of European cultural domination and the stigmatization and marginalization of African cultures and peoples. This process he saw as the beginning of creole society through the interaction of African and European in a "fixed superiority/inferiority relationship first by the *adaption* of both groups to their new environment, then of 'blacks to white norms' and of *interculturation* between both groups." In other words, Brathwaite argued that Caribbean creole society emerged both from the *assimilation* of Blacks to the dominant European cultural norms and behaviors *and* by the inadvertent *interculturation* of Whites into Black norms and behaviors and vice versa.

In a later work, *The Development of Creole Society in Jamaica,* Brathwaithe highlights the ways in which the Whites adopted/adapted to the ways of the enslaved people as evidenced by their language and accent, their dress—e.g., the use of head ties by White Caribbean women—and by their choices of food.[8] This, he argues, contributed to the creation of Caribbean creole society—a society of which Whites, Blacks, and their mixed offspring were all part, although with different levels of power and inclusion. These mixed offspring of European colonizers, colonial officials and businessmen, and non-European women (and possibly men) have been part of the colonial history of most of the postcolonial world. In the Anglophone Caribbean as in Zambia (see the preceding essay by Juliette Bridgette Milner-Thornton), South Africa, and elsewhere, the category "colored" emerged to refer to this group, which often performed a buffer role between the hegemonic European ruling class and the subordinated African working classes and was incorporated into the colonial censuses of many countries. The status and positioning of these mixed people and their descendants are central to the continuing discourses around color and phenotype that are central to Caribbean life today and still perceived as relevant to the allocation of privilege and prestige. At the same time, however, they also symbolize past and present European, social, sexual, cultural, and economic dominance. No doubt this contributes to the "contradictoriness" of which Brathwaithe speaks. For his part, Glissant saw Caribbean creolization as the future for the increasingly globalized world as the world itself, subject to the increasing movement of peoples, becomes much more of a creolized space.

Shalini Puri observed that the notions of hybridity and mixing are represented in the national icons—mottos, anthems, coats of arms, and so forth—of many Caribbean territories established at independence. Puri identifies a clear link between the emergence of state discourses of hybridity and efforts to construct the postcolonial nation-state in Latin America and the Caribbean. She notes:

> This recognition of the creolizing power of the state, combined with different demographic dynamics elsewhere in the Caribbean, makes for

the prominence of hybridity in Caribbean political nationalisms. It is, in other words, no accident that in the Caribbean and Latin America the rise of discourses of hybridity and the rise of (proto) nationalisms coincide.[9]

These occurrences suggest further that these discourses of hybridity such as Jamaica's national motto—"Out of Many: One People"—or that of Guyana (popularly known as the Land of Six Peoples)—"One People, One Nation, One Destiny"—had a political end in that they served as the "rhetorical glue" that could hold those new "nation-states" together.[10] These identities of mixing and hybridity therefore have become important tropes of post-independence discourse in the region, an independence led primarily by the Afro- and Euro-creole elites. With the emergence of late-20th-century Indo-Caribbean identity movements in the southern Caribbean countries of Guyana and Trinidad and Tobago, this rhetoric of mixing became challenged by the Indian rhetoric of purity, which deeply challenged the national hybrid identity.

For most of Caribbean history however, the existing hybrid identity was one shaped by Africa, Europe, and to a lesser extent the indigenous Caribbean people. Social constructionist scholars have identified what Diane Austin Broos refers to as the "notion of heritable identity" through which ethnic groups in the contemporary Caribbean "trace their identities and behaviours to historical factors especially those located in slavery."[11] Lisa Douglass, for example, found that "Jamaica whites" are seen as the descendants of the old slave plantocracy and their continued class and color privilege is derived from this. Her study of late-20th-century Whites in Jamaica, however, found that "the histories of most of the white families on the island are very short, with European ancestors who came only in the last century to Jamaica."[12] Recent White entrants, however, benefit from the status and privilege accorded Whites for these historical reasons.

Daniel Segal in his work on preindependence Trinidad noted that the origins of the "colored population" are located figuratively in the sexual union of a European master and an African slave. In his words:

This highly conventionalised tale of origins of 'the coloured middle-class' located natural male desire and dominance as the cause of mixing and memoralised this 'mixing' as the beginning of a distinctively West Indian social order. . . . The telling of history thus imbued each 'race' with a singular status and hierarchical value.[13]

In this gendered construct of mixing however, this tale is differentially understood: on the one hand as African (Black) women selling out to European (White) slave masters in search of upward mobility or possible manumission[14] via mixed offspring, or on the other as the rape of African slave women by European slave masters.

Caribbean and Trinidadian mixed or hybrid identity therefore was identified as creole and understood as a continuum of various shades of "Blackness" and "Whiteness"; hence color and shade became important signifiers of status in Caribbean cosmologies. Caribbean "Blackness" therefore became identified with Caribbean "creoleness," especially in countries like Trinidad and Tobago and Guyana where *both* are hybrid notions. As noted by Segal, "Indeed the 'mixing' of the disparate 'races' was identified as being emblematic of both Trinidad and more generally, the West Indies." He notes further that local discourse stresses the symbolic localness of being mixed; in other words, "pure" races exist outside of Trinidad and arrived from other places. "Mixing is what happens locally."[15]

In other words, in Trinidad and Tobago it is possible to be identified as African and also as "mixed"—they are not mutually exclusive. Indianness, however, continues to be a "pure" identity. This view is supported by Sarah England, who observes that in the Trinidad and Tobago context, "the absorbency of blackness can be contrasted with the purity of Indianness which is exclusive rather than inclusive." When Indian is mixed with anything else it becomes something other than Indian by definition.[16] This significant distinction could be attributed to a number of factors—the salience of Hindu notions of "purity" and dread of "polluting" influences and the negativism associated with "Blackness" and by extension "Africanness," which give it a polluting character, similar to the US one-drop rule. This was vividly reflected in a report of an antiracism workshop organized by two women's organizations in 1995, which stated:

The individuals present described their heritage in terms that included: Indian, East Indian, Carib, Venezuelan, Spanish, French Creole,

European and African. Several individuals ended their description with the phrase "as far as I know." . . . It was notable that the only participants who indicated a single ethnic identity were those of Indian descent, these individuals further made distinctions of caste or religion nuancing this identity."[17]

The tension between these two strands of identity formation has been central to notions of citizenship in Trinidad and Tobago, although it is not normally discussed in these terms. Interestingly, purist notions of Africanness are also incompatible with the hegemonic hybrid national identity. Still today many people have difficulty in identifying themselves as African—a source of constant disappointment to Afrocentric groups and individuals. The public creole mainstream, therefore, is perceived as a hybrid space, a place where prior "pure" identities become mixed. But it is also a place, possibly due to its identification with "Blackness," which is seen as impure, vulgar, immoral, sexual, and masculine. What I demonstrate in this chapter—and is clearly demonstrated in other chapters in this book—is that the situation of mixed-race people today in various countries has a great deal to do with the dominant colonial influence. While various nations share common features, they also demonstrate unique trajectories and configurations of mixedness, depending, for example, on the former colonial power and the cultural heritage of those who trace their lineage to it (for example, language and religion). This is evident even within the circum-Caribbean region, as can be seen from the chapter in this book on Mexico. Contemporary forces of globalization are currently stirring up the cultural categories to a significant degree, but it does not override them.

Trinidad and Tobago: A Background

The Republic of Trinidad and Tobago is the most southerly state in the Caribbean archipelago, located between the Caribbean Sea and the North Atlantic Ocean just seven miles north of Venezuela. Tobago lies a few miles northeast of Trinidad and is more similar in topography to the other islands north of it than it is to Trinidad. In 1889, Trinidad was administratively linked to Tobago, creating the two-island colony of Trinidad and Tobago. While the Caribbean population comprises primarily the descendents of former enslaved Africans, since the 19th century, Trinidad and Tobago as well as the nearby mainland countries Guyana and Suriname have had significant South Asian (in Trinidad and Tobago and Guyana referred to as "Indian") populations as well as other minorities. Small numbers of Indo-Caribbeans are also present in other countries of the region such as Jamaica, Guadeloupe, and Belize.

The differences in historical development are most obvious in the contrast between the demographic composition of the two islands; Trinidad's ethnic diversity on one hand and Tobago's predominantly African population on the other. Trinidad and increasingly Tobago are also multireligious.

The population of Trinidad and Tobago according to the 2011 Census was 1,328,019, with 50.1 percent male and 49.9 percent female.[18] With respect to ethno-demographics, people who for census purposes define themselves as African (34.2 percent) and Indian[19] (35.2 per cent) comprise the majority of the population. The "mixed" group appears to have increased significantly since the 2000 census from 20.5 percent to 22.8 percent, perhaps due in part to a trend toward identification as "mixed." This coincides with a 5 percent decline in the number of people identifying themselves as Indians between 2000 and 2011. In 2011, for the first time the "mixed" group was subdivided into Mixed—African/Indian (7.7 percent) and Other Mixed (15.1 percent). The other minorities—White/European, Chinese, Syrian/Lebanese—though small in number, are highly represented in the social and economic elite. Small numbers of mixed descendants of indigenous people also exist, mainly in the northeastern town of Arima and sections of the south and central areas of Trinidad. Of those recorded in the census, 6.2 percent did not respond to this question. The population of Tobago is 85.2 percent of African descent, a decline from 92 percent in 2000 reflecting the small but increasing group defining themselves as Mixed—African/Indian (4.3 percent) and Other Mixed (4.2 percent).[20] The proportion of Indo-Trinidadians in Tobago remained stable at 2.5 percent.[21]

The largest religious groupings are Roman Catholics and Hindus. The remainder include Muslims, other Christian denominations such as Anglicans, Seventh-day Adventists, Pentecostals, Evangelicals, and Afro-Christians such as the Spiritual Baptists. A small but significant number of Orisha[22] (Shango) practitioners also exist, as well as those with no religious affiliation.

With relatively equal numbers of the two main ethnic groups—Africans and Indians—a dynamic of ethnic competition has emerged that shapes contests for political and economic power. Control over state power and the opportunities for political patronage that accompany this ensure the continuation of a racialized ethnic politics that shapes many aspects of economic, cultural, and social life and encourages mistrust among groups. Scholars have also observed and theorized a strong ethnic dualism which characterizes all aspects of social life. This refers to an accepted but shifting alterity or contrasted otherness between the stereotypes, behaviors, customs, festivals, and other cultural elements associated with each of the two main ethnic groups, combined with an equally strong identity of mixing and interculturalisms.[23]

Mixing in Historical Perspective

The Caribbean has often been described as the most historically globalized of all regions, and many of the characteristics of globalization have been part of its historical experience. This includes the exploitation of cheap and sometimes unwaged labor, the large-scale movement of people and goods, the involvement of transnational trading and manufacturing companies, and the negative effects of a brutally competitive capitalist economic system. The majority of the African-descended population trace their ancestry to the imported enslaved persons brought from the African continent during the slave trade of the 16th to 19th centuries. Today, the region is experiencing new manifestations of this phenomenon through the economic restructuring of global neoliberalism. The most significant so far has been the destruction of the main agro-based plantation and peasant production systems with the removal of protective mechanisms such as the European Union quotas for preferential markets. Interestingly, these preferences were negotiated as partial reparations for the extreme exploitation and dehumanization of colonialism generally and the slave and postslave era in particular, from which Europe gained so much. The current context acknowledges no such debt and calls on all countries to operate as if they are beginning from the same starting point and urges them to aim for the same conclusion.

This has been especially devastating in the banana-producing countries of the region such as Jamaica, Dominica, St. Lucia, St. Vincent and the Grenadines, and Grenada, where the removal of preferential quotas to the European Union has all but devastated the banana export industry. As noted by Jessica Byron, the agricultural sectors, which once ensured some degree of employment and social peace have now been dislocated, opening the way for increased global criminal activity such as narco-trafficking and the trade in small arms with its tremendous potential for corruption and destabilization.[24] She notes further:

> In the 1990s, several elements of the equation had changed. In the international economy, processes of globalisation and liberalisation have intensified, leading to marked reductions in the levels of protection accorded to the OECS[25] in their international and regional trade. Earnings from commodity trade and concessionary financial flows have shrunk while the economies have switched to a deepening reliance on tourism, the offshore financial sector[26] and remittances. From 1990-1996, the OECS regional growth rate averaged 2.4. percent per annum in contrast to 5.6. percent per annum during the 1980s. The OECS state apparatus struggles to find the administrative and technical capacity to perform the roles of the regulatory state and the competitor state dictated by global neoliberalism.[27]

Even in oil- and gas-rich Trinidad and Tobago, the sugar industry, livelihood for over 30,000 people, has suffered a similar fate. Yet the oil and gas base of the economy has provided some sort of cushion relative to other parts of the region and indeed the world. As a result, over the last five years Trinidad and Tobago has seen a new influx of immigrants from other parts of the region but also from Africa, China, India, Latin America (especially Venezuela), and the Middle East.

So while contemporary globalization and the global movements of people are seen as an impetus for new manifestations of "race-mixing" in many parts of the world, as clearly evidenced in many chapters in this book, for the Caribbean this began much earlier, becoming central to Caribbean histories and identities and continuing to influence modern life in many ways. Prior to the 1950s in Trinidad and Tobago, concerns related to intermarriage were primarily in relation to "Whites" and "Blacks" or "Coloreds." By the 1980s and 1990s, however, the concern had shifted to relationships and intermarriage between persons of African and Indian heritage. For most of the indentureship period, there was a great imbalance in the number of Indian men to Indian women in Trinidad. For example, between 1891 and 1917, when indentureship ended, the ratio of women emigrants to every 100 males ranged from as low as 39.22 in 1906 to 49.22 in 1916.[28] Despite this, according to Bridget Brereton, as late as 1871, the "Protector of Immigrants" stated that "there is not probably at this moment a single instance of an indentured immigrant who cohabits with one of the negro race."[29] (The "Protector of Immigrants" was a colonial civil servant appointed to look after the interests of the Indian indentured immigrants. The office was instituted in response to complaints in India about the treatment of indentured immigrants in colonies such as Trinidad.) Brereton suggests that, up to 1900, sexual unions between Indians and Africans remained rare, and there were until then no known cases of legal marriage between these two groups.[30]

One recent study has sought to explain the reasons for this, citing distance and separation among other things.[31] There is, however, evidence of unions of Indians, especially Indian females with European plantation males, continuing the old plantation tradition. In spite of this, concerns over women "cohabiting with males of other races" were expressed in letters to the British Colonial Office on many occasions.[32]

This situation contrasts greatly with that of the Chinese immigrants (fewer in number) who first arrived in the region in 1806 and later between 1853 and 1866 as indentured laborers. In the context of an even more skewed sex ratio, many Chinese men took African- descended women as wives or partners, resulting in a significant mixed Afro-Chinese population.[33] Indeed as early as 1807, this was already observed as characteristic of Chinese immigrant men who were described by one colonial official as follows:

[T]hey are indifferent about the colour or condition of the females they cohabit with . . . they willingly submit to the law which enacts that the offspring shall follow the condition of the mother.[34]

Relatedly, Barry Higman notes that during that early period when slavery was still in existence, there were cases where Chinese immigrants formed relationships with slave women, paid for their manumission (freedom), and financially supported their children.[35]

The situation continued during later migration as well. Walton Look Lai notes that in this period there was an effort by the British to encourage family migration; nevertheless, the numbers of females continued to be quite low. In the 1860s, therefore, of the 2,645 Chinese immigrants who landed in Trinidad, 309 or 11.7 percent were female.[36] In some cases men left wives in China and so had two families—a mixed Trinidadian family and a Chinese family. In some instances the Chinese wife and family would come to Trinidad, resulting in some uncomfortable situations. Interestingly, today the Chinese population of Trinidad and Tobago is described very inclusively as evidenced on the current Chinese Trinidadian and Tobagonian Facebook page:

Community

The Chinese Trinidadian and Tobagonian community is a diverse mixture that includes first-generation immigrants from China, Trinidadians whose ancestors have lived in Trinidad for many generations, and diasporan Trinidadians and Tobagonians, who have primarily settled in the United States, Canada and the United Kingdom. The Chinese Trinidadian community includes people of unmixed and mixed Chinese ancestry, although the latter usually appear as mixed race in census figures in Trinidad and Tobago. Most Trinidadian Chinese originate from Guangdong province, especially among the Hakka people.[37]

Mixing and Ethnic Categorization

The 1931 census, according to R. R. Kuczynski, recorded a population of 115,705 Indians resident in the colony who were not born in India. Of these, 1,713 were recorded as being born "of Indian fathers only," while 805 were recorded as being born "of Indian mothers only."[38] Here we see the beginnings of what later became known as the "*dougla*" population of Trinidad and Tobago. In 1931, these persons were recorded as part of the Indian population, and if these records are correct, then more mixed children were born to Indian men than Indian women.[39] As noted in another publication, this is noteworthy in a context where Indian women are normally the ones accused of deserting their "race" to form liaisons with men of other "races." It also reflects the situation in which men maintain their status (in this case caste status) in hypergamous unions while women inherit the status of their husbands and therefore lose their status if they marry "beneath" them. The latter situation is therefore more stigmatized.[40] Interestingly, in that same 1931 census, persons with one Chinese parent were categorized as Chinese.

In the subsequent census, 1946, data on Indian creoles and Chinese creoles (i.e., persons of mixed Indian/African and Chinese/African heritage) were collected but these data were combined in the new category of "mixed or colored."[41] On this occasion, however, the report noted, "There are also included in these figures those who described themselves as 'Indian-creoles' numbering 8,406. These are persons whose parents either father or mother, were from India or of Indian race."[42]

Since 1960 also, the category "mixed" has been used in the census to include persons with parents of different ethnic groups. It is a somewhat amorphous category, as it is unclear what groupings are involved. What is clear from this is that racial/ethnic categorizing continues to be very much a case of self-definition and social context, a factor that was highlighted by sociologist Lloyd Braithwaite in his 1957 article "Sociology and Demographic Research in the British Caribbean." He noted that the term "race" was used loosely, partly in a biological sense and partly in a social sense. The categories used combined race and nationality and were based on popular categorizations used in everyday speech and a mixture of self-definition by the respondent and identification by the enumerator.[43] This continues to be the case today.

The impact and importance of international forces and local events is also evident. For example, one important result of the Black Power Movement of the 1970 period was a shift in self-definition among the African-descended population. This was reflected in an increase in the number of people defining themselves as African by 40,000 and a decline in the mixed population of 3,000 between 1960 and 1970. Between 1970 and 1980, there was a further increase of 32,000, or 8 percent, in the African group and an even larger increase of 40,000, or 31percent, in the mixed group.[44]

Today, at the dawn of the 21st century, the new migrations that are taking place into Trinidad and Tobago from China, other parts of Southeast Asia, Latin America, Africa, and the Middle East are not yet captured by demographic analysis. The International Organization for Migration (IOM) gives the rate for immigration in 2010 at 2.6 percent, with 54 percent of these being female migrants.[45] Always a region of high out-migration, the projected rate of migration from Trinidad and Tobago for the period 2010–2015 is given as 3.0 per 1,000 people.

Mixed Ethnic Categories

Segal introduced the phrase "racial accounting" to describe the "fractional and genealogical accounting"—such as "half this; quarter that"— used by Trinidadians to trace their "mixed" ancestry in pre-independence Trinidad. He noted that while numerous lexical items emerged to describe mixed offspring of Europeans and Africans, often through a range of colors—red, brown, off-white, sapodilla brown—only one lexical item was used to identify mixtures of Indian and African—*dougla*— and no term has emerged since then to describe mixtures of Europeans and Indians even though they have a longer history in Trinidad and Tobago.[46] Additionally, Indians were never placed on the creole color spectrum.[47] In the section below I discuss two mixed ethnic categories that have emerged into popular usage and the debates and negotiations surrounding their usage.

Dougla

The emergence of the strongly pejorative term *dougla*[48] to refer to offspring of Indian and African parentage reflects the distaste with which such unions were and to a lesser extent are perceived among most of the Indo-Trinidadian community. According to Puri, the *douglas* occupy a "vexed position" as they "pose [a threat] to the logic of pure racial stereotypes and disrupt the racial accounting which depends on clearly differentiable races."[49] The figure of the *dougla* represents the contradictions characteristic of Trinidad and Tobago's ethnic system; it represents the ethnic fluidity that is accompanied by a clear ethnic dualism that is constantly reinventing itself. The existence of the *dougla* represents and contradicts these boundaries.

It is, however, not a fixed category and often disappears after one generation.[50]

This "vexed position" is still very real, although less so today than in the past. Douillet, writing in 2006, found that although mixed

(African-Indian) couples were common, some contemporary Indo-Trinidadians, especially Hindus, still had a negative perception of intermarriage and indeed often treated *douglas* as "creoles," still associated with low castes and polluting in relation to food, marriage, and so forth.[51] Douillet mentions coming across several Indo-Trinidadian women who were ostracized or thrown out of their family homes immediately after their parents learned of their involvement with an Afro-Trinidadian man.[52] She opined:

> Indo-Trinidadians commonly believe douglas to be "Creoles" (not Indian) and attribute to them all the stereotypically undesirable physical and behavioral characteristics of Africans. . . . Indo-Trinidadians I talked to often considered dougla children as ugly, especially if their complexion is dark or their hair "hard." Other discourses about mixed couples involve the notion that mixed couples mix "the blood" that should remain pure.[53]

Acceptance by Afro-Trinidadian relatives is somewhat easier, however ethnic stereotypes, prejudice, and ambivalences also characterize these relationships. England notes, for example, that while the negativity associated with being *dougla* has been significantly reduced, the exclusion from Indianness associated with *dougla* identity continues to be a source of distress. It also becomes a basis for assumptions and stereotypes about character, aptitudes, tastes, cultural skills, and sexuality, making it difficult for those identified as *douglas* to embrace both sides of their family and culture and forcing them "into a false essentialization of themselves simply as Afro-Trinidadian."[54] She continues:

> Almost all blamed the sources of their distress on Hindu notions of purity that creates its own one-drop rule by automatically categorizing anyone mixed with African into the Afro-Trinidadian population. For others, their status as biracial was an opportunity to challenge the binary thinking of racial/cultural pluralism and embrace both sides.[55]

There is a growing agreement among anthropologists and students on Trinidad and Tobago ethnicity that although many of the structural and occupational aspects of the Hindu caste system no longer exist in

Trinidad and Tobago, caste values[56] continue to govern and influence some relationships both among Indians, Hindus in particular, and with various other groupings in the society. Central to this is the notion of hierarchy: this refers to the general acceptance of a preordained hierarchical system within which groups are placed. The feeling among Hindus in particular and Indians in general is that, based on this structure, some people are high and others are low. This may no longer be related to notions of ritual pollution and ritual purity, but is probably now related largely to behaviors seen as indicative of a low nation or caste (*jati*).

This notion of caste hierarchy has been further influenced by the creole hierarchical structure based on color, ethnicity, and class thatIndians encountered on arrival in the region. This system reinforced traditional notions of hierarchy, in particular the negative associations with Blackness and positive association with light skin color, which is characteristic both of the Hindu caste system and the European color/class structure. In this doubly hierarchized color/caste system, African peoples were placed at the bottom of the scale along with, or probably just below, the dark-skinned South Indians locally referred to as "*madrassis*" in the new hierarchical structure. In an adaptation to the Caribbean context, European Whites were placed at the top of the hierarchy. For the majority of Indians, the word "black" still has a decidedly pejorative meaning and whereas marriage with Africans/creoles is less desirable, marriage with Europeans is more easily accepted and in some instances welcomed. Indeed, Segal suggests that the fact that no term emerged to describe the issue of Indian-European unions reflects a perception of less distance and greater similarity.[57] This, he concluded, "imposed a silence on the results of such mixing."[58]

Gender and Restrictions on Exogamy[59]

Issues of gender are also implicated in the shaping of these relations. Rules of kinship, family, sexual intimacy, and marriage are some of the mechanisms through which ethnic, class, and caste hierarchies have been reproduced. Whether through matrilineal or patrilineal systems they reflect the link between patriarchal (male-dominance) and other forms of elite dominance such as ethnicity and class.

Rules of hypergamy[60] and hypogamy[61] govern marital and intimate relations in all patriarchal societies to varying degrees. Within the caste system, different restrictions define the behavior of groups and marriages between members of different castes are normally unacceptable except in certain circumstances. In the rare instance where it is allowed, it must be a hypergamous union—that is, between a woman of lower and a man of higher caste, but not vice versa. In the hierarchy constructed in Trinidad and Tobago, therefore, marriage of Indian men to Afro-Trinidadian women (women of presumed lower "nation") would be slightly more acceptable than the other way around.

As has been argued elsewhere,[62] in the reconstructed social space of Trinidad and Tobago, caste values may continue to affect marriage between castes, but they become far more important in relation to marriage with other ethnic or ethnic/religious groups, which come to be perceived in castelike terms. To a large extent this could explain the abhorrence conventionally felt by Indians generally and Hindus especially to exogamous unions, especially to exogamous unions with members of groups perceived to be "lower" than their own.

Afro-Trinidadian males see this as evidence of the discriminatory feelings harbored by Indian males against them.[63] Issues of sexual competition are also involved in the identification of African males with overactive sexuality as a consideration on both sides. Studies on intermarriage show that stated attitudes against it are generally much stronger in the Indian, especially Hindu, population.[64] This however may be changing, especially among young people, as evidenced by the increased visibility of mixed African-Indian unions and individuals.

The ideology of "mixing," on the other hand, is so entrenched in creole culture that although sometimes criticized or remarked upon it is seen as an inevitable part of life. At the same time however, because of the tradition of seeing interethnic unions as attempts to improve social or ethnic status, it is sometimes treated with suspicion by some Afro-Trinidadians and criticism by others who see it as a sign of self-hate. Women especially are often perceived of as "race traitors" seeking to improve the color and hair of their offspring, while Afro-Caribbean men have been criticized for marrying women of other groups and rejecting "their own."[65] This was especially remarked upon by Braithwaite in 1953 in relation to the castelike class/color context of Trinidad in the mid-20th century,[66] where light-skinned women could "trade caste (color) for class" by marrying dark-skinned professional men.[67] At that time, men's superior economic status and accepted role as breadwinner facilitated this pattern of hypergamy. In this context of ethnic competition and tension, I argue that rules of hypergamy are central to the understanding of "mixing" in Trinidad and Tobago, especially on the part of the caste (*varna*) influenced predominantly Hindu population.

In 1961, an election year and a period of intense interethnic rivalry, the Mighty Dougla penned a poignant calypso summarizing the challenges of existing in this society. The words of the calypso went as follows:

> Suppose they pass a law
> They don't want people living here anymore
> Everybody got to find they[their] country
> According to your race originally
> What a confusion I would cause in the place
> They might have to shoot me in space.
>
> Chorus
> Because they sending Indians to India
> And the Negroes back to Africa
> Can somebody just tell me
> Where they sending poor me
> I am neither one nor the other
> Six of one, half a dozen of the other
> If they really serious about sending back people for true
> They will have to split me in two.

Despite the continued ambivalence[68] towards the concept of *dougla,* this term has in many ways, become a metaphor for the Trinidad and Tobago social and cultural reality.[69] In other words, this term reflects the shift from the hegemonic "creole"—i.e., European-African—notion of mixed identity to the *dougla* concept of mixing. This was reflected, for example, in the title of the 2009 magazine *Dougla: A Celebration of Trinidad and Tobago.* In the opening editorial the editors optimistically remark:

Dougla is a bi-monthly publication that aims to celebrate the perfect mix that is Trinidad and Tobago. Our pages capture the beauty and uniqueness of our country, the rhythm and essence of our culture, and the spirit and exuberance of our people. Our name comes from the word, "dougla" which in Trini speak refers to a person of mixed race. Although a percentage of our population is of obvious mixed ethnicity, we believe everyone has a mixed perspective. The reason is simple: our society is as cosmopolitan as they come.

Virtually every Trinbagonian grows up with an understanding and appreciation of different cultures, lifestyles and people. Our all-embracing society creates individuals with dynamic perspectives and limitless potential. For us, dougla is a Mentality, not an ethnicity. In T&T, we are all douglas.[70]

Further evidence of the mainstreaming of the idea of the *dougla* is the inclusion of the category "Mixed—African/East Indian" in the 2011 census in addition to another category, "Other Mixed." This would be the first time since the 1946 census that a category for African-Indian mixtures was included.

Spanish

The local identity of "Spanish" owes its origin to the history of Trinidad, which was a colony of Spain for three centuries (1498–1797), and to its location close to Venezuela and the continuous migration between the two countries. People popularly understood as "Spanish" therefore could be understood as mixed descendents of the indigenous people of the region, first colonized by Spain, African enslaved or free people and Spanish colonizers, settlers or planters or migrants from Venezuela, especially those that traditionally inhabited the Northern Range cocoa-producing valleys of Trinidad, known popularly as "cocoa panyols." In her article "What is a Spanish?" Aisha Khan reported on this conversation:

INDO-TRINIDADIAN WOMAN: My boyfriend is a Spanish—Indian and
    Negro.
AK: Isn't that a dougla?

WOMAN: Well, I doesn't use that word, I calls it Spanish. He have green
    eyes, like, and soft hair, I doesn't say dougla.
AK: How about if he had dark eyes and hard hair?
WOMAN: Oh! Then he'd be dougla, not Spanish.[71]

This exchange and Khan's analysis of the category "Spanish" provides
an excellent example of the ways in which ethnic categories as cultural
resource become available for use by persons as they negotiate their
way through the complexities of ethnic relations and identifications in
everyday life and bring out clearly the fluidity and social character of
ethnic identities and categories. She concludes that there is more than
one way to be called a "Spanish," including through appearance/phe-
notype or through heritage; something we could extend to all Caribbean ethnic identities especially "mixed" ones. What also becomes
clear is that ethnic categories have relevance primarily in the context
within which they exist, bringing to mind the work of Michael Omi and
Howard Winant on racialization—the extension of racial meanings to
groups that were previously unclassified—and racial formation—"The
socio-historical process by which racial categories are created, inhabited, transformed and destroyed."[72]

Today, with the increasing mobilization of indigenous communities,
all of which are now mixed in Trinidad and Tobago, the term "Spanish"
is being deconstructed to reveal the hidden indigenous presence that
to a large extent was considered irretrievably lost. Whitehead noted
in 2005 that native identities—in particular, hybrid native identities—
"threatened the colonial schema of 'racial' identity and directly challenged the validity of the existing classification."[73] He referred here
specifically to the "Black Caribs" of St. Vincent and later Belize and
Honduras and observed:

Such hybrid identities were thus threatening to established forms of
colonial, political and social authority, even creating at times a common
interest in the suppression of the ethnically ambiguous on the part of
persistent colonial rivals such as the British and French. This was precisely the case with the eighteenth century emergence in the Lesser
Antilles of the so-called Black Caribs.[74]

In a similar vein, the term "Spanish" therefore in many ways emerged to silence the indigenous presence within this hybrid identity. Indeed many communities and individuals popularly known as "Spanish" until recently were unaware of their indigenous heritage and many continue to be. Today, some have begun to reconceptualize themselves as at least partly indigenous and it is accepted that this would be a mixed or hybrid ethnic category.

This matter is explored by anthropologist Maximilian Forte, who looks at it from a different angle when he observes that "[f]rom this early point . . . there is no evidence to suggest that race, and racial purity, were either indigenous concerns or part of a philosophy rooted in indigenous culture."[75] He continues:

> In the case of Trinidad . . . we see a similar pattern of intercultural and interethnic amalgamation, between long-time Spanish settlers and indigenous inhabitants, in an underdeveloped colony long neglected by Spain. While there is no doubt that the indigenous population acquired some of the cultural practices and beliefs of their Spanish cohabitants, what is most often remarked upon is the housing, dress, and material sustenance of the Spanish settlers, as barely distinguishable from that of the aboriginals. This Spanish-indigenous fusion became formed to the extent that even today, many of those who could be called Carib, and who in different situations identify themselves as Carib, go by the ethnic label of "Spanish" or "Payol" (from Español). [76]

This however has not diminished the intensity of the struggles for recognition and for land rights by activists from these communities. One arena has been the census: the category "Amerindian" was used in 1960, succeeding "Carib/Aboriginal Indian," which was used in 1946.[77] In 2011, as a result of activism among First Nations groupings, the category "Indigenous" was included in the census for the first time.

Concluding Remarks

The Caribbean presents to us centuries of "race mixing" with complex and intriguing results. The diversity of experiences of this phenomenon suggests strongly that a number of local social and historical factors shape the ways in which mixing is experienced and understood both by the persons involved as well as by their societies. Any comparison of this region with other regions covered in this book further highlights these issues. In Trinidad and Tobago a number of critical factors appear to determine this experience, such as: the power relations among ethnic groups in the societies involved, the ways in which those power relations shape the intimate relations, and the conflictual and ethnicized legacies of colonialism and postcolonial population movements. Also significant are the gendered rules of hypogamy and hypergamy and the patriarchal competition among men, which affect the different ways through which women and men enter into mixed relationships.

In the ethnicized political context of Trinidad and Tobago, it has often been stated—in venues ranging from political platforms to annual calypso festivals—that *douglas* hold the key to a more "harmonious" society or "national unity." So far, however, there has been no coalescing of *douglas* into a social or political category whose members could consciously act as a buffer between the two main ethnic groups. It is left to see what the increases in the population defining themselves as "mixed" in censuses will have on the national psyche and individual identities. The flow of new migrant groups into Trinidad and Tobago society will also contribute to and complicate this process.

In a context of new global migrations and movements of people, societies are being confronted more than ever with the reality of mixed identities and ethnicities. The diverse history of "race mixing" and cultural and ethnic hybridity in Trinidad and Tobago and the Caribbean can provide many clues to understanding this phenomenon in all its complexity.

NOTES

1. Shalini Puri notes, however, that North Atlantic–based hybridity scholarship has marginalized Africa and the Caribbean in its discussions due to a number of structural and theoretical reasons (2004: 29–30).
2. Hinny: hybrid offspring of a stallion and a female donkey (similar to a mule, which is the offspring of a mare and a male donkey).

3. Hence the development of the term "mulatto," developed around the 1590s, from the Spanish or Portuguese *mulato,* "of mixed breed," lit. "young mule," from *mulo,* "mule," from Latin *mulus* (fem. *mula*) "mule," possibly in allusion to hybrid origin of mules. Fem. *mulatta* is attested from the 1620s. http://www.etymonline.com/index.php?term=mulatto, accessed on December 27, 2011.

4. Young 1996: 7.

5. *Ibid.:* 8.

6. *Contradictory Omens: Cultural Diversity and Integration in the Caribbean,* Mona: Savacou, 1974; see also *The Development of Creole Society in Jamaica, 1770–1820,* Oxford: Clarendon Press.

7. Edouard Glissant, *Le Discours Antillais.* Paris: Editions de Seuil, 1981.

8. *The Development of Creole Society in Jamaica, 1770–1820.*

9. Puri 2004: 47.

10. *Ibid.*: 49.

11. Austin-Broos 1994: 12.

12. Douglass 1992: 6.

13. Segal 1993: 86.

14. Manumission: freedom.

15. Segal 1993: 83.

16. England 2010: 208.

17. Wells 2000: 201–2. Spanish was italicized in the original quote perhaps because it was used in popular discourse but was not a census category.

18. Trinidad and Tobago Central Statistical Office 2011: 15–16.

19. Mainly from today's India, Pakistan, and Bangladesh and a minority from Afghanistan.

20. Trinidad and Tobago Central Statistical Office 2011: 16.

21. Ibid: 15–16.

22. Orisha (Shango) worship: a Yoruba-derived religious tradition based on the acknowledgement of a pantheon of deities known as the Orishas (Orixa Brazil) originally from Nigeria but now present in Brazil, Cuba, Puerto Rico, Trinidad and Tobago, and more recently the United States.

23. Miller 2004; Reddock 2007.

24. Byron 2000: 138.

25. OECS (Organization of Eastern Caribbean States): Grenada, St. Vincent and the Grenadines, Dominica, Antigua and Barbuda, St. Kitts and Nevis, and St. Lucia.

26. These industries of course open the way for an increase in commercial sex work and money laundering.

27. Byron 2000: 138.

28. Reddock 1998: 41.

29. Brereton 1979.

30. *Ibid.*: 83. The Reverend John Morton according to Dennison Moore in his 1876 testimony did state that "a few children are to be met with, born of Madras and Creole parents and some also of Madras and Chinese parents—the Madrasee

being the mother" (Moore 1995: 238, cited in Regis 2011). Madrasses were immigrants from Madras in South India, usually of darker skin color than the Northern Indian migrants from Bihar and Andhra Pradesh who comprise the majority.

31. Diptee 2000.
32. Reddock 1994: 102. See the Letters of Mohammed Orfy –DPRO 1915-1918: CO 571/4 W.I. 22518 of 1916; 571/4455 Enc. Cited in Rhoda Reddock, "The Indentureship Experience: Indian Women in Trinidad and Tobago," in Shobhita Jain and Rhoda Reddock (eds.), *Plantation Women: International Experiences*, Oxford: Berg, 1998: 44.
33. Brereton 1981: 100.
34. Cited in Higman 2006: 14.
35. *Ibid.*: 33.
36. Look Lai 2006: 57.
37. http://www.facebook.com/pages/Chinese-Trinidadian-and-Tobagonian/116456681735929, accessed on December 26, 2011.
38. Kuczynski 1953.
39. *Ibid.*.
40. Reddock 1994: 104; see also Rhoda Reddock, "Constructing Race: Ethnic Categorisations, Colonial Censuses and their Post-Colonial Legacies, The Case of Jamaica and Trinidad and Tobago", paper presented to the 54th International Congress of Americanists, University of Vienna, July 2012.
41. Kuczynski 1953: 339.
42. Trinidad Registrar-General's Department 1948: 31.
43. Braithwaite 1957: 524.
44. Abdullah 1985: 446. Some uncertainty has been expressed about the final census figures for 1970. It was felt that some underenumeration may have taken place due to the ongoing political and social unrest, which culminated in the declaration of a state of emergency two weeks after census day. The difference between the census count and the midyear estimates derived from the 1960 census however was not appreciable according to leading demographer Jack Harewood (1975: 11).
45. http://www.iom.int/jahia/Jahia/activities/americas/the-caribbean/trinidad-and-tobago/cache/offonce/.
46. Historian Bridget Brereton advises that the terms "overseer child or baby" were sometimes used to refer to children of European plantation staff and Indian females. These terms are however not widely used today.
47. Segal 1993: 93.
48. Derived from the word *dogla*—the issue of inter-*varna* marriage. It was defined by Platts (1884: 534) as originally referring to "a person of impure breed, a hybrid, a mongrel; a two-faced or deceitful person and a hypocrite" (cited by Regis 2011).

49. Puri 1997: 130.
50. Although in Merle Hodge's novel *For the Love of Letitia*, one character is described as being a half-dougla.
51. Douillet 2006: 270.
52. *Ibid.*
53. *Ibid.*: 172.
54. England 2010: 208.
55. *Ibid.*: 209.
56. Haraksingh 1992, cited and developed in Reddock 1999.
57. Segal 1993: 93–99.
58. *Ibid.*: 100.
59. Exogamy: marriage based on rules that prescribe marriage outside of one's group or aimed at excluding persons holding certain relationships, usually associated with the incest taboo.
60. Hypergamy: a rule of marriage in which a woman of lower status marries a man of higher status. A hypergamous system is one in which men conventionally marry women of lower status.
61. Hypogamy: marriage in which a woman of higher status marries a man of lower status—seldom sanctioned in any society.
62. Reddock 1994.
63. Reddock 1997.
64. St. Bernard 1999.
65. Reddock 1998.
66. In that context it would be a rare occurrence for the opposite to occur. This situation is much less prevalent today however the basic premise of women marrying up and men marrying equal or "down" in class, color, age, and economic terms continues.
67. Braithwaite 1970: 43.
68. Ferne Regis (2011) argues that based on her fieldwork between 2001 and 2010, this has been shifting with some persons actually publicly claiming this identity.
69. Although for some it is also perceived as evidence of Indian social, economic, and political ascendency.
70. *Dougla* 2009, 1.
71. Khan 1993: 198.
72. Omi and Winant 1994: 55.
73. Whitehead 2005: 225.
74. *Ibid.*
75. Forte 2011. http://indigenousreview.blogspot.com/2011/05/carib-identity-racial-politics-problem.html, May 1, 2011, accessed on December 27, 2011.
76. Forte 2011.
77. These were the only years that these categories were included in the national census.

4

In the Laboratory of Peoples' Friendship

Mixed People in Kazakhstan from the Soviet Era to the Present

SAULE K. UALIYEVA AND ADRIENNE L. EDGAR

The billboard on display outside a bank in Almaty, Kazakhstan's largest city, depicts a mixed couple (see figure 4.1). The man, who appears ethnically Kazakh, is wearing jeans and a flannel shirt and speaking on a cellphone, his arm draped around a well-dressed woman who is flashing a credit card. She is clearly "European," in local parlance—Russian, Ukrainian, or perhaps an ethnic German. In the background is an American-style bar, complete with barstools and an old-fashioned juke box. Overall, the image is that of a cosmopolitan, affluent couple enjoying a night on the town.

A great deal has changed in the last two decades in Kazakhstan, a vast Central Asian land with a highly diverse population. Since achieving independence from the Soviet Union in 1991, Kazakhstan has jettisoned Marxism-Leninism in favor of unbridled capitalism, replaced dependence on Moscow with an opening to the rest of the world, and abandoned proletarian internationalism for a resurgent sense of Kazakh ethnic consciousness and an embryonic, multiethnic "Kazakhstani" identity. Despite this transformation, much of the country's political and cultural life is still shaped by the legacy of seven decades of Soviet rule. In particular, views of ethnic mixing and mixed people continue to bear the stamp of the Soviet era.

In many ways, the experience of ethnically mixed people in Kazakhstan has been radically different from that of their counterparts in the United States and Western Europe. The most striking difference is that the word "race" was virtually absent from Soviet discourse and remains

Figure 4.1

relatively uncommon in Kazakhstan today. The Soviet state categorized its citizens by "ethnicity" or "nationality," not by race. Moreover, these categories were conceived of in cultural and historical terms, not biological or genetic, particularly in the formative Soviet years between the 1917 revolutions and the Second World War. In the well-known formulation of Joseph Stalin, who along with Vladimir Lenin was one of the two main architects of Soviet nationality policy, "A nation is an historically evolved, stable community of language, territory, economic life, and psychological makeup manifested in a community of culture."[1] From the founding of the Soviet state until its collapse in 1991, Soviet ideology vigorously opposed racial and ethnic discrimination, while all Soviet ethnic groups were officially equal under the law.

As historians of the Soviet multiethnic state have argued, the Soviet state itself was a "maker of nations," institutionalizing ethnicity by creating territorial republics based on ethnic criteria and promoting "national languages" and "national cultures" within them. The state also practiced a kind of affirmative action, actively recruiting members of underrepresented nationalities into higher education, jobs, and Communist Party membership.[2] Every Soviet citizen had a single nationality, fixed at the age of 16 and registered in his or her identity document. Being "mixed," in this context, was not understood as interracial (as in the United States) or interfaith (as in prerevolutionary tsarist Russia); it was "interethnic" or sometimes "inter-national."

Contrasting sharply with the antimiscegenation attitudes prevalent in the United States, the Soviet state beginning in the early 1930s supported ethnic mixing both in theory and practice. This was originally a response to the eugenicist ideas then prevalent in Nazi Germany and elsewhere. Soviet theorists attacked their ideological opponents by arguing that differences between groups were due to history and culture, not biology. All ethnic groups were equally capable of flourishing, given the right (i.e., socialist) conditions. Moreover, Soviet anthropologists challenged the notion that ethnic or racial mixing led to degeneracy and pathology—an idea that had wide currency in the 1930s not just in Germany, but among West European and American scholars. Soviet anthropologists conducted studies designed to show that mixed individuals were just as healthy and productive as people of supposedly pure racial background. Ethnic mixing, in the official view, was a positive manifestation of social progress.[3]

In the world's first socialist society, intermarriage was seen as contributing to the eventual merging of the Soviet nations into a single Soviet people. Intermarriage was also closely associated with modernity, and in particular with the arrival of modernity in "backward" areas such as Central Asia. Soviet analysts argued that mixed couples were more likely to abandon traditional ways and adopt a modern, typically Soviet lifestyle, thereby setting an example for other Central Asians to follow. This modernity was often understood in terms of Russian-ness or European-ness, since mixed families were more likely to speak Russian at home and lead an urban, European lifestyle. (Although there was no official policy of Russification in the USSR, Russian was the dominant culture and non-Russians were encouraged to become competent in Russian as a second language.) Official Soviet policy had certain similarities with the Latin American ideology of *mestizaje*, which also celebrated multiethnic and multiracial hybridity.[4] The Soviet approach to intermarriage in Central Asia, with its overtones of Russification, also resembles the attempts of Australia and New Zealand to "Europeanize" their indigenous populations through ethnic mixing (though Russification in the Soviet case was always envisioned as cultural and not biological).[5]

Despite these obvious ideological and cultural differences, the idea of race was not completely absent in the Soviet Union. Historians have noted an undercurrent of racial awareness and racial prejudice on the popular level, coexisting uneasily with the official position of antiracism.[6] Moreover, race crept in through the back door of Soviet ethnic discourse. The postwar period saw a rising interest in the "ethnogenesis" of the various Soviet nations and a primordialization of ethnic identities within individual non-Russian republics. These developments were the result, in part, of the Soviet institutionalization of ethnicity within "national" republics, which gave the titular nationality of each republic a vested interest in seeing their own "nation" as eternal and immortal— even those that were essentially inventions of Soviet nationality policy.[7] The "ethnos" (a term used to refer to ethnic group or ethnicity by Soviet scholars beginning in the 1960s) was increasingly seen as a biological or genetic unit.[8] Indigenous scholars within each national republic began tracing the roots of the republic's titular nationality, identifying its "genotype" and "genofond."[9] All this meant a covert racialization of the discourse of ethnicity in the late Soviet Union. One result of this reification of Soviet ethnic categories in the postwar Soviet Union was an obsessive interest in interethnic relations, marriages, and families. Just as US scholars have argued that the study of multiracial people is predicated on scientifically questionable assumptions about the reality of race, the study of interethnic marriage and families in the Soviet Union relied on a belief in the existence of distinct and pure "ethnoses."[10]

From the 1960s until the collapse of the USSR, an avalanche of Soviet scholarly publications sought to show that the number of interethnic marriages and mixed families was increasing throughout the Soviet Union—evidence that the much awaited merging of Soviet nations was taking place. Kazakhstan was celebrated as the republic with the highest rates of intermarriage in Central Asia and one of the highest in the Soviet Union. In Kazakhstan, the proportion of mixed families rose from 14.4 to 23.9 percent between 1959 and 1989.[11] By contrast, the total number of mixed families in the USSR in the late 1980s was around 15 percent. The Kazakh Soviet Socialist Republic was lauded as a showcase of ethnic harmony and Soviet-style "friendship of the peoples."

A caveat here: Soviet and post-Soviet statistics on mixed families should be treated with caution. First, they do not distinguish between marriages among culturally close groups such as Eastern Slavs (Russians, Ukrainians, Belorussians), which would be considered "interethnic" in US terms, and marriages of Slavs to Kazakhs and other Muslims, which we would consider interfaith and in some cases interracial. Interethnic marriages within the Slavic population and the Muslim Central Asian population were extremely common and were scarcely considered intermarriages by their participants. (In tsarist Russia, where the tsar's subjects were categorized mainly by religion rather than ethnicity, only interfaith marriages had been viewed as crossing an important identity boundary.) For the Soviets, all interethnic marriages were created equal (just as all ethnic groups were equal) and all would equally further the "friendship of peoples" and the ultimate goal of creating a Soviet people. The second reason for caution has to do with the peculiarities of the Soviet (and now post-Soviet) system of ethnic classification. Soviet citizens had to declare a single nationality when they received their personal identity documents at the age of 16. Even children of interethnic marriages, who in reality had two or more possible identities, were forced to choose just one official nationality. Thus, when mixed people married other mixed people, as they often did, the official statistics did not reflect the diversity of their backgrounds. Moreover, Soviet citizens historically could be and were ethnically "miscategorized" for a variety of reasons. In some cases this was due to bureaucratic error; in other instances, Soviet citizens themselves claimed the "wrong" nationality due to fear of persecution or the desire to be associated with a more prestigious nationality. This, too, distorted the statistics on mixed couples and families.

Despite these caveats, it is likely that the higher reported rates of ethnic mixing in Kazakhstan reflect certain distinctive features of the country's history and ethnic composition. Russian encroachment and colonization in the 18th and 19th centuries had led to the presence of a large Russian settler population within Kazakhstan. Stalinist deportations, mass migrations, and wartime evacuations in the 20th century had brought numerous other ethnic groups—Germans, Ukrainians, Chechens, Ingush, Koreans, Armenians, Azerbaijanis, Uyghurs, Tatars, and others—to Kazakhstan, creating a diverse population celebrated in Soviet propaganda as a "laboratory of peoples' friendship." As a result, mixed people in Kazakhstan come in a seemingly endless variety of combinations—Kazakh Russian, Kazakh German, Korean Ukrainian, Armenian Russian, Kazakh Tatar, and so on. Today one finds numerous families in which interethnic marriage has taken place across multiple generations. The situation in some ways resembles what Farida Fozdar and Maureen Perkins describe in their chapter on Australia as a "multiplicity of hyphenations," in which no single type of mixture predominates within the population.[12] Kazakhstan, like Australia, finds itself with an extremely diverse population of immigrants, though for entirely different historical reasons.

With the collapse of the Soviet state and communist ideology in 1991 and the rise of an independent nationalizing state in Kazakhstan, the context in which ethnic mixing occurs has changed significantly.[13] Kazakhstan has experienced a surge of ethnic Kazakh consciousness, even as the post-Soviet government seeks to ensure the peaceful coexistence of its multiethnic population. The proportion of mixed marriages has declined as the population has become more heavily Kazakh, in part because of the emigration of ethnic Russians (who tend to intermarry at higher rates than other Soviet ethnic groups). Between 1989 and 2004, the Russian share of the population in Kazakhstan decreased from 37.4 percent to 27.2 percent, while the Kazakh share increased from 40.1 to 57.2 percent.[14] Other factors besides demographic change have played a role in the declining proportion of interethnic marriages. With the resurgence of religious belief and practice in the post-Soviet era, religious identity plays a growing role in marriage decisions. Language has also become more of a stumbling block to intermarriage; the state now promotes Kazakh as the official language, and use of Russian as a lingua franca within the republic has declined. The proportion of mixed families has now shrunk to around 18 percent of the population.[15]

Despite changes in the political and social context, independent Kazakhstan is still largely shaped by the Soviet legacy in its approach to ethnic mixing. The concept of intermarriage—and the view of ethnicity as monovalent and immutable—remains that of the Soviet era. Debates about racial mixing and multiculturalism in other parts of the world have had little impact so far in Central Asia. Kazakhstani citizens continue to have a single passport identity, even though many are "so mixed that they don't know who they are," in the words of one Kazakh scholar. While there is no official policy on ethnic mixing, multiethnicity continues to be publicly celebrated in ways reminiscent of the Soviet-era ideology of "friendship of the peoples." Billboards and magazine advertisements commonly depict smiling multiethnic couples and families. Yet just as there were tensions between Soviet identity and individual national identities before 1991, the current Kazakhstani state's promotion of multiethnicity and a civic identity coexists uneasily with a resurgent Kazakh ethnic identity. As in many other polyethnic societies, mixed people in Kazakhstan are particularly affected by these tensions.

This chapter examines the experiences of mixed people based on more than 40 in-depth, open-ended interviews conducted in Kazakhstan with ethnically mixed individuals, some of whom came of age in the Soviet era and others since 1991.[16] How do they negotiate and express their complex identities within a society that compels them to choose just one nationality for official purposes? How has the end of Soviet-style internationalism and the official promotion of Kazakh language and identity in the past 20 years affected mixed families and individuals? Our interviews have included mixed people in a variety of combinations—Russian Kazakh, Kazakh Tatar, Russian Korean, Armenian Ukrainian, Russian Azerbaijani, Russian Ingush, and others. Of our various respondents, only people of mixed Central Asian/European background (for example, of mixed Russian-Kazakh parentage) would be considered mixed race in US terms. However, it is important to stress that this is *not* the main way "Eurasians" are understood in Kazakhstan, where views of the fault lines within the population differ from those in the United States. While there is a recognition that one can often distinguish Kazakhs from Russians visually, the broader category "Asian" in Kazakhstan is nevertheless primarily defined in religious, linguistic, cultural, and geographic, not racial, terms. Kazakhs, Tajiks, Tatars, Turkmens, Azerbaijanis—all are "Asians" because they are Muslims, speak Turkic or Persianate languages, and hail from the Soviet "East," not primarily because of their physical features (which in any case vary widely).

Mixed People, Identity, and "Official Nationality"

In the Soviet Union, each individual had a single nationality, permanently inscribed in his or her internal passport—the basic Soviet identity document. The range of possible identities was defined by the Soviet classification system, which had been elaborated in the early decades of the USSR's existence by Soviet ethnographers and bureaucrats.[17] An individual could not declare an identity that was not officially recognized, nor could he or she claim a nationality that was not the official identity of one of his/her parents. A person of mixed background had to choose either the mother's or the father's nationality upon receipt of identity documents at the age of 16. This declaration of identity was actually a formal process in which the young person went alone to the government office, made his or her choice, and received the passport. There was no officially recognized mixed identity, nor was it possible to declare more than one nationality. What is striking about the Soviet case is that individuals were free, within certain constraints, to choose their own official identity; the state made no attempt to force them into one category or another. Children who were part "Asian" and part "European" were free to choose either as their primary identity. In a colony such as Zambia, by contrast, British authorities actively sought to prevent Eurafricans from claiming the British identity of their fathers.[18]

In some ways this situation resembles the US racial classification system prior to 2000, when individuals had to choose just one racial category for the census even if they were of mixed descent.[19] However, there were several important differences. Official nationality categorization intruded much more on popular awareness in the Soviet system, since the internal passport with its "paragraph 5" identifying nationality was used constantly in everyday life. Long before the US government began practicing affirmative action and requesting racial identity on forms for statistical purposes, the Soviet state was tracking and managing the ethnic composition of its various institutions and practicing its own form of affirmative action.[20] Second, in contrast to the US system where individuals are able to combine an ethnic or racial identity with American citizenship to become "hyphenated Americans"—a practice also common in Australia[21]—there was no official "Soviet" nationality that could be hyphenated with—let alone trump—one's ethnic identity. As we will see, many mixed people in Kazakhstan felt that their true identity was Soviet, but this was not officially recognized by a system that forced them into a single ethnic box.

Moreover, this Soviet identity was closely associated with Russian-ness. Those mixed individuals who identified with a Soviet culture that was Russian-speaking and Moscow-oriented are now left to contend with a post-Soviet Kazakhstan that is attempting to reverse decades of Russification and revive the Kazakh language and culture. The Soviet system of ethnic classification has been retained by post-Soviet Kazakh-stan, and it has led—and continues to lead—to tensions for mixed indi-viduals. (The one change is that individuals may now decline to state their nationality.) Many of them describe being torn by the need to choose between two parents, or by a painful mismatch between official and subjectively experienced identity. Others express intense nostalgia for the Soviet period, when internationalism was valued and exclusivist nationalism was condemned.

Soviet and post-Soviet social scientists have devoted a great deal of attention to analyzing and explaining the choice of passport identity on the part of mixed children. They have recognized that, in the words of A. A. Susokolov, a leading specialist on interethnic marriage in the late Soviet era, "the offspring of an international marriage may have a self-consciousness that does not coincide with what is written in the passport."[22] However, they rarely question the principle that every indi-vidual, including those who are mixed, *needs* to choose and possess a single identity in order to be a well-adjusted member of society.

The identity a mixed person chooses is influenced by a num-ber of factors, among which the individual's subjective conscious-ness is of relatively little importance. If the father is of an "Eastern" or "Muslim" nationality (i.e., indigenous to Central Asia or the Cauca-sus—this includes Kazakh, Turkmen, Uyghur, Azerbaijani, and many other groups), the children are usually expected to identify accord-ing to the father because of patriarchal conceptions of the family. As Alina Bugulbaeva, a 20-year-old student and product of a mixed

Kazakh-Russian marriage, said, "I feel that if my father is Kazakh, that means I'm a Kazakh too. In my documents I am also registered as a Kazakh."[23] If the father is of European ethnic background (Russian, German, Ukrainian, etc.) respondents report that there is less overt pressure on children to choose the father's nationality. This allows them in principle to choose what is closer to their subjective consciousness; however, ethnically mixed adolescents may feel even more torn between their two identities in the absence of a firm expectation that they will automatically choose one or the other. "Olzhas Dubrov," the 19-year-old son of a Russian father and Kazakh mother, recalls, "In my identity papers, when I chose which nationality, I faced the question— either offend Mom or offend Dad . . . it's very hard to choose between two nationalities that are close to you.[24]

In addition to the tradition of taking the father's identity, there are other reasons for choosing an official nationality that have little to do with subjective self-identification. Mixed children sometimes were urged by their parents to avoid choosing a nationality that could potentially expose them to persecution. Certain ethnic groups within the Soviet population, including Chechens and Ingush (ethnic groups from the North Caucasus), Koreans, and Germans had faced mass deportation to Kazakhstan in the 1930s and 1940s because of Stalin's suspicions that they were collectively "disloyal" to the Soviet state. If mixed children could avoid identifying with one of these stigmatized groups, they generally did so. In other cases, mixed children chose an identity as an expression of their political views.

There was no well-developed individual or collective multiracial identity in Soviet Kazakhstan, nor does such an identity exist today except perhaps in embryonic form. The Soviet legacy of associating each individual with just one nationality seems to have hindered the emergence of a distinct mixed identity. Here again there are similarities to the situation in Australia described in this volume by Fozdar and Perkins, where "mixed race is a much more atomized affair" and mixed people have been unable to organize themselves as a group with common interests.[25] A few Kazakhstanis who grew up in the post-Soviet period consciously claim a mixed identity, but in such cases "mixed" seems to mean belonging to—and moving freely between—two distinct cultures, rather than an identity distinct from both. Mixed people raised in the spirit of Soviet internationalism often denied feeling mixed at all. They were more likely to consider themselves Soviet and to identify strongly with the Russian/Soviet common culture. One mixed Russian-Kazakh woman said firmly of her parents' marriage, "I wouldn't really call it a mixed marriage. They were both Soviet people."[26] Similar sentiments were expressed by a number of respondents who grew up in the 1960s and 1970s. Marina Abdurahmanova, a 50-year-old architect of mixed Kazakh and Russian parentage, commented,

> I can't really say that I feel like a Kazakh or a Russian. It's hard to say. I don't know, I, well, I simply feel like a human being. I identify more with what we had under socialism—internationalism. I am a person for whom it is really not important what nationality I am. That is, in spirit I am very close, you might say, to this principle of internationalism.[27]

Respondents over the age of 35 or 40 often expressed nostalgia for the internationalism of the Soviet period. (This internationalism, it should be noted, was of the proletarian variety and had nothing to do with contemporary notions of globalization. It encompassed primarily the peoples and nationalities of the USSR and the communist bloc.) Susanna Morozova, daughter of a Ukrainian mother and an Armenian father, declared, "No, of course I don't feel like an Armenian, there is nothing Armenian in me except perhaps in my external appearance. I feel, right now I really feel like a 'Soviet person.' I probably have this nostalgia for Soviet times, not specifically Russian but Soviet . . . for me these were not just empty words, that we are one family, that all people are brothers, that all nationalities are equal."[28]

Respondents who grew up in the late Soviet era described schools, institutes, workplaces, and apartment buildings where the population was multiethnic and people socialized without regard to ethnicity. They went to pioneer camp, joined the Komsomol, did their stint in the army, went to study in Moscow if they were strong enough students—all with a multiethnic cohort of friends and colleagues. The Soviet Union, unlike many countries with multiethnic populations, did not feature ethnic segregation or self-segregation in housing, education, or jobs—the ever-present state assigned people to jobs, institutes, dormitory rooms, and apartment buildings without regard to ethnicity. Large cities such as Almaty tended to be very ethnically diverse. Susanna recalled, "The ethnic composition of our school was very diverse, but I remember that there were just three Kazakh children in our class. The rest were Russians, Ukrainians, a lot of Germans, there were Korean girls, Tatars, a very mixed bunch, but everyone spoke Russian."[29]

As Susanna's comment suggests, the lingua franca of Soviet society was Russian. In many cases, mixed people report that they felt like Russians because of their strong attachment to the Russian language and culture. This was true even of those without a Russian parent and therefore with no possibility of officially claiming Russian identity. A mixed Armenian-Ukrainian or Korean-German family in Kazakhstan almost always spoke Russian at home. Susanna, our Armenian-Ukrainian respondent, at one point told her mother that she felt Russian: "And she said, 'how can you possibly be Russian?' I told her, well, I speak perfect Russian, I got an 'A' in Russian class [she laughs]. She said, 'No, honey, you have to know your roots, where you're from.'"[30] Nikolai Vladimirovich Hon, an ethnic Korean married to a mixed Russian-Korean woman, said, "In the 1970s, I felt part of the Soviet people. Now I am actually closer to Russia. Although I feel—I fear— that they would not accept me there."[31] Hon's comment reflects the poignant situation of a man who is linguistically and culturally Russian (as are most Soviet Koreans) yet unlikely to be accepted as a Russian in Russia because of his physical appearance. Kazakhstanis are aware of the disturbing rise of racism and xenophobia in post-Soviet Russia, which seems to be a reaction to the feelings of humiliation engendered by "defeat" in the Cold War and loss of the Soviet empire. Most of our respondents expressed relief that Kazakhstan has avoided this problem so far.

For some respondents, Kazakhstani identity has replaced "Soviet" as a nonethnic or supraethnic identity. "Kazakhstani" is a civic identity referring to the state while "Kazakh" refers to the ethnic group; thus, one can be Kazakhstani without being ethnically Kazakh. Although Lesya Karataeva, a 39-year-old mixed Russian-Kazakh woman, is officially Kazakh like her father: "I can't say that ethnic identity is most important for me. . . . I don't think of myself as a Kazakh, living here in Kazakhstan. And when I travel abroad I really can't say that I feel Kazakh, you know? But Kazakhstani. Kazakhstani, that's my identity.

Yes. And perhaps to an even larger degree an Almaty resident. I identity myself more with the residents of this city than with an ethnic group."[32]

Areas of Contention: Language, Names, and Religion

Soviet nationality policy saw language as one of the most important components of national identity. Each "national-territorial republic" in the Soviet Union had its own "native language," officially encouraged through policies of "nativization" that required native-language schools, textbooks, newspapers, and elites in each Soviet national republic. Officially, then, there was no policy of Russification in the Soviet Union. Nevertheless, there were strong incentives for people to acquire Russian-language proficiency in non-Russian republics such as Kazakhstan. Russian was promoted as the common language for people throughout the USSR, and all children were required to learn it as a second language. Higher education and careers in the Soviet bureaucracy required a good knowledge of Russian. And despite the official rhetoric about the importance of the national language in Kazakhstan, in reality the Kazakh language was frequently denigrated and treated as a second-rate or backward tongue by Russian speakers.

As a result, ethnic Kazakhs in Kazakhstan often didn't speak their own "native language" in the Soviet period; instead, many spoke Russian, the lingua franca of the USSR. Mixed families were among the most likely in Kazakhstan, apart from monoethnic Russian families, to use Russian at home. There were also many monoethnic German, Armenian, Korean, and Tatar families who spoke Russian as their first language. Moreover, many "full-blooded" Kazakhs did not speak Kazakh fluently or use it regularly at home. Sixty-four percent of Kazakhstan's Kazakhs were fluent in Russian at the end of the Soviet era; many in urban areas had attended Russian-language schools and had a poor knowledge of Kazakh.[33] Even monoethnic Kazakh families wanted their children to speak Russian perfectly, to ensure their future success in Soviet society. In the post-Soviet era, the newly independent state of Kazakhstan has sought to consolidate a sense of national identity in part by reviving the Kazakh language, increasing the use of Kazakh in education and the workplace, and requiring knowledge of Kazakh for government jobs.[34]

This has created an uncomfortable situation for those Kazakhs and mixed people who grew up speaking mainly—or only—Russian.

The derogatory term "shala-Kazakh," which literally means half-Kazakh, is most often used today to refer not to the product of a mixed marriage, but to any Kazakh who is linguistically and culturally Russified. The synonym "asphalt Kazakh" further conveys the idea that the Russified Kazakh is predominantly an urban phenomenon. As Kazakh author Jumabai Jakupov noted in his provocative book, *Shala Kazakh: Proshloe, Nastoiashchee, Budushchee* ("The Shala-Kazakh: Past, Present, and Future"):

> The existing demographic situation [in the Soviet era] with the pre-dominance of Russians led to an astonishingly rapid russification of the Kazakhs. In the course of just one or two decades an entire generation grew up among the Kazakhs that did not know its own language.[35]

The experiences described by our respondents confirm Jakupov's analysis. "Maira Ahmetova," a 57-year-old Kazakh woman from Almaty, recalled, "schooling was completely in the Russian language . . . lessons in Kazakh were not mandatory. It was voluntary, and in reality we learned Kazakh very poorly, by the end of school we hardly knew it at all. Even though in my family, my parents knew Kazakh and spoke Kazakh with each other. Yet they always tried to speak Russian with us." Asked why her parents always spoke with their children in Russian, Maira answered:

> Because they themselves knew Russian poorly, and at that time it was prestigious to know Russian. And their dream was that we would have a good command of Russian. They thought that we would know Kazakh in any case, but that didn't turn out to be true. It turned out that we spoke Russian well, and Russian became like our native language. We hardly know Kazakh.[36]

Several respondents reported that their parents were afraid the children would later suffer in Soviet society if they did not speak perfect, unaccented Russian. Ruslan Isaev, 38, son of a mixed Ukrainian/Russian father and a Kazakh mother, said about his parents, "They always spoke only in Russian. . . . I was of course surprised and asked why they never spoke with me in another language, but my father said, we thought it wasn't necessary, we were afraid that you would speak Russian with an accent and so forth."[37]

For people such as 34-year-old Timur Sergazinov, of mixed Kazakh-Russian parentage, lack of knowledge of the Kazakh language complicates their identification as Kazakhs. Timur explains:

> If I could speak [Kazakh], I would feel that I belonged both here and there. . . . Not knowing Kazakh, I'm already not considered "one of us" by the Kazakhs. They called me "shala-Kazakh." . . . But even so I still consider myself a Kazakh.

Despite his assertion of Kazakh nationality, Timur expresses unease at the prospect of a Kazakhstan where everyone is expected to speak Kazakh: "We all [my sisters and I], since we are Russian-speaking, our internal cultural specificity was formed by that . . . we still feel more like Russians, no matter what. And overall I think that, no matter how much I love my motherland, if the [Kazakh] language question were to be posed very rigidly, we would probably have to emigrate to Russia. Somewhere like, say, Omsk, cities like that where Kazakhs live, too [he laughs]."[38] (Omsk is a Russian city in southern Siberia, close to the Kazakh border.)

Timur's comments reveal the somewhat uncomfortable position in which Russified Kazakhs find themselves in post-Soviet Kazakhstan. Though they form a large proportion of the Kazakh population, and generally the most urbanized and educated part, russified Kazakhs are sometimes made to feel like second-class citizens in independent Kazakhstan. A linguistic strategy that sought to ensure their elite status in the Soviet Union has rendered them less than fully functional in the post-Soviet era. One could even argue that these "shala-Kazakhs"— whether fully Kazakh in parentage or mixed—form an identity group in their own right. When asked whom they hoped their children would marry, several Russified urban Kazakhs indicated that they would object just as strongly to a rural, Kazakh-speaking Kazakh as they would to a Russian son- or daughter-in-law. They would like their children to marry Russian-speaking Kazakhs like themselves.

During the Soviet period, Russian had greater prestige and offered greater opportunities than Kazakh; thus, parents were concerned that their children could not succeed in society without a perfect knowledge of Russian. Many Kazakh parents were relatively unconcerned with making sure that their children spoke Kazakh. The situation in the post-Soviet period has been reversed, with greater incentives for "shala-Kazakhs" to learn Kazakh. Larger numbers of Kazakh parents are sending their children to Kazakh-language schools, recognizing that there may be greater career opportunities for those who know Kazakh.[39] However, a lack of high-quality classes, funding, and time makes it impossible for many Russian-speaking adults to learn Kazakh. As Marina Abdurahmanova, a mixed Kazakh-Russian woman married to a Kazakh man, lamented, "It's easier for me to learn English than Kazakh." She and her husband and daughters all speak Russian at home, and she worries that her daughters may be disadvantaged by their lack of fluency in Kazakh in the new Kazakhstan.[40]

Closely related to questions of language and identity is the issue of naming. Mixed children in Kazakhstan often have a complicated relationship to their names, especially if the name does not correspond to their self-identification. Moreover, the dominance of Russian culture made many with "ethnic" (i.e., non-Russian) names feel socially awkward or marginalized in the Soviet era.

Children in Kazakhstan may be named in several different ways. Sometimes the grandparents choose the child's name—a traditional Kazakh practice that occurs most often if the parents are young and want to show deference to their elder relatives. In mixed families, this may mean that the first name, patronymic (a middle name based on the father's first name, an originally Russian practice that is used throughout the former Soviet Union), and surname have different ethnic origins. Anna Kadylbekovna Nugumanova, aged 21 (Kazakh father, Russian mother), has a Kazakh surname and patronymic, but a Russian first name. Anna remarks in an interview, "The two grandfathers gave us our [first] names, one Russian, the other Kazakh. My sister was named by the grandfather on my father's side, a Kazakh. Her name is Rimma, in honor of his older sister, my aunt. And I was named by my grandfather on my mother's side, the Russian one . . . he named me Anna, in honor of my great-grandmother."[41] In some families, a first name is chosen because it blends harmoniously with the child's surname and patronymic. Thus, a child with a Russian surname and patronymic (i.e., a Russian father) would be given a Russian first name; a child with a Kazakh surname and patronymic would receive a Kazakh name.

Another common naming practice among mixed families is to choose names that sound "international"—in other words, not associated with a specific nationality. Thus, instead of an obviously Kazakh name such as Jumabai or an unmistakably Russian name such as Sergei, a child would be given a generically "Eastern" name or a name that simply sounds modern and melodious to the post-Soviet ear. Examples of "international" male names in Kazakhstan would be Timur, Ruslan, and Elias; female equivalents would include Karina, Alina, and Diana. (Again, it is important to note that the Kazakhstani idea of internationalism is part of a post-Soviet dynamic that has little to do with Westernization or globalization.) One can also find names that result from a combination of these strategies—parents concerned with the sound of the name who also show respect to their elders by naming the child after its grandfather.

Several respondents reported feeling ashamed of their obviously non-Russian names in the Russian-dominated environment of the Soviet period. Susanna Morozova (maiden name Aivazyan) 37, is the product of an interethnic marriage between an Armenian man and a Ukrainian woman. Susanna's misgivings about her name are worth quoting at length:

> The problem was that I never liked my first or last name. Because they are not very easy to pronounce and often, when they called roll in class, the teachers, the classmates pronounced my name wrong. And I remember that as a child I simply dreamed of changing not my ethnic identity, but simply my first and last names. On the one hand I kind of liked the fact that I was Armenian, that I was so unusual, and that there was only one such child in my class and only two of us in our apartment complex. On the other hand, and this was probably just a case of adolescent socialization, I wanted to be like everyone else, all those girls named Julia or Lena, say, Ivanova [typical Russian names]. . . this was my dream. When I hinted to my parents that I wanted to register myself as a Russian when I received my identity documents, and perhaps even change my unusual name, my father was incensed.[42]

Sazhida Avrorovna Dmitrieva (maiden name Valilulina), aged 51, child of a Tatar father and a Russian mother, had similar problems with her obviously Tatar first name. "My mom picked out this name. It's Tatar . . . but Grandma (on my mother's side, the Russian one) was categorically opposed to it, and when I used to visit her, she tried to call me by Russian names, like 'Sveta' [note: short form of Svetlana]. I was small then, but this really irritated me and I didn't love her because of this. I didn't answer my grandmother, I became angry with her when she tried to call me by a Russian name."[43]

Sazhida was angry at her grandmother's refusal to use her true name, because she understood—even as a small child—that her grandmother was rejecting the Tatar part of Sazhida's identity. Yet Sazhida too was ambivalent about her Tatar name and ashamed of being "different."

In the depths of my soul it was difficult for me to live with this name. All around there were Lenas, Katyas, Svetas, Olyas [diminutive forms of Elena, Ekaterina, Svetlana, and Olga] and there I was with this name. I was even, to be honest, ashamed of my name for a very long time. Only in later years do you understand that it's better to be unique than to be one of many with the same name. Yes, I wanted to be like everyone else and I was even ashamed to go to Pioneer [the Communist Party's children's organization] camp, because when you meet new people they can't always remember your name at first [she laughs]. . . . Really, I was ashamed of my name.[44]

The ambivalence described by Susanna and Sazhida reflects the mixed messages received by many multiethnic people in the Soviet Union. The Soviet state officially celebrated ethnic mixing and declared all ethnic groups to be officially equal, yet Russian was somehow more equal than the others. Mixed children often felt out of place in this Russian-dominated environment. Moreover, families were not always pleased to welcome a son- or daughter-in-law of another ethnicity. In the post-Soviet era, at least, the dominance of Russian culture has diminished and it is easier to take pride in one's Kazakh—or Tatar or Armenian—roots.

Along with the resurgence of the Kazakh language, the issue that has been most problematic for mixed individuals and families in post-Soviet

Kazakhstan is the problem of reconciling two or more religious faiths. In the officially atheist Soviet Union, the suppression of religion and resulting inability of families and communities to practice their faiths openly meant that religious identity played less of a role in marriage and child-rearing decisions. The religious map of Kazakhstan is every bit as varied as the ethnic map. Ethnic Kazakhs and other native Central Asians are traditionally Sunni Muslim, while the European population of Kazakhstan (Russians, Ukrainians, Germans) is mainly Christian—Orthodox, Catholic, and Lutheran. Sunni Tatars, Shiite Azerbaijanis, Orthodox Armenians, Korean Christians, and Ashkenazi Jews are part of the mix. After 70 years of Soviet rule, many people were committed atheists or indifferent to religion, while others believed privately but had no opportunity to practice their faith openly. "Muslim" and "Christian" became part of one's cultural and ethnic identity, without necessarily indicating a specific set of beliefs or adherence to the rules associated elsewhere with these faiths. (Muslims in Central Asia, for example, regularly eat pork and drink alcohol without any sense that this makes them "less Muslim.")[45]

With the revival of religion in the post-Soviet era, the issue has taken on new importance for mixed couples and families. Because the religious revival is still relatively new and many people remain largely secular in orientation, there is still room for children of mixed marriages to experiment with different religious practices—or to adopt none at all. Nevertheless, mixed people sometimes report feeling confused about their religious identity or forced to choose between the religious traditions of their parents.

Timur Besembaev, a 20-year-old student of mixed Kazakh-Russian parentage, recalled: "I went to church a few times, a few times to the mosque. . . . My grandmother on my father's side definitely wanted to make a Muslim out of me."[46] Timur Sergazinov described his conflict with his Kazakh father over religion. As a child he learned about Christianity from his maternal grandmother, a Russian Orthodox Old Believer. Yet in 1991, when Timur was 15, his father tried to introduce him to Islam:

> I was already acquainted with Christianity through my grand-
> mother. . . . When I said something about Christianity, he said, why are
> you talking all the time about Christianity? I had this conflict with my
> father. I told him that God is one, that any religion is simply a method, a

means of communicating with Him. In principle, there is no difference. He said, what do you mean no difference, of course there's a difference! Either you're a Muslim or you aren't. He has these rigid principles on this issue.

Interestingly, this father who insisted on his son's Muslim identity was a lifelong Communist who had never shown any outward evidence of religious belief (such as praying, fasting, or attending mosque services) in the Soviet era.

For Sazhida Dmitrieva, who is of mixed Russian and Tatar (and hence mixed Christian and Muslim) parentage, the post-Soviet religious revival has also been problematic. "I consider myself a child of the Soviet Union, and nationality wasn't so important for us, and religion didn't play any role at all. But now it seems more complicated to me in this respect, that people have become more religious," Sazhida explained. "My grandmother was religious; the Tatar women used to gather and pray, celebrate all the Muslim holidays. This did take place, but we children were not raised religiously or taught about religion. Somehow it wasn't accepted back then [i.e., in Soviet times]. Now it has become fashionable, and so it's become very difficult for me to define myself. I am really suffering from a split personality because of this issue!" Because of her own confusion, Sazhida believes that interfaith marriages should be avoided.[47]

Susanna Morozova, who has christened her children in the Russian Orthodox faith, said that she would try to steer them away from interfaith marriages. She believes that such unions are simply too difficult for all concerned:

The husband is Kazakh, the wife Russian, and everyone has to make some compromises, concessions. They raise the children: should we speak this language or that? Sometimes there are conflicts with the husband's or wife's relatives: "Why are you speaking more in Russian at home? Why don't you speak Kazakh? Why did you christen the children? Why didn't you take them to the mosque?" Although I'm not very religious, I still think this is important for the future—that the future husband and wife speak in one language and were raised in one faith. Assuming, of course, that they are religious believers.[48]

Since the fall of the Iron Curtain, Kazakhstan has become a much more open society. Its citizens travel the globe, surf the Internet, study abroad, consume foreign goods, and learn English in addition to Russian and Kazakh. Yet the circumstances and dilemmas of being mixed in Kazakhstan are still for the most part inherited from the Soviet era. This should not be surprising, since most people in Kazakhstan had little exposure to Western scholarship or popular culture before 1991. Their ideas about politics, culture, and ethnicity derived largely from their experience of being ruled by Moscow. Most Kazakhstanis are surprised to hear that interracial marriage was once illegal in the United States; many have never heard of Tiger Woods or other icons of U.S. multiraciality. The word "race" is heard more often today than in the Soviet era, perhaps because of greater exposure to Western discourse, yet ethnically mixed people still describe their experiences mainly in terms of Soviet understandings of "nationality." They tend to emphasize official or "passport" nationality and language as primary indicators of identity. When Kazakhstanis mention racism, they mainly have in mind the situation in Russia, where right-wing xenophobia against people from Central Asia and the Caucasus is flourishing.

Few people in Kazakhstan seem able to conceive of an identity as mixed or multiracial. While there is much discussion of the "shala-Kazakh," this term does not refer to the offspring of mixed marriages but to Kazakhs who are linguistically and culturally Russified, a phenomenon that is primarily a legacy of Russian and Soviet rule. There have been no demands for a change in the way people are categorized by nationality, nor has the idea been challenged that a well-adjusted individual needs to have a single officially designated ethnic (or "national") identity. One sign of the globalization of the past 20 years is that citizens of Kazakhstan may—and sometimes do—intermarry not just with other former Soviet nationalities, but also with foreigners such as Turks, Afghans, Chinese, Americans, and Western Europeans. As Kazakhstan gains further exposure to Western discourses of race and multiraciality, the prevailing ideas about identity may change. At present, however, Kazakhstan is very much part of a post-Soviet discourse on ethnicity and not a full participant in a global conversation about mixed race.

NOTES

1. Stalin, "Marxism and the National Question," p. 5.
2. The pioneer of the argument that the USSR was a "maker of nations" was Ronald Grigor Suny in *The Revenge of the Past*. See also Slezkine, "The USSR as a Communal Apartment." On the origins of ethnic preferences in the Soviet Union, see Martin, *The Affirmative Action Empire*.
3. Hirsch, *Empire of Nations*, pp. 253–58, 265.
4. Miller, *The Rise and Fall of the Cosmic Race*; Tilley, "Mestizaje and the 'Ethnicization' of Race in Latin America," pp. 53–68.
5. For more on Soviet intermarriage in comparative context, see Edgar, "Marriage, Modernity and the 'Friendship of Nations.'"
6. On race and racism in the USSR, see Weitz, "Racial Politics without the Concept of Race"; Roman, "Another Kind of Freedom."
7. Martin, "Modernization or Neotraditionalism?"; Laruelle, "The Concept of Ethnogenesis in Central Asia."
8. The leading theorist of ethnos in the late Soviet Union was ethnographer Iu. V. Bromlei. See his *Etnos i etnografiia*. On the evolution of the theory of ethnos, see Hirsch, *Empire of Nations*, pp. 313–15; Laruelle, "Concept of Ethnogenesis." On the similarities between conceptualizations of race and ethnicity as "communities of descent," see Ann Morning's chapter in this volume.
9. Tishkov, *Rekviem po etnosu*, chap. 1; Bromlei, *Etnos i etnografiia*.
10. For an example of this argument in the US context, see Spencer, *Challenging Multiracial Identity*.
11. Susokolov, *Mezhnatsional'nye braki v SSSR*, p. 140; Topilin, "Mezhnatsional'nye sem'i i migratsiia," p. 76.
12. See Fozdar and Perkins, "Antipodean Mixed Race: Australia and New Zealand," in this volume.
13. The term "nationalizing state" is from Brubaker, *Nationalism Reframed*.
14. Fierman, "Language and Education in Post-Soviet Kazakhstan," p. 110.
15. *Etnodemograficheskii Ezhegodnik Kazakhstana*, p. 168; *Demograficheskii Ezhegodnik Kazakhstana*. pp. 178, 197.
16. Our interviews were conducted between 2008 and 2010 in two Kazakhstani cities: Almaty (the largest city and former capital) and Ust-Kamenogorsk (a provincial city in the northeast). Most respondents permitted the use of their real names; those using pseudonyms are identified with quotation marks. Interviews were conducted in Russian. All translations are by Adrienne Edgar.
17. On ethnographers and the classification of nationality in the early USSR, see Hirsch, *Empire of Nations*, chaps. 3 and 4.
18. See Juliette Milner-Thornton's chapter in this volume.
19. DaCosta, *Making Multiracials*, pp. 1–2.
20. Martin, *Affirmative Action Empire*, pp. 9–15.

21. Fozdar and Perkins, "Antipodean Mixed Race."
22. Susokolov, *Mezhnatsional'nye braki*, p. 131.
23. Interview with Alina Bugubaeva, Ust-Kamenogorsk, February 2009.
24. Interview with "Olzhas Dubrov," Ust-Kamenogorsk, January 2009.
25. See Fozdar and Perkins, "Antipodean Mixed Race."
26. Interview with Lesya Karataeva, Almaty, April 19, 2010.
27. Interview with Marina Aitkalievna Abdrakhmanova, Almaty, April 15, 2010.
28. Interview with Susanna Sergeevna Morozova, Ust-Kamenogorsk, April 10, 2010.
29. Ibid.
30. Ibid.
31. Interview with Nikolai Vladimirovich Hon, Ust-Kamenogorsk, April 5, 2010.
32. Interview with Lesya Karataeva.
33. Fierman, "Language and Education in Post-Soviet Kazakhstan," p. 101.
34. Ibid., pp. 111–12.
35. Jakupov, *Shala Kazakh*, pp. 9–10.
36. Interview with "Maira Ahmetova," Almaty, April 11, 2010.
37. Interview with "Ruslan Isaev," Almaty, April 20, 2010.
38. Interview with Timur Sovetkairovich Sergazinov, Ust-Kamenogorsk, April 5, 2010.
39. Fierman, "Language and Education in Post-Soviet Kazakhstan," pp. 111–12.
40. Interview with Marina Abdurahmanova.
41. Interview with Anna Nugumanova, Ust-Kamenogorsk, February 2010.
42. Interview with Susanna Morozova.
43. Interview with Sazhida Avrorovna Dmitrieva, Ust-Kamenogorsk, April 7, 2010.
44. *Ibid.*
45. On the specificities of Islam in Central Asia, see Khalid, *Islam after Communism.*
46. Interview with Timur Beisembaev, Ust-Kamenogorsk, June 2009.
47. Interview with Sazhida Dmitrieva.
48. Interview with Susanna Morozova.

5

Competing Narratives

Race and Multiraciality in the Brazilian Racial Order

G. REGINALD DANIEL AND ANDREW MICHAEL LEE

Brazil's Ternary Racial Order

Brazil and the United States were the two largest slaveholding nations in the Americas.[1] Both inherited European norms granting Whites privileged status relative to other racial groups. Yet they defined Black-White relations differently in their respective racial orders. This encompasses ideological beliefs as well as institutional and social practices establishing racial categories, group boundaries, and membership.[2] The US binary racial order distinguished Blacks from Whites by reference to the "one-drop rule," which defined as Black everyone of African descent. It has supported legal and informal racial discrimination preventing Blacks from having contact with Whites as equals in most aspects of social life, particularly in terms of miscegenation.[3] At the turn of the twentieth century, these restrictions culminated in Jim Crow segregation.

Brazil, by contrast, has displayed widespread miscegenation and cultural blending. It implemented a ternary racial order characterized by fluid racial markers distinguishing individuals as White, multiracial, and Black based on physical appearance rather than ancestry.[4] Moreover, there was no legalized racial discrimination. Social inequality was supposedly based on class and culture. This earned Brazil the reputation of being a "racial democracy." In the 1970s, Brazil's Black Movement began challenging the racial democracy ideology. Activists underscored the existence of pervasive, if largely informal, racial discrimination. In order to mobilize against racism, they have sought to unite Blacks and multiracials as African Brazilians and differentiate them from Whites. This narrative seeks to transform Brazil's ternary racial order into a binary one similar to the United States. By 2001, various individuals, along with Brazil's Multiracial Movement, countered with a narrative supporting Brazil's ternary racial order and the right of individuals as well as the nation to identify as multiracial.

Drawing from Omi's and Winant's racial formation theory,[5] we define these competing narratives as racial projects that exhibit both cultural and political initiatives endeavoring to bring about social structural change. The cultural initiatives involve identity politics that strive to rescue identities from distortion and erasure by the dominant society; the political initiatives seek to reorganize and redistribute resources, and have called upon the state to play a key role. This chapter examines these racial projects as they relate to the intersection of Black and multiracial identity politics and the politics of collecting racial data as in the census and affirmative action. In order to achieve their objectives, these projects have engaged in what racial formation theory defines as rearticulation. This entails redefining racial identities and political interests by recombining familiar ideas and values in new ways.[6]

Brazil's racial democracy was popularized in anthropologist Gilberto Freyre's *The Masters and the Slaves* (1933), *The Mansions and the Shanties* (1936), and *Order and Progress* (1959). Freyre argued that the Portuguese colonizers, compared to their Anglo–North American counterparts, were receptive to miscegenation and generous in differentiating multiracials from Blacks. However, these phenomena were motivated by self-interest, and related respectively to the ratio of European men to women and the ratio of Whites to Blacks.[7]

In Brazil, Europeans were a minority and mostly single males; Africans slaves were a majority. The scarcity of Portuguese women gave rise to miscegenation between White men and women of African descent as had been the case with Native American women. Historically, these relationships were largely consummated through coercion and violence such as rape, fleeting extramarital relations, and concubinage, rather than mutual consent. Whether through coercion or consent, Portuguese civil and ecclesiastical authorities condemned miscegenation. Yet official reprimands failed to have the desired effect. Consequently, authorities turned a blind eye to interracial intimacy. The interracial family was informally legitimized notwithstanding legal barriers to racial intermarriage.[8] The shortage of White women limited not only any collective outcry against these relationships but also opposition from the lawful wives. In practice, common-law unions involving White males and women of color were prevalent. Seventeenth-century Portuguese law recognized "common law" marriage as one of "virtually every kind of union"[9] approved to increase the population. These relationships produced legitimate offspring alongside widespread clandestine and fleeting liaisons involving births outside of marriage, especially the progeny of slave women of African descent who were raped by or were concubines of White masters.[10]

European Brazilians were greatly outnumbered by Blacks in Brazil. Consequently, they differentiated multiracials from Blacks and relied on their collaboration in maintaining the racial order. Mixed-race slave offspring often received socially tolerated affection, as well as economic and educational support, from their White fathers. As was the case with interracial intimacy, the dearth of White women mitigated interposition from the legal wives. These offspring were often assigned tasks as domestics, artisans, and overseers. They were given preferential liberation over Blacks, who overwhelmingly were slaves.[11] Multiracials entered the free classes early in the colonial period. They filled interstitial roles in the economy, particularly in the artisanal and skilled trades, due to both a shortage of European labor and the need for workers in situations where slave labor was considered impractical. They were barred from holding public office, entering high status occupations in the clergy and governmental bureaucracy, and experienced limitations on educational attainment. Yet Free Colored urban artisans and skilled laborers, long before abolition, advanced into the arts, letters, and liberal professions. Still their social advancement was generally facilitated through (and controlled by) patrons in the White elite.[12]

Because Whites were a minority, multiracials, who were a majority of Free Coloreds, performed a critical role in the civilian militia. The

Portuguese monarchs often viewed Free Colored militia as a means of expanding the frontier. They secured Brazil's borders against foreigners and provided a military brake on independence-minded Whites. Whites viewed Free Coloreds as natural allies against the Black slave majority. The inclusion of Free Coloreds in the state's security apparatus, however, contributed as much to their own circumscribed status as to the superordinate position of Whites. Free Colored militia could hardly overthrow Whites while holding slaves in their place. Any revolt would bring them into opposition to the crown as well as the colonial government, resulting in reprisals in the event of defeat.[13]

In Anglo–North America large numbers of European settlers arrived as families, the gender ratio was comparatively more balanced, and there was a rapid natural increase of the population, which reproduced European patterns of conjugal life. Yet during the early seventeenth century, there were no laws prohibiting interracial intimacy despite strong social prejudice against it. Small numbers of Blacks and Whites, particularly African slaves and White indentures, intermarried or formed common-law unions and had offspring, alongside more prevalent clandestine contacts that involved births outside of marriage. These were largely the offspring of coercive liaisons as in rape or concubinage involving White masters and indentured or slave women of African descent.

In the late seventeenth century, European Americans began passing antimiscegenation legislation criminalizing interracial intimacy. By the mid-eighteenth century, interracial marriages in the Southern and some Northern colonies were proscribed and stigmatized where they were not legally prohibited. These regulations also began enforcing rules of hypodescent that designated multiracials as Black in order to preserve White privilege and racial "purity."[14] Moreover, hypodescent conveniently exempted White landowners (particularly slaveholders) from the legal obligation of passing on inheritance and other benefits of paternity to their multiracial offspring. The status of White women as legal wives afforded them greater leverage to oppose such actions. Also, European Americans established numerical dominance early in the colonial period. This diminished any need to utilize multiracials as interstitial labor, or to differentiate multiracials from Blacks to gain their collaboration, whether slave or free, against Black slaves.

Whereas European Americans consigned all individuals of African descent to the same inferior status, European Brazilians granted multiracials a social location somewhat superior to that of Blacks, but significantly inferior to that of Whites. This assured that African Brazilians collectively were retained at the bottom of society. Yet select multiracials have been rewarded through what Degler refers to as the "mulatto escape hatch."[15] This informal social device allows some "visibly" multiracial individuals (because of talent, culture, or education) token vertical mobility and with it the rank of situational "Whiteness." That said, the escape hatch has broader implications. It has allowed millions of individuals who have African ancestry, but who are phenotypically White, or near-White, to become self-identified and socially designated as such with all the privileges of Whiteness. In the United States, the one-drop rule can transform into Black and subject to its accompanying social indignities an individual who appears otherwise White. In Brazil, the escape hatch makes it possible for such individuals to completely escape Blackness and its social liabilities. It thus serves as a form of social control by guaranteeing that many individuals possessing the sociocultural capital to serve as voices in the antiracist struggle are co-opted into silence.

Nineteenth-century scientific racism espoused by European and European American thinkers considered miscegenation and cultural blending deleterious. The Brazilian elite's solution to this predicament was Whitening through miscegenation and the Europeanization of Brazilian culture. It was posited on inegalitarian integration (or *assimilation* in disguise) that *perpetuated* only one—the European—with the goal of presenting a Whiter national image (figure 5.1—see point b).[16] The White racial state thus encouraged and subsidized European immigration and passed legislation restricting that of Blacks.[17] Freyre argued, however, that Brazil was characterized by egalitarian integration (figure 5.1—see point a) involving a reciprocal *transracial/transcultural* blend of Europeans, Africans, and Native Americans. This had an invigorating rather than enervating impact on Brazil. His work helped undermine nineteenth-century scientific racism and its 1930s and 1940s variants. It also formalized Brazil's image as a racial democracy and gave it social scientific legitimacy.

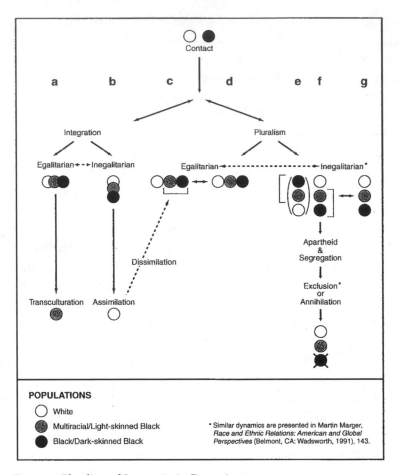

Figure 5.1. Pluralist and Integrationist Dynamics

In the 1950s, Brazilian and foreign social scientists were commissioned by the United Nations Educational, Scientific, and Cultural Organization (UNESCO) to discover the formula for Brazil's impressive achievement. Empirical data did not, however, correspond to their expectations. They found that discrimination involved an interweaving of class, culture, and physical appearance, rather than ancestry, as in the United States. Moreover, darker-skinned individuals were disproportionately found at the bottom of society.[18] The popular saying that "money Whitens," which was utilized as proof of Brazil's racial democracy, paradoxically evinced the tacitly ignored fact of White privilege. These data made the racial democracy ideology more crucial. It was staunchly defended by the ruling elite during the military dictatorships that dominated Brazil between 1964 and 1985.

During military rule, racial mobilization was deemed "racist" and a threat to national security. Individuals who organized to address a problem the White-dominated state declared nonexistent risked detention, incarceration, and even torture. Many were imprisoned; others emigrated or were exiled. By 1969, university faculty like those conducting cutting-edge race relations research at the University of São Paulo were branded as subversives and given compulsorily retirement. Moreover, no racial data were collected in the 1970 census. Officials argued that racial categories were ambiguous and thus virtually meaningless. Their true motivation was to promote the belief that race was insignificant in shaping social stratification, thus depriving researchers of data confirming how poorly African Brazilians fared in terms of key social indicators.[19]

The Black Movement and the Binary Racial Project

The gradual return to civilian rule beginning in the 1970s opened up the political opportunity structure and provided space to reformulate racial meanings, as well as forge an oppositional racial ideology and alternative racial institutions. This rekindled the militancy of the Black Front (*A Frente Negra*) and the Black Experimental Theater (*Teatro Experimental do Negro*) of the 1930s and 1940s before their decline during the dictatorship of Getúlio Vargas (1937–1945). Mobilization was also fueled by the growing racial tension in Brazil, the US civil rights movement, African decolonization, and the change in Brazil's foreign policy targeting new markets in Africa.

Black consciousness first emerged in "cultural" phenomena, which were less threatening to military authorities. These included study groups focusing on African/African Brazilian history and culture, and the urban "Black Soul" movement composed of underemployed working-class African Brazilian youth inspired by US cultural developments in music and film. They adopted English-language terms such as "soul" and "Black-power kids," colorful clothing, elaborate handshakes, and

"Afro" hairstyles. Disparaged by the cultural establishment for being "un-Brazilian," these constituted a culture of opposition that rejected traditional African Brazilian culture (e.g., *samba*) now seen as co-opted by European Brazilian society and central to maintaining the racial democracy ideology.[20]

These social forces set the stage for the Unified Black Movement (*O Movimento Negro Unificado*, or MNU). Coinciding with the anniversary of the abolition of slavery, the MNU emerged out of May 1978 protests in several major cities. The specific impetus was events in São Paulo. The police murdered an African Brazilian taxi driver, and three African Brazilian youths were expelled from a yacht club where they were part of a volleyball team. These incidents were not unusual, but were catalytic in the formation of the MNU.

The MNU enjoyed considerable publicity in the late 1970s and early 1980s although it gained greater attention abroad, particularly from academics, than in Brazil. It garnered some support from Brazilian intellectuals, the church, and workers' organizations. Those social justice advocates who viewed African Brazilians as part of a transracial working class believed the MNU's race-specific strategy deviated from the main course of social reform. The political and cultural establishment expressed hostility toward the organization. At best, it was deemed "un-Brazilian" and a mindless imitation of the US civil rights movement. Brazilian activists were cognizant of and influenced by that movement, attributable to awareness of transnational racial formations facilitated by the growing forces of globalization, particularly in the media. At worst, the MNU was considered racist in the manner of a reverse type of apartheid (figure 5.1—see point e).[21]

The MNU's efforts were aided by a new generation of (mostly White) social scientists who helped reinstate the race question on the 1980 census. They provided rigorous analyses of the 1940, 1950, and 1980 censuses and the National Household Surveys of the 1970s and 1980s, which documented glaring racial disparities in employment and earnings. Blacks (*pretos*) and multiracials (*pardos*) achieved lower financial returns than Whites on their investments in education, particularly at higher educational levels. In addition, they had a lesser chance of entering the university, had higher rates of infant mortality and incarceration, and were handicapped by the cumulative disadvantages of persistent racial discrimination.

These data confirmed activists' contention that the racial divide, in terms of overall socioeconomic stratification, was primarily located between Whites and African Brazilians and secondarily between multiracials and Blacks. Indeed, social scientists did not find the differences between Blacks and multiracials to be statistically significant.[22] These findings challenged a core principle of the racial democracy ideology, which supported the idea that the social location of multiracials was intermediate to that of Blacks and Whites. Still while the location of multiracials was closer to Blacks than to Whites, it was not exactly the same. Other researchers in the 1990s found differences between Blacks and multiracials to be statistically significant, justifying a consideration of multiracials as distinct from Blacks.[23] Multiracials have been able to enter the primary occupational tier in greater numbers, get promoted more easily, and earn more than Blacks. Rates of intermarriage and residential integration among Whites and multiracials are comparatively higher than between Whites and Blacks.[24]

The MNU's leadership was drawn primarily from the urban middle class, which hindered its appeal to the African Brazilian masses, who were largely unaware of its existence.[25] Yet by the 1980s, the MNU had become part of a larger Black Movement composed of political and cultural organizations that challenged Brazil's racial democracy ideology. In support of this aim, on May 11, 1988, two days before the official celebration of the centennial of the abolition of Brazilian slavery, activists organized a protest of several thousand individuals who marched through downtown Rio de Janeiro decrying racism in Brazil.[26] Similarly, the 1988 constitution, for the first time, declared racial discrimination to be a crime without bail or statute of limitation, and punishable by imprisonment.[27]

Yet the constitution's antiracist article seemed more rhetoric than a societal commitment.[28] Also, attorneys have found it challenging to establish a legal basis for criminal complaints even with the passage in 1989 of the necessary constitutional enabling statute—Law 7716—commonly referred to as the "Lei Caó" (Caó Law). Guimarães maintains this is due in part to the fact that racism as defined by the statute (and interpreted by the judiciary) is limited to acts of "segregation or exclusion based on skin color or race,"[29] particularly in public services and business establishments. This type of blatant discrimination is rare in Brazil. When it occurs, the "racial" motive is hidden beneath informal rules, processes, and "code words" (e.g., "good appearance," "service elevator").[30]

Moreover, the judicial system can present formidable obstacles to litigating criminal cases involving charges of racism. Police officials frequently do not take complaints seriously. Sometimes they fail to conduct preliminary investigations. When evidence is gathered, police often neglect to forward it to the public prosecutor's office. Prosecutors have been known to settle cases with financial penalties that are so small that they fall short of either compensating the aggrieved parties or deterring future racially discriminatory behavior. Although cases are more publicized and investigated, they can take years before final resolution.[31]

Since the 1970s, the Black Movement has rearticulated a "new" African Brazilian identity grounded in a positive valuation of Blackness. This identity interrogates Brazil's Whitening ideology and the European aesthetic bias that permeates mass culture and holds sway over the public imagination in determining one's perceived worth. Activists believe miscegenation and fluid racial categories and identities have thwarted African Brazilian unity and social progress. They seek to transform Brazil's ternary racial order into a binary one that unifies Blacks and multiracials as African Brazilians and distinguishes them from Whites.[32]

In 1980, the Brazilian Institute of Geography and Statistics (IBGE) moved quietly in this direction when it combined *pretos* and *pardos* as a single non-White group in analyzing and publishing data. The IBGE still maintained its three categories—*branco, pardo, preto* (or four, if one includes *amarelo* [yellow] to designate individuals of Asian ancestry)— in collecting data. Yet previously, IBGE had advanced the national narrative that projected a more integrated (albeit Whiter) national image. By 1990, activists petitioned IBGE to replace *pardo* and *preto* with *negro* (African Brazilian) in collecting data, which called attention to the state's role in maintaining racial categories.[33]

Activists were unsuccessful in getting IBGE to make this change on either the 1990 census—which was delayed until 1991—or the 2000 censuses. Nobles explains that the term *negro* conveyed a politicized identity mobilized against the state and long-entrenched patterns deemed fundamental to maintaining racial civility and social cohesion. The terms *branco, pardo, preto, amarelo,* and *Indígena* (Native American) were included.[34] The data for *pretos* and *pardos* were combined for certain statistical work. In terms of public presentation, the relevant categories were "White" and "non-White."[35] Data on both censuses indicated little change. In 1991, *brancos* remained slightly more than half of the population (52 percent); *pretos* decreased from 5.9 percent in 1980 to 5 percent in 1991; and *pardos* increased from 38.8 percent in 1980 to 42.6 percent in 1991. The 2000 data indicated that *pretos* were 6.2 percent of the population, which is a slight increase over the 5 percent on the 1991 census; *pardos* decreased from 42.6 percent in 1991 to 39.1 percent in 2000; and *brancos* were still a majority (53.7 percent).[36]

Bailey found that since the late 1980s Brazilians have increasingly acknowledged racism, particularly in public opinion surveys.[37] Twine and others have noted, however, that individuals commonly toe the "politically correct" line about racism, yet have difficulty identifying racism in their own thoughts, behavior, or experience. Moreover, they speak of individual rather than institutional racism and do nothing to interrupt either.[38] Support for institutional changes increased in the 1990s when President Cardoso initiated deliberations on implementing affirmative action. State agencies followed suit by specifying quotas for hiring African Brazilians.[39] Affirmative action received an enormous boost from the 2001 UN World Conference on Racism, Racial Discrimination, Xenophobia, and Related Intolerance, in Durban, South Africa. The conference legitimized discussions on racism at the global level, which helped marshal Brazilian civil society and public opinion against racism as well as support for affirmative action.[40]

After taking office in 2003, President Lula stressed his commitment to racial equality and affirmative action. His cabinet included four African Brazilians, among them Matilde Ribeiro in the newly created position of special *secretary* of policies for the *promotion of racial equality.* Lula appointed the first African Brazilian Supreme Court judge, Joaquim Benedito Barbosa Gomes. He ordered three ministries to recruit African Brazilians to fill at least 20 percent of senior posts. Lula also promised that African Brazilians would account for at least one-third of the federal government within five years.[41]

Opponents argue that race-based affirmative action is a solution imported from the United States that is unsuitable in Brazil. Moreover, Brazilians define affirmative action as quotas, rather than target goals, due in part to frequent misrepresentations of US policies as quotas in the United States and global media.[42] Critics believe the most egregious racial inequalities can be eliminated with class-based programs aimed at eradicating poverty and supporting improvements in public elementary and high school education, sanitation, medical and dental care, affordable housing, and employment. Race-specific initiatives that increase access to university education, job promotion, and so on would primarily benefit the small African Brazilian middle class, which already has the qualifications to benefit from these policies.[43] Supporters respond that racial quotas are a legitimate means of expanding opportunities for all African Brazilians, despite imperfections.[44]

A critical site for the affirmative action debate has been policies at several of Brazil's most prestigious universities: Rio de Janeiro State University (UERJ), the Northern Fluminense State University (UENF), and the University of Brasília (UnB). Only 3 percent of students admitted to Brazilian universities have typically identified as African Brazilian and only 18 percent have come from public schools, where most African Brazilians are enrolled. The enrollment of African Brazilians in elite institutions has doubled (and in some cases tripled) as a result of affirmative action.[45]

UERJ and UENF became the first public institutions to comply with October 2, 2001, legislation in the state of Rio de Janeiro that required universities to reserve a 40 percent quota for African Brazilians in its entering class. This figure corresponded to the fact that roughly 45 percent of Brazil's 175 million (currently 197 million) people identified as African Brazilian. The legislation also mandated a 50 percent quota for graduates from public secondary schools. They are overcrowded, underfunded, and of lesser quality compared to the private schools attended by wealthier, mostly White Brazilians.[46]

Affirmative action directives have forced Brazil to formally define racial categories. However, the results have been ambiguous. Racial quotas provide individuals with an incentive to accommodate a wide range of phenotypes or emphasize ancestry over phenotype as *Afrodescendentes* (African-descended) in order to qualify. Some applicants who were typically White-designated and White-identified did this to increase their chances of admission.[47] This is a real conundrum since many Whites have some African phenotypical traits and large numbers have African ancestry. The universities intervened to clarify the intended targets of affirmative action.[48]

Schwartzman states that negotiations resulted in modifications of the original law affecting UERJ and UENF, which conditioned eligibility on applicants identifying as either *negro* or *pardo*. The new law eliminated the term *pardo* since it was assumed to be included within *negro*. There were also concerns that many *brancos* would feel comfortable identifying as *pardos*. Class factors were also taken into consideration. Students benefiting from racial quotas needed to prove their families earned no more than 300 *reais* a month (about US$150). Otherwise, affluent African Brazilians would be the primary beneficiaries since they have the sociocultural and academic capital to score high on the entrance exam (*o vestibular*).[49] At UnB, the term *negro* was the only one used from the beginning. Also, there were no recommended income qualifications or quotas for public school students. The solution for potential "abuse" was to require candidates seeking admission under the quotas to participate in a university-organized photo session and have their photographs examined by a committee. Due to public opposition, UnB recently substituted photographs with an interview.[50]

More than 70 percent of Brazil's 98 public universities have affirmative action programs. Most rely exclusively on students' self-identification. Many include additional socioeconomic criteria, or restrict eligibility to public school students. Affirmative action in university admissions appears promising. Yet critics have expressed concerns about the decline in some admittees' entrance exam scores, which they interpret as a lowering of academic standards. Supporters counter that racial quotas are not the problem. The focus, they say, should be on improving education earlier on in preparation for college, particularly on the entrance exam. Notwithstanding efforts along those lines, increased African Brazilian admission rates primarily further the goal of equal opportunity. Retention rates and equal outcome have been less successful and require sustained efforts.[51]

Lula's administration endorsed the Racial Equality Statute, which supported programs benefiting African Brazilians. This legislation was submitted to Congress in 1998 but was not approved by the Senate until 2005.[52] The statute recommended a 20 percent quota for African Brazilians in government jobs and public universities, enterprises with more than twenty employees, and actors in television programming. In addition, 30 percent of political party candidates were to be African Brazilians. On November 25, 2005, the legislation went to the House of Representatives for a vote. It met with resistance and was eventually modified in order to reach a compromise with the House's conservative members, particularly on the constitutionality of mandated quotas. The revised statue passed in the House on September 9, 2009.[53]

The approved statute removed mandated quotas in universities and the media, along with the public health care system's requirement to identify patients by race. Yet it permitted guaranteeing spaces, if not actual quotas, for African Brazilians in high schools and colleges. The quota for political parties was reduced from 30 percent to 10 percent. The statute mandated teaching African and African Brazilian history and culture in the public schools, providing government incentives for businesses whose work force is at least 20 percent African Brazilian, and a prison term of up to three years for individuals practicing racism on the Internet. On April 25, 2012, Brazil's Supreme Court in a 10-to-0 vote ruled in favor of racial quotas in public universities and in combating racial inequality more generally. This ruling ended the first of several legal challenges to programs at many of Brazil's elite universities.[54]

The Multiracial Movement and Ternary Racial Project

Black Movement political organizations require de facto that participants identify as *negro*. They view multiracial identifiers as a strategy used by the White elite to undermine African Brazilian unity. Activists overlook, or outright reject, the possibility of a multiracial identity formulated on egalitarian or antiracist premises.[55] This may alienate sympathetic individuals who unequivocally acknowledge they are African-descended, but cannot translate this into adopting *negro* as an appropriate means of self-identification. Burdick suggests this may originate in the awareness that their experiences have differed from darker-skinned individuals.[56] Schwartzman indicates that in everyday parlance, the term *negro* is not consistently used to encompass *pretos* and *pardos* (although the latter is rarely used outside of bureaucracies). It is often restricted to darker-skinned individuals. It is thus synonymous with *preto*, which differentiates it from *mestiço* or *mulato*.[57]

Many Black Movement activists want to sensitize individuals to African ancestry by adopting US-style binary racial thinking based on the one-drop rule. They contend that the absence of the negative factor of legal discrimination and the one-drop rule has undermined African Brazilian mobilization. It is indisputable that the one-drop rule was implemented to deny African Americans equality, but also had the unintended outcome of forging group identity. This, in turn, enabled African Americans to mobilize in the civil rights movement of the 1950s and 1960s, which dismantled legalized segregation and achieved the passage of historic civil rights legislation. Yet imposing ancestral definitions of racial identity in Brazil is fraught with irreconcilable contradictions. African ancestry (not to mention African phenotypical traits) is widespread among self-identified and socially designated Whites. It also remains to be seen whether these individuals are welcomed as "assumed African Brazilians" (*negros assumidos*).[58]

Social anthropologists Peter Fry and Yvonne Maggie, along with journalists Ali Kamel and Antonio Risério, among others, have warned about imposing a binary racial project on Brazil.[59] The Brazilian Multiracial Movement (*O Movimento Pardo-Mestiço*), which was established in 2001 in Manaus, Amazonas, was the first collective challenge to this binary racial project. This is not surprising given the concentration of multiracials in Amazonas who have a strong identification with Native American ancestry. They promote a ternary racial project that reaffirms the cultural and racial blending that has historically characterized Brazil. According to Jerson César Leão Alves, general secretary of the movement, individuals and the nation should have the right to identify as "multiracial" (*mestiço*).[60]

By 2007, the Multiracial Movement succeeded in establishing two official days celebrating multiraciality. These celebrations are now recognized at the municipal and state levels in parts of Amazonas. The Day of the Caboclo (*Dia do Caboclo*)—which pays tribute specifically to individuals of Native American and European descent[61]—and the Day of Multiraciality (*Dia do Mestiço*) take place respectively on June 24 and 27. They encompass festivities that include musical performances as well as arts and crafts exhibits celebrating multiraciality.

The June 27 date refers to the twenty-seven multiracial representatives elected during the First Conference for the Promotion of Racial Equality held in the city of Manaus, Amazonas, April 7–9, 2005. It is also a reference to the month when a multiracial woman, after persistent opposition, was registered as the only multiracial representative at the First National Conference for the Promotion of Racial Equality, which occurred in Brasília, June 30–July 2, 2005.[62] Indeed, Black Movement activists and supporters have expressed aggressive opposition to multiraciality in the form of "multiracialphobia" (*mestiçofobia*) or "antimultiracial racism" (*racismo antimestiço*).[63] This is a radical and ironical departure from historical attitudes toward mixed race. It is evident in microaggressions where individuals are the perpetrators, mezzoaggressions involving Black Movement organizations, as well as macroaggressions involving institutions that structure the behavior of actors in the political and cultural economy,[64] which multiracial activists argue is abetted by the state. Indeed the White-dominated state has greeted the movement with indifference, if not outright hostility.

The Multiracial Movement has sponsored six educational seminars on multiracial identity politics and the rights of multiracials.[65] Movement activists stress the importance of addressing Black inequality and respecting a Black identity. However, they argue that neither should this be achieved at the expense of multiracial-identified individuals nor does it justify disregarding their grievances in the pursuit of racial equality. During a session of the General Committee convened by the Chamber of Deputies in Brasília on November 26, 2007, to discuss the Statute of Racial Equality, multiracial activists criticized the legislation, particularly what they considered its erasure of or discrimination against multiracials.[66] At the same hearing, Helda Castro de Sá, current president of the movement, who represented the Association of Caboclos and River Peoples of the Amazon (Associação dos Caboclos e Ribeirinhos da Amazônia), voiced these concerns. She expressed the same uneasiness in March 5, 2010, when speaking at the Public Hearing on the Constitutionality of Affirmative Action Policies for Access to Higher Education convened by Minister Ricardo Lewandowski of the Federal Supreme Court. Identical concern was expressed by Dr. Juliana Corrêa

Ferreira, an attorney who *offered amicus curiae* ("friend of the court") testimony on behalf of the Multiracial Movement during hearings before the Federal Supreme Court on April 25, 2012. She criticized racial quotas and the racist implications of requiring multiracial applicants interested in being considered under quotas to self-identify as negro.[67]

Similarly, in the United States beginning in the 1980s, interracial couples and multiracial adults began forming support groups that among other things pressured the state to revise racial data collection standards to permit a multiracial identification. The oldest of these groups still in existence as of 2012, I-Pride (Interracial/Intercultural Pride), was founded in 1979 in Berkeley, California. By the 1990s, I-Pride joined more than fifty grassroots organizations, including a national umbrella organization called Association of MultiEthnic Americans and eventually Project RACE (Reclassify All Children Equally), which served as the foundation of the Multiracial Movement. These organizations and individual activists supported a "combined format" that included a separate multiracial category on the race question but also allowed individuals to check all applicable boxes corresponding to their backgrounds.

Traditional civil rights organizations expressed concern over tabulating data on underrepresented groups of color for the purposes of enforcing civil rights legislation and other initiatives, particularly affirmative action, aimed at tracking and rectifying racial inequality. Specifically, they argued that a stand-alone (or separate) multiracial category would lead to a loss of numbers. That said, on October 31, 1997, the Office of Management and Budget, the branch of government responsible for implementing changes in federal statistical surveys, rejected the stand-alone and combined formats. It recommended instead, a "mark one or more" format, which was supported by traditional civil rights entities. This format was implemented in the 2000 census. The "mark one or more" format—unlike the combined format—required fewer changes on existing forms and allowed for data continuity. Furthermore, the data could be retrofitted in each of the existing single-racial categories, facilitating the continued enforcement of civil rights legislation.[68] The "mark one or more" format was also a response to opponents who contended that a stand-alone multiracial category would undermine African American solidarity as it has supposedly done in Brazil.

Brazilian multiracial activists and supporters keep abreast of developments in the United States. They have been in communication with some US multiracial activists in formulating strategy in dealing with the collection of racial data as well as opposition from Black activists and the state. Globalization has increased local awareness of concerns and developments relating to mixed-race people elsewhere. For example, Brazilian multiracial activists have expressed solidarity with the *Yo Soy Mestizo* campaign (I Am Mestizo) in Bolivia in response to moves to erase mixed-race individuals in the collection of census data in support of an Indigenous identity.[69]

Yet Brazilian activists and supporters draw their inspiration primarily and directly from Brazil's long history of multiraciality. There is limited global influence in the direction of identifying as mixed race given that multiraciality has been a normative part of the Brazilian racial order since the colonial era. The social significance of being multiracial in Brazil is neither impacted nor informed significantly by the flow of racial ideas from across the world. In contradistinction to mixed-race identities, the new formations of African Brazilian identity have been heavily impacted by political initiatives like affirmative action from the United States, as well as New World Black cultural practices, which themselves are to some extent part of the global interchange of Black cultural symbols increasingly shared by large numbers of individuals in the African diaspora, particularly the Black Atlantic.[70]

If there is any global influence in terms of the multiracial phenomenon, it is Brazilian influence on the international discussions of mixed race, rather than the other way around, with the following qualification: traditional Brazilian mixed-race formations have been severely criticized for being officially articulated as egalitarian and integrationist, meaning transracial/transcultural. Yet, they have been imbued with a racial romanticism that espouses naïve notions of racial democracy while euphemizing whitening and Europeanization through racial and cultural blending. This has perpetuated assimilationist ideologies based on inegalitarian integration, which has operated to blur racial distinctions in order to mask racial inequalities and impede strategies to eradicate them. Thus, Brazil's global influence has been accompanied by a *rearticulation*, rather than a *reproduction*, of Brazilian mixed-race formations. This essentially involves repetition of Brazilian multiracial identity with a difference in support of racial difference without hierarchy, that is to say, difference based on equality. This discourse also underpins the mixed-race formations espoused by Brazil's Multiracial Movement.

That said, it is difficult to determine the long-term strength and impact of Brazil's Multiracial Movement. It is localized primarily in the states of Amazonas, Roraima, and Paraíba, and involves a relatively small number of active participants, although they have grown in numbers over the past decade. Beyond the leadership and active membership, there is a wider circle of participants, readers of multiracial publications, and other devotees who participate in movement activities; beyond that, there is a general constituency of potential supporters sympathetic to the movement's objectives. At best the movement may be able to prevent the erasure of multiracials in data collection.

In fact, this was expressed in Bill PLC 180/2008 *Projeto de Lei da Câmara* that provided the specifics for the implementation of quota policies. The legislation recommends reserving at least 50 percent of university openings for the largely poor students who have graduated from public high schools. This is also where the majority of African Brazilian students are enrolled. The bill targets self-identified *pretos*, *pardos*, and *Indígenas* in university and federal technical school admissions at minimum equal to their proportion in each of Brazil's 26 states and the capital, Brasília, based on the most recent census where the institution is located. In states with large Black and multiracial populations, such as Bahia, this could result in a significant increase in the number of African Brazilians in public universities. States in southern Brazil, which are largely White, could still have relatively few African Brazilians. The bill was approved by a full Senate vote in August 2012, and awaited final presidential approval.[71]

On August 29, 2012, President Dilma Rousseff signed the law (LEI No 12.711), stating that the implementation of the specifics of quota policies must be premised not only on inclusion, which allows a greater number of students to gain access to the universities, but also meritocracy and educational excellence. Rousseff vetoed just one point from the text approved by Congress, Article 2, which created a coefficient to select students who could join the vacancies for the quotas. Accordingly, the state decided that the National Secondary Education Examination (ENEM), which is an alternative to the vestibular entrance examination, will be used to determine the filling of reserved vacancies. While some institutions (e.g., UERJ) have opted to replace the vestibular with the ENEM as the only basis for selection, others employ it only partially and maintain their own selection process. Universities may adopt additional mechanisms.[72]

The ENEM now serves as one parameter of the new system. Additional measures must be implemented to compensate for any differences between students who entered under the quotas and those under the universal admissions. Many federal universities already provide such assistance, for example, through tutoring. These supplemental measures will provide a leveling effect, so that those students with disadvantages are sufficiently prepared for their course work. The universities and federal institutes have been given four years to implement the percentage of quotas established by law. The rules and timetable for transition will be established by legal regulations, released later this year, in time to ensure the enforcement of the law next year.[73] The fact that the language in the approved legislation clearly distinguishes *pretos* and *pardos*, rather than combining them as *negros*, would seem to be an important victory for the Multiracial Movement. Yet whatever impact either of Brazil's competing narratives on race and multiraciality has in these matters, the White-dominated state is the final arbiter.

A New Brazilian Racial Order?

The Black Movement has achieved remarkable success in undermining the racial democracy ideology. Public discourse increasingly includes references to "racial diversity" and "multiculturalism" (egalitarian pluralism), instead of the traditional reference to "racial unity" (egalitarian integration).[74] Group pluralism premised on a distinct African Brazilian center of reference is considered a legitimate feature of Brazil's racial order, compared to the traditional image of integration. Yet the goal is still to integrate African Brazilians as equals in terms of occupation, income, education, and political representation, particularly through affirmative action and other initiatives targeting racial discrimination. Indeed, statistics indicate that Blacks and multiracials compose 63 percent of the 53 million individuals living in poverty and over 70 percent of the more than 16.2 million individuals or 8.5 percent of the population living in extreme poverty, defined as family per capita income of 70 *reis* (US$43.70) or less per month.[75]

Bailey and Telles found that many Brazilians consider racial democracy an unfilled potential that may be realized in the future; others cling to the ideology of racial democracy.[76] The cornerstones of that ideology—miscegenation, multiraciality, and egalitarianism—have been hypocritically multiracial and served to erase racial distinctions in the manner of what Bonilla-Silva refers to as "colorblind racism."[77] This deliberately masked and deflected public attention away from, as well as undermined policies to eliminate racial inequities.

Similar patterns exist throughout Latin America. Sue points out that the ideology of *mestizaje,* cultural blending, and racial democracy have been central to nation making in Mexico. Still there has been a preference for Whiteness. As in Brazil, lighter-skinned Mexicans dominate the upper echelon of society and darker-skinned individuals are overrepresented at the bottom.[78] Ualiyeva and Edgar noted similarities with the official Soviet-era "friendship of the peoples" ideology. Intermarriage was considered a means of melding the Soviet nations into a single "Soviet people." Historians have also observed an undercurrent of racial awareness and prejudice on the popular level in the Soviet Union, which coexisted uneasily with the official position of antiracism in a manner similar to Mexico's and Brazil's ideologies.[79]

The census debate in Brazil has sought to address this social oppression, which has been imbedded in the collection of racial data. The objective is to deconstruct the very racial categories and identities that underpinned racism and racial hierarchy, which bolstered and were reinforced by the racial democracy ideology.[80] Consequently, an African Brazilian identifier such as *negro* that combines *pretos* and *pardos* into a single category is a logical step in the pursuit of these goals. Analyzing data in binary form is one thing. Erasing multiracials from data collection and analysis, and from Brazil's national consciousness, is another matter. Indeed, the proposed formulation of Blackness essentially precludes a multiracial identification in the antiracist struggle.

The 2010 census data do not, however, signify a major shift in normative patterns of Brazilian self-identification. Individuals identifying as *brancos* still compose almost half of the population, although they decreased from 54 percent in 2000 to 48 percent in 2010; *pardos* increased from 40 percent in 2000 to 43 percent in 2010; and *pretos* increased from 6.2 percent in 2000 to 7.6 percent in 2010.[81] These statistics do indicate that Brazil has an African Brazilian (or non-White) majority, but one that is composed overwhelmingly of *pardos*. Some attribute the decrease in the percentage of Whites and growth in the percentage of African Brazilians to the Black Movement's success in furthering a positive valuation of Blackness. Others consider this an opportunistic response to the perceived benefits of affirmative action.

Whatever the case, the die has been cast in terms of affirmative action, which many Multiracial Movement activists and supporters have contested as being divisive, even racist. The debate on these policies continues apace. Some individuals contend they will heighten group consciousness of Brazilians as *brancos* and *negros*, but do little, if anything, to reduce racial inequality.[82] Conversely, the "new" expressions of multiraciality could give renewed credence to the racial democracy ideology while masking continuing racial inequality, as well as eschewing meaningful strategies aimed at eradicating it. What is clear is that Black and multiracial activists are rearticulating racial designations differently from traditional Brazilian racial commonsense. Those designations have been individual "free-floating," and frequently illusive, physical markers, combined with cultural and socioeconomic criteria. They are now increasingly posited as racial reference groups, with ancestral criteria also factored into the calculus.[83]

Yet a genuinely new Brazilian racial order calls for a critical rearticulation of Blackness rooted in the lived experiences that make diverse identities and cultural productions possible, rather than formulated as the antithesis of Whiteness.[84] It also necessitates a critical rearticulation of multiraciality that embraces Whiteness without negating Blackness, which could serve as an "intellectual weapon" and "theoretical wedge"[85] in the pursuit of "colorblind antiracism."[86] Accordingly, multiraciality would serve as a conceptual tool for collaborating across more racially porous collective subjectivities to create a more equitable racial order where racial distinctions no longer determine, or have considerably less significance in determining, the distribution of wealth, power, privilege, and prestige. This rearticulation of multiraciality diverges from the hypocritical variant that has historically characterized the racial democracy ideology. It is, in fact, what Brazil's racial democracy is supposed to have been but never was.

NOTES

1. This manuscript borrows from material in G. Reginald Daniel, *Race and Multi-raciality in Brazil and the United States: Converging Paths?* and *Machado de Assis: Multiracial Identity and the Brazilian Novelist.*

2. Daniel, *Machado de Assis.*

3. Hypodescent designates racial group membership of first-generation multiracial offspring of European Americans and Americans of color exclusively based on their background of color. Successive generations, except those of African descent, have more flexibility in self-identification, including the option to identify as White. The "one-drop rule of hypodescent" ("one-drop of blood") applied to Blacks precludes any choice in identification. The rule did not become a normative part of the legal apparatus in the United States until the early twentieth century (circa 1915), although ancestral quanta defining legal Blackness have historically varied according to local. Statutes and even court decisions were necessarily more precise than social custom. Indeed, expressions in formal law appear later than evidence of perceptions and practices that were customary long before they were written down (see Winthrop D. Jordan, "Historical Origins of the One-Drop Rule in the United States"). And there have always been exceptions to the rule. Control over the boundaries between White and Black has always been relative rather than absolute (see Daniel, *Race and Multiraciality*). Some individuals of known African ancestry have been accepted as Whites due to local customs or have less African ancestry than law stipulated. Many phenotypically European individuals have made a clandestine break from the African American community and passed as White. Yet the one-drop rule gained currency as the "commonsense" definition of Blackness over the course of the seventeenth and eighteenth centuries. This was increasingly the case during the nineteenth century and definitively so by the 1920s (F. James Davis, *Who Is Black? One Nation's Definition*).

4. Oracy Nogueira, "Preconceito Racial de Marca e Preconceito Racial de Origem (Sugestão de um quadro de referência para a interpretação do material sobre relações raciais no Brasil)."

5. Michael Omi and Howard Winant, *Racial Formation in the United States: From the 1960s to the 1990s.*

6. Ibid., 99, 131.

7. Oliver Cox, *Caste, Class, and Race: A Study in Social Dynamics*; Marvin Harris, *Patterns of Race in the Americas.*

8. Carl N. Degler, *Neither Black nor White: Slavery and Race Relations in Brazil and the United States*; Marvin Harris, *Patterns of Race in the Americas*; Muriel Nazzari, "Concubinage in Colonial Brazil: The Inequalities of Race, Class, and Gender"; Anthony John R. Russell-Wood, *The Black Man in Slavery and Freedom in Colonial Brazil*; Júnia Ferreira Furtado, *Chica da Silva: A Brazilian Slave of the Eighteenth Century.*

9. Donald Pierson, *Negroes in Brazil: A Study of Race Contact at Bahia.*

10. Degler, *Neither Black nor White.*

11. Anthony John R. Russell-Wood, "Colonial Brazil."

12. John Burdick, "The Myth of Racial Democracy"; Emilia Viotti da Costa, *The Brazilian Empire: Myths and History.*

13. Herbert S. Klein, "Nineteenth-Century Brazil"; Russell-Wood, "Colonial Brazil."

14. Davis, *Who Is Black?*

15. Degler, *Neither Black nor White*, 140.

16. Anani Dzidzienyo, *The Position of Blacks in Brazilian and Cuban Society*; Abdias do Nascimento, *Mixture or Massacre? Essays on the Genocide of a Black People*; Thomas A. Skidmore, *Black into White: Race and Nationality in Brazilian Thought.*

17. Most European immigrants came from Italy, followed by Portugal and Spain, with Germany a distant fourth. There were also arrivals from Syria, Lebanon, China, and Japan. Brazil passed an immigration law in 1907 prohibiting Black immigration and limiting Asian immigrants to an annual rate of 3 percent of the current Asian population. In the early twentieth century, Japanese immigrants arrived to work on coffee plantations. They replaced earlier Chinese immigrants who were deemed inassimilable and undesirable. See Jeffrey H. Lesser, *Negotiating National Identity: Immigrants, Minorities, and the Struggle for Ethnicity in Brazil*; Jeffrey H. Lesser, "Are African-Americans African or American?: Brazilian Immigration Policy in the 1920s."

18. Charles H. Wood and José Alberto Magno de Carvalho, *The Demography of Inequality in Brazil.*

19. Peggy Lovell-Webster, "The Myth of Racial Equality: A Study of Race and Mortality in Northeast Brazil."

20. Pierre-Michel Fontaine, "Transnational Relations and Racial Mobilization: Emerging Black Movements"; Michael George Hanchard, *Orpheus and Power: The Movimento Negro of Rio de Janeiro and São Paulo, Brazil, 1945☒1988.* Myriad racial projects have been conduits of Black identity ranging from popular music, dance, and art to electoral politics, and so on. These include carnival groups such as the *blocos afros* (Olodúm and Ihê Aiyê) that originated in the 1970s and Grupo Cultural Afro-Reggae, which appeared in the 1990s, along with traditional forms of expression in dance and music (e.g., *samba, capoeira*) and religion (e.g., *candomblé*).

21. Thomas A. Skidmore, "Race Relations in Brazil."

22. Rebecca Reichmann, "Brazil's Denial of Race"; Carlos Hasenbalg, "Race and Socioeconomic Inequalities in Brazil"; Peggy Lovell-Webster and Jeffery Dwyer, "The Cost of Not Being White in Brazil."

23. Ana Maria Goldani, "Racial Inequality in the Lives of Brazilian Women."

24. Edward E. Telles, *Race in Another Country: The Significance of Skin Color in Brazil.*

25. Skidmore, "Race Relations in Brazil."

26. John Burdick, "Brazil's Black Consciousness Movement."

27. Skidmore, "Race Relations in Brazil."

28. This was also true of the 1951 Afonso Arinos Law, which prohibited racial discrimination in public accommodations and treated infractions as misdemeanors rather than felonies. The legislation was in response to an incident involving Katherine Dunham, an internationally recognized African American dancer, while she visited São Paulo on tour in 1950. Dunham had advance reservations at a hotel, which had been confirmed in person by her White secretary. Yet she was denied entrance to the hotel. The constitution also affirmed protection of African Brazilian cultural practices and granted land titles to surviving occupants of *quilombos*, communities established by runaway slaves prior to emancipation in 1888 (see Daniel, *Race and Multiraciality*; Antonio Sérgio Alfredo Guimarães, "Measures to Combat Discrimination and Racial Inequality in Brazil"; Skidmore, "Race Relations in Brazil"; Mala Htun, "From 'Racial Democracy' to Affirmative Action").

29. Guimarães, "Measures to Combat Discrimination," 140.

30. Ibid.

31. Benjamin Hensler, "*Nao vale a pena* (Not Worth the Trouble?): Afro-*Brazilian* Workers and *Brazilian* Anti-*Discrimination* Law"; Tanya Katerí Hernández, *Racial Subordination in Latin America: The Role of the State, Customary Law, and the New Civil Rights Response*; Robert J. Cottrol, *The Long Lingering Shadow: Slavery, Race, and Law in the American Hemisphere*.

32. Daniel, *Race and Multiraciality*.

33. Ibid.

34. Since the 1950 census, Native Americans had been classified as *pardo*. Beginning in the 1990 census, they were listed separately. See Melissa Nobles, *Shades of Citizenship: Race and the Census in Modern Politics*.

35. Nobles, *Shades of Citizenship*.

36. Marcelo Paixão, "Waiting for the Sun: Account of the (Precarious) Social Situation of the African Descendant Population in Contemporary Brazil"; Instituto Brasileiro de Geografía e Estadísticas (IBGE), *Censo Demográfico 2000: Características gerais da população. Resultados da amostra. Tabelas de resultados*.

37. Stanley Bailey, "The Race Construct and Public Opinion: Understanding Brazilian Beliefs about Racial Inequality and Their Determinants."

38. France Winddance Twine, *Racism in a Racial Democracy: The Maintenance of White Supremacy in Brazil*.

39. Kevin Hall, "Brazil Program Will Set Aside Jobs for Blacks: Government Plans to Address Inequities"; Mala Htun, "Quotas for a Racial Democracy"; Mala Htun, "From 'Racial Democracy' to Affirmative Action: Changing State Policy on Race in Brazil"; Mark Margolis, "Brazil's Racial Revolution: Affirmative Action Has Finally Come of Age, and Latin America's Most Diverse Society May Change in Ways Few Had Ever Imagined."

40. Daniel, *Race and Multiraciality*.

41. Htun,"Racial Quotas for a Racial Democracy"; Larry Rohter, "Racial Quotas in Brazil Touch Off Fierce Debate"; Telles, *Race in Another Country*.

42. Daniel, *Race and Multiraciality*.

43. Guimarães, "Measures to Combat Discrimination"; Sales Augusto dos Santos, "Ação afirmativa e mérito individual."

44. Jon Jeter, "Affirmative Action Debate Forces Brazil to Take Look in the Mirror"; Ricardo Rochetti, "Not as Easy as Black and White: The Implications of the University of Rio de Janeiro's Quota-Based Admissions Policy on Affirmative Action."

45. Jeter, "Affirmative Action Debate"; Rohter, "Racial Quotas."

46. Antonio Sérgio Alfredo Guimarães, "Ações afirmativas para a população negra nas universidades brasileiras"; Daniela Galdino and Larissa Santos Pereira, "Acesso à Universidade: Condições de Produção de um Discurso Facioso"; Sérgio da Silva Martins, Carlos Alberto Medeiros, and Elisa Larkin Nascimento, "Paving Paradise: The Road from 'Racial Democracy' to Affirmative Action in Brazil"; Delcele Mascarenhas Queiroz, "A negro, seu acesso ao ensino superior e as ações afirmativas"; Nilma Lino Gomes and Aracy Alves Martins, *Afirmando Direitos: Acesso e permanêcia de jovens na universidade*; Ahyas Siss, *Afro-Brasileiros, cotas, e ação afirmativa: Razões históricas*.

47. Jeter, "Affirmative Action Debate"; Rochetti, "Not as Easy as Black and White."

48. Luisa Farah Schwartzman, "Seeing Like Citizens: Unofficial Understandings of Official Racial Categories in a Brazilian University"; Luisa Farah Schwartzman, "Who Are the Blacks?

49. Michael Astor, "Brazil Tries Quotas to Get Racial Equality"; Raquel Villardi, "Acesso à universiadade por meio de ações afirmativas: Estudo da situação dos estudantes com matrícula em 2003 e 2004 (Junho)."

50. Schwartzman, "Seeing Like Citizens"; Schwartzman, "Who Are the Blacks?"

51. Jon Jeter, "Affirmative Action Debate"; Daniel, *Race and Multiraciality*.

52. Mario Osava, "Rights—Brazil: Blacks Demand Adoption of Promised Measures."

53. The original and approved statutes recognize *candomblé* and other African-derived religions as a matter of religious freedom, *capoeira* as an official sport worthy of governmental support, and *quilombadas* (surviving escaped-slave communities) as deserving protection and financial assistance. The approved statute removed the clause relating to the definition of official recognition of *quilombadas*. "Brasília–DF. Comissão geral para debater o estatuto da igualdade racial"; Mariana Oliveira, "Estatuto da Igualdade Racial divide movimento negro."

54. Mari Hayman, "Brazilian Supreme Court Approves Racial Quotas in University."

55. Daniel, *Race and Multiraciality*.

56. John Burdick, "The Lost Constituency of Brazil's Black Movement."

57. Schwartzman, "Seeing Like Citizens," 248.

58. Mike DeWitt and Adam Stepan, "Brazil in Black and White." For example, journalist Nilza Iraci identifies as African Brazilian but could be considered White. In a conference on racism in the early 1990s she heard an activist comment, "I didn't know our organization is already accepting Whites." When defending the rights of African Brazilian women in another meeting, Iraci was questioned by a White colleague, who stated, "But why are you saying all these things when you aren't even African Brazilian?" See Francisco Neves, "Two Brazils."

59. Peter Fry, "Politics, Nationality, and the Meaning of Race"; Ali Kamel, *Não somos racistas: Uma reação aos que querem nos transformar numa nação bicolor*; Peter Fry and Yvonne Maggie, "Política Social de Alto Risco"; António Risério, *A utopia brasileira e os movimentos negros*; Pierre Bourdieu and Loïc Wacquant, "On the Cunning of Imperialist Reason"; Schwartzman, "Seeing Like Citizens."

60. Jerson César Leão Alves, e-mail correspondence with G. Reginald Daniel, October 9, 2007. Freyre expressed similar sentiments. He maintained that the term *moreno,* which encompasses individuals designated as *preto, pardo,* and *branco* (if the latter have dark hair and eyes) (brunette), had increasing salience over other designations. "Brunettism" (*morenidade*) corresponds more closely to Brazil's "beyond-race" (*alem raça*) reality. The term may reflect this encompassing "brownness" synonymous with a transcendent "Brazilianness," which jettisons the perceived color bias in other terminology. It can also be employed as a form of race-neutrality (or even Whitening) to avoid the stigma of Blackness or ignore racial inequality. See Edith Piza and Fúlvia Rosemberg, "Color in the Brazilian Census"; Nobles, *Shades of Citizenship*; George Reid Andrews, *Blacks and White in São Paulo, Brazil, 1888⊠1988.*

61. People of predominantly European and Native American backgrounds were the first multiracials to emerge in colonial Brazil. They reside primarily in the North (*caboclos*), West (*mamelucos*), and the Sertão region of the Northeast (although the *Sertanejos* generally have more African ancestry than the other two groups).

62. Jerson César Leão Alves, e-mail to G. Reginald Daniel, October 10, 2007; "Coloque de volta MESTIÇO no censo do IBGE," Naçãomestiça http://www.nacaomestica.org/.

63. "Racism against Multiracials in Brazil."

64. Marc P. Johnston and Kevin L. Nadal, "Multiracial Microaggressions: Exposing Monoracism."

65. "Abertas inscrições para o V Seminário Sobre a Identidade Mestiça."

66. "Brasília–DF. Comissão Geral para debater o Estatuto da Igualdade Racial."

67. "Mestizo Identity Elimination Public Policies and Color, Race, Ethnicity Classificatory Systems"; "Racial Quotas in Brazil Require Browns Identify Themselves as Negro."

68. Daniel, *Race and Multiraciality,* 220–35.

69. Jerson César Leão Alves, e-mail correspondence with G. Reginald Daniel, October 9, 2007; "Mestizos brasileños expresan apoyo a los mestizos bolivianos,

Nota Contra La Discriminación Hacia Los Mestizos Bolivianos," http://nacao-mestica.org/blog4/?p=6450.

70. Livio Sansone, *Blackness Without Ethnicity*.

71. Paola Lima, "Vai à sanção política de cotas em universidade fed-erais," Senado Federal, Agência Senado, Portal de Notícias, http://www12.senado.gov.br/noticias/materias/2012/08/07/vai-a-sancao-politica-de-cotas-em-universidade-federais.

72. Nádia Franco, "Dilma sanciona Lei de Cotas e veta apenas artigo que criava mecanismo de Seleção," *Terra*, August 29, 2012, http://noticias.terra.com.br/brasil/noticias/0,,OI6113370-EI306,00-Dilma+sanciona+Lei+de+Cotas+e+veta+apenas+artigo+que+criava+mecanismo+de+selecao.html

73. Nádia Franco, "Dilma sanciona Lei de Cotas e veta apenas artigo que criava mecanismo de seleção."

74. Nobles, *Shades of Citizenship*; Stanley R. Bailey, *Legacies of Race: Identities, Attitudes, and Politics in Brazil*.

75. Ford Foundation 2011, http://www.fordfoundation.org/regions/brazil; Juli-ana Barbassa, "Brazil Launches Program to End Extreme Poverty"; Luciana Marques, "Um em cada dez brasileiros é extremamente pobre: Governo esta-belece renda familiar per capita de 70 reais por mês como piso abaixo do qual cidadão já se encontra em situação de miséria."

76. Bailey, *Legacies of Race*; Telles, *Race in Another Country: The Significance of Skin Color in Brazil*.

77. Eduardo Bonilla-Silva, *Racism Without Racists: Color-blind Racism and the Persistence of Racial Inequality in the United States*.

78. Christina A. Sue, "Negotiating Identity Narratives among Mexico's Cosmic Race."

79. Saule Ualiyeva and Adrienne Edgar, "In the Laboratory of Peoples' Friendship: Mixed People in Kazakhstan from the Soviet Era to the Present."

80. Paul R. Spickard, Rowena Fong, and Patricia L. Ewalt, "Undermining the Very Basis of Racism—Its Categories."

81. Taylor Barnes, "For the First Time, Blacks Outnumber Whites in Brazil."

82. DeWitt and Stepan, "Brazil in Black and White."

83. Bailey, "The Race Construct."

84. bell hooks, *Yearning: Race, Gender, and Cultural Politics*.

85. Naomi Zack, *Race and Mixed Race*.

86. Daniel, *Machado de Assis*.

6

Antipodean Mixed Race

Australia and New Zealand

FARIDA FOZDAR AND MAUREEN PERKINS

In this chapter we consider the ways in which mixed-race identities are constructed in Australia and New Zealand, both relatively new nation-states with histories as British settler societies.[1] Australia and New Zealand have experienced little debate in the public sphere about mixed race and minimal impact from international discussion on the subject. Even media coverage of Barack Obama as mixed race at the time of his election did not trigger a conversation about racial terminology. Likewise when Australia's former prime minister John Howard commented that he would prefer a multiracial policy rather than a multicultural one, the comment fell into a void.[2] The issues that have claimed most prominence in relation to race in both Australia and New Zealand have been the effects of migrant intake and the interaction between colonizers, other immigrants, and indigenous peoples.[3] Surveying the literature, we argue first that race as a category and mixed race as a subset are important concepts in theorizing and studying the lived experience of Australians and New Zealanders and that both deserve more scholarly attention. Second, we note the different ways in which the histories of the two nations, and particularly public policies of multiculturalism and biculturalism, have impacted the discourse of multiraciality. We also suggest that processes of globalization have produced an apparent need for "authenticity" among indigenous populations with mixed heritages in both nations. And finally we argue that it is likely that, in a global context, mixed-race individuals may come increasingly to hold cosmopolitan identities oriented to global perspectives.

Australia and New Zealand are relatively young countries, built around a model of the nation-state as it emerged in Europe in the seventeenth and eighteenth centuries. This model implies close links between ethno-racial and political identity, and as such fits uncomfortably within settler societies, which have generally grown through constant migration of people from different ethnic and racial backgrounds, often resulting in mixed offspring. It also necessitates, in Australia's case, a forgetting of the dispossession of the original inhabitants, and in New Zealand, a fraught relationship between its White and indigenous populations based on a contested treaty.[4]

Neither Australia nor New Zealand has formally named mixed-race populations, in the way that Brazil, Mexico, South Africa, colonial India, and some other countries have. This is partly because neither has a single racial group with whom the dominant Whites have mixed—mixing has occurred across a range of groups. The result is that there is no single population of mixed-race people to which an identifier can be applied. In both nations, most indigenous people of mixed race identify as indigenous and the rest of the mixed population come from such diverse backgrounds that no single identifier would suffice. The closest these nations come to recognizing this racial diversity is through a multiplicity of hyphenations (such as Anglo-Celtic, Vietnamese-Australian, Fijian-New Zealander, Cypriot-Turkish-Australian), with many citizens identifying with a number of different heritages, which is not dissimilar from the ways mixed-race Canadians tend to identify (see chapter on Canada, this volume). An interesting aspect of such identifications is that the "Australian" or "New Zealander" part of the hyphen is automatically presumed to be White (see also Mahtani 2002a).

Race (as opposed to ethnicity) is rarely an explicit focus of current policies in Australia and New Zealand, and neither country offers a color option in their census.[5] Tilbury has argued that there is a need for a name to identify the White population in Australia, just as the term "Pakeha" is used in New Zealand,[6] but here we argue further that there is a need for mixed race to be acknowledged and named. This is not to suggest a "group-making project" that would see those of mixed race identified as a "multiracial community" in a collective sense, seeking support and resourcing in the manner of other ethnic communities, as has occurred over a number of decades in the US.[7] Rather, we suggest that the material realities of the experience of mixed-race people are better understood by acknowledging color/race as distinct from ethnicity.

In this chapter we use several examples to illustrate the complexities of dealing with mixed race in contexts characterized by what Steve Vertovec calls "super-diversity."[8] Vertovec defines superdiversity as "a condition . . . distinguished by a dynamic interplay of variables among an increased number of new, small and scattered, multiple-origin, transnationally connected, socio-economically differentiated and legally stratified immigrants."[9] While he does not comment on mixed race as a consequence of this diversity, he explores differences in immigration statuses, labour market experiences, gender, age, languages, religion, and race to illustrate what he means by the "diversification of diversity." He suggests such diversity, resulting from processes of globalization, requires a rethinking of racial and ethnic categorization, recognition of the conjunction of race and ethnicity with a range of other variables, and addressing the question of the appropriate orientation of the state towards its peoples. In the cases of Australia and New Zealand superdiversity is the result of large numbers of racially and ethnically diverse migrants joining predominantly White settler societies, with a smaller proportion of indigenous peoples, within policy contexts that have increasingly encouraged the mixing of populations. In such instances, the "ethnic group" and even the "mixed-race group," is insufficient as a unit of analysis. We argue that such societies offer a different context for the consideration of racial and ethnic boundaries and hybrid identities. However we suggest that before a truly cosmopolitan imagination and identity beyond race can be developed it is necessary to acknowledge race and mixed race as categories of difference.

Australia

Prior to federation in 1901 the Australian population was made up of individuals from a variety of countries of origin and racial backgrounds, including significant numbers of gold miners from China, indentured workers from the Pacific nations, and smaller numbers of camel drivers from Afghanistan, joining convicts and free settlers from Britain. Even as early as the First Fleet in January 1788, not all those settling in Australia claimed British ancestry. Cassandra Pybus's research reveals that at least a dozen Black convicts arrived in these boats, and thousands of people of African ancestry (often mixed offspring of masters and slaves from the US) had settled in Australia by the late 1830s, mixing with the White and Indigenous populations.[10]

Despite, or perhaps because of, this diversity, the first piece of legislation that the Australian Parliament passed was an immigration law popularly known as the White Australia Policy (the Immigration Restriction Act, 1901), effectively limiting entry to Whites only. The policy sprang from concerns that settlers from Asia would change the racial and cultural character of the colonial outpost, reflecting a fear of the "Yellow Peril."[11] It resulted not only in fewer migrants from non-European backgrounds coming to Australia, but also in many who had lived in Australia prior to federation returning to their countries of origin. The result was that by 1947 Australia was one of the "Whitest" countries in the world, with only 0.25 percent of its population being non-European (excluding Aboriginal people).[12] In 1958 a new Migration Act signaled the beginning of the end of the White Australia Policy, due to the economic demand from the labor market and recognition of the policy's fundamental racism.

During the 1960s increasing numbers of "mixed-race" (albeit English-speaking Christian) migrants from Asia arrived, although they were not provided the assisted passage to migrate that the British were.[13] In the early 1970s, as a result of increasingly diverse migrant populations and recognition of the economic value of migrants, multiculturalism became a defining feature of Australian policy, as it did in Canada around this time.[14] Policies supported the rights of migrant groups to retain their cultural identities and, through the provision of resources, cultural activities such as language retention. While this has been criticized as a limited "food and festivals" version of valuing diversity,[15] it was an improvement on the monoracial monoculturalism of earlier times.

While multiculturalism started as a political discourse, it found its way into the general conceptualization of the nation among many

Australians desperate for some unique feature to characterize their national identity.[16] However, there remained an undercurrent of Euro-centrism.[17] Multiculturalism focused more on the right of migrant groups to maintain cultural differences than on racial categorizations and identification. One result was that migrant groups were treated in monolithic essentialist terms, ignoring their internal diversity. And while government rhetoric criticized the formation of ethnic enclaves as inhibiting integration, multicultural policies encouraged migrants to establish ethnic community structures.[18] Ethnic groups were encouraged to play up their homogeneity in order to access ethno-specific resources, leading to strategic essentialism in the discourses around diversity. This approach tended to encourage single identifications, marginalizing those with multiple ethnic and racial roots. This meant that those who traversed group boundaries were problematic.

Multicultural policies did not remove racial division, of course, but resulted in what Jon Stratton has called "culturalism," according to which "race works as a signifier of [culture]."[19] A strong emphasis on "British-ness" as the basis of mainstream Australian culture was retained, often referred to in terms both of values and physical features.[20]

The last decade has witnessed a retreat from multiculturalism in government policies and as a core aspect of Australian identity.[21] This has many underlying causes: processes of globalization, including increasingly diverse migrant intakes; a questioning of the national character; a shared sense that together with other Western nations Australia faces a global threat from Islam; and a divisive national debate over how "boat people" (asylum seekers) should be treated. The result has been, in Robert Putnam's terms, a "hunkering down" and closing off towards others, and a growing sense of suspicion towards anyone who could be seen as an outsider (read non-White, non-Christian).[22] Thus concern for the last decade or more has been focused on three main targets: the influence of Islam and Muslim migrants; black Africans; and asylum seekers. All three groups are seen as "visibly different," and various measures have been implemented either to keep them out (asylum seekers) or to ensure cultural assimilation.

Since the end of World War II, seven million people have migrated to Australia. Over the last decade Australia has taken, on average, around 120,000 new migrants annually, including around 10 percent under its humanitarian program.[23] A quarter of Australia's 22 million people were born overseas, and over 40 percent were either born overseas themselves or have at least one parent born overseas. Migrants still largely come from European countries, with the greatest proportion of overseas-born from the United Kingdom (15.3 percent) and New Zealand (14.8 percent), but growing numbers come from China, India, and Japan.[24] Recent humanitarian intakes from Africa contribute further to the racial diversity. However, the CIA Handbook[25] states that "ethnic groups" in Australia consist of "White 92%, Asian 7%, aboriginal and other 1%," indicating far lower levels of diversity than most public discourse assumes. It is unclear what "White" means in this context—people only of European origin, or Caucasians (including from the Indian subcontinent, the Middle East, and north Africa), or whether it includes people of mixed race. It is interesting to consider why the CIA would classify people in this way, and interesting that one commentator has been using this race-based statistic recently in public debates on issues of diversity.[26]

The fact is that no information about the numerical size of the mixed-race population exists as information that could provide such statistics is not available. The Wikipedia entry for "mixed race" in Australia relies on census data on "mixed marriages" based on country of origin of marriage partners rather than race—thus a migrant White Briton and a White Australian would be classified as a "mixed marriage." It is unlikely such a marriage is significantly "mixed" ethnically, let alone racially. Carmen Luke and Allan Luke similarly report that one in six marriages are between an Australian-born and overseas-born, but again this tells us little about the racial composition of these marriages and their offspring.[27]

Mixed Race in Australia

There are two main categories of mixed-race populations in Australia, those with mixed Aboriginal/non-Aboriginal ancestries, and those with mixed White and other ancestries. The life chances and identities of the two differ significantly. In this section we outline some of the features of both groups.

Color is, as always, a key issue. Blackness is understood as a signifier of authentic Indigeneity, and lightness of skin color indicative of a suspect mixedness. For example, Australian media recently reported the case of a young Aboriginal woman who was told that she was too White to work for an Indigenous rights charity as they needed someone who "looked Indigenous."[28] In another instance, a class action was taken against a journalist by a group of Indigenous people who objected to his criticisms of white-looking Aboriginal people claiming Aboriginal identity.[29] Further cases of identity premised on skin color rather than on cultural identity illustrate the complexities of racial identification. There are a growing number of stories of Australians who have discovered that rather than having presumed Aboriginal roots, they were of African or other "Black" heritage (for example, Sri Lankan). One example is writer Mudrooroo Nyoongah (aka Colin Johnson), the son of a part–Black American part-Irish father and a White (Irish-descendant) mother. Growing up, he experienced considerable social marginalization—he had dark skin, grew up in a boys' home, and spent his young adulthood in jail. He claimed an Aboriginal identity, and his literary success is partly a result of linking his experiences to Aboriginal politics.[30] Similarly, Gordon Mathews, Australia's first "Aboriginal" diplomat, was adopted as a child and presumed to be one of the Stolen Generations,[31] whose career progression through the diplomatic service was aided by formal and informal affirmative action processes for Aboriginal Australians. However he eventually discovered he was of mixed Sri Lankan ancestry.[32] Debate has arisen as a result about what constitutes an authentic Aboriginal identity, and whether being raised as an Aboriginal is sufficient, or whether blood is requisite.

A significant feature of mixed-race Aboriginal people is the decision to self-identify as Indigenous. Greg Gardiner and Eleanor Bourke quote estimates suggesting that between 83 percent and 88 percent of the offspring of mixed Indigenous marriages identify as Indigenous.[33] Only 22 percent of Indigenous people report some European ancestry,[34] although the actual proportions are much higher. Significant academic debate arose from the 1996 census, which indicated an increase in the Indigenous population of 50 percent in the previous ten years. The increase has been variously attributed to a recruitment of the offspring of mixed marriages into the Indigenous population, affirmation of Indigenous identity among the Stolen Generations, and inadequate conceptualization of categories.[35]

Such identification has both positive and negative consequences. In some contexts, "passing" or looking White is a benefit; in others there are advantages to identifying as Black. On the one hand Aboriginality is strongly associated with social disadvantage and marginality, but on the other, identifying as Aboriginal can help secure access to rights through land claims and various positive discrimination mechanisms. Indigeneity is also desirable as an identity of right or legitimacy.[36] According to Ghassan Hage the first owners of the land enjoy a degree of prestige associated with a sense of "belonging" that White Australians and others, all migrants at some point, do not have.[37] They also "have" culture in a more obvious way than other Australians.[38] Many would argue, however, that the stigma and poor socioeconomic outcomes associated with Indigeneity provide little incentive to claim Aboriginality.

Positive or negative, Aboriginal identity remains associated in the minds of many Australians with Blackness—the lighter one is, the less likely one is to be seen as authentic. There are many Aboriginal people for whom this would be an important and insulting misrepresentation of their heritage.[39] However, movements for indigenous rights in many countries including New Zealand, South Africa, Australia, Hawaii, Fiji, Canada, the US, Malaysia, India, Papua New Guinea and other Pacific nations, have often been supported through an identity politics that rests on the notion of a fundamental, extraordinary connection of the original, darker-skinned population with the land. This has become particularly important in a globalized context where such authenticity holds some cachet.

In addressing this question Yin Paradies (described on his website as an Aboriginal-Anglo-Asian Darwinian living in Melbourne) suggests that the strategic essentialism of pan-Aboriginality, while useful politically, has had some negative impacts leaving "an increasing number of Indigenous people vulnerable to accusations of inauthenticity."[40] Paradies uses his personal experience as an example of the complexity of mixed race in Australia. He refuses to privilege one identity over others, despite an imperative "that anomalous individuals choose to be either exclusively Indigenous or exclusively non-Indigenous."[41] His preference, he says, is to create a hybrid space of multiplicity. He notes that presumptions of inauthenticity adhere to a lack of cultural markers such as language, class, "morality," cultural knowledge, and so on, but perhaps most importantly to "Indigenous looks." He argues:

> Fair-skinned Indigenous people experience "racism scorn and disbelief" from other Indigenous and non-Indigenous people alike, whose perennial interrogation of their identity leads to acute anxiety. . . . This intense questioning of authenticity . . . is due to the profound disruption that white-skinned Indigenes represent for the Black-white racial dichotomy, so fervently clung to in Australia.[42]

It is easy to assume that the relevant categories for Indigenous mixed-race people are White and Indigenous, but in fact there has been much mixing across diverse racial lines within the Aboriginal community. Christine Choo, for example, tracks historically the relationship between Chinese and Indigenous communities, noting the stigma within the Chinese community of marrying someone of darker skin, and the attempts by authorities to control sexual contact between Indigenous women and Asian men.[43] Indigenous people also produced offspring with Afghan camel drivers and Malay fishermen in the northern parts of Australia, which has left many with recognizably Muslim names, some shared aspects of culture, and mixed racial features.[44]

The second dimension of racial mixing in Australia is between the White population and racialized others, usually newer migrant communities, particularly after the de-legislation of the White Australia Policy. However it remains an open question as to how these changes in immigration policy and processes of globalization are affecting the mixed-race composition of Australia because of the absence of race statistics.[45] It is possible to make some comments based on information about mixed marriages, where "mixed" refers to marriages between those whose country of birth is different from their spouse. Using 2006 census data, Siew-Ean Khoo tries to deal in a more sophisticated way with the "overseas-born" category to determine rates of racial mixing.[46] She argues that the next generations of Australians are far more ethnically and racially diverse than previous generations. The result, one already evident in marriage patterns among the young, is that Australians are more likely to interracially marry than at any time in Australia's history. While very high proportions of Australian children report their parents as having Australian or European ancestry (85 percent of the zero-to-twenty-four-year age group), 31 percent report having more than one ancestry (compared with 21 percent in the over-sixty-fives). As shown in figure 6.1, 7 percent of the total population, or just over a quarter of those with multiple ancestries, report a combination of Australian/European and a non-European ancestry and this ethnic and racial diversity is growing. While proportions of marriages to overseas-born spouses have been stable over the last decade, there has been an increase in partners from Asia, the Middle East, and the Americas. Khoo argues this is partly attributable to the greater engagement of Australia with countries in Asia and North America as part of the process of globalization, but also to the younger generation traveling to these places for work and holidays, as well as growing numbers of overseas students from Asia and working holiday-makers living in Australia for a number of years and developing partnerships as a result. She suggests the increased propensity of the younger generation to identify as having mixed or multiple ancestries may herald an age of postmulticulturalism or cosmopolitanism. Australia's recent policy shift to encourage temporary work migrants, who now number around 90,000 a year, is likely to increase this phenomenon.

Qualitative studies find Australian mixed-race families do not report feeling in any way stigmatized or disadvantaged, and they tend to see hybridity and the "third space" produced by their union[47] as positive and empowering.[48] For example, one participant in a study claims, "We are a multi-racial nation and we should flaunt it."[49] However, it has been argued that there are regional differences in the perception of these unions. Luke and Luke focus on two Australian cities, Darwin and Brisbane, which have different histories of diversity and orientations to hybridity.[50] Due to Darwin's long history of interracial mixing it is common to find people who share, for example, Torres Strait Islander, Aboriginal, Indonesian, and Chinese heritages or Filipino, Malay, and American backgrounds. Brisbane, on the other hand, has tended to have a more recent racial diversity in its migrant population, de facto segregation, and a majority of specific migrant groups. It is also politically conservative. Interracial mixing is found to be a less positive experience in Brisbane. Luke and Luke argue that due to the political climate and assimilationist policies and practices in Brisbane, there is limited

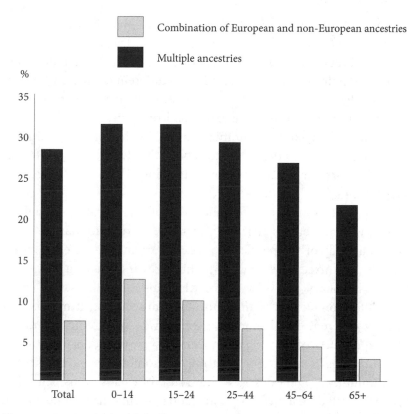

Figure 6.1. Percent Stating Multiple Ancestries or a Combination of European and Non-European Ancestries, by Age Group, 2006. Source: Siew-Ean Khoo, "Generational Change in Ethnic Composition and Inter-ethnic Marriage: Implications for Australian Multiculturalism in the 21st Century." Draft for presentation at "A New Era in Australian Multiculturalism?" workshop, Melbourne, November 19–20, 2010.

opportunity for acknowledging, let alone engaging with, race, ethnicity, and cultural difference, compared to Darwin. Thus, Luke and Luke find, consistent with other scholars, that context affects the experiences of mixed-race populations.[51]

However, as we have stated earlier, there remains scant research on mixed-race Australian populations. The exception is Perkins's collection of autobiographical reflections on the experience of being mixed race in Australia.[52] Contributors' experiences vary, but all explain that they have felt "different" on the grounds of physical appearance, not fitting easily into discrete Black, White, or Asian categories. This sense of difference has not always resulted in a negative marginality, but it has been a trigger for self-reflection, and, at its best, leads to a celebration of mixedness and a recognition of the diversity of Australian identities. The collection illustrates, however, the very different context for mixed-race Australians compared to those in the US who have started to form collectives designed to promote rights and recognition.[53] In Australia, mixed race is a much more atomized affair. There is no critical mass of mixed-race people attempting to lobby collectively, and the terminologies of race have been primarily the domain of the Indigenous population.

To illuminate some of the complexities of this debate, particularly for those who are read as racially ambiguous, we refer to Margot Ford's work. In a study of the politics of race in Darwin, she notes the ways in which her mixed-race daughter, while growing up, struggled with social exclusionary practices in everyday Australia. She says, "Dina's milky coffee complexion is an important characteristic. It marked her as visibly different, but her racial identity was ambiguous to others. Dina's experiences of growing up in Darwin were mixed, having to deal with sometimes being included within, and sometimes excluded from, her community."[54] Dina describes her sense of exclusion as being less like a brick wall than a piece of plastic food covering that can be pushed and will stretch, but never quite let her across. "There's still interaction. You can touch these people, you can play with them, but you can never ever be on their side of the world." Ford concludes that her daughter's experiences of belonging in Australia are therefore ambivalent.

More recently interest has been in the racial mixing of the growing communities of African descent, many of whom came to Australia in the 2000s as part of Australia's commitment to settling refugees. Resources such as *Working It Out* have been designed by and for those in so-called African-Australian relationships to assist with understanding cultural differences. The challenges for White mothers of children of African descent in Australia have also been the subject of research, particularly their desire to ensure that their children have access to positive engagements with their African-ness, in what is a highly asymmetric cultural environment.[55]

In order to recognize the diversity of racially mixed people in Australia, Perkins argues against the color blindness that assimilation holds up as an ideal, suggesting that more color consciousness rather than less is required to understand the impact of race on social, economic, and cultural experiences in Australia.[56] In the Australian context, where the terms "Black" and "White" have meant Indigenous and non-Indigenous (until recent humanitarian entrants from African countries), terms of "mixed" identity carry a residue of colonial racist usage and, as we have seen, are generally rejected by Aboriginal communities. For the growing numbers of those who are racially mixed in other ways, racial awareness recognizes an important parameter of experience and opportunity as well as identity. To some extent, such identities are becoming valorized as evidence of the success of multiculturalism, as is the case in Canada.[57] However Perkins argues that in the general refusal to consider "mixedness," Australian culture makes national loyalty and a sense of belonging difficult for those non-White Australians who are not Indigenous. Processes of globalization, most notably large-scale migration from increasingly racially and culturally diverse countries, and challenges to the rights of mixed-race Aboriginal people to claim their status as Indigenous, have meant mixed race remains a significant, if underresearched, feature of the Australian social landscape.

New Zealand

New Zealand has a different racial profile from Australia and a different relationship to its indigenous people, the Maori. The colonization of New Zealand was based on the Treaty of Waitangi, signed in 1840, guaranteeing governance to the English monarch, but, ambiguously, it also gave complete rights over properties and resources to Maori.[58] Formal and informal challenges to the meaning of this document have meant an ongoing tradition of resistance and movements calling for Maori self-determination.[59] Such resistance has often revolved around claims for biculturalism in government policy—a policy orientation markedly different from Australia's multiculturalism. Biculturalism implies that the key racial and cultural relationship is between the two groups unique to New Zealand, Maori and Pakeha (White New Zealanders), with related "moral, political, and social obligations."[60] In the context of the economic and social disadvantage of Maori, rights claims are frequently linked to racial heritage.

In terms of migration, New Zealand is similar to Australia, specifically in relation to historical attempts to limit the country's racial diversity. It too had an Immigration Restriction Act that excluded those not from England and Ireland, using a language test.[61] This was eventually lifted in 1974, as part of the worldwide phenomenon of the opening up of borders, allowing much more diverse populations to migrate. As well as Maori and Pakeha, New Zealand has significant migrant communities from China who came as gold miners in the 1870s and then more recently as business immigrants and students; other Asians including Japanese, Vietnamese, Cambodians, and Koreans; Lebanese; Indians (both from India and from Fiji); Pacific Islanders from the Cook Islands, Tonga, Samoa, Fiji, Tokelau, and Niue; and more recently South Africans, Filipinos, Iranians, Iraqis, and migrants and refugees from African nations.[62]

This diversity shows up in New Zealand's census, where data is analyzed on a number of levels, with level 1 collapsing the population into European, Maori, Asian, Pacific peoples, MELAA (Middle Eastern, Latin American and African—introduced in 2006 and reflecting the changing nature of the population), and "Other." This provides some insight into the proportions of mixed-race, as opposed to simply mixed-ethnic, populations as outlined below. Because of the quality of its statistics, and the growing diversity of its population, New Zealand has become increasingly sophisticated about considerations of racial, ethnic, national, and mixed identities.[63]

Debate continues among Maori, Pakeha, and New Zealanders of other descents about their own ethnic identities, culture, and rights, and whether biculturalism is the best model for their nation. Within this debate are questions about the place of mixed-race Maori and others and their right to legitimately claim a particular racial heritage.

Mixed Race in New Zealand

In 1995 Ranginui Walker wrote:

> For every Maori that marries a Pakeha he or she doubles the Maori population! Because the children will identify with Maori. Because they are rooted in the land. Pakeha are not.[64]

Walker comes from a mixed background, but he clearly privileges not so much Maori culture but race, bloodline, as connected in an essential and mystical way, to the land. Maori call themselves "*Tangata Whenua*," which means the "people of the land," and their creation story, like so many, sees Maori created from the earth. However, the story also involves migration from an ancestral homeland one thousand years ago, and Maori greeting rituals include the *whakapapa*, a scripted identification of one's ancestry that should be traceable back to one of the seven canoes (or tribes) that made this voyage. This is the heritage, Walker argues, that is passed down, through the blood, even to mixed-race children. However, the relationship between race and culture in this context is complex.

In the late nineteenth and early twentieth centuries concerns about depopulation and fears of "alien races" resulted in attempts to quantify the numbers of Europeans, Maori, and others living in New Zealand.[65] In the 1921 census, enumerators were instructed to classify people of mixed Maori and other races by proportion of blood based on ancestry—those with over 50 percent were to be categorized as Maori of full blood, those with less than 50 percent were to be designated "half-castes." However, there was also a cultural aspect to this classification—half-castes were to be enumerated under the Maori as opposed to the European census only if they lived as Maori rather than European.[66] Since the 1970s census questions have focused on identification rather than blood, and since 1986 the census has allowed multiple ethnic affiliations, both changes resulting from shifts in migrant intakes and to a growing recognition of the complexity and subjectivity of ethno-racial identities. Consequently growing numbers of New Zealanders are identifying with multiple roots, as a result of ethnic mobility and ethnogenesis of new categories, but also a growing pride in indigeneity. Those of Maori descent tend to identify as Maori though—in the 2006 census, 81 percent of those identifying as having Maori descent also chose Maori as their ethnic group, although many also identified with other ethnic groups.[67] This may indicate the positive effect biculturalism has had on identification as Maori.

There are high levels of intermarriage among Maori and non-Maori in New Zealand, although social interaction generally remains somewhat limited. Colleen Ward reports that 1996 census data reveals half of partnered Maori have non-Maori spouses.[68] The 2006 census shows 47 percent of Maori identify with multiple ethnicities.[69] Thus mixed identities are common among Maori.

However mixedness is experienced ambivalently by many. In Farida Fozdar's research into Maori and Pakeha relationships and identity construction, most Maori interviewed had mixed ancestry.[70] Some chose to highlight their Maori-ness, others to focus on their mixedness. Maori respondents were generally ambivalent about their Maori identities. Similar to the issues raised by Paradies in relation to Indigenous Australians, some Maori denied themselves a legitimate Maori identity due to self-perceived racial inadequacy, some due to cultural inadequacy. Reasons for not seeing themselves as authentic Maori included the fact that they were not "Black" enough physically (Black being the contrast category, rather than the more technically correct "brown," due to the American-style identity politics adopted by Maori), and did not have the language, culture, a Maori name, or knowledge of their ancestry. Some felt they did not have a sufficient proportion of "Maori blood" or the right physical features. Some felt that since they were partly White, they were therefore not authentic Maori. As one respondent said, "There are no true Maoris left in New Zealand at all. We've all got a bit of white in us." Few Maori were willing to identify as "authentic" Maori —their mixed heritage and acculturation within mainstream New Zealand society meant they saw themselves as "White Maori," "Pakeha Maori," or "McDonald's Maori." For most, however, their racial identity was not particularly important, with most saying it was seldom salient in their interactions or sense of themselves.

On the other hand, a few respondents had adopted a specifically bicultural identity, regardless of proportion of "Maori blood," as a political stance and chose their networks of interaction to support that identity. This identity was a "project identity," "created consciously . . . to precipitate political struggle."[71] As such, support for this identity was important. Those who had taken this identity were engaged in processes of identity solidification—learning their culture, attending language classes, changing their names, and surrounding themselves with other Maori who could provide a "plausibility structure" both to support the ethno-racial identity and to provide information about the content of that identity.[72] Pride in claiming such an identity is influenced by the political climate—at the time of the research several decades of pro-Maori bicultural policies had produced an environment where there was less stigma attached to being Maori.

The importance of skin color in terms of identity but also for socioeconomic outcomes such as health, education, and employment, is significant, according to Paul Callister.[73] He refers to the phenomenon known as the "browning of New Zealand" as high birth rates, greater mixing, and increased identification as Maori begin to change the complexion of the country. Without some way of measuring skin color, though, he notes, it is impossible to measure the effects of color on outcomes.

Recent research by Ward found significant differences between Maori, Pakeha, and dual-heritage (mixed Maori Pakeha) students in the strength of their ethnic identity and various other factors.[74] Maori had stronger ethnic and national identities, engaged in more ethnic exploration, reported more discrimination, and held less liberal views about parental authority (they were less likely to support children's rights or parental obligations) and other values than Pakeha students. Importantly for this paper, those of mixed heritage fell between the two. Ward analyzes the results in terms of acculturation theory, arguing that those of dual heritage are well placed to negotiate the demands of two cultures.[75] She rejects the deficit model of identity often attributed to mixed-race offspring that focuses on psychological stress and instability. Instead she argues dual-heritage adolescents absorb the cultural influences of two traditions. Noting the importance of context, Ward suggests that "the development of a positive bicultural identity in dual heritage Maori-Pakeha youth is sanctioned in New Zealand"[76] and thus such youth see themselves as both Maori and Pakeha, and see this biracial and bicultural identity as positive.

New Zealand may well be an unusual case as many White New Zealanders, and some Maori, identify aspects of Maori culture as the factor that differentiates them as a national grouping from, say, Australians. Maoriness is thus a fundamental part of many New Zealanders' sense of identity, regardless of racial background.[77] It may well be argued that this phenomenon simply reflects a support of ethnic trendiness and appreciation of cultural differences. However, in New Zealand it appears to be both more universally held and more consistent.

However, mixed race in New Zealand is not simply a matter of White and indigenous racial and cultural mixing. Senka Bozic-Vrbancic argues for a recognition of the multiple dimensions of identity construction among mixed-race New Zealanders, demonstrating that for those of mixed Maori and Dalmatian (Croatian) backgrounds particular class (shared working-class backgrounds due to interactions on the gumfields) and gender structures, overlaid with discourses of national (New Zealander), racial (Maori), and ethnic (Dalmatian) identities, delimit subject formation and agency.[78] Using Laclau she suggests that in such cases "a single subject may occupy many different subject positions but it is important to stress that the meaning of each subject position is constituted with respect to its differential relations within the entire system of subject positions."[79] The two women whose life histories and identities she tracks have almost identical racial and ethnic backgrounds, but radically divergent identities. This supports the argument by Penny Edwards, Debjani Ganguly, and Jacqueline Lo that mixed race is much more complicated, transcending biology through the influence of history, location, culture, socialization, desire, and memory.[80]

Significant proportions of the New Zealand population are mixed Pacific Islanders—Samoans, Tongans, and Cook Islanders who have mixed heritages with White New Zealanders, Maori, less commonly Asians, and with each other. However little has been written about their experiences and identities.

The fact that the New Zealand Census has for over two decades allowed multiple ethnic identifications indicates a recognition of the complexity of racial mixing in New Zealand, as well as processes of globalization (see Morning, this volume). In the 2006 census one in eight people affiliated with more than one ethnic group.[81] This was much higher among some groups than others, particularly for Pacific Island peoples and Maori, where half identified with more than one group. Similar to the trend in Australia, the rate of multiple affiliations is higher among younger age groups, where it reaches almost 20 percent.[82]

Antipodean Mixed Race, Cosmopolitanism and Directions for the Future

It is clear that "people of so-called mixed race reflect the arbitrary and contested logic of racial distinctions."[83] However, as we have seen, rather than meaning that such individuals must identify with one or the other side (what Miri Song calls "monoracial prescriptiveness"), increasingly, in contexts where diversity is seen as a positive thing, they are able to take on hybrid identities that recognize multiple heritages. David Parker and Miri Song note the movement in discourses around mixed race from pathologization to celebration. Research such as that of Barbara Tizard and Ann Phoenix, who studied young people of mixed parentage in the UK, has found that a majority see their mixed heritage as an asset, rather than having a negative, pathological self-identity, and the few Antipodean studies outlined above generally back this up, while recognizing the importance of the spatial, cultural, and political context.[84]

However this celebration of difference should not become an assumption of the superiority of the mixed-race person as the person of the future and as biologically advantaged, with the corollary of a sense of inferiority for the monoracial and monocultural person.[85] Further, as Rainier Spencer argues, such celebration may be at the expense of recognizing the very real disadvantage associated with Blackness (of whatever shade).[86] He criticizes the American multiracial identity movement and its celebration of "Generation Mix" for feeding into the same logic that traditional biological racism supports—that race, in this case mixed race, produces racial superiority, "super powers unavailable to monoracial blacks."[87] We do not wish to adopt such a stance, which implies a biological superiority to mixedness. We do suggest, however, that the opportunity to engage with the world from a body that simply does not fit established racial categories offers a person particular potential to develop an identity and attitudes that support a cosmopolitan outlook in the context of a globalized world.

The use of mixedness to achieve particular political ends has resulted in concerns about the potential for fragmentation that a focus on race-based classification and attendant access to resources might entail. We argue that the growth in numbers of mixed-race individuals offers an opportunity to rethink racial categorization, and to move towards a recognition of hybrid identities with more cosmopolitan outlooks, but that this very fact illustrates not the irrelevance of race and ethnic categorization, but the ways in which mixing across such categories offers fundamentally different types of subject positions with different types of experiences. Such crossings both challenge the "ethnic absolutism"[88] of much identity politics that presumes ethnicity and race overdetermine identity, behavior, and attitudes, and simultaneously recognize the importance of race in influencing these aspects of subjectivity.

It is as yet unclear how mixed race and hybridity in terms of identity and outlook are related. Indeed, in the Australian context (and, we would add, the New Zealand context), Luke and Luke argue that the interracial family

> is not the stable source of microgovernmentality and normativity described in traditional family studies, nor is it the site of partiality, nonidentity, and lack implied in some traditional multicultural studies. They are nothing less than sites of fluctuating hybridity, mimicry, heteroglossia, and transformation—where identities, relations of power, cultural practices, and intergenerational continuities are reconstructed and reframed in historically grounded but unprecedented ways, and where "new" human subjects are innovatively crafting themselves.[89]

They are a particularly fascinating phenomenon in the Antipodean context where decades of policy designed to exclude the racially different have given way to a social and political context in which mixing is, to some extent, encouraged.

We wish to link this conceptualization to the growing literature on globalization and its relation to cosmopolitan identities. The literature on superdiversity and cosmopolitanism tends to ignore mixed race. It is odd that while, as Vertovec suggests, superdiversity in England and Europe has produced new challenges for the social sciences including new patterns of inequality and prejudice, and issues around cross-cultural "contact," cosmopolitanism, and integration,[90] there has been little focus on mixed race as an aspect of this superdiversity. Likewise, in Ulrich Beck's proposed research agenda for cosmopolitanism, mixed race does not feature.[91] Instead other aspects of globalization such as consumption of global cultural commodities, dual citizenship, language diversity, cross-border mobility, global communications patterns, ecological crises, and aspects of transnationalism and national identities are identified. Yet we would argue that significant features of cosmopolitanism are found in the mixed-race experience. Bronislaw Szerszynski and John Urry identify cosmopolitanism as including extensive mobility, willingness to take risks involved in dealing with others, awareness of one's culture, and most importantly, an openness to other peoples and cultures.[92] We argue it is likely that the growing phenomenon of mixed race will produce an intercultural or cosmopolitan identity, as those of mixed backgrounds tend to be more mobile, open to engaging with others, and critically aware of their own and others' racial and cultural distinctiveness and yet similarity. Certainly they are less likely to have a monocultural monoracial commitment. This may bring about "a global identity shift . . . neither the integration of home and host culture values (hybridisation) nor the bicultural strategy which results from acculturation experiences, but rather an identity in which the [individuals] define themselves as world citizens."[93]

Whether this also holds true for indigenous mixed-race people remains to be seen—so far a growing body of evidence indicates that processes of globalization have produced a fixation with authenticity among both Australian and New Zealand mixed-race indigenous populations, which appears to signal a move in the opposite direction in terms of localizing identity around Blackness rather than universalizing it. This may be the result of the particular political contexts in which these groups are negotiating access to resources and respect, and as such may be a stage in a process towards a more global perspective.

Little research focusing on mixed race exists in Australia and New Zealand. This has been due partly to a reticence to discuss race and partly to presumptions about exclusive racial/cultural categories, a product of over thirty years of multicultural and in New Zealand's case, bicultural, policies. It may be that such policies have privileged exclusive identities based on essentialist notions, encouraging identification with a single culture, in order to access resources. The result is a research focus on cultural integration, rather than questions of race and mixing. It is also related to the fact that race has been the preserve of the Indigenous people in Australian studies, as it is in New Zealand.[94] There is therefore a clear need for more research on Antipodean mixed race. Maureen Perkins suggests that studies of those who cross such boundaries are an important aspect of developing a better understanding of similarity and difference:

Far from fragmenting society, mixed race studies emphasizes human universals: everyone has colour, mixedness and ethnic identity and none of these is determined by biology or nationality. . . . In a very different way from the naïve optimism of proponents of the melting pot, mixed race is helping to unravel race itself.[95]

Thus we do not wish to argue for movement beyond racial classification. As Song suggests, while the notion of transcending race is appealing, as it implies moving beyond racist identification, it is a long way off. While people continue to use race "in their thinking, interactions, and behaviours in their everyday lives, we as social scientists need to continue documenting such usage."[96] Awareness of mixed race may shed light on the process of identification beyond single racial categories, and therefore beyond orientations to single geographic spaces and sets of values and practices. Mixed race is emblematic of processes of globalization, as is cosmopolitanism. In this chapter we have offered a view of these processes and their interaction from the perspective of the Antipodes.

NOTES

1. "Antipodean" here refers to the British Antipodes, i.e., Australia and New Zealand (literally "feet against feet," on the other side of the world). It is a word that carries colonial and imperial resonances, as if Britain were the center from which other places are measured, but it is now often used to signify Australasian identity, sometimes with a sense of proud assertiveness.
2. Norington, "Free World." Howard was of course referring to his preference for an imagined nation made up of people of different colors sharing a single culture, as opposed to a nation full of people of mixed race. It is the fact that he used the term "race," which was unusual.
3. This chapter follows the practice of using a capitalized "Indigenous" to refer to Aboriginal Australians, but a lower case "indigenous" when referring to a broader category that includes non-Australian indigenous peoples or as a synonym for Maori in New Zealand. This is the practice that is most widely used in Australia and New Zealand.
4. Jones and Brady, "Interview"; Durie, TeMana.
5. New Zealand was a leader in terms of allowing ethnic self-identification in its census (Callister et al. 2009), while Australia has allowed multiple ancestries to be named (Perkins 2004). The 2001 Australian Census asked for ancestry to be identified ("For example, Vietnamese, Hmong, Dutch, Kurdish") and instructed that more than one ancestry could be chosen "if necessary."

6. Tilbury, "What's in a Name?"
7. DaCosta, *Making Multiracials.*
8. Vertovec, "Super-diversity"; see also Aspinall and Song, this volume.
9. Vertovec, ibid., 1024.
10. Pybus, *A Touch of the Tar*; Pybus, *Black Founders*; Pybus, "Tense and Tender Ties."
11. Jupp, *From White Australia.*
12. Ibid., 10.
13. Ibid., 21.
14. See Mahtani et al, this volume.
15. Hage, *White Nation.*
16. Stratton and Ang, "Multicultural Imagined Communities."
17. Castles and Davidson, *Citizenship and Migration*; Jupp and Nieuwenhuysen, *Social Cohesion*; Goot and Watson, "Immigration, Multiculturalism."
18. Cox, *Migration and Welfare.*
19. Stratton, *Race Daze*, 14.
20. Stratton and Ang, "Multicultural Imagined Communities"; Forrest and Dunn, "'Core' Culture Hegemony."
21. Joppke, "The Retreat of Multiculturalism"; Tilbury, "The Retreat from Multiculturalism."
22. Putnam, *E Pluribus Unum*; Fozdar, "Constructing Australian Citizenship"; Fozdar, "The Choir Boy."
23. DIAC, "Fact Sheet 2."
24. Ibid.
25. CIA, "Australian People."
26. The equivalent entry for New Zealand, taken from statistics from the 2006 census, identifies the population as made up of 56.8 percent Europeans, 8 percent Asians, 7.4 percent Maori, 4.6 percent Pacific Islanders, 9.7 percent mixed, and 13.5 percent other.
27. Luke and Luke, "Theorizing Interracial Families."
28. ABC, "Aboriginal Woman."
29. Kissane, "Case against Bolt.
30. Pybus, *Black Founders*; Clark, "Unmasking Mudrooroo." Mudrooroo's family background is not clear, with the author denying his sister's published account of their ancestry.
31. The "Stolen Generations" is the term commonly used to refer to the 20th-century practice of forcibly separating mixed-race children from their Aboriginal mothers and Aboriginal communities in order to be brought up in the White society.
32. Pybus, *Black Founders.*,
33. Gardiner and Bourke, "Indigenous Populations."
34. Paradies, "Beyond Black," 357.
35. Gardiner and Bourke, "Indigenous Populations."

36. Povinelli, *The Cunning of Recognition*.
37. Hage, *Against Paranoid Nationalism*.
38. Attwood and Arnold, *Power, Knowledge*.
39. See, for example, Rodriguez, "But Who Are You"; Boladeras, "The Desolate Loneliness."
40. Paradies, "Beyond Black," 355.
41. Ibid., 357.
42. Ibid., 359.
43. Choo, "Chinese-Indigenous." See also Choo et al., "Being Eurasian."
44. Ganter, *Mixed Relations*.
45. For criticism, see Perkins, "Australian Mixed Race."
46. Khoo, "Generational Change."
47. See Bhabha, "Cultures in Between."
48. Luke and Luke, "Theorizing Interracial Families."
49. Owen, *Mixed Matches*, 167.
50. Luke and Luke, "Theorizing Interracial Families."
51. Katz, "Mixed Race across Time and Place"; Holloway, Wright, and Ellis, "Constructing Multiraciality in U.S. Families and Neighborhoods."
52. Perkins, *Visibly Different*.
53. DaCosta, *Making Multiracials*; Spencer, *Reproducing Race*.
54. Ford, *In Your Face*, 7.
55. Stopford, "Mothering Children."
56. Perkins, "Australian Mixed Race."
57. See Mahtani et al., this volume.
58. Bellich, *The New Zealand Wars*.
59. Durie, *TeMana*; Cox, *Kotahitanga*; Walker, *KaWhawhai*; Walker, *Nga Tau Tohetohe*; Awatere, *Maori Sovereignty*.
60. Spoonley, *Racism and Ethnicity*, 93.
61. Goodyear, "The Differences," 20.
62. Goodyear, "The Differences."
63. See Callister et al., *Who Are We*.
64. Walker, "Maori Sovereignty," 35.
65. See Smithers, *Science, Sexuality*, for similar phenomena in Australia and the US.
66. Goodyear, "The Differences," 7.
67. Ibid., 10.
68. Ward, "Acculturation, Identity," 245.
69. Goodyear, "The Differences," 11.
70. See Tibury, *Some of My Best Friends*. Fozdar's project analyzed interviews with 22 Maori and Pakeha about their friendship networks, ethnic identity, and attitudes to race relations issues.
71. Tsolidis, "Re-envisioning Multiculturalism," 6.
72. Berger and Luckmann, *The Social Construction*.
73. Callister, "Skin Color."

74. Ward, "Acculturation, Identity."
75. See also Nakashima, "The Invisible Monster."
76. Ward, "Acculturation, Identity," 255.
77. King, *Being Pakeha.*
78. Bozic-Vrbancic, "After All."
79. Ibid., 539.
80. Edwards et al., 'Pigments," 2.
81. Goodyear, "The Differences."
82. Kukutai, "Ethnic Self-prioritisation," 1.
83. Song, *Choosing Ethnic Identity,* 63; Tizard and Phoenix, *Black, White,* 114.
84. Parker and Song, *Rethinking "Mixed Race,"* 3.
85. Ibid., 9.
86. Spencer, *Reproducing Race.*
87. Ibid., 213.
88. Gilroy, *Between Camps.*
89. Luke and Luke, "Theorizing Interracial Families," 249.
90. Vertovec, "Super-diversity."
91. Beck, "The Cosmopolitan Perspective," 79–80.
92. Szerszynski and Urry, "Visuality, Mobility."
93. Sussman, "The Dynamic Nature," 368.
94. Perkins, "Australian Mixed Race."
95. Ibid., 195–96.
96. Song, *Choosing Ethnic Identity,* 146.

7

Negotiating Identity Narratives among Mexico's Cosmic Race

CHRISTINA A. SUE

We in America shall arrive, before any part of the world, at
the creation of a new race fashioned out of the treasures of
all the previous ones: the final race, the cosmic race.
José Vasconcelos, 1925

In contexts such as the US, "multiracialism," "mixed-race families,"
and "race mixture" are terms that signal relatively new phenomena
linked to recent immigration trends, intermarriage patterns, and a
shifting racial terrain.[1] However, in places such as Mexico, ideologies
and practices of race mixture (*mestizaje*) have been around for centuries. In colonial times Spaniards developed an elaborate caste system
to maintain a socio-racial hierarchy in light of the race mixture that
was occurring between the indigenous, Spanish, and African populations.[2] In this hierarchy, Spaniards were on top and Indians and Africans at the bottom, with mixed-race individuals falling somewhere in
the middle depending on the composition of their mixture. The ideology and practice of race mixing continued after Mexico gained independence from Spain (in 1821) and played a prominent role during the
era of the Mexican Revolution (1910–1920). As part of revolutionary
and postrevolutionary rhetoric, the ideology of *mestizaje* became a central focus of nation-building efforts. At the same time, however, there
was a strong value placed on whiteness, something which continues to
this day. In fact, contemporary Mexican society represents a pigmen-
tocracy where light-skinned individuals dominate the top social strata

and dark-skinned individuals are overrepresented at the bottom of the socioeconomic hierarchy.[3]

Given the aforementioned history, Mexico provides an interesting context to study dynamics related to race mixture. It represents a situation in which a mixed-race citizenry is not a new phenomenon spurred by recent globalization trends, but is instead an integral part of Mexican history, society, and ideology. Mexico is also a country with a strong national ideology—a set of beliefs promulgated and institutionalized by government officials and intellectuals—which simultaneously promotes race mixture and privileges whiteness. Mexico differs, however, from countries that have similar histories and ideologies of race mixture. For example, unlike Brazil[4] and Trinidad and Tobago,[5] Mexico has not had a census category for race since 1921; consequently, official discussions about how to measure or define the mixed-race population have been absent. Additionally, the relationship between hybridity and national identity has not been questioned or challenged in Mexico as it has been in these other two countries. Therefore, Mexico represents a case in which societal notions of hybridity are very much taken for granted and naturalized compared to other countries in the region.

Given that Mexico is stratified by color, the Mexican case also presents an opportunity to investigate the role of color within the mixed-race (*mestizo*) population, which represents up to 90 percent of the Mexican citizenry.[6] Examining color differences within the *mestizo* population allows us the opportunity to assess whether or not processes of identity construction vary by color.[7] Despite the potential that the Mexican case holds for understanding race mixture dynamics, mixed-race identity formation, and color, there has been little research on the topic. At this point we know little about what it means to be mixed race in Mexico, how mixed-race Mexicans construct their identities, and how color may influence the identity construction process.

In an attempt to fill this gap in the literature, in this chapter I address issues related to the identity construction of Mexico's mixed-race population, using the national ideology of *mestizaje* and Mexico's color hierarchy as a conceptual backdrop. I ask: *How do mestizos of different hues construct their identities within the context of a national ideology, which simultaneously privileges race mixture and valorizes whiteness?* I address this question by discussing different components of individuals' mixed-race identities, including notions of ancestry, race, and color. Before delving into my findings, I provide some background on Mexico.

Revolutionary and Post-revolutionary Mexican National Ideology

At the turn of the 20th century, Mexican elites (government officials and state-sponsored intellectuals) faced two major dilemmas in the process of nation building. First, they were trying to modernize their country during a time when European scientific racist theory was equating whiteness with modernity and racial hybridity with backwardness.[8] "Modern" societies such as the US and French Indochina were relying on a version of scientific racism that viewed "mixed-bloods" as marginal and degenerate. Furthermore, in French Indochina the *métis* were seen as threatening attempts to create a culturally cohesive national society.[9] These perspectives posed a problem for Mexico, which had a predominantly non-white, racially mixed population. The second dilemma surfaced in the wake of the Mexican Revolution, Mexico's ten-year bitterly fought civil war. Mexico's leaders faced the task of having to unite a divided country, rebuild the image of the nation, and foster national pride.

Using national ideology as a vehicle to solve both dilemmas, Mexican elites first challenged scientific racism by reframing hybridization as something positive, arguing that the *mestizo*, a racial hybrid, was actually a stronger, superior race.[10] They also declared hybridity to be a distinct attribute of Mexican society.[11] An ideology promoting the positive attributes of *mestizaje* was popularized by José Vasconcelos, a Mexican writer, philosopher, and politician. Privileging mixture over purity, Vasconcelos predicted the global creation of mixed-race societies, a theory he outlined in his classic 1925 text, *The Cosmic Race*, in which he characterized the *mestizo* as superior to all existing races.

The national ideology of *mestizaje* and the glorification of the *mestizo* also worked to unite the country and foster nationalist sentiment.[12] By highlighting the mixed-race character of Mexico's population, Mexican elites drew on notions of shared blood to emphasize commonality among all Mexicans. As such, understandings of race became fused with understandings of national identity. National subjects were racialized and the *mestizo* was deemed the Mexican national prototype. This prototype was constructed not only on an ancestral (*mestizos* were defined as being of both indigenous and European heritage), it was also associated with a particular physicality—markers of Mexicanness included having brown skin and embodying a mixture of European and indigenous features.

Despite the fact that the mixed-race brown-skinned individual was lauded as the ultimate symbol of Mexicanness, light skin and European traits were prized. The value placed on whiteness was a theme that ran through the *mestizaje* ideology. One of the perceived benefits of the race-mixing process was the anticipated cultural and biological erasure of Mexico's indigenous and African-origin populations.[13] In treating race mixture as a vehicle for whitening, Mexican elites challenged mainstream eugenic thought, which posited that race mixing leads to darkening and racial degeneracy. They relied, instead, on another strand of genetics—the neo-Lamarckism version—which was less deterministic in its stance on race mixture.[14] Some interpretations of neo-Lamarckism viewed race mixture as an avenue to whiten and improve a country's racial stock. This was the position adopted by many Mexican elites. Thus, Mexico's early-20th-century national ideology simultaneously valued race mixture and whiteness. Despite the prominence given to ideas of *mestizaje* and whitening in national thought, it is unclear if these elite perspectives have "trickled down" to affect the way in which contemporary Mexicans construct their identities.

The racialization of Mexicanness and the privileging of whiteness in Mexico present certain dilemmas for Mexican nationals—dilemmas related to the authentication of their racial and national identities. The topic of authenticity and the way in which individuals and groups engage in practices to authenticate particular identities has been well addressed in the literature.[15] For example, King-O'Riain (2006), in her study of Japanese American beauty pageants, found that half-Japanese beauty queens made racial claims regarding their Japanese ancestry to authenticate their identities as Japanese Americans since their mixed-race backgrounds jeopardized their membership in the Japanese American community.

Similar processes of authentication arise around the intersection of racial and national identities. Individuals whose race or phenotype does not align with racialized images of their country need to work to authenticate their national identities. In the case of Mexico, light-skinned individuals with predominately European features face the dilemma of potentially being viewed as marginal to the Mexican community as their phenotype contrasts with the prototypical brown-skinned Mexican. Consequently, they need to engage in strategies to reassert and authenticate their identity as Mexican. That being said, their light skin tone and European features are highly prized in Mexico. Moreover, whiteness in Mexico signals power, status, and dominance, as those with light skin and European features are overrepresented at the top rungs of society. Thus, light-skinned Mexicans are faced with the task of navigating around these conflicting images of whiteness. On the other hand, brown-skinned individuals who possess a phenotype that embodies a European-indigenous mixture conform to stereotypical representations of Mexicanness and are thus viewed as racially authentic; their status as Mexican is generally not subject to question. However, these individuals face the stigma of having brown skin and indigenous (and sometimes African) features in a society that privileges whiteness. In this chapter I address how Veracruzanos manage these dilemmas in the process of constructing their identities.

The Site and Research Methodology

In this study, I rely on ethnographic and qualitative data collected in 2004 and 2005 in the Port of Veracruz and Boca del Río, two adjacent cities in the state of Veracruz. Veracruz differs from other parts of Mexico due to the historical presence of African slaves and Cuban immigrants.[16] The indigenous population is very small, comprised mostly of migrants from neighboring towns and states. As such, the Indian question is less salient compared to some other regions of Mexico. However, consistent with other areas of Mexico, there is a wide range of phenotypic distinctions within the *mestizo* category in Veracruz, distinctions that correlate with different positions in the socioeconomic hierarchy. As such, Veracruz is an optimal site for studying color dynamics within the *mestizo* population.

In Veracruz, I engaged in participant observation for over a year and conducted 112 semistructured interviews. Using the snowball technique, I purposefully selected respondents who varied in terms of gender, age, class, education, and color. None of my respondents self-identified as members of the indigenous population. The vast majority asserted a mixed-race heritage and would therefore be considered *mestizos* by academics and government officials, although my respondents frequently did not use the term *mestizo*, preferring instead to identify in terms of color.

In this chapter I refer to respondents using color descriptors based upon my classification using the following categories: light, light brown, medium brown, and dark brown. These descriptors are not meant to be definitive, but instead, are used to give readers a general idea of where individuals fall on the Veracruz color continuum. I also asked respondents how they identify and I reference these identifications in the text; specifically, I contrast the experiences of "white Veracruzanos" (those who self-identify as white) and "brown Veracruzanos" (those who self-identify as brown [*moreno*]).[17]

Being *mestizo* in Mexico entails more than simply claiming a mixed-race identity. *Mestizos* of all hues need to negotiate their claims to a mixed-race status in the context of the national ideology, social norms, color hierarchies, and conceptions of the nation. In addressing how mixed-race individuals understand and construct their identities, we need to recognize that color plays a prominent role with respect to individuals' self-perception and how they are viewed by others. As mentioned previously, light- and brown-skinned Veracruzanos are positioned differently in society and therefore face different circumstances and dilemmas related to the interplay between their racial and national identities. Because of this, they have different goals—light-skinned *mestizos* strive to authenticate their Mexicanness without compromising their privileged racial status, while brown-skinned *mestizos* strive to overcome the stigma of their non-European ancestry and phenotype. Given these distinct goals, these two groups develop different strategies when constructing and asserting their identities.

Mixed-Race White Identities

Light-skinned Veracruzanos generally identify as white, but also claim a mixed-race heritage. Among other things, this illustrates how being white in Veracruz does not require being racially "pure" as race is largely defined by phenotype as opposed to ancestry. In other words, in Mexico, like other Latin American countries such as Brazil,[18] there is no contradiction whatsoever to being white *and* mixed race. This contrasts with societies such as the US where race is highly dependent on ancestry and "being white" typically implies having only European ancestors. Not only is the racial status of Mexican whites in no way threatened by claims of a mixed-race heritage, Mexicans who self-identify as white also have something to gain by asserting a mixed-race identity—they reaffirm their identity as Mexican since being Mexican implies being mixed race. This reassertion by whites of their national identity is important since their phenotype does not align with that of the prototypical Mexican.

The Compatibility of Whiteness and Hybridity

In Veracruz, I found that individuals who self-identified as white (henceforth "white Veracruzanos") made a point of emphasizing the mixture beneath their white façade. For example, in a focus-group discussion, Bella, a 48-year-old light-skinned high-school teacher, asserted, "Here in Mexico there are no real whites . . . we are a mixture. There are those who are light in color but not white like the pure white race." Like Bella, Concha, a 43-year-old light-skinned upper-class homemaker, also reproduced the notion of white racial impurity in our conversation. Although Concha is unsure about her racial heritage, she tends towards the assumption that she is mixed. She explained, "Here the majority of people are *mestizos* . . . regularly people here have some indigenous ancestry, even if it is a great-grandparent, a great-great grandparent or something like that. . . . Perhaps me too. I don't know." Despite Concha's inability to confirm that she has any non-European ancestors, she finds the idea that she is mixed a realistic possibility, given that she is Mexican. Bella and Concha demonstrate how white Veracruzanos bring themselves into the symbolic fold of the mixed-race Mexican nation when asserting their identities.

Judy, a 35-year-old light-skinned university professor, engages in similar mixed-race rhetoric but in a more exposed forum. In her classroom she makes a point of disseminating an image of Mexico that includes hybridity. Judy told me that she always teaches her students that "we are a hybrid people, a people that can't be proud of a pure race." Character-izing Mexico as the vanguard of the mixed-race trend, she emphasized that "in other countries there was racial mixture but it wasn't as deep of a mixture . . . here in Mexico it definitely occurred very, very strongly." Judy, like others, narrates Mexican history through the lens of hybridity, highlighting Mexico's long-standing history and entrenched practice of race mixture. Her continual use of "we" in this context signals that she includes herself, a white Veracruzana, in this narrative. She impli-cated herself in the *mestizaje* discourse even more directly in a separate conversation, when she told me that, although she "looks white," she believes that if I took her "blood," it would not "come out 100 percent European." Judy's phenotype belies her mixed-race identity. However, instead of using her phenotype to claim racial purity, Judy chooses to assert what she assumes are her hybrid origins.

Other white Veracruzanos either identified as being mixed race or were similarly open to the idea that they are racial hybrids. For example, Jessica, a 21-year-old light-skinned university student, made no attempt to claim racial purity. To the contrary, she was very open to the possibil-ity that she may have non-European heritage, despite her fair skin, green eyes, and blonde hair. In our conversation, Jessica said she gets her phe-notype from her mother's side of the family, but she also highlighted the brownness of her father's family. She described her father as "somewhat African" based on his "curly hair" and "thick" facial features. Although Jessica is unsure about the details of her non-European lineage, she not only accepts but, in some way, showcases, her identity as mixed race.

Tying his identity construction to nationalist sentiment is Antonio, a 55-year-old light-skinned employee of PEMEX, the Mexican state-owned petroleum company. Antonio was not bashful in asserting a mixed-race background. This point surfaced in response to my ques-tion about what it means to be Mexican. He said,

> I am proud to be Mexican . . . It fills me with pride that we have origins in cultural roots that are very old. . . . The truth is that I am a prod-uct of the mixture of races and I consider them my own even though I am not a direct descendant of the first inhabitants of this part of the country . . . mixture happened in my family but stopped various genera-tions ago. The native features have been diluted because there has been

mixture with the Caucasian races. Those are what have predominated over the races, over the native race. But on my mother's side, they do have some characteristic signs of those who have indigenous blood.

Despite Antonio's claim to being primarily descended from the "Caucasian races," he still acknowledges his indigenous ancestry and, furthermore, connects this ancestry to feelings of Mexican pride. Like other whites, Antonio's claim to indigenous heritage is mainly symbolic—it does not compromise his whiteness nor the societal benefits associated with it.[19] However, his claim to hybridity works to legitimize his Mexicanness because of the interconnectedness between notions of national identity and race—to be Mexican is to be mixed. As such, claiming a mixed-race status assists whites in positioning themselves more centrally within the boundaries of Mexicanness.

White Veracruzanos' identity constructions include claims not only to mixed heritage but also to whiteness. However, asserting a white Mexican identity can be challenging given the fact that, in Mexico, whiteness connotes not only wealth and power, but potentially also domination, exploitation, and a history of Spanish colonization. Consequently, showcasing or flaunting one's whiteness or European heritage (especially when one embodies this heritage) can elicit negative reactions. As such, white Veracruzanos need to tread lightly, taking care to claim a white identity in ways that do not appear to be pretentious or arrogant. Furthermore, emphasizing one's whiteness can be perceived as antinationalistic—a white identity can be read as evidence of an allegiance to one's Spanish as opposed to one's indigenous or Mexican heritage. In light of the multiple symbolisms associated with whiteness, light-skinned individuals need to carefully manage their assertions of a white identity.

Softening Claims to Whiteness

White Veracruzanos manage this symbolic quagmire by engaging in strategies to avoid being perceived as pretentious or antinationalistic. Many are discreet in asserting their whiteness; when they claim whiteness, they try to mitigate the potential negative impact of their claim by exhibiting humility, downplaying their whiteness, and asserting their Mexicanness. To "soften" their claim to whiteness, individuals oftentimes pause, giggle, or hesitate prior to identifying as white. For example, when I asked Jessica, the 21-year-old university student, about her racial identity, she responded, "Well [laughs], I am, uh, white, the white race with features that are uh . . . well European." Jessica is usually quite articulate; her uncharacteristic stumbling likely signals that she was treating the topic with care or uncertainty. Demonstrating reluctance to strongly assert his whiteness, Giovanni, a 28-year-old light-skinned fisherman minimized, but did not fully negate, a white identity. At one point in our conversation, he referred to himself as white, albeit after pausing, but later playfully downplayed his lightness, pointing to his sun-tanned arms and saying that he is not completely white.

Corazón, a 56-year-old light-skinned working-class homemaker, also skirted around a direct claim to whiteness. She described herself as not being "overwhelmingly" white but "more or less" white. To this she added, "Well, not very white but neither am I brown . . . a lot of people say I'm white." After making this indirect assertion of whiteness by referencing others' perceptions of her, Corazón moved to contest this outside classification, stating, "Who knows why they think I am white because nothing about me is white . . . I consider myself to be neither white nor brown." Throughout our conversation, Corazón deployed a number of discursive maneuvers to frame her white identity. Although she is clearly identified as white by fellow Veracruzanos, she refused to unequivocally accept this label. Instead, she claimed a marginal whiteness and sprinkled discursive cues such as giving pause, lowering her voice, and introducing qualifiers such as "well" and "more or less" to downplay her whiteness. Finally, Corazón exemplifies a dynamic that will be covered in the next section—she passed the classificatory torch to others, claiming whiteness indirectly through outside classification. In doing so she establishes a link between herself and whiteness, but sidesteps potential accusations of white arrogance associated with this claim. In the case of Corazón, she evoked outsiders' classifications only to challenge them, further entrenching her demonstrations of humility.

"People Say I'm White"

The strategy of evoking outside classifications as a way to assert one's whiteness while concurrently avoiding the appearance of pretentiousness is common among white Veracruzanos. Illustrating this dynamic is Javier, a 28-year-old navy employee with light-brown skin. When I asked Javier about his racial identity, he laughed, and then responded: "Look. I feel like what I am, right? Many people call me *güero* [whitie] and, well, I say, 'What part [of me is] white?'. . . Maybe it is because I descend from a family of whites. My mom, my grandparents, my aunts and uncles are all white." In his response, Javier avoids presenting himself as white but nonetheless positions himself as white via a discussion of how he is viewed in society. Moreover, he fortifies others' classifications of him by referencing his white family. Later in our conversation he told me that it makes no difference to him that he is labeled "*güero*," despite the fact that, in Veracruz, being called *güero* is generally a compliment. By challenging and demonstrating indifference to being labeled white, Javier is able to indirectly claim whiteness in a socially acceptable way.

Respondents sometimes referenced conversations with other Veracruzanos about their racial status. For instance, Gloria, a 48-year-old retired healthcare worker with light-brown skin, told me that she always feels compelled to contest others' descriptions of her as white. On one occasion, I witnessed this dynamic when Gloria, her friend, and I were chatting. At one point, Gloria referred to herself as brown but her friend immediately corrected her, saying, "You are white." Gloria remained silent, neither accepting nor rejecting this characterization. Her silence had the result of leaving the standing classification of her as white intact. On another occasion, I observed a mother and her daughter engage in a discussion about the color of the daughter's skin. The mother described her daughter as wheat-colored (*trigueño*) but the daughter reminded her mother that all of her friends characterize her as white. Referencing outside classifications allows whites to assert their whiteness while retaining an appearance of humility. Similarly, whites who claim European ancestry are careful to do so in a way that does not compromise their Mexicanness.

"I Have European Ancestry but I Am Mexican"

When discussing their racial identity and European (predominately Spanish) ancestry, white Veracruzanos often made a point of concomitantly asserting their primary identity as Mexican and emphasizing their loyalty to Mexico, dynamics that represent national authentication strategies. One way they accomplished this was to provide assurances that, despite being of European descent, they in no way feel European. The issue of loyalty to Spain versus Mexico has important historical antecedents. During colonial times there was a contentious relationship between *peninsulares* (Spanish-born Spaniards) and *criollos* (people of full Spanish descent born in the New World). This tension played an important role in Mexico's War of Independence. For this and other reasons, although European ancestry and related phenotype are privileged in Veracruz, individuals who embody this ancestry claim it with caution.

Examples of individuals performing the delicate balancing act between asserting European heritage and demonstrating loyalty to Mexico are plentiful in Veracruz. To take one case, Cristina, a 20-year-old light-skinned university student, negotiated this balance while also using the strategy of evoking others' classifications. When I asked Cristina how she identifies racially, she gave an indirect, roundabout answer: "When I was in Italy, a lot of people thought I was Russian or from Ireland because they are said to be tall and very white. They never thought I was Mexican. I would tell them, 'I am Mexican,' and they would say, 'No, no, you aren't Mexican. You are Russian or something else.'" When I asked Cristina how she felt about the mischaracterization of her nationality, she told me, "It felt bad because I am Mexican . . . I love Mexico." In her comments Cristina does not negate her whiteness but simply takes issue with the misclassification of her as non-Mexican. In doing so, she effectively claimed whiteness via others' perceptions, but was also able to reaffirm her Mexicanness. Cristina maintained her position as "Mexican first" in other parts of our conversation. On the topic of her ancestry, she informed me she has indigenous, Italian, Portuguese, and Spanish roots. However, she contextualized this background by asserting, "I am Mexican, right? I don't think that because I have a grandma who is Italian. . . . I don't identify with the Spanish or with the Italian or anything like that . . . Mexican, yes." In saying this, Cristina clearly positions her European ancestry as second to her identity as Mexican. Like other white Veracruzanos, by referencing yet minimizing her European ancestry vis-à-vis her

Mexicanness, Cristina is able to claim whiteness while maintaining national loyalty.

Concha, the 43-year-old light-skinned upper-class homemaker, also made a point of stressing her Mexicanness when I asked about her race. She began, "My mom, well, is the daughter of Spanish with Italian. My dad is the son of a Spaniard with a Mexican but one who was the son of a Spaniard. . . . We are of Spanish descent. But we are Mexicans, born in Mexico." White Veracruzanos, such as Concha, often highlighted their Mexican identity at the closing of discussions of ancestry. This placement signals a sense of finality or definitiveness about the assertion of one's Mexicanness. It also transmits the idea that, despite one's race, color, or heritage, one is, above all, Mexican.

In our conversation, Elena, a 48-year-old light-skinned working-class homemaker, was determined to continually assert a Mexican national identity. For instance, when I asked Elena about her racial identification, she responded, "Well, I feel like I am not in any category because I feel like, in Mexico, we are all Mexicans." On the topic of her ancestry, she said she is "completely mixed," elaborating, "I have family descendants who are completely Mexican, from the mountains. . . . I consider myself to be Mexican because I was born here but I believe that three or four generations back I have a little Spanish blood." Summing up her identity, Elena confidently proclaimed, "I am neither from the Selva Lacandona[20] nor from any other country. I am from Mexico." With this conclusion, Elena positioned herself as neither wholly indigenous nor wholly foreign, but as unequivocally Mexican.

To conclude, since white Veracruzanos' phenotypes are dissimilar to that of the prototypical Mexican, they are sometimes perceived as more marginally Mexican in symbolic terms. Furthermore, because whiteness is associated with wealth, power, and a history of colonization, flaunting one's whiteness can be interpreted by other Mexicans as pretentious. At the same time, however, whiteness affords individuals with a certain degree of privilege in Mexico, a society that values whiteness. In this section, we saw how individuals who self-identify as white and mixed race manage these dilemmas in a way that avoids them appearing pretentious or antipatriotic, yet does not dismiss their association with whiteness.

Mixed-Race Brown Identities

Brown-skinned Mexicans face a different set of dilemmas and circumstances than their light-skinned counterparts. They embody stereotypical Mexicanness and are, therefore, not under the same kind of pressure to constantly reaffirm their national identity. However, they do
face the stigma of having brown skin and indigenous and/or African-
origin features in a society that privileges whiteness. As such, brown-
skinned Veracruzanos develop different strategies when constructing
their identities with regards to race, color, and ancestry. Unlike whites,
they typically do not defer to outside classifications nor do they make
a point of expressing national loyalty when discussing their identities.
Instead, most matter-of-factly identify as *moreno* (brown) and mixed
race, without engaging in particular discursive maneuvers to frame
these aspects of their identities in a particular light. Regarding ancestry,
self-identified *morenos* (henceforth "brown Veracruzanos") much more
overtly reference their European heritage compared to whites. These
patterns suggest that the identity expressions of mixed-race, brown-
skinned Veracruzanos are in some ways less problematic, in that they
do not threaten social norms and nationalist sentiment in the same way
that claims to whiteness and European ancestry do for light-skinned
Veracruzanos.

Being mixed is a central ingredient to the identity construction of
brown Veracruzanos. Two patterns emerged surrounding their claims
to a hybrid status—they gave equal weight to their multiple ancestries
or they privileged their European ancestry. Notably, another potential
discourse—one which privileges indigenous or African ancestry—was
conspicuously absent from brown Veracruzanos' identities. This is
likely due to the fact that these ancestries are stigmatized in Veracruz,
especially when one's phenotype reflects the traits of these heritages.

Jennifer, a 42-year-old light-brown-skinned working-class homemaker, illustrates a matter-of-fact balanced claim to hybridity. She told
me, "I have as much Spanish blood as Cuban blood" (which she later
referred to as "white" and "Black" blood, respectively). Also illustrating this pattern is Salvador, a 24-year-old light-brown-skinned laborer.
When I asked him about his racial descent, he told me: "My mom, you
could say, is totally mixed and my dad came out more Spanish. My dad

is tall, white, with green eyes. My mom is a little brown, robust and she has all of the features of a *mestizo*, you could say." Jennifer and Salvador give fairly equal weight to both sides of their families and, consequently, both sides of their ancestries.

Highlighting One's European Origins

More typically, however, brown Veracruzanos emphasized their European ancestry. Pilar, an 18-year-old light-brown-skinned gas station worker, exemplifies this framing. She explained, "I am mixed because my grandma, her parents were Spanish. I even have family that is very white and even has blue eyes. And on my grandfather's side, well, they were . . . well, more indigenous you could say. . . . So I am, more than anything, *mestiza* . . ." Later in our conversation, Pilar discussed her family more in-depth, reemphasizing the whiteness of particular members: "My grandma is still alive and she looks very white and she has blue eyes, like my great-grandma . . . and I also have uncles that are white. Only I came out more brown because of my dad but my mom is also white." Although Pilar acknowledges her non-European ancestry, she highlights her European roots. Furthermore, like others, she was less detailed and enthusiastic when discussing her non-European ancestors.

The lack of detail is understandable given that, in Veracruz, the interfamily transmission about non-European ancestry is much less common and readily shared compared to information about European ancestors. This oftentimes leaves individuals having to speculate about the ancestry of brown-skinned members of their family, which may partly explain why some highlight their European ancestry. It is also likely that individuals are emphasizing their European ancestry to capitalize on the higher value placed on that ancestry in society.

The fact that families engage in more concerted efforts to pass on information about European ancestors compared to non-European ancestors revealed itself in the interview context as well as in everyday conversation. Brown Veracruzanos often relayed detailed stories about their European ancestors, information passed on by their parents and grandparents. Moreover, they frequently exhibited a palpable enthusiasm when referencing a tall, light-skinned, blonde, blue- or green-eyed member of the family. Comparable stories, detailed information, and expressions about indigenous and African ancestors were highly uncommon. Non-European ancestors, when acknowledged, were rarely humanized with a face, name, or story.

Some individuals claimed indigenous heritage in a perfunctory manner, merely assuming they had this ancestry because of their phenotype, other family members' phenotypes, or the national narrative of *mestizaje*. Moreover, when they claimed indigenous ancestry, they frequently relegated indigenous ancestors to the distant past. For Veracruzanos of African descent, knowledge transmission surrounding African ancestry was tenuous at best, but more frequently absent. The general lack of familial information about African heritage is compounded by the fact that the African contribution to Mexico's population is neglected in 20th-century Mexican national ideology; the *mestizo* has traditionally been defined as a mixture between indigenous and Spanish, not African, populations.[21]

Since brown Veracruzanos face the stigma of having brown skin and non-European features in a society that privileges whiteness, they often move to distance themselves from their indigenous and/or African backgrounds. At the same time, they emphasize their European heritage, establishing a connection, albeit tenuous, to the privileged realm of whiteness. Since the meaning surrounding claims to European ancestry is different for brown-skinned compared to light-skinned Veracruzanos (i.e., claims to European ancestry coming from brown-skinned individuals are less likely to be read as pretentious and do not threaten their Mexican identity), brown-skinned individuals are afforded more leeway when highlighting their European lineage. However, the fact that brown Veracruzanos tend to emphasize their European ancestry does not mean that they completely negate other aspects of their heritage.

Relying on the National Ideology of Mestizaje

Brown Veracruzanos draw upon Mexico's national ideology of *mestizaje*, which emphasizes the mixed European and indigenous heritage of Mexico's population, to construct an understanding of their personal identities, especially when they do not have much information about their ancestral histories. Consequently, many Veracruzanos claim a mixed-race identity absent of specific knowledge of the components of their mixture. The fact that many Veracruzanos identify as mixed, without specifically tying this claim to knowledge of ancestors who are from two discrete races, indicates that a mixed-race identity can be an identity in and of itself. In other words, being mixed race in Veracruz is not necessarily a logical outcome or consequence, which flows from concrete knowledge that one's ancestors are of distinct races. For example, Vanesa, a 30-year-old working-class homemaker with medium-brown skin, told me she identifies as *mestiza* because of her parents. However, when I probed more deeply, asking Vanesa about her parent's background, she responded, "Wow. The truth is that I don't remember. I have never investigated that." Like other Veracruzanos, Vanesa's identity as mixed exists absent of information about distinct ancestries.

Belinda, a 46-year-old working-class homemaker with dark-brown skin, also identified as mixed, but in our conversation hinted that this identity has been influenced by national messages about race mixture. When I asked about her racial identity, she told me, "Well, I have heard that we are mixed, right? That the Mexican mixture was made with, I believe, the Spanish and from there they made 'the race.' What race, I don't know." Belinda draws on the national ideology in the context of being unsure about her personal ancestry. Some Veracruzanos referenced being exposed to the national ideology in books they had read in school. They used this information to fill in gaps about their own racial heritage. For example, Alicia, a 25-year-old navy employee with dark-brown skin, said the following when I asked about her racial background: "According to the books I read, the Spanish race with Mexicans . . . right now I don't remember the word but a combination of races . . . Spaniards and *mestizos* or *mestizos* and Spaniards . . . combined, let's say it like that [laughs]." Like other Veracruzanos, Alicia draws on outside information regarding the national population to construct her individual history. Both Belinda and Alicia illustrate how, when unsure about their *personal* heritage, individuals rely on what they have learned about the *nation's* heritage to construct an understanding of their own background. The effect of the national narrative of *mestizaje* is most powerful when individuals lack concrete information about their ancestors. Under these conditions, Mexico's national ideology helps to guide and shape own identities.

However, Veracruzanos do not adopt and employ Mexican national ideology comprehensively. Instead, they select particular strands of national ideological thought, molding them to fit their personal situations. Brown Veracruzanos often draw on the national ideology to surmise that they have indigenous ancestry since information about European ancestry is much more frequently discussed within the family.[22] Silvia, a 54-year-old retired daycare worker with dark-brown skin, has specific knowledge of her European ancestors but relies on Mexico's national ideology to deduce that she has indigenous ancestry. Silvia told me, "We are . . . well, we are *mestizos* because of the blood. . . . Our grandparents were the ones that left us that blood . . . my grandma, on my mom's side, was almost authentic Spanish. She was . . . big and very white. Yes . . . but we are *mestizos*. We are no longer from the . . . what are those called? The first of our race? The, the first indians that were here?" Like other Veracruzanos, Silvia self-identifies as mixed even though she only has a vague understanding of the non-European aspect of her mixture. Silvia points to her European ancestry in the context of her family but roots her understanding of her indigenous ancestry in the context of her nation. These examples demonstrate how and under what conditions the national ideology of race mixture becomes a source of information in the construction of mixed-race identities. Furthermore, the differences in identity construction noted in the previous sections between white and brown Veracruzanos demonstrate how color and position in society affect the identity construction process of mixed-race individuals.

Conclusion

We can extract a number of concluding thoughts based on the identity construction dynamics of the mixed-race individuals discussed in this chapter. First and foremost, there is much that lies beneath the surface of mixed-race identities. As I demonstrated, mixed-race Veracruzanos engage in a rich and dynamic process of identity construction as they negotiate notions of ancestry, race, and color. As part of this process, they draw upon Mexico's national ideology of race mixture to construct their individual identities. In this chapter we also saw how color matters for identity construction dynamics—light-skinned *mestizos* face different dilemmas when navigating societal and national ideological messages compared to their brown-skinned counterparts. Consequently, these two groups adopt distinct strategies, which lead to diverging identity paths. For light-skinned Veracruzanos, their phenotype contrasts with the image of the prototypical brown-skinned Mexican. Furthermore, although whiteness is privileged in society, flaunting one's whiteness can be read as a display of arrogance. Given the multiple connotations surrounding whiteness, light-skinned Veracruzanos engage in identity work to assert their whiteness in a way that weds them to the nation but dodges possible accusations that they feel they are racially superior.

Brown-skinned Veracruzanos of mixed European and indigenous heritage, on the other hand, are under less pressure to authenticate their national identity as they embody stereotypical representations of Mexicanness. However, they face the dilemma of needing to construct their identities in a context where whiteness is valued and non-European features are stigmatized. In some cases, brown-skinned Veracruzanos respond by choosing to emphasize their European ancestry, thus positioning themselves more closely to whiteness. However, when unsure of their racial origins, they turn to the national ideology of *mestizaje,* which emphasizes the mixed European-indigenous heritage of the nation, to claim indigenous ancestry. In contrast, individuals of partial African descent rarely offer information about their African ancestry as blackness is stigmatized in Mexico and the national ideology does not recognize the African root of Mexico's population. Taken as a whole, the dynamics identified in this chapter illustrate how national ideology and color interact to influence the identity construction of Mexican *mestizos.*[23]

The findings from this chapter also reveal how, in Mexico, a mixed-race identity can be a stand-alone identity. In other words, a mixed-race individual is not necessarily understood to be a person immediately descended from two (or more) distinct racial groups since the process of race mixture has a long history in Mexico and individuals are not always able to trace their lineage back to particular ancestors. Because national leaders have disseminated a historical narrative and ideology which highlights the hybrid nature of the Mexican citizenry, many Mexicans simply assume that, as Mexicans, they have mixed-race origins. Therefore, being mixed race in Mexico is the norm, not the exception. Although this may be true for other countries in Latin America, as mentioned in the introduction, this norm is more invisible and entrenched in Mexico, given that it has not been publicly questioned or challenged. Consequently, although recent changes associated with globalization will surely affect what it means to be mixed race across the globe, for Mexicans these changes may not be as dramatic as in other countries since being mixed in Mexico continues to be the undisputed national "status quo."

NOTES

1. "Black" and "white" are not capitalized in this chapter because they are not racialized in the same way as they are in the US. For an overview of the state of the literature on these topics, see Telles and Sue, "Race Mixture."
2. Katzew, Casta Painting.
3. Flores and Telles, "Social Stratification in Mexico"; Villarreal, "Stratification by Skin Color in Contemporary Mexico."
4. Daniel and Lee, this volume.
5. Reddock, this volume.
6. There is no direct measure of the mestizo population, although, in Mexico, it is generally understood that this population is a default category for those not classified as indigenous. In 2010, roughly 7 percent of the population five years or older spoke an indigenous language (http://www.inegi.org.mx), a common measure of indigenous status (Fernández et al., "Estimaciones de la Población Indígena en México).
7. The analytic relationship between color and race is complex. Some scholars argue that color and race are conceptually distinct (Golash-Boza, "Does Whitening Happen?"; Harris, "Introduction: Economies of Color"), while others treat color as an analytic subset of race (Sue, "An Assessment of the Latin Americanization Thesis"; Telles, Race in Another America). Although this discussion is beyond the scope of this chapter, I adopt the latter position.
8. Stepan, The Hour of Eugenics; Stern, "From Mestizophilia to Biotypology."
9. Stoler, "Sexual Affronts and Racial Frontiers."

10. Gonzalez Navarro, "Mestizaje in Mexico"; Stepan, *The Hour of Eugenics*; Vasconcelos, *La Raza Cósmica*. As in Trinidad and Tobago (Reddock, this volume), in Mexico, *mestizaje* was conceptualized as involving both the biological and cultural merging of the races.

11. Gonzalez Navarro, *"Mestizaje in Mexico"*; Knight, *"Racism, Revolution, and Indigenismo"*; Stepan, *The Hour of Eugenics*; Stern, *"From Mestizophilia to Biotypology."*

12. Lomnitz, *Exits from the Labyrinth*; Urías Horcasitas, *Historias Secretas del Racismo en México.*

13. Hernández Cuevas, *African Mexicans;* Hernández Cuevas, *África en el Carnaval Mexicano;* Knight, *"Racism, Revolution, and Indigenismo."*

14. Stepan, *The Hour of Eugenics.*

15. Cornell and Hartmann, *Ethnicity and Race*; Erickson, *"The Importance of Authenticity"*; Fine, *"Crafting Authenticity"*; Grazian, *Blue Chicago*; Peterson and Anand, *"The Production of Culture Perspective."*

16. Roughly 200,000 slaves were brought from Africa in colonial times (Vaughn, "Race and Nation") and approximately 2,716 Cuban individuals arrived between 1870 and 1900 (García Díaz, "La Migración Cubana).

17. Approximately one-fifth of my respondents identified as white and most of the remaining individuals identified as *moreno*. Approximately one-fifth of the respondents had noticeable African ancestry.

18. Daniel and Lee, this volume.

19. Waters, *Ethnic Options.*

20. This is a reference to a region of Chiapas that is predominately indigenous.

21. Sue, *"Racial Ideologies."*

22. The same national narrative that highlights indigeneity also excludes blackness. African heritage is generally excluded from both familial and national narratives.

23. The dynamics I describe in this chapter did not seem to be affected by gender or class status.

PART II

Places with Newer Populations of Mixed Descent

8

Multiraciality and Migration

Mixed-Race American Okinawans, 1945–1972

LILY ANNE YUMI WELTY

"When I left Okinawa and came to America, I recognized the cultural diffcrences, 'In America, even the rice is independent! In Japan, the rice sticks together.'"[1]

"As a kid I was told things like, '*Amerika he kaire* (Return to America)' and 'Yankee, go home!'" I did not even know what Yankee was. Okinawa was home, not America."[2]

Human migration and racial mixing facilitated the mixing of people, creating "third spaces"[3] where cultural and linguistic fragments of two majority groups combine to form a hybrid community. This chapter examines the history of multiracial American Japanese who grew up in Okinawa and the US during the post–World War II period through the 1970s. I contextualize their lives historically and document them with oral history interviews focusing on people who grew up in Okinawa. Their transnational lives provide insight on the human experience of multiraciality. The reason for focusing on Okinawa is twofold: the first because of Okinawa's status as a repeatedly colonized space, by Japan in 1879, and later by the US from 1945 to 1972; and secondly on the basis as a place where a "third space" hybrid culture exists for mixed-race people as a result of the long term US military presence.[4] After World War II, many children sired by US troops were left behind in the care of their Japanese mothers and the Japanese government.[5] In Okinawa, US hegemony persisted for twenty years longer than it did on mainland Japan, and long after the 1972 reversion,[6] it continues to have an effect on mixed-race people living on the islands.[7] A transnational militarized borderland served as the backdrop as they came of age with the dual influence of the US, via its military bases, and the Japanese national project. This first generation of American Okinawans is now entering their fifties or sixties, and their history is yet to be told in English.

It is important to study this age group for several reasons. First, many of them have a more concrete sense of their own identity than people who are in their teens or twenties. As individuals near middle age, not only are they more comfortable in discussing their childhood, but also many years have passed, allowing them to reflect on their lives with greater thought. Second, in the academic literature on multiracial people following World War II, their voices are largely absent while the focus is on their parents, caretakers, or adoptive parents.[8] Placing mixed people at the center of the analysis reveals how parents may occupy different roles in the family. The direct perspective from the mixed-race people themselves enhances the historical understanding of what it meant to grow up mixed in Okinawa. Third, beginning with occupied Japan as a birthplace for mixed people who embody a third culture in a semicolonized space, and later looking at this group as American immigrants, my research offers new openings for discussion about the current models of racial formation of mixed and marginalized people and how race is reinforced historically across borders. The postwar environment created the contingencies that made the hybrid culture possible. Drawing on previous studies of multiraciality and hybridity, I focus on the individuals without ignoring their international origins.[9]

Colonialism, Imperialism, and Identity

Multiracial people in Okinawa possess a history that is deeply affected by colonization and imperialism, on three levels. Following Leo Ching's analysis of Colonial Taiwan, multiracial people in Okinawa were influenced by a tripartite colonization: Japan, the US, and as a mixed-race person within a colonized body in Okinawa.[10] Multiracial people in Okinawa were an unsettling reminder to other Okinawans of the ever-present US occupation of the islands long after the formal departure of American forces in 1972. Alongside monoracial Okinawans, multiracial people had become provisionally incorporated into Okinawan society.[11] Multiracial Okinawans did not fit into the available racial categories in Okinawa because they were not accepted as Japanese, nor as

Okinawans, even though many could not even speak English, but rather spoke *Uchinaguchi* (the Okinawan-Ryûkyûan indigenous language) or Japanese. Their mixed racial heritage was stigma, yielding visible features regarded as non-Japanese. Multiracial Okinawans occupied a cultural third space that could be defined either on or off of the military bases. Within this third space, there were two tiers: those who could speak English and might have connections to the military bases, and those without access to the opportunities English and the bases provided. Colonialism was evident within multiracial Okinawans as well as within the Okinawan population.

The first period of colonization occurred when Japan abolished the monarchy of the Ryûkyû Kingdom and established Okinawa Prefecture in 1879 as a part of the Japanese nation-building and modernity project of the late nineteenth century. The Japanese government erased Okinawan history, culture, and language and replaced it with all things Japanese. As stated by multiracial Okinawan activist Fija Bairon,

> All I was taught was that Okinawa has that dark history and that Okinawans are supposed to be Japanese. I was a person who didn't know Okinawa. Or, more appropriately, I was someone who had been educated in a way to not know anything about Okinawa. Neither my teachers nor parents would teach me that Higa is a Japanese pronunciation of a name, which used to be pronounced Fija. But now my identity is Okinawan and I speak *Uchinaguchi* and I decided that calling myself Higa wouldn't make much sense. Higa is Japanese and that is not my identity. I am Fija, an *Uchinanchû*, and I speak *Uchinaguchi*.[12]

The Soviet state took similar measures to institutionalize a national language and culture in Kazahstan (see Ualiyeva and Edgar in this volume). Japan banned Okinawan indigenous music in schools, and forced Okinawans to change their names to Japanese ones. As late as the 1940s, Okinawan students caught speaking *Uchinaguchi* and not standard Japanese in school were punished and forced to wear wooden plates that read *hogenfuda,* or dialect card, around their necks.

The effects of colonization did not stop there. The influence of the late-nineteenth- and early-twentieth-century nation-building project traveled overseas with immigrants to the Americas and shaped the

Okinawans who were part of the diaspora. The distinctions between Japanese and Okinawans carried over to overseas Nikkei communities (Japanese emigrants and their descendants who reside outside of Japan) in Peru and Brazil, through the maintenance of separate social and occupational circles. In the early twentieth century in Peru, where Okinawans made up at least 50 percent of the immigrants from Japan, the Nikkei maintained a self-chosen separation between the communities of *Naichijin* (those of the main islands of Japan proper), and *Uchinanchû* (those from the prefecture of Okinawa).[13] Both cultural and physical differences between Okinawans and mainland Japanese created systematic divides between the two communities. *Naichijin* perceived Okinawans as hairy, dark, lazy, uncivilized peoples of the southern islands, who were *dôjin* (savages of the dirt), wasting away too much time on the tropical beaches of the southern hinterland. As Japan's nation building project gained momentum domestically, its influence over the identity of people abroad changed too. Over time, diasporic Okinawans became identified and identified themselves as Japanese.[14]

The next era of colonization occurred following World War II, when Japan, as part of its wartime losses, granted the US access to Okinawa's strategic military location.[15] It is widely understood by historians and activists that, as Julia Yonetani states, the Japanese "military protected the interests of the Japanese state at the expense of Okinawan civilians."[16] The US military returned the governance of the islands back to Japan in 1972 but continues to occupy large areas in Okinawa. The US occupation thus represented a second colonization of the islands and served as a reminder of Okinawans' subordinate position in their own country. As stated by Rinken Teruya, *Uchinâ* pop singer and Okinawan activist, "It seemed not so much as though the U.S. military were inside Okinawa but as though Okinawa were alone, trapped inside the metal fences of the U.S. military."[17] Clearly, the anxiety expressed by Rinken reflects the difference from the mainland: Okinawans—not mainland Japanese— had to deal with the extraterritoriality of the ever-present US military installations. The US military can move freely off base into Okinawan cities, whereas most Okinawans cannot enter the US bases, unless they work there or have been granted special access. The militarized borderland catalyzed increased interactions between Americans and Okinawans, leading to the births of a growing number of multiracial people.

The third aspect of colonization is the colonized body of multiracial people in particular. Many multiracial children were easy to recognize by people in Okinawa because of their mixed-race phenotype. These physical characteristics went beyond a benign label of inherited genetics to a stigma of illegitimacy and an association with the military. Multiracial people embodied the colonial power relations between the US and Japan and Okinawa, with both Japan and Okinawa occupying subservient roles. Due to their mixed status, multiracial people became politically marked and inherently colonized. The idea of tripartite colonialism is complicated by the nature of their national and racial identities (see Aspinall and Song, this volume). In short, they visually represented the colonized status of the population. I employ here the definition of colonialism whereby a powerful body exerts full or partial control over another body creating an "other" for purposes of self-identification or ascribed identification or both.

As Japanese and American colonialism took shape in Okinawa, multiracial American Okinawans migrated between Okinawa and the US during the 1970s and into the 1980s. They used various methods, such as faking language ability or ignoring signs in Japanese prohibiting things like smoking, and often strategically deployed multiple identities as forms of engagement and resistance to weather racism and also discriminatory and pejorative identification. They advantageously used their various identities as adoptees, as immigrants, as Americans, as Japanese, or as Okinawans to resist the negative effects of single-identity pegging. They resisted pejorative identities and discriminatory situations by choosing whatever identity suited them best under the circumstances. Their racial ambiguity provided them with situational agency. When analyzed historically, it is evident that mixed-race people have employed strategies to find greater opportunities for success for a very long time.[18]

Life Histories

My main research methodology is oral history. Many of the people who shared stories of their lives are bilingual in Japanese and English, or Japanese and *Uchinaguchi*. The interviews were done in both the English and Japanese languages, and often involved code switching between the two. The difference between those who lived in Okinawa and those who lived in the US rests largely on the way they were educated, their choices about visiting and their later migration. In this chapter, I will argue that for mixed-race people migration was not a one-way process, but rather it represented a back and forth between countries. These individuals had transnational lives because their families helped strengthen the push and pull factors.

It is important to look at a variety of peoples' stories to get a richer understanding of the multiracial experience. Rather than categorize mixed people from their appearance, language abilities, or socioeconomic status and make definitive statements on those bases, analyzing their personal choices (and not just the choices of their parents) provides a window into better understanding the historical context in which mixed-race people have lived. It is true that certain life experiences, such as having a single parent, and English fluency influence individuals tremendously. However, those things are usually out of the individual's control. Much of the environment that their parents chose affected these individuals during childhood. Parents—especially those making a household with partners who come from different countries—shape the lives of these individuals in ways that parents from a single country do not. As Fernando Herrera Lima stated, "Transnational families are therefore vehicles—better yet, agents—for both material exchanges and the creation, re-creation and transformation of cultures."[19] The parents' choices of household language, educational language, and country of residence affect their children. As adults, these mixed people have the freedom of choice to maintain international connections and keep their nuclear families spread across continents or determine to what degree the families that they establish will transcend the international separation they experienced in their earlier lives.

Studying mixed-race people with transnational identities is complicated because the definitions of identity, nationality, and kinship become fluid and messy, often defying scholarly convention. Despite the flux transnational families endure, they provide individuals with stability that nurture the "strength of ties with family members back home or in other places."[20] These individuals are neither Japanese nor American, but rather both Japanese and American, and on top of that Okinawan. I will focus on their lives in the context of immigration,

migration, and transnationality. It is important to remember that the one-way migration process is too simple a model, and the US was not always the final destination.[21] Many people go back and forth between countries, and the connections between people and places are still very much active.

I discuss several examples of transnational multiracial identity. Each person's experience is unique and together they represent the different ways that multiracial identity is manifested in their transnational life stories. All of the people are living either in Okinawa as half American or in America as half Okinawan. In other words, being mixed race is not universal, and the environment matters. Some had the agency to make the choice to go to the US; for some the choice was made for them. For others, the trips were yearly, while others made the pilgrimage for the first time as adults. These trips provided multiracial people with the interactions that galvanized identity consciousness and an awareness of their language skills and appearance. Making the trip to the US can be difficult for multiracial people who may not have a direct connection to their extended family. Among those who went to the US, some stayed while others returned.

Having a nuclear family that spanned borders and an ocean meant being away from parents and other relatives for extended periods. As a result, some individuals spent a concentrated amount of time with one part of their family but had to miss seeing other family members. In the case of Cindy, after her parents' separation, her father purchased tickets for her to visit his family every summer, during which she was completely immersed in American culture.[22] She saw herself as having one foot in each country and was always homesick no matter where she resided.

Cindy's parents met and married in Okinawa. Her mother was born and raised in Naha. Her father came to Okinawa after he was drafted to fight in the Vietnam War. Cindy and her sister were born in Okinawa and shortly thereafter they moved to Texas to be near her father's family. After several years, her mother grew tired of the violence in the home, and her parents divorced.[23] Cindy's mother brought her two daughters back home to Okinawa, and lived in Naha with no direct access to the American lifestyle on the bases. Cindy recalled her childhood without base privileges: "I was on the outside of the fence, and didn't even know what I was missing by not being a military card holder in Okinawa."[24] From the age of seven, every summer Cindy took an international flight, traveling 7,500 miles from Okinawa to Texas by herself, and went to visit her father and his family. For three months, she was complete immersed in English. She became bilingual and had no difficulties living in either place. At first she went to a Japanese elementary school, but later she switched to the Christ the King International School. She attended college in Texas to be near her extended family, and then went to Tokyo University for her master's degree. Several years ago, she returned to Okinawa with her own family. The constant movement back and forth she experienced as a child slowed in her adult life because of her father's passing. Cindy is an example of how mixed-race people move transnationally, but in order to understand the larger picture, we must analyze how governments also facilitate the transnational identities experienced by multiracial Okinawans.

Both the US and the Japanese government played roles in shaping the transnational lives of mixed-race Okinawans. The US military deploys soldiers in various places every four years with or without their families, often resulting in parents and children becoming separated from one another. The Japanese government's nationality laws relating to patrilineal citizenship prevented many mixed-race children with Japanese mothers from receiving Japanese citizenship, and because of questions of paternity, the US did not grant citizenship to some mixed-race people, leading them to become stateless.[25] Although they could choose to self-identity as Okinawans, they did not have a choice when it came to nationality, unlike the children of interethnic marriages in Kazakhstan (see Ualiyeva and Edgar, this volume). Laws pertaining to race and citizenship, as well as the absence of parents, impeded the ease of the transpacific passage.

For mixed-race adults, making the pilgrimage to the US was a hugely uncertain and emotional decision, especially if contact with one's parents had been lost. Rosa's parents met in Okinawa.[26] Her father, who is Mexican American, came to Okinawa on his way to fight in Vietnam. When Rosa was born, her parents were not married, and she thus received only Japanese citizenship. During the war, Rosa's father traveled between Okinawa and Vietnam, repeatedly returning to see her and her younger brother. When she was five years old, he returned to the US with the intention of sending for his family. They sent letters back and forth until she was eleven years old. Rosa's English was better than her mother's, so she read the letters and wrote back to her father on her mother's behalf. She received Christmas gifts from her Mexican American grandparents. Her father eventually wrote to Rosa's mother that he was ready to get married and bring the family to the United States. Rosa's mother knew he lived in a trailer house, and declined the offer. Even as a single mother in Okinawa, she could support her two children and have a better quality of life than she could anticipate in America. This flexibility of citizenship and implicit choice of residence reflected agency and an advantage that maximized options and global position.

Rosa attended the Okinawa Christian School through fourth grade. At reversion in 1972, all Japanese citizens in Okinawa began to attend Japanese schools administered by the Japanese Ministry of Education, unless they paid tuition to attend a private international school. At the time, her brother was going to start at a Japanese primary school. Although Rosa was permitted and wanted to stay at OCS, her mother— who felt that children in the same household should have the same education—persuaded her to switch to a Japanese elementary school by promising to buy her a piano. Changing schools and adapting to the Japanese curriculum was very difficult for Rosa, so she decided that going to the US might help. Her mother convinced her to stay in Okinawa. In the sixth grade, for some unknown reason, her father stopped writing. Rosa all but gave up on contacting him. When she turned forty, she felt she should try one more time.

She began her search by writing to three people with his name. She received one letter back, and it was from her father. She went to visit him in Texas in 2005 for the first time. Rosa recalled the visit: "When I saw him, all of my ideals as a father figure were forgotten and I accepted that he was just a human. I could forgive him."[27] It had been thirty-five years since they had last seen each other.

Despite being separated by thousands of miles for decades in some cases, American Okinawans still feel a connection to the family that is abroad. Rosa needed to bring closure to her family history and did this by finding her father and restarting the relationship that had been lost. It was her courageous decision to reach out and make the pilgrimage.

As an adult, she had greater control and could make deliberate choices that children can not always make. She reflected, "You improve your life yourself. It's not your parents, and not other people around you."[28] Rosa considered getting American citizenship, and she may live in the US in the future: "I don't think going to the States and living there will make me happy, but I still want to open up my options, and then think about what I can do."[29]

Returning to Okinawa as an adult meant coming home for some American Okinawans. Lona lived in Okinawa and the US each for years at a time and received her education in both places. Lona's parents met and married in Yokohama, and she was born at the Tachikawa Air Base in 1960. She received US citizenship through her father, but she was unable to get Japanese citizenship due to the nationality law that granted citizenship only to children of Japanese fathers.[30] She came to Okinawa with her family, because her civilian father's job was connected to the military. Lona and her older brother both went to Okinawa Christian School (OCS) and were educated in English. The school was so strict that "students could get a detention for speaking Japanese, because the teachers knew we could cheat on tests that way."[31] She was there from age eight to age seventeen. Then the family went to various places in the US, from Oklahoma to Oxnard, and she graduated from high school in California. She recalled the stark racial difference: "In Oklahoma it was all White people. I felt like I died."[32] At age twenty, Lona returned to Okinawa alone, without her parents. She took advantage of her ambiguous phenotype and did some modeling in Okinawa during her twenties.

Although she has lived in the US, she prefers to live in Okinawa, where she has spent the past twenty years. She is considering returning to California to be closer to her aging parents. Despite living in America and having parents who live there now, Lona identifies with her Okinawan identity. She has a strong desire to be in Okinawa because of her business and because her daughter, whose father is also mixed-race American Okinawan, currently attends a middle school where she receives a bilingual education. Factors like family, employment, education, and the age at which one lives in a certain location matter in deciding where to be. As a parent herself, the decision to return to the US is a difficult one for Lona.

For some mixed-race people, making the journey to the US served to reinforce Okinawan identity. Fija Bairon came to California to search for his extended family after he finished high school in Okinawa. He lived in Los Angeles for several years, attending community college with the goal of learning English. Leaving Okinawa changed his perception of the US, Okinawa, and himself. "Me, who had claimed before 'I am an American' and had vowed to give up Japan and Okinawa, to never return, had been drawn exactly in the opposite direction. It was like a bow being pulled towards America, but when the string was released the arrow flew directly towards Okinawa. BOOOOM, I had changed. I had finally become Okinawan."[33] For Fija, coming to the US with limited English skills and an Okinawan cultural background contextualized his Okinawan identity. He passed for American, but did not feel at home in the United States. Physical separation from Okinawa emphasized another dimension of their perceived identity for many multiracial Okinawans. Coming to America amplified their Okinawanness. For some, it was only upon reaching adulthood that multiracial American Okinawans could restart relationships, go to the US, or return home to Okinawa.

Family ties underpinned transnationalism for multiracial Okinawans. In addition, economics also play a part in the luxury of international travel. However, being born and raised in Okinawa and calling it home does not guarantee that one is perceived as or feels like a native. Ted, who was born in 1961, lived most of his life in Okinawa except for four years during college when he went to his father's home state of Alabama. Even so, he said, "I felt like an outsider in Okinawa."[34] He is highly competent in spoken Japanese, yet struggles with written Japanese because he attended an English-speaking school at his father's insistence. His American father was in the military for a short time, and later opened up his own business and stayed in Okinawa. Ted comes from a family of six children, who all have US citizenship and attended an international English school. His immersion in an English-language school limited his access to the Japanese-speaking sector of Okinawa.

Speaking English and visiting the US did not mean Ted was a native to the US either. When they were young Ted and his siblings had an opportunity to visit the US about once every six years. Each of the six children took turns on a trip alone with their father to visit their family in Alabama when he returned yearly to the US for a business trip. Later, the children rotated through Alabama for four years each, attending college and spending time with their grandparents and extended family. When they went to the US, they were told they were foreigners, and that they spoke strange English. They were not embraced completely by American society. Now, two of the six siblings are still in Okinawa; the other four live in the US and they return home to Okinawa to visit their mother. According to Ted, "I have no complaints about living here. My wife's family, who is Okinawan, and my mother live in Okinawa. I have the most family here than anywhere else."[35] Ted said he is thankful for having English skills but realized that living in Okinawa requires more Japanese, and he wished he went to a Japanese school. He said, "It's really hard to do business in Okinawa as a foreigner."[36] Though he spent most of his life and continues to have close family on Okinawa he feels doubly displaced there, both as a mixed-race Okinawan and an English speaker in a primarily Japanese-speaking society. These personal reactions to racial and linguistic difference reflect a microcosm of the institutionalized policy of difference evident in governmental immigration restrictions.

American and Japanese government officials and government policies often worked as gatekeepers preventing multiracial American Okinawans who could not prove paternity from permanently immigrating to America. But proving paternity and obtaining proper visas were only part of the problem, since racial discrimination permeated Japanese and American society in the postwar era. In the US, institutionalized segregation was the law of the land and this included the American military overseas, as seen in the all White, all Black, and all Nisei battalions during World War II. When the US Occupation Army took over the governance of Japan in 1945, the Japanese—who had just suffered a crushing defeat and whose sociopolitical systems were already very hierarchical—readily embraced new notions of racism in the form of 1940s American ideology and iconology.[37] The racial continuum spanned gradients of both pigment and nationality, with people of European descent occupying a higher position, and little value placed upon people of African descent. Racial segregation permeated even the red-light districts; prostitutes were divided into "separate districts to be reserved for use by U.S. officers, White enlisted men, and Black enlisted men."[38] These differences of status were transferred to the children born from the unions between Americans and Japanese. Japanese society placed this *de facto* hierarchy of color onto the mixed-race people born on their soil and granted those who where half White a slightly more privileged position than those who were half Black. This ideology of discrimination based on race would continue into the occupation of Okinawa despite the end of *de jure* segregation in the US in 1964.

By the time Elizabeth was born in Okinawa in 1960, times had changed, but it was not a racial utopia for multiracial Black Okinawans. Her experiences as a multiracial Black Okinawan woman fostered her desire to leave for someplace more welcoming. She had the agency to make decisions as a young girl and as a high school student that aimed at relieving tension related to her racial background. These decisions would have a significant effect on her multiracial and transnational identity, and on her language ability as an adult.

Her physical differences and her monoracial classmates brought her tremendous challenges in the Japanese schools she attended as a young girl. She said, "Children would call me bad names like *kuronbo*, they would throw stones, throw sand, and try to start fights with me. Black is equated with dirty in Japan, and because I had black skin they said I was dirty. I never fought back. I cried all the way home. Everyday I cried. Everyday."[39] As a result, at the age of ten she made the decision to stop going to a Japanese school, and instead went to the international Okinawa Christian School, even though no one in her family spoke English. It was there that she became Christian and finally learned English. Elizabeth's choice as a young girl ultimately helped her make the decision to attend college and come to the United States in her late teens.[40] According to Elizabeth, it was a very common thing for many of her friends from the international school to go to universities abroad, since there were few choices in Okinawa. The high school one attends in Japan has a huge influence on which college one can enter, and Elizabeth was at a disadvantage since she had attended an international school.

Elizabeth went to the United States for the first time when she finished high school at the age of eighteen to attend Bethel College in Minnesota. When she arrived, she said, "So, this is my father's country. This is the kind of place where he grew up." When asked why she chose to go to the US for college, Elizabeth said she initially wanted to go to a university in the American South where there were a lot of Black people. In fact, she was initially accepted into a community college in Georgia and was drawn to the South, where people looked like her. Perhaps this demonstrated her Asian cultural values and her desire to find a larger group in the US of which she could become a part. Coming alone and without any family, she sought means to ease the transition into the United States. However, she ended up going to Bethel because it ultimately seemed like a better fit than a community college. One of her teachers at OCS was a Bethel alumnus and encouraged Elizabeth and her classmates to attend. Her dual language abilities in English and Japanese gave her the freedom to make this choice, widened her opportunities, and eased her transition upon her return to Japan.

Governmental immigration restrictions prevented Elizabeth from staying in the US after she graduated. She possessed only Japanese citizenship and could obtain only a student visa. After she finished college in the early 1980s, she had to return to Japan when her visa expired. Fortunately for Elizabeth, she was able to come to the US for at least a few years. Many other multiracial people who wanted to immigrate to the US could not do so because they could not prove their American paternity. To address this problem, Congress passed the Amerasia Homecoming Act of 1982 to allow anyone of part-American heritage to get around the strict immigration rules and avoid having to prove paternity.[41] Although multiracial children could now legally immigrate from nearly all Asian countries where US troops had been stationed, there was one oversight: children born in Japan were not covered.[42] Even though Elizabeth qualified according to the act's general language, because she was from Japan, it did not apply to her case. As it was not possible for her to live in the US, she began considering other options.

Elizabeth said that her future husband would have to be able to live in Japan—to her, it was home. She figured that African American men would not want to go to Japan to live with her, since they had families in the United States. The man she married, whom she met at Bethel College, was an Ethiopian immigrant.[43] Despite dealing with obstacles that prevented her from easily immigrating to the US, Elizabeth was able to make choices about her life. Her Japanese citizenship and, ironically, US immigration restrictions allowed her to bring her husband with her to Japan, where the "people and the rice stick together."[44]

Conclusion

Many multiracial families carry the burden of migration and international marriage. Such families span the globe because their households are multinational. When parents split because of jobs or divorce, individual family members must piece together what is left of the family relationship often by navigating great distances. Parents' decisions are immensely influential, and the case of multiracial Okinawans is especially complex because of differences in race, language, and nationality. Sometimes because of language barriers, parents occupy different roles in the family. As I pointed out in each story, the way they influenced their children in different ways affected their childrens' identities as multiracial persons.

Historian Paul Spickard has argued that a great majority of immigrants have maintained ties with other countries and have come and gone between the US and another place. He stated that these transnational individuals highlight the inaccuracy of the "American myth of one-way migration." Similar to the Japanese American *Kibei* during World War II, mixed people left Japan and returned to the United States.[45] Many mixed-race people had to split their time between their extended families in Okinawa and their extended families in the States. Immigration for them was not unidirectional. Their multicultural immersion with parents of different nationalities and their multiraciality allowed them to have transnational lives, and I argue that this shaped their multiracial identities.

Their marriage preferences and the choices of partners they made—a Japanese, an American, or another mixed-race person—suggest varied cultural preferences. Whether they decided to put their own children in international schools, like Lona, or in Japanese schools, like Ted, also reveal certain preferences. Those choices reflect particular responses to a social environment, and the choices the parents and the children made reflect society's values. The social pressures to adapt and respond to a divided family (or to prejudice because of a multiracial background) have shaped how American Okinawans cope with their multiracial identity, as youth, as parents themselves, and now in middle age. There were often severe structural constraints that shaped their identities. Governmental policies promoted transnationalism through the

movement of military personnel, while other policies restricted immigration, preventing family unification or permanent residency. Religion
also worked to shift the parameters of multiracial identity for those
who had the dual influence of English education in conjunction with
Christianity.

The official US occupation of Japan lasted only seven years, while
the occupation of Okinawa lasted twenty-seven years. Not only was the
nature of the occupation different, but the advocates for mixed-race
people during the postwar period also took different approaches due to
their resources, the racial environment, and the family circumstances of
the children. In Okinawa, institutions like the Pearl Buck Foundation
assisted children within their existing environments in a variety of ways
and tried to support the single-parent homes, many of which were low
income. Often referred to as *haafu*, or half, mixed-race people in both
Okinawa and Japan experienced similar kinds of discrimination based
on their mixed-race background. However, mixed-race Okinawans had
the privilege of time: many were born well into the 1960s, not immediately following World War II, under the more spartan conditions experienced by mixed-race people in Japan. Mixed-race people in Okinawa
also had more sympathetic institutions and schools in place to provide
support for their specific needs.

American Okinawans were granted upward social mobility in the
1970s and 1980s that was usually accessible only to people of higher
social class and status, such as the children of international business
people.[46] Multiracial American Okinawans had international lives that
gave them the opportunity to be bilingual, bicultural and, for some,
well traveled at a young age, even if in many cases their parents were
not bilingual or had never even left their own countries. American
Okinawans enjoyed the social capital of being bilingual and bicultural,
despite the fact that they did not come from elite backgrounds, and their
lives were enriched by those experiences. They were shaped in Okinawa
by one set of social and national dynamics, the culture of indigenous
Ryûkyû coupled with Japanese and US colonialism. Then they dealt
with the trauma of having to leave that and live in the US, where they
were shaped by a different set of social and national dynamics distinct
to the 1970s and 1980s. People like Rosa, who lived only in Okinawa,
occupy a bilingual and bicultural third space that is not transnational

by definition, but they nonetheless possess many of the same character-istics, because of the access to American culture and English speakers provided by the US military presence.

In conclusion, each of the aforementioned life stories shows that: (1) immigration is not a one-way process, but rather back and forth; (2) many mixed-race people who came from working-class backgrounds had transnational lives; and (3) with regards to immigration the US was not necessarily the final destination. American Okinawans' lives were difficult since their families spanned continents and oceans, and the nuclear families of some were splintered for various reasons. They faced challenges because their multiraciality and transnational lives visibly marked their foreignness, whether in Okinawa or in America, even as they varied in terms of how foreign they actually were in terms of lan-guage, culture, and identity. Paradoxically, some American Okinawans led privileged lives because their transnationalism fostered bilingual skills that proved to be an asset during the prosperous economic years of the 1980s in Japan. English-language ability gave them choices others did not have. The definitions that shaped American Okinawan identity are fluid and complex and scholars must remain flexible in the way we discuss and define migration, multiraciality, identity, and transnation-ality in the lives of multiracial people from Okinawa.

NOTES

1. This research was made possible by a Fulbright Fellowship through the Institute of International Education in Japan from 2008 to 2009. I want to thank the mul-tiracial American Okinawans who were willing to talk with me about their lives.

    Elizabeth Kamizato (alias), interview with Lily Anne Yumi Welty, Osaka, Japan, December 23, 2007. She was implying that the consistency of the rice was similar to the countries' respective cultural values: individual independence in the US and group dependence in Japan.

2. Kina Saeko (alias), interview with Lily Anne Yumi Welty, Chatan, Oki-nawa, October 19, 2009. Saeko is Okinawan and Black, and speaks Japanese *Uchinaguchi*.

3. Teresa K. Williams-León, "International Amerasians: Third Culture Afroasian and Eurasian Americans in Japan" (MA thesis, Department of Asian American Studies, University of California at Los Angeles, 1989), 2.

4. George H. Kerr, *Okinawa: The History of an Island People*, revised edition (Boston: Tuttle, 2000); Williams-León, "International," 2; *Time Magazine*, July 15, 1946, quoted in Cynthia Enloe, "It Takes Two," in *Let the Good Times Roll: Prostitution and the U.S. Military in Asia*, edited by Saundra Pollock Sturdevant and Brenda Stoltzfus (New York: New Press, 1992); for Korea, see Ji-Yeon Yuh, *Beyond the Shadow of Camptown: Korean Military Brides in America* (New York: New York University Press, 2002); for Korean Amerasians, see Margo Okazawa-Rey, "Amerasian Children in GI Town: A Legacy of U.S. Militarism in South Korea," *Asian Journal of Women's Studies* 3:1 (1997), 71–102.

5. Cynthia Enloe, *Bananas, Beaches and Bases: Making Feminist Sense of International Politics* (Los Angeles: University of California Press, 2000), 44.

6. Asato Eiko, "Okinawan Indentity and Resistance to Militarization and Maldevelopment," in *Islands of Discontent: Okinawan Responses to Japanese and American Power*, edited by Laura Hein and Mark Selden (New York: Roman and Littlefield, 2003), 229. "Reversion" refers to May 15, 1972, when the "U.S. finally ended direct military rule of Okinawa and the islands 'reverted' back to Japan."

7. Stephen Murphy-Shigematsu, translated by Sakai Sumiko, *Amerajian no kodomotachi: shirarezaru mainoriti mondai* [*Amerasian Children: Understanding the Minority Problem*], (Tokyo: Shueisha Shinsho, 2002); Marika Suzuki, "Empowering Minority Youth in Japan: The Challenge of the AmerAsian School in Okinawa" (MA thesis, Stanford University, December 2003); Akemi Johnson, "Island *Haafu*, Tokyo *Haafu*: Learning English at the AmerAsian School in Okinawa" (senior honors thesis, Brown University, 2004; Fukuchi Hiroaki, *Okinawa no konketsuji to haha tachi* (*Okinawa's Mixed Bloods and Their Mothers*), (Naha: Aoi Umi Shuppansha, 1980).

8. Sawada Miki, *Haha to ko no kizuna: Erizabesu sandāsu hōmu no sanjūnen* [*The Bond between a Mother and Child: Thirty Years of the Elizabeth Saunders Home*], (Kyoto: PHP Kenkyujo, 1980); Matsushita Shizuko, (1951) "Konketsuji wo sodatete" (Raising multiracials), *Fujinkoron* 37:12 (December 1951), 76–78; Lloyd B. Graham, "The Adoption of Children from Japan by American Families 1952–1958" (dissertation, Department of Social Work, University of Toronto, 1958); Mattie H. Briscoe, "A Study of Eight Foreign-Born Children of Mixed Parentage Who Have Been Adopted by Negro Couples in the U.S." (MA thesis, Atlanta University School of Education, 1956); Heide Fehrenbach, *Race After Hitler: Black Occupation Children in Postwar Germany and America* (Princeton, NJ: Princeton University Press 2005); Robert Fish, "The Heiress and the Love Children: Sawada Miki and the Elizabeth Saunders Home for Mixed-Blood Orphans in Postwar Japan" (PhD dissertation, Department of History, University of Hawai'i at Manoa, 2002).

9. Paul R. Spickard, *Mixed Blood: Intermarriage and Ethnic Identity in Twentieth Century America* (Madison: University of Wisconsin Press, 1989); Homi K. Bhabha *The Location of Culture* (New York: Routledge, 1994); Maria P. P. Root, editor, *The Multiracial Experience: Racial Borders as the New Frontier* (Newbury

Park, CA: Sage, 1996); G. Reginald Daniel, *More than Black? Multiracial Identity and the New Racial Order* (Philadelphia: Temple University Press, 2002); Fernando Herrera Lima, "Transnational Families: Institutions of Transnational Social Space," in *New Transnational Social Spaces: International Migration and Transnational Companies in the Early Twenty-first Century*, edited by Ludger Pries (New York: Routledge, 2001); Zlatko Skirbis, "Transnational Families: Theorising Migration, Emotions, and Belonging," *Journal of Intercultural Studies* 29: 3 (August 2008).

10. Leo T. S. Ching, *Becoming "Japanese": Colonial Taiwan and the Politics of Identity Formation* (Berkeley: University of California Press, 2001); Naomi Noiri, "Two Worlds: The Amerasian and the Okinawan," *Social Processes in Hawai'i* 42 (2007), 211–30.

11. Hiroaki, *Okinawa no konketsuji to hahatachi.*

12. Fija Bairon and Patrick Heinrich, "'Wanne Uchinanchu—I Am Okinawan': Japan, the U.S. and Okinawa's Endangered Languages," *Asia Pacific Journal: Japan Focus* (November 22, 2007). http://japanfocus.org/-Fija-Bairon/2586, accessed July 14, 2009. In the Okinawan-Ryûkyûan language, *Uchinanchu* means "Okinawan" and *Uchinaguchi* means the "Okinawan-Ryûkyûan language."

13. Steven Masami Ropp, "The Nikkei Negotiation of Minority/Majority Dynamics in Peru and the U.S.," in *New Worlds, New Lives: Globalization and People of Japanese Descent in the Americas and from Latin America in Japan,* edited by Lane Ryo Hirabayashi, Akemi Kikumura-Yano, and James Hirabayashi (Palo Alto, CA: Stanford University Press, 2002). *Naichijin* means "Japanese" in the Okinawan-Ryûkyûan language.

14. Ryan Masaaki Yokota, "Okinawan Nationalism(s): From Independence to Autonomy, and from Diasporic Nationalism to Indigenousness" (PhD dissertation, Department of History, University of Chicago, 2013).

15. John W. Dower, *Embracing Defeat: Japan in the Wake of World War Two* (New York: W.W. Norton, 1999), 54; Kerr, *Okinawa: The History,* 466.

16. Julia Yonetani, "Future 'Assets,' but at What Price? The Okinawa Initiative Debate," in *Islands of Discontent: Okinawan Responses to Japanese and American Power*, edited by Laura Hein and Mark Selden (Lanham, MD: Rowman & Littlefield, 2003), 257.

17. James E. Roberson, "Uchinâ Pop: Place and Identity in Contemporary Okinawan Popular Music," in *Islands of Discontent,* ed. by Hein and Selden, 209.

18. Ingrid Dineen-Wimberly, "Mixed-Race Leadership in African America: The Regalia of Race and National Identity in the U.S., 1862–1916" (PhD dissertation, Department of History, University of California Santa Barbara, 2009).

19. Fernando Herrera Lima, "Transnational Families: Institutions of Transnational Social Space," in *New Transnational Social Spaces: International Migration and Transnational Companies in the Early Twenty-first Century*, edited by Ludger Pries (New York: Routledge, 2001), 91.

20. Skirbis, "Transnational Families," 231.

21. Paul Spickard, *Almost All Aliens: Immigration, Race, and Colonialism in American History and Identity* (New York: Routledge, 2007).

22. Cindy Brown (alias), interview with Lily Anne Yumi Welty, Kadena, Okinawa, July 7, 2009.

23. For further information on war brides, see Takeshi Ueki, *Sensou hanayome: go jyu nen wo kataru kusanonen wo shinzen taishi* [*War Brides: Fifty Years of Discussions, Grassroots Friendship Ambassadors*], (Tokyo: Bensei Shuppan, 2002); Teresa K. Williams, "Marriage between Japanese Women and U.S. Serviccmen since World War II," *Amerasia Journal* 17:1 (1991), 135–54; Ji-Yeon Yuh, *Beyond the Shadow of Camptown: Korean Military Brides in America* (New York: New York University Press, 2002); Bok-Lim C. Kim, "Asian Wives of U.S. Servicemen: Women in Shadows," *Amerasia Journal* 4:1 (1977), 91–115.

24. Brown (alias), interview, July 7, 2009.

25. Keiko Kozeki, *Nihonjin Keiko: Aru konketsu shōjo no shuki* [*Japanese Keiko: The Memoirs of a Multiracial Girl*], (Tokyo: Bunka Hōsō Shuppanbu, 1967).

26. Rosa Morimoto (alias), interview with Lily Anne Yumi Welty, Kadena, Okinawa, September 27, 2009.

27. *Ibid.*

28. Rosa Morimoto (alias), interview with Lily Anne Yumi Welty, Ginowan, Okinawa, June 27, 2009.

29. *Ibid.*

30. William Wetherall, "Japan's Nationality Law: A Primer and Guide to Other Articles," January 1, 2007. http://members.jcom.home.ne.jp/yosha/yr/nationality/Nationality_primer.html, accessed January 14, 2011; Oshiro Masayasu *Konketsuji: Okinawa kara no kokuhatsu kokuseki no nai seishun* [*Mixed Blood: Indicted Youth without Nationality from Okinawa*], (Tokyo: Kokusai Johosha, 1985). Prior to 1985, the Japanese nationality law dictated that Japanese citizenship was granted to the children of Japanese fathers and not to the children of Japanese mothers who did not have Japanese fathers. A case decided that year, *Sugiyama v. Japan,* overturned the 1950 Nationality Law on the grounds that it legalized sexual discrimination; the principle of patrilineality was thus declared unconstitutional.

31. Lona Blake (alias), interview with Lily Anne Yumi Welty, Chatan, Okinawa, September 15, 2009.

32. *Ibid.*

33. Fija and Heinrich, "'*Wanne Uchinanchu*–I Am Okinawan.'"

34. Ted Duvall (alias), interview with Lily Anne Yumi Welty, Ginowan, Okinawa, September 21, 2009.

35. *Ibid.*

36. *Ibid.*

37. One example of the racialized objects include the Sambo-like *dakko chan* (huggie) doll.

38. Dower, *Embracing Defeat*, 130.

39. Kamizato (alias), interview, December 23, 2007.

40. Many mixed-race Vietnamese Amerasian refugees similarly came to the US as teenagers without their families. However, multiracial Okinawans were not sponsored by the US Amerasian Homecoming Act of 1986, and could not come with their families.

41. Spickard, *Almost All Aliens,* 352. Most of the 100,000 people who came after the passage of this act were Vietnamese.

42. The rationale for excluding children born in Japan was that their emigration could damage the diplomatic relations between Japan and the US.

43. Kamizato (alias), interview, December 23, 2007.

44. *Ibid.*

45. *Kibei* were Japanese Americans born in the United States in the early twentieth century to Issei, the first generation of immigrants from Japan. Paul Spickard, *Japanese Americans: The Formation and Transformation of an Ethnic Group* (New Brunswick, NJ: Rutgers University Press, 2009), 96–98.

46. Stephen Murphy-Shigematsu, "Multiethnic Lives and Monoethnic Myths: American-Japanese Amerasians in Japan," in *The Sum of Our Parts: Mixed Heritage Asian Americans,* edited by Teresa Williams-León and Cynthia L. Nakashima (Philadelphia: Temple University Press, 2001), 212–13.

9

The Curious Career of the One-Drop Rule

Multiraciality and Membership in Germany Today

MIRIAM NANDI AND PAUL SPICKARD

It is impossible to write about racial intermixture in Germany without mentioning that the very word "race" (*Rasse*) is no longer used in the German language except when people talk about dogs or horses.[1] The Nazis disowned, displaced, and eventually killed all those races they considered inferior—in particular, obviously, the Jews, who would probably not be considered a race apart in the United States, where race works more along color lines than in Germany. Six million people were killed because of Germany's obsession with race, and, to a certain degree, Germany is still traumatized by guilt and shame. Thus, Germans avoid the word "race" and tend to use the word *Ausländer* (foreigner) for people of non-German ancestry. In an academic context, the word "ethnicity" (*Ethnizität*) is sometimes used to denote racial difference, but it is rarely used in everyday language.

In a similar vein, people of mixed race would never call themselves "mixed race" (*rassisch gemischt* or *Mischling*), because these terms are associated with the Nazi past. There is no German term for people of mixed race. People who were considered to be *Halbjude* (literally a half-Jew) were not officially subject to the Nazi race penalties laid down in the Nuremberg race laws. But such mixed people could still be deported to a death camp, and they were not allowed to attend university nor to marry. Since the Nazi race ideology was firmly grounded in biologistic terms—Judaism was considered to be not a religious choice, but a biological trait—today's German ideas about difference are at least officially structured around ideas of language, religion, and national origin, not biology.

A common term that is applied to people of color (this is also a term that does not exist in German) would be *Menschen mit Migrationshintergrund*, which does not translate very well; literally it means "people with a migration background." This term is used for people who either migrated to Germany themselves or have one or two parents who hail from a non-German country. Officially, it refers to both White and non-White German residents of foreign background, and is therefore not strictly speaking a "racial" term in the Anglophone sense. In terms of common usage, however, when German people speak about *Menschen mit Migrationshintergrund*, they usually mean people whose alleged difference is either visible or audible: people who are of a darker pigmentation than other Germans and people who speak imperfect German (and the two categories leak into each other).

Furthermore, there is no German equivalent for "interracial marriage"—which again would bring back nightmares about *Rassenschade* ("race shame"), the Nazi term for sexual intercourse between Christian and Jewish Germans. During the Third Reich, interracial marriages were forbidden; sexual intercourse between a non-Jew and a Jew meant that the man involved would be sent to prison (women were not, which has to do with the Nazi idea of female passivity). Understandably, there are no statistics on how many biracial marriages in Germany there may be, nor is there any contemporary notion of how "race" or "multiraciality" would be determined in Germany. The National Census (*Statistische Bundesamt*) does, however, take binational marriages (*binationale Ehen*) into account, but the term "binational marriage" for them also includes Austrian-German and any other international matches. In these statistics, binational marriages are determined strictly and exclusively by the passports of the partners and take no other factors into account.

Nonetheless, although the word *Rasse* is not used, Germany is in some senses a racial nation. That is, long before Nazism, and even before there was a single German state (it was founded in 1871), German intellectuals defined Germany as an embryo nation that was made up of all the people who were ethnically German, a designation usually constructed on linguistic lines. Exactly what sorts of people were to be included among ethnic Germans has varied according to time, context, and the political purpose of whoever was doing the deciding. Usually, all the Germanic-speaking peoples were included. Yet the grounds for deciding which languages were Germanic have not always been clear— Dutch has seldom been included despite its manifest similarity to the northwest German dialects, whereas several local language groups in what are currently Austria, Hungary, Poland, and the Czech Republic have usually been reckoned to be Germanic.[2] It was the bold aim of the eighteenth- and nineteenth-century thinkers who first imagined a modern German state to unite all the peoples they regarded as German-speaking into a single nation-state.[3]

Usually the idea of Germanness has also taken on an explicitly racial tone. The racialist pseudoscience that came to dominate so much European thinking in the late nineteenth and early twentieth centuries based much of its analysis on linguistic divisions between peoples that were believed to stand for underlying, immutable, biological differences that were called racial.[4] Johann Gottfried von Herder, the Enlightenment philosopher, posited a unified German *Volk*, united by their common language, as the basis of the German nation-to-be.[5] His contemporary, the poet Friedrich Schiller, wrote of an "*inneres Reich*," a mystical inner consciousness that he believed all ethnic Germans shared in common.[6] Johann Gottlieb Fichte wrote about

cultivating a new race of men . . . Germans to Germans. . . . [W]hat the German in and of himself, independently of the fate that has now befallen him, is and has always been in his essential character, ever since he came into existence. . . . [H]is aptitude for and receptivity to a culture such as we envisage lies already in this essential character and separates him from every other European nation.[7]

Such ideas have been echoed by German thinkers in every generation, from Herder and Fichte in the eighteenth century, through Wagner and Nietzsche in the nineteenth, and down to our own day.[8] They have been partly offset by more progressive intellectuals such as Gotthold Ephraim Lessing (1729–81), who spoke up for tolerance toward other religions and cultures against influential thinkers of his time. His drama *Nathan der Weise* (*Nathan the Wise*) describes how the Jewish merchant Nathan and the enlightened Muslim ruler Saladin bridge the gaps between the three book religions (Judaism, Christianity, and Islam). The play was forbidden by the church during his lifetime and banned by the Nazis in the 1930s, but it does give evidence of a minor-key alternative evolving alongside the dominant melody of the racial nation. Since the 1970s, *Nathan der Weise* has been a prescribed text for German high school students.[9]

Ideas about the uniqueness of the German race were codified in the 1913 German law of citizenship, which was based on the principle of *jus sanguinis*, the law of descent. That is, one is German if one's ancestors were German (Herder would have said, if they spoke the German language). By contrast, France since the first days of the republic has embraced the principle of *jus soli*, the law of place of birth: anyone born in France is reckoned a citizen, irrespective of that person's ancestry. Britain and the United States embrace both *jus sanguinis* and *jus soli* as grounds for natural-born citizenship. German citizenship law in the twentieth and twenty-first centuries has consistently clung to the *jus sanguinis* principle, although in 2000 a small opening was made to some native-born children of permanent-resident immigrants. Under current law they are not granted citizenship at birth, but they can apply for naturalization after they have completed education in German schools.[10] At least officially, people who have fluency in the German language are considered culturally German, regardless of their pigmentation or ancestry, although as we shall see, there are practical limitations.

In Germany today, race works less along purely biologistic lines than it used to three-quarters of a century ago. Furthermore, the post–World War II German government has owned up to the Holocaust in a forthright way and continues to keep it before the public. Every large town has a Holocaust memorial. In the southern German university town of Freiburg, for instance, the names of all the local Holocaust victims (Jews, Roma, homosexuals, disabled people, and others) are engraved into the cobblestones of one of the main streets in the old part of town. People quite literally stumble over Germany's troubled racialized past. High school, even primary school curricula are replete with Nazi and

German-Jewish history. One of the first songs that coauthor Miriam Nandi learned at primary school was "Shalom Chaverim," a traditional Hebrew tune. Thus, a lot of Germans feel they have dealt with their racist history, and so they are quite reluctant to talk about race any more. It is understandable that many Germans should be squeamish about resurrecting a term that has so much negative history, and, indeed, the word *Rasse* is more or less banned from public discourse.

That, however, is as much a matter of linguistic avoidance as it is of social substance. In actual German social life, racialized issues persist in new forms, targeting new peoples. As Neil Gregor has observed, "Contrary to popular assumption and official projection, race did not go away, but . . . was merely refocused and recoded away from overtly biologized notions of difference to cultural ones."[11] We would amend Gregor's formulation, and suggest that biologized notions of difference continue to hold considerable power in German everyday life alongside racialized cultural markers such as Muslim identity. To put it simply, although ethnic Germans don't use the word *Rasse*, they tend to perceive Muslims, Africans, and Asians as not being Germans, particularly when they are not very educated, even if they are in fact native to the country and are citizens and tax-payers. The distinction they are making is a racialized one, even though they don't use the word *Rasse* to mark it.

It is not just Germans who don't want to use the word "race." When in 2008 one of the authors proposed, to the leaders of a conference in Finland, a panel on "Migrants, Race, and Membership," he was politely informed that "race" was a word no longer used in Europe, and that it would be better to substitute "ethnicity" instead.[12]

Over the last two decades there have been regular reports in the German press of racialized attacks by neo-Nazis, skinheads, and other extremists perpetrated against immigrants, particularly Muslims and people of color.[13] But racialized distinctions are also a fact of everyday life on German streets, in shops and classrooms, where ordinary, non-extremist ethnic Germans often simply fail to perceive that their non-White or non-Christian-descended neighbors are in fact Germans. These unarticulated racialized distinctions have great impact on the lives of racially mixed Germans.

In 1998 the government, a coalition of the Social Democratic Party (SPD) and the Green Party attempted to adapt German law to the *jus soli* principle and allow for dual citizenship. The conservative Christian Democratic Union party (CDU) then launched a huge campaign against it. In almost every large town in Germany the local divisions of the CDU set up stalls where people could sign a petition against the new law. An old lady in inner-city Freiburg came rushing to one of the stalls, saying, "Where can I sign that petition against foreigners?" This summarizes the spirit in which the campaign was launched, even though the CDU still today vociferously denies allegations of racism. The reform was passed eventually in 2000, but it brought only a small improvement, due to the massive public protest encouraged by the CDU. Second-generation migrants who were born in Germany or people of binational origin can now have dual citizenship until the age of twenty-three. Afterwards, they have to choose between keeping their German passport and retaining the other nationality.

A more recent example is Thilo Sarrazin, a German politician, who topped the bestseller lists with his 2010 book *Deutschland schafft sich ab* (literally, *Germany Abolishes Itself*). Sarrazin articulated intensely negative stereotypes about Turkish-Germans and Arabic-Germans. He claimed that Germany's immigrant Muslim population was unwilling to assimilate and tended to rely on social services. Sarrazin (whose family name, ironically, is derived from the word "Saracen," meaning Arab or Muslim) calculated that their population could well outnumber the ethnic German population within a couple of generations at the current rate of growth. He also suggested that their intelligence was lower than that of White Christian Europeans.[14] What is worrying, perhaps, is not so much the fact that Sarrazin wrote the book, but that the first edition sold out within a few days. Germany is more caught up with its racist past than most Germans would like to admit, and Germany's residual racism is also felt by multiracial people. Due to Germany's vexed relationship with its Nazi past, discussions of race are silenced, but that does not mean that race simply went away. It has morphed and taken on new forms, as the following discussions will illustrate.

Race, Pop Culture, and Football

Despite such signs of residual racism, many Germans would claim that they have learned from the past to such an extent that Germany has now entered a postracial era in which one's pigmentation or one's grandfather's home address is no longer important. With globalization in full swing, Germany has witnessed increasing economic and cultural relationships with the rest of the world. From the late 1950s onwards, Germany signed bilateral recruitment agreements with Italy, Spain, Turkey, Greece, Morocco, Yugoslavia, and Tunisia. These agreements permitted so-called guest-workers (*Gastarbeiter*) to work in blue-collar jobs for a period of five years. The initial aim of this policy, which was espoused both by the German government and by Germany's first-generation migrants, was that the guest-workers would return to their countries of origin after a few years. Most of them, however, stayed, even if their children (who were obviously born in Germany) were not granted citizenship. Today, Germany has, probably unwittingly, become one of the most multicultural and multiethnic countries in Europe. According to Eurostat, 12 percent of the residents in Germany have "a migration background." Accordingly, binational marriages have doubled in the last decade. In 2010, every ninth marriage in Germany was a binational one. One child out of three is born in a binational family setting, according to the Association for Binational Marriages and Partnerships (*Verband Binationaler Familien und Partnerschaften*), a community-based group in Berlin.[15]

German politics and German pop culture are replete with people who have a migration background: such as Tunisian-German rapper Bushido, Indian-South-African-German singer Xavier Naidoo, Turkish-German politician Cem Özdemir, and Russian-German writer Wladimir Kaminer, to name but a few important figures. The current minister of economy, one of the most powerful people in Germany, Phillip Rösler, is of Vietnamese origin and was adopted by ethnic German parents as an infant.

Many Germans today like to see themselves as *weltoffen* ("open towards the world"), as a globalized people. German pop culture may serve as an example who this new increasingly globalized and postracial German identity is performed in these days. The popular casting show *The Voice of Germany* recruited a number of mixed-race or queer artists, all of whom were very popular with viewers. Benny Fiedler, a dark-skinned nineteen-year-old singer, who was adopted by ethnic German parents as child, topped the download charts with his version of the song "Eiserner Steg" by the ethnic German singer-songwriter Phillip Poisel. Similarly, the Iranian-German student Benam Moghadamm was particularly popular with the audience. Kim Sanders, a fairly light-skinned African American who migrated to Germany in the early nineties, recalled being replaced by a blonde model for a music video in the early nineties. In 2012, she was celebrated for her musical versatility not just by her coach Nena, but also by the German viewers. Another successful candidate was the Black, bisexual artist Percival Duke, originally from Texas, now a permanent German resident. His "coach," Rea Garvey, received hateful emails for dropping him in the semifinals. The winner of the show was Ghanaian-German high-school student Ivy Quainoo, who received standing ovations with the Berlin audience of the program. Even if other candidates like the Polish German postman Fanel Cornelius and the ex-GI and African American soul artist Butch Williams did not make it to the final round, about one-third of the contestants of the popular program were at least racially ambiguous. Interestingly, these people were never asked to explain their ethnic background by the host of the show, nor was race an issue in the media representation of the artists. It was assumed that they were German.

Similarly, the German football team that mesmerized soccer fans all over the world during the 2010 World Cup appears to be the epitome of a new, cool, perhaps postracial Germany, since some of its strongest players are hyphenated Germans. Mesut Özil, a young Turkish-German who was also referred to as "the German Zidane"[16] in the international press, scored a left-footed half-volley from the edge of the penalty box against Ghana in the final group game, ensuring that Germany would make it into the second round. Sami Khedira, son of a Tunisian father and a German mother, moved from VfB Stuttgart to Real Madrid for a fee that was so high it was never disclosed. The most successful player on the young team was Polish-German Miroslav Klose, who is obviously White and has German citizenship; but again, in Germany race works less along strict color lines than in the United States. Klose's parents came from Poland, and Klose himself speaks German with an accent. He is thus viewed as a *Person mit Migrationshintergrund*, even if he is an extremely cool one.

The most intriguing example, however, is that of the Boateng brothers, who both have a Ghanaian father and a German mother. Jérôme

Boateng grew up with his mother in a middle-class area of Berlin. Kevin-Prince Boateng, who called himself a "ghetto kid" in an interview with the *Berliner Zeitung*,[17] spent his youth with his father in Berlin-Wedding, a rough neighborhood widely thought to be home to myriad social problems such as unemployment, violence, and drug traffic.

We would like to take the case of the Boateng brothers as a starting point for our discussion of multiraciality in Germany, a phenomenon that is complex and certainly goes beyond the new, cool, ostensibly postracial Germania paradigm. Germany's relationship with race and racial intermixture continues to be vexed and vexing, particularly but not exclusively when class comes into play, as the case of the Boateng brothers illustrates.

Months before the beginning of the World Cup, the media, from tabloid to highbrow, rallied around the Boateng brothers and focussed almost exclusively on the alleged difference between the two brothers. While Jérôme was usually represented as hardworking, reliable, and polite, if a bit quiet, Kevin-Prince was portrayed as performing antics, loving crowd-pleasing moments, and risking letting his tremendous talent go to waste. The conservative paper *Die Welt* opened its diatribe against the young footballer with the words "Fits of anger, loose tongue, lack of discipline, things never went well for Kevin-Prince Boateng in sports and in life."[18] Unlike his brother, who was portrayed in very similar terms as his White teammates, Kevin-Prince was often photographed in a gangster pose, displaying his twenty-six tattoos. The photographs taken of Kevin-Prince tended to overemphasize his physicality, while Jérôme was hardly ever portrayed without his shirt on. The press recorded with relish that Kevin-Prince prayed before a match (quite unusual and exotic in the German context), which allegedly clashed with his taste for the ghetto melodrama *Blood In, Blood Out*. It was also reported that Kevin-Prince developed a shopping addiction due to his personal problems and that he owned about two hundred caps, twenty leather jackets, a Lamborghini, a Cadillac, and a Hummer, the cost of which added up to six figures. At the time when Kevin-Prince decided to play internationally for Ghana rather than Germany, his friends reported that Kevin-Prince could not find Ghana on the map.[19]

To be fair, nobody forced Kevin-Prince to take off his shirt or talk about his shopping habits with journalists. He later admitted to having been naïve in his handling of public attention. But even if Kevin-Prince had his own share in the construction of his public image, the media nevertheless produced a fable of the two brothers which falls into a binary pattern of normal and exotic, disciplined and extravagant, public school boy and gangster, White and Black. The media representation of Kevin-Prince reproduced almost every single stereotype about young men of color, while Jérôme appeared to be every bit as German as his teammates. Jérôme was also seen as far less interesting and hot for that reason, while his brother appeared to be fascinating, exotic, and sexy.

One of the reasons for the split in the representations of the Boateng brothers has to do with class. While multiracial people with a middle-class background are often accepted as normal Germans, even if their pigmentation is dark, working-class or unemployed migrants have to face a number of unflattering clichés. It is partly the fact that Kevin-Prince grew up in Wedding that sets him apart from his brother, as well as from everyone else, in the mind of the average German. To a certain extent, Wedding makes him Blacker, as living in that neighborhood also blackens (on a metaphorical level) Russian Germans. People may get away with hailing from a different climate and speaking German with an accent, but they have to face a lot of negative stereotyping as soon as it becomes clear that they are members of the working class, or worse, unemployed. In reality, then, when Germans talk about *Menschen mit Migrationshintergrund*, they usually do not mean the Canadian diplomat's daughter or even the Chinese PhD student. They really are referring to an unemployed Turkish-German migrant who never leaves his *Kiez*, his Turkish-German neighborhood. To many Germans, even though they would see themselves as cosmopolitan, class is as important as physical appearance. To a certain extent, we are witnessing a classing of race; that is, issues of race become more pressing as soon as the person in question is working class or lives on social welfare. Race is the issue, but lower-class status activates and reinforces it.

Another trope that was associated with the Boateng brothers is that of "successful integration" (*gelungene Integration*) versus "failed integration" (*mißlungene Integration*), a particularly German cliché that appears almost every day in public discourse. A large part of the German population is convinced that migrants are supposed to assimilate to German culture, a process that they call *Integration*. Conversely, the public assumes that migrants, particularly but not exclusively when they are from a Muslim background, are not willing to undergo the process of integration, and they are reproached for it. Exactly what is meant by *Integration* is hardly ever explained; we can only speculate that it includes things like having the capacity to speak flawless German, pursuing an occupation, and having ethnic German friends. Thus, hyphenated Germans are more often than not portrayed in terms of good migrants, who have managed to integrate themselves into German society, versus bad migrants, who do not speak proper German, who live on public welfare, and so on. Depending on the political leanings of the observer, either of these two sorts of immigrant is assumed to make up the larger part of Germany's migrant population. Jérôme, then, obviously, is the good migrant, in that he appears to have chosen to stick with his German side. Kevin-Prince, by contrast, despite his obvious football success—he played for Tottenham Hotspur and then for AC Milan—was still viewed in terms of difference and failure: he lacked discipline, he lived in a fantasy world, he did not fit in, he was rootless (he was not really German, but on the other hand he could not find Ghana on the map, either).

The problem with these binaries is not that they were completely wrong—after all, Kevin-Prince did have twenty-six tattoos and Jérôme Boateng probably was genuinely reliable and hardworking—but that they were a fixed representation of reality. The multiracial subject appears to have only two options: either to try to pass as White or to take up the pose of the ghetto kid, and thus inhabit a space of exoticized difference. There appears to be very little room for in-betweenness or inhabiting a "third space" in the media representation of multiracial subjects. A multiracial person is thus trapped in an "apparatus of power," as Homi Bhabha puts it, with very limited choices: either stick with your German side or become a ghetto kid and face the consequences.[20] Yet it seems obvious that multiracial people like Jérôme and Kevin-Prince inhabit precisely that liminal space in between races, cultures, and even classes (Kevin-Prince has long left Wedding, but Wedding seems never to have left him). It is ludicrous that people of color would have to choose between such extremes when there are certainly more than two possibilities. As Kwame Anthony Appiah points out in a different context: "If I had to choose between . . . Uncle Tom and black power, I would, of course, choose the latter. But I would like to have not to choose. I would like to have more options."[21]

Germany's Racial Rules of Citizenship

To make matters worse for migrants in Germany, the pressure to choose is not only a symbolic one, on the level of representation, but also part of the German juridical system. According to the *jus sanguinis* principle, a person receives a German passport, not if she is born in Germany, but if she has a German mother or father. It is virtually impossible to have two passports.[22] As a consequence of the *jus sanguinis* rule, a six-figure number of Russian migrants of German ancestry were granted permanent residence in Germany in the early nineties, many of them speaking very little German and having no possibility to get into workforce. Meanwhile, the father of coauthor Miriam Nandi, who migrated to Germany from India in 1963, acquired a PhD from a renowned German university, pursued a professional career, was married to a German woman and had four children with her, was required to pass an "integration test" before qualifying for his German passport. And then he had to renounce his Indian citizenship, a move that caused him a lot of pain and regret. Officially, the goal of the forced choice is to facilitate "integration." But one wonders whether the reasons do not run deeper and have their origins in nineteenth-century German nationalism. German nationalism was based much less on citizenship (á la French nationalism) than on language and culture. In German nationalist thought, Germany was defined as a *Kulturnation*, a cultural nation, a term that is still used and intuitively understood by most educated Germans. Viewed through the lens of German nationalism, people can only belong to one culture, therefore to one nation; it is quite simply impossible to be in between.

On one hand, Germany's long-standing racial definition of citizenship would seem to favor unmarked inclusion in the nation for people of mixed ancestry. After all, they are part German. Several scholars describe the "return" to Germany in the 1980s–2000s of tens of thousands of *Aussiedler* (emigrants) after as much as several generations spent in places like Poland and the Ukraine. Many of these people were remote descendants of long-ago German émigrés who lived and inter-married in foreign lands. The returnees often had little actual German ancestry and less German culture, but they were welcomed into Ger-man society and fast-tracked for citizenship because they were deemed to be blood Germans. By prioritizing and recognizing people as Ger-man who have only the smallest shred of actual German ancestry, lan-guage, or culture, this amounts to a one-drop rule.[23]

For instance, Mira Foster tells the story of Anna, a middle-aged woman who came to West Germany from Poland in 1981 with her hus-band and child. They came for a visit, but stayed on because of politi-cal instability back home that accompanied the temporary defeat of the Solidarity movement. Growing up in Poland, Anna did not know much about her family history. A cousin who had migrated to Germany earlier informed her that they shared a German grandfather, although Anna's branch of the family never learned about that ancestry, as the family split over World War II. Anna applied for and received German citizenship based on her German name and her descent from a German grandfather, though she did not speak much German and felt culturally Polish. Foster described Anna's situation and the benefits she received with her German citizenship:

> Anna's newly received German citizenship ensured her legal member-ship in the German community. Her family was eligible for an apart-ment, welfare support, and a German language course. Like many other Poles who immigrated to Germany during the seventies and eighties, they did not speak German. Socialized and educated in Poland, they had Polish biographies and were familiar with neither German custom nor culture. Many of them had never visited a country on the other side of the Iron Curtain. Their German roots were merely a distant family his-tory put aside or even forgotten due to the prevailing memories of the Nazi invasion and destruction of Poland during the Second World War as well as the nationalist pressure in communist Poland.

German culture and identity never took in Anna's case. Thirty years on, she still said of herself, "I am Polish. Despite having the German passport, which is only a paper, I always stress the fact that it is only a paper, which allowed me to live here, but it is not me, this is not what

I feel. Me, being German, . . . never in my life will I identify with Germany, never." Yet despite her persistent self-identification as Polish, Anna stayed on in Germany after Solidarity's eventual triumph several years later, in part because her children were becoming unproblematic Germans in culture and identity.[24]

Similarly, people whom the German government reckoned to be descended from long-ago German migrants to Russia and the Ukraine were allowed to move to Germany in the late twentieth century and granted an expedited path to citizenship. The so-called Volga Germans entered the Russian Empire during the reign of Catherine the Great, nearly a century before a German national state came into existence. Many had mingled and mated over the intervening generations with Russians, Ukrainians, and other eastern peoples. Few spoke German or had much knowledge of German culture. According to historian Abraham Friesen, many of the original Ukrainian German migrants came, in fact, not from regions that later became part of the German state, but from the Netherlands and other places.[25] So when their descendants were granted *Aussiedler* status in Germany, people who in fact had no actual ancestral connection to German citizenship, and whose ancestors had in the intervening generations mixed with foreign peoples, were reckoned to be Germanic by blood nonetheless because of a quasifictive historical tie, and on that basis they were initially accorded an unproblematic place in German society.

Karina* was born in Kirgizstan.[26] She has a complicated ethnic background, some small part of which was German once upon a time, but that was a very long time ago. She relates her identity wanderings in the passage below. She has felt herself to be, and has been treated by others, depending on the period of her life and the context of the moment, by turns as Kirgiz, Soviet, Russian, German, perhaps a bit Armenian or Tatar, and finally as European.

> My affiliation to [German] ethnicity arises from a surname. My biological father is half-Armenian and half-Tatar. My mother is German (half-Swabian and half-East-Prussian). Her maiden name is Polish with a Russian ending. I had the Armenian name of my paternal biological heritage. My grandmother, whose ethnic affiliation qualified us to go to Germany, her maiden name was full German.

In Germany, we, as the Russian-Germans, have been received like a wild horde of "fucking Russians" (sorry), who threatened in every way the German way of life. The people couldn't consider us as ethnic Germans, especially because we looked, behaved and talked like Russians. . . . I never felt so Russian before, just Soviet, and easily slipped over into a new glorious and awesome identity, unified with all the proletarians of all the ex-Soviet countries into a proud working-class German subculture named "The Russians." The teens like me (I was twelve when we moved to Germany) formed our own kind of behavior, speaking Russian and a kind of slang that distinguished us from the adults but emphasized our Russian origin, even though almost none of us had Russian genetic roots. . . . [S]tigma created . . . this defensive social identity. . . .

I never have spoken and thought so much like a German as [when I lived for a year] in France . . . and learned to accept who I had become. If the French asked me "Where are you from?" I said that I'm living in Germany and was born in Kirgizstan. "So you are Kirgiz?" they followed. "No, I'm Russian." It was frustrating for both sides . . . because it was obvious that the French hadn't any idea where Kirgizstan is and that Kirgiz are Asians and that I didn't look like them. Further, there was an awareness of racial difference, which I unknowingly sensed.[27]

The tide has turned immensely for Russian Germans since the early nineties. By now, they face almost as much negative stereotyping and discrimination as Turkish Germans. Real estate prices drop dramatically as soon as a neighborhood becomes known as Russian-German. Other Germans are advised against putting their children into schools where the majority of the students are Russian Germans. One of our authors usually has one or two Russian-German students in her English literature classes. The ethnic German students are often reluctant to co-operate with them when she assigns group work tasks, or they make expressions of distaste when they hear the Russian-Germans speak English with a heavy Russian accent. One of her Russian-German students was particularly gutsy and confronted his fellow students with their impolite behavior. He said, "I don't speak good English, but that does not mean I am a bad person." That opened their eyes. The class cooperated extremely well afterwards.

German and White: The One-Drop Rule Works

Some people mix German parentage with another West European nationality such as Irish or Dutch. It is for this group only that the one-drop rule that is the German ideal and that is mandated by German citizenship law actually works in everyday social life.

Katje* is an Irish-German woman with hazel eyes, dark brown hair, and a peachy complexion. Her mother came to Germany from County Galway as a young woman and married Katje's German father. Katje grew up in northwest Germany, unimpeded by her mother's foreign birth. She was, in her eyes and in the eyes of other Germans, simply a German girl who had an Irish mother.[28]

Even some people who have no German ancestry at all, but some other West European parentage, are accorded places in German society as more or less full Germans. Roberto's* father came from Chile in the 1970s, fleeing the murderous Pinochet regime. The son of an elite family, he attended a German university and ultimately earned a doctorate. In Germany he met a fellow student from the Netherlands, married, and together they had a son. Later the couple divorced, but both remained in Germany. Roberto was raised by his mother in a north German city.

Roberto, tall and loose-limbed, with dark brown hair and eyes and light olive skin, has a Dutch passport. He speaks both Dutch and Spanish, but with a child's vocabulary and a German accent. His English, by contrast, is fluent and unaccented, courtesy of a half year of high school in Illinois and a year of university in Manchester. He regards himself, if not quite as a German, then as something pretty close:

> I wouldn't really say, I don't feel like a German. In a lot of places I go to,
> I am not only considered to be [German], but also . . . I take a very Ger-
> man standpoint or point of view. . . . Discussing Israeli politics and the
> Holocaust in Germany when you're at an English university and you're
> surrounded by five guys from Pakistan, who are all pretty bright, who
> all know what they're talking about, and one of them is saying, "Let's
> compare Israel's foreign policy to Germany's not-so-foreign policy from
> that time" [World War II]. And something in me . . . there is this little
> switch you have in a German mind . . . which is, whenever Israel or any-
> thing like that shows up, you have a little red light going "Be careful, be

careful." You . . . can't say half of what you think you may want to say, but that's something that really kicks in. I'd probably start out by saying if Israel was doing the same, there'd probably be no Palestinian population any more. . . . I probably argue from a very German perspective.

There were some incidents as a schoolboy where Roberto felt singled out as foreign, and some of his mother's family would like him to choose to be Dutch. But despite his lack of a German passport he feels and is treated as a *de facto* German on a daily basis and in all his relationships. His ethnic German girlfriend, from a prosperous, well-respected family, was flabbergasted that he was being interviewed as part of a study of immigrants' children, because, as she said, "You're German, aren't you?"[29]

Part-African, -Turkish, -Arab, or -Asian: Not So German

Unmixed people of Turkish, African, Asian, or Arab descent are the objects of daily discrimination, even when they were born and grew up all their lives in Germany.[30] Several dozen other interviews, undertaken in conjunction with this study but to be reported elsewhere, give ample evidence of the daily racialization that such people endure. To take just one example, Nehir* was born to two Turkish immigrant parents and raised in Hamburg. She has dark hair and eyes and olive skin. She speaks fluent, unaccented German, as well as fairly fluent, but German-accented English. She encountered an employer who shouted at her, "Don't speak to me in German! I can't understand your German because your accent is so thick! Speak to me in English!" She replied, rubbing her cheek, "I know my skin has an accent."[31] Several German women who have unmixed foreign ancestry, and who wear a headscarf, reported having clerks scrutinize them closely whenever they would enter a store, eyes following their every move, apparently on the assumption that they were likely to steal something. Several young German men of Arab or Turkish descent reported being rousted by police while simply walking or cycling down the street.

Although there is a welcome in Germany for mixed people whose non-German parent hails from Northwest Europe, the same cannot be said for mixed people whose non-German ancestry comes from darker, more pigment-rich peoples. In our interviews, people of mixed German-and-Turkish, German-and-Arab, German-and-African, and German-and-Asian ancestry all testified to being racialized as foreigners, even though they were born and raised in Germany and perform German culture perfectly. They remain racialized Others within German society.

Kristin's* father came to Dortmund straight from medical school in Istanbul. He married a German nurse who worked in the same hospital and settled down to build a practice and raise a family. Kristin and her family would make yearly trips to visit relatives in Turkey, but they spoke only German in the home, went to church, ate German food, and otherwise lived lives that were indistinguishable from those of their unmixed ethnic German neighbors. Both families were supportive of the marriage, but other ethnic Germans (even casual acquaintances) took it upon themselves to harass Kristin's mother with personal questions about headscarves and the daily oppressions they assumed she must be suffering as the wife of a Turk.

Kristin has had her share of strange encounters with ethnic full-Germans:

> I get asked all the time. It started when I went to kindergarten and elementary school, and [it continues] until now: The people ask, "Where are you from?" and I say "Okay, I'm from Germany." "No, where are you really from?" And I say, "I'm from Germany.". . . And they say, "No, because you're not really German. You look dark." And then I say, "Okay, my father's from Turkey.". . .
>
> I'm really into soccer and I'm really into the German team. . . . Then in the end Turkey had to play against Germany [in the European championships]. Then all of these friends . . . they [had been] really nice to me . . . we were sitting together, and . . . I was suddenly Turkish. I couldn't understand it. My best friend, we were . . . really mad at them . . . because they were really hurtful. . . . It would have been different if I was from Spain or something. I think it was such a hostile atmosphere because they don't really like Turkish people. . . . I mean, they see I'm not speaking with an accent, I can't speak Turkish, my father is more German than Turkish, so [on ordinary occasions] I'm accepted. . . I'm a German. But at this point . . . I was an outsider, because they said, "You can't be for the

Germans because you're half Turkish.". . . They were doing that because they don't like Turkish people. . . . I feel German.

Kristin performs Germanness perfectly. All of her friends are ethnic Germans. Should she marry, she is certain that it would be to an ethnic German man.

I met some Turkish guys that I was just talking to on a friendly basis. And there was this one guy and we were just friends and we were just talking about things. We had just met and he was a really modern guy. He speaks German fluently. So you really would assume that he's really assimilated in Germany, a really nice guy. . . . And at one point he said, "I would never, ever marry a German girl." And I was like "Whoa, why?" And he said, "No, because I would only marry a girl from Turkey." I asked why, and he said, "Because they are pure, they're virgins, they have to be a good housewife, and you can't find that in a German girl.". . . I said, "You have a German girlfriend." He said, "Yeah, and that's fine with me. I will have German girlfriends until I will marry a Turkish girl." I was so shocked. . . . I asked him, "You have sex with your girlfriend, don't you?" He said, "Yeah, that's fine with me. I have these German girls that I can . . . have sex with and that's fine with me, but my future wife has to be a virgin and she has to be pure." And I said, "Okay, I won't talk to you again.". . . [For] guys like that, I wouldn't be accepted, because these guys want to have really, really Turkish women. I'm not the one, because . . . I'm German to them. . . . My dad would put his hands together and throw me out of the house if I come and say, "I'm going to marry a Turkish guy."[32]

Monica* was born in Germany, raised in Germany, attended German schools, carries a German family name, speaks unaccented German, and holds a German passport. Yet no White person except her father and the interviewer in this study has ever treated her as if she were a German, because her mother came from West Africa. For most of her life she grew up in a small town where she, her mother, and her sister were the only people with any apparent non-German ancestry. Monica feels conflicted. At one and the same time, she feels fully German inside and longs for that to be recognized by the people around her.

On the other hand, she feels more comfortable in large cities like Berlin where there are other African-descended people. "In the inner city [of her current, very homogeneous north German town] I'm always the only one who looks different. Then if I walk through the city . . . Afro shops. . . . Where are they? . . . There are no Black people around. If I walk through the city then everybody was looking." Monica tells of being pushed on the bus by a White German man and ordered out of a bus shelter into the pouring rain by a White German woman on account of her color. She tells of White German female students shunning her, but White German male students coming on to her, with the assumption that she was an easy sexual mark because of her racial mixture.

> When we had to do some group work, I don't know if it was my skin color, . . . but the girls didn't want to be with me in one group. . . . And it's like always the only person who comes to me are boys, but the girls excluded me. . . . I don't think that [the boys] want to be friends. Maybe they want more. . . . Maybe they think it's interesting with some exotic woman. Because when we got [to be] friends then it all ends up that they were saying that they were in love. And when I said no, they went away. So stupid.

Monica is ashamed of a certain wish for Whiteness that is close to her core. "No [I did not want to be African]. Because I never knew any African kids, just White. . . . I don't have African friends. Just German or mixed. But Polish, Croatian, but not Blacks." Monica's boyfriends have all been unmixed White Germans. When she was interviewed, she had processed her hair so that its naturally tight curls would be straight. Then, after the interview, she wrote:

> [I]t is hard to reflect on one's own life and starting to realize that I never knew where I belonged to. It is hard to realize that my wish to have a blond and blue-eyed boy friend and kids might have something to do with a subconscious wish of being an ethnic German. But I was surrounded by White people all my life and the whole time I never even realized or thought about being different. It even happened that White people started gossiping about Blacks in front or even with me, strange! Because they even forgot that I am coloured, too.

When I was young I denied my African identity. I even was ashamed of having a Black mother. I am feeling so bad when I am thinking about my behavior towards her. But now I can proudly say that I am proud of having such a beautiful and special and coloured mother and I am glad that she knows it. I never had Black friends, because they didn't want to. The Black boys wanted to have a relationship with me, but I wasn't into Black, so they called me a Nazi. The girls hated me because their men wanted me. So what should I have done? I tried to.

It is a struggle to live between two identities. And I just now started to read a lot about my other identity. Because I am proud of being different. Even if it's not that easy sometimes. But I am willing to learn more about my African roots. Even my wish of becoming a teacher. I want it because I want to be kind of a role model for other Black children (foreigners in general). Because I don't know any Black teacher or foreign teacher at all. And I am sure they would feel better and they might feel that I am able to understand them better, because I know that it can sometimes hurt to be different. I haven't been supported by my teachers. But look where I am standing now. I have reached it by myself and I am willing to guide them [on] their way, because I believe that you can become whatever you want and if you have a teacher that supports you, it might become easier to achieve your goal.

You asked me what my children would be and I answered German. But it will still be important for me that they know where their second part is coming from and I will teach them to be proud of it. I think that my parents missed that part. I don't want to say that they did it with purpose. I am sure they just wanted for us to be accepted and that we should not even think about being different than the others.[33]

Monica's example may be an extreme one. Not all African-Germans or Asian-Germans had similarly nasty experiences, but most people of mixed-race descent whose pigmentation is darker than the German average are more likely to be checked by the police, have troubles when crossing the border, and so on. Only a few people in Germany see such racial profiling as problematic.

Furthermore, there is a recent trend among the German middle class to shut themselves against social groups that they might find threatening: migrants, people of color, people on public welfare. In a primary school in a middle-class area in Freiburg, several parents launched a petition asking for the establishment of a new class where only students whose parents were academics would be allowed. As only a small number of migrants have a degree, this would have led to an establishment of an all-White, all middle- and upper-class schoolroom. The headmistress would not hear of that, of course, but the fact that campaigns like that can be launched is worrisome.

Conversely, people who are regarded as having successfully integrated into German society always risk being regarded as inauthentic, either by the immigrant community or by the White majority, particularly when their pigmentation is ambiguous and they can pass as White. Miriam Nandi is often confronted with remarks such as "But you don't look one bit Indian" and "But you don't have a migration background, you don't even speak Bengali," which sounds almost like a reproach. By contrast, her youngest brother and her son (whose father is ethnic German) who are slightly darker are often complimented on their "tan" and often called *Inder* (Indian).

There is not one version of multiraciality in Germany. There are, at least potentially, thousands of stories that can be told by thousands of people in thousands of different ways. In this chapter we have tried to lay out the background for thinking about race and mixed race in Germany. The overriding idea of a unitary German *Volk*, described in terms of culture but defined by blood ancestry, determines membership in German society. Yet it does so unevenly. One might imagine that *jus sanguinis* would mean an ironclad one-drop rule of citizenship and social acceptance. But it turns out that mixed people whose non-German ancestors are White enjoy readier access to membership than do those whose non-German parentage hails from Africa, Asia, or the Middle East. Moreover, class distinctions lay across racial ones in complicated ways. Middle-class status may not make a person like Kristin or Monica seem more acceptable to monoracially White Germans, but being identified with working-class origins definitely makes Kevin-Prince Boateng darker and more foreign in the public mind.

So race in Germany is a tricky business, and so is racial mixedness. For many Germans, perhaps, guilt and shame about race are almost as disabling as straightforward racism. Perhaps the fear of being labelled "racist" prevents White Germans from actually confronting their own racism and coming to terms with it.

NOTES

1. This chapter combines the work of two writers: a literary critic of South Asian and German parentage who has lived as a mixed person in Germany all her life, and an American who in 2009–10 interviewed a dozen Germans who have mixed ancestry as part of a larger study of adult children of immigrant families.
2. Lockwood, *Informal History of the German Language*; Ammon et al. *Variantenwörterbuch des Deutschen*; Sanders, *German: Biography of a Language*.
3. Kohn, *Prelude to Nation-States*; Brubaker, *Citizenship and Nationhood in France and Germany*; Barbieri, *Ethics of Citizenship*.
4. Brace, *"Race" Is a Four-Letter Word*; Ripley, *Races of Europe*; Grant, *Passing of the Great Race*; Grant, *Der Untergang der großen Rasse*; Coon, *Races of Europe*; Coon, Garn, and Birsell, *Races*; Gobineau, *Inequality of Human Races*. The relationship between linguistic categories and racial categories has sometimes been quite complex. Yet there was in late-nineteenth- and twentieth-century ethnology an explicit link between group-average physical characteristics (such as hair, eye, and skin color, head shape, and limb and torso length) and linguistic features, alleged moral tendencies, and imputed intellectual capacities; Keane, *Ethnology*, 228; Hutton, *Race and the Third Reich*; Bartholomew, *World Atlas*, 22–23.
5. Barnard, *Herder on Nationality, Humanity, and History*; Barnard, *Herder's Social and Political Thought*.
6. Barbieri, *Ethics of Citizenship*, 12.
7. Fichte, *Addresses to the German Nation*.
8. Blickle, *Heimat: A Critical Theory of the German Idea of Homeland*; Miller-Idriss, *Blood and Culture: Youth, Right-Wing Extremism, and National Belonging in Contemporary Germany*; Chin, *Guest Worker Question in Postwar Germany*; Chin, "Guest Worker Migration and the Unexpected Return of Race."
9. There are also a number of film adaptations of the play, the earliest dating from 1922 and directed by the German-Jewish artist Manfred Noa. Stefan Drössler, liner notes to *Nathan der Weise* (orig. München: Filmhaus Bavaria, 1922), directed by Manfred Noa, written by Hans Kyser, based on the stage play by Ephraim Lessing (Edition Filmmuseum, 2nd ed., 2007); http://www.editionfilmmuseum.com/product_info.php/language/en/info/p26_Nathan-der-Weise.html, retrieved on April 16, 2011.
10. Göktürk, Gramling, and Kaes, *Germany in Transit: Nation and Migration, 1955–2005*, esp. 149–91; Senocak, *Atlas of a Tropical Germany*, xxxix–xli.
11. Gregor, review of *After the Nazi Racial State*.
12. The organizers' scruples about this term seem to have stemmed from a kind of politeness: the notion that race is an outmoded and nasty concept, so one should use another term in its place. A lot of White Americans make a similar rhetorical move, perhaps not always with such benign intentions. See, for example, such racially essentialist diatribes against Muslims and Mexicans, couched

in the language of religion and culture rather than overtly referring to race, as Huntington, *The Clash of Civilizations and the Remaking of World Order*; Huntington, *Who Are We? The Challenges to America's National Identity*; Buchanan, *The Death of the West*; Bawer, *While Europe Slept: How Radical Islam Is Destroying the West from Within*. These are examples of the racialization of religious and cultural identities and expressions. On the racialization of religion concept, see Goldschmidt and McAlister, *Race, Nation, and Religion in the Americas*; Blumenfeld, Joshi, and Fairchild, *Investigating Religious Oppression in the United States*; Rana, *Terrifying Muslims*.

13. Göktürk, Gramling, and Kaes, *Germany in Transit*, 105–48; Braun and Koopmans, "The Diffusion of Ethnic Violence in Germany."

14. Sarrazin, *Deutschland schafft sich ab* [*Germany Abolishes Itself*]; Schwarz, *Die Sarrazin Debatte*; Deutschlandstiftung Integration, *Sarrazin: Eine deutsche Debatte*.

15. www.verband-binationaler.de, retrieved on February 22, 2011.

16. Zinedine Zidane is a footballer of legendary achievement and Algerian descent who led the French national team to a World Cup title in 1998 and another World Cup finals appearance in 2006. "Ozil Flattered by 'German Zidane' Label"; http://soccernet.espn.go.com/news/story?id=815628&cc=5739, retrieved on August 19, 2010.

17. "Die große Rotation," *Berliner Zeitung* (August 1, 2007).

18. The German original sounds even more degrading than the English translation: "Ausraster, ein loses Mundwerk, Disziplinlosigkeit—im privaten wie im sportlichen Leben des Kevin-Prince Boateng ist bisher wenig glatt gelaufen." "Kevin-Prince Boateng Ghetto Kid aus Wedding," *Welt Online* (May 17, 2010); http://www.welt.de/sport/fussball/article7668946/Kevin-Prince-Boateng-Ghetto-Kid-aus-Wedding.html.

19. Oehmke, "Boah, Bruder, da ist Bierhoff dran."

20. Bhabha, *The Location of Culture*.

21. Appiah, "Identity, Authenticity, Survival," 163.

22. Up until 1975, you could receive a German passport only if your father was German. Therefore, Miriam Nandi had an Indian passport for the first months of her life and only received German citizenship when the law was changed a few months after her birth.

23. Bade, *Auslander, Aussiedler, Asyl*; Troen and Bade, *Returning Home: Immigration and Absorption into Their Homelands of Germans and Jews from the Former Soviet Union*; Igenhorst, *Die Russlanddeutschen*; Rock and Wolff, *Coming Home to Germany? The Integration of Ethnic Germans from Central and Eastern Europe in the Federal Republic*; Münz, "Ethnic Germans in Central and Eastern Europe and Their Return to Germany," 242–52; Roll, "Young Ethnic German Immigrants from the Former Soviet Union"; von Koppenfels, "*Aussiedler* Migration to Germany"; Bade and Oltmer, *Aussiedler: deutsche Einwanderer aus Osteuropa*; O'Donnell and Reagin, *The Heimat Abroad*.

24. Foster, "Successful Immigrants? The Stories of Polish Immigrants in Germany."
25. Friesen, *In Defense of Privilege: Russian Mennonites and the State Before and During World War I.*
26. Asterisks denote pseudonyms. Karina and the other people who speak in this chapter were interviewed in Germany in 2009. The interviews were conducted in varying mixtures of English and German and transcribed verbatim. We also quote from follow-up emails we received from some of the respondents. Some portions that originally were in German have been translated into English for the convenience of our readers.
27. Interview with Paul Spickard, June 24, 2009, Münster, Germany.
28. Interview with Paul Spickard, April 27, 2009, Münster, Germany.
29. Interview with Paul Spickard, January 30, 2009, Münster, Germany.
30. Göktürk Gramling, and Kaes, *Germany in Transit*; Mandel, *Cosmopolitan Anxieties: Turkish Challenges to Citizenship and Belonging in Germany*; Abadan-Unat, *Turks in Europe.*
31. Interview with Paul Spickard, June 22, 2009, Münster, Germany.
32. Interview with Paul Spickard, July 7, 2009, Münster, Germany.
33. Interview with Paul Spickard, March 6, 2009, Münster, Germany.

10

Capturing "Mixed Race" in the Decennial UK Censuses

*Are Current Approaches Sustainable in the Age
of Globalization and Superdiversity?*

PETER J. ASPINALL AND MIRI SONG

Can current ethnic and racial classification systems capture the growth
of "mixed-race" people in the UK? This question frames the focus of this
chapter. In a comparative study of national censuses around the world,
Ann Morning (see chapter in this volume) found that states can differ
markedly in the ways in which they employ forms of ethnic and racial
classification. One interesting geographical finding is that while countries
in North America and Oceania tend to use ethnic and racial classifications, European and African countries are much less likely to do so. There
are, of course, important historical and societal explanations for such
differences. There are myriad reasons for why and how specific countries come to classify their diverse populations in particular ways, and
this includes a state's willingness to recognize and enumerate so-called
mixed-race people—though which kinds of people are regarded as mixed
race can vary, often arbitrarily, across disparate societies. However, even
in societies where there is official recognition of a mixed group, such as
the Métis in Canada, such a group may remain largely invisible, especially
in relation to more "visible" forms of mixture (see Mahtani et al., this volume). It is simply a fact that, in each society, certain forms of mixedness
are more socially salient than others (Morning, this volume).

This certainly holds true in the case of the UK. Our focus is upon the England and Wales census classification of "mixed" people in particular, and we examine whether this classification system is effective in capturing the growing diversity of its mixed population. Official forms of data collection on ethnicity are often reductionist, whereby respondents are asked to shoehorn their choices into predesignated categories on a "best fit" basis,[1] so categorizing a highly heterogeneous population presents major challenges. While many scholars of ethnicity have argued for its fluid, multidimensional, and socially constructed nature,[2] the challenge of the decennial census is to capture the country's ethnic diversity in recognition of the fact that its classification system and findings will have saliency across government for the succeeding decade. In Britain, it has also deployed measures of religion, national identity, and language to address this complexity.[3]

A critical examination of official classification systems is important for various reasons, but the growing diversity of the British population makes this issue especially pressing.[4] While regional variations clearly apply, the emergence of superdiversity in cities such as London can significantly shape the ways in which "ordinary" people and officialdom conceptualize and understand notions of ethnic, racial, and religious difference, and their significance.[5] Complex webs of migration and transit contribute significantly to this growing diversity, and are important in shaping contemporary understandings of citizenship, ethnic and racial difference, and belonging.

Whilst Kibreab has observed a tendency in post-modernist literature to assume that the globalization process has given rise to the "erosion of spatially bounded social worlds" which has then led to "deterritorialisation of identity,"[6] studies such as by Waldinger and Fitzgerald indicate that people's allegiance to place may be multiplied to encompass countries of origin and the host society, thereby creating new connectivities, including transnational forms of identity, multiple forms of belonging, and complex patterns of rights and memberships.[7] Caglar argues that a "growing number of people define themselves in terms of multiple national attachments and feel at ease with subjectivities that encompass plural and fluid cultural identities."[8] Where migrants form interethnic unions, the patterns of those connections and identities for their offspring may be even more diverse.

Over the last few decades there has been an unprecedented rise in flows of global migration. In Britain, what we now see is an increasing number of country origin groups not captured by the census classifications. The ONS has estimated that in 2010–11 there were 56 overseas-born country of birth groups each comprising 25,000 or more people in the UK, some of which conceal multiple ethnicities, such as South Africa, Kenya, Zimbabwe, and Uganda.[9] Just five of these groups had matching census ethnic labels. Many groups (such as Somali, Filipino, and Sri Lankan) are currently hidden and invisible in "Other" categories attached to the "White," "Asian," "Black," and "Chinese/other ethnic groups" headings.

Another key source of growing diversity in multiethnic Western societies is the growth of intermarriage and "mixed race" people[10] (and see Mahatani et al., this volume). Like Canada, the US, and Australasia, Britain has experienced an increasing rate of interethnic relationships and a commensurate rise in the "mixed race" population over the last few decades. The 2001 Census enumerated a total of 661,034 "Mixed" persons resident in England and Wales, representing approximately 1.3 percent of the total population. The largest mixed group was "White and Black Caribbean" (35.9 percent), followed by "White and Asian" (28.6 percent) and "Other Mixed" (23.6 percent), with a smaller "White and Black African" (11.9 percent) group.

The "Mixed" group is now one of the fastest growing segments of the British population as revealed by the findings of the 2011 England and Wales Census.[11] Demographers having predicted a "Mixed" population in excess of one million, 1.2 million "Mixed" people were enumerated.[12] This represented a growth in the intercensal decade of 85 percent, varying from 80 percent for the White and Black Caribbean category to 110 percent in the case of the White and Black African category. Population projections had, indeed, predicted the "Mixed" group to rise to 1.2 million by 2020, though still smaller in this projection than the pan-ethnic (South) Asian (3.5 million) and Black (1.6 million) groups.[13] Revised projections indicate a "Mixed" population of 1.6 million by 2031.

After three decennial censuses, which have included a question about ethnicity (starting with the 1991 census), it is now timely to revisit the conceptualization of the "Mixed" group (and methods of capture) in the context of globalization, migration, and the growth of mixed unions and people. Over the last decade there has been an unprecedented growth in the literature on the "mixed race" population in Britain and how it identifies in ethnic/racial terms. In general, there has been little fresh thinking on how we can measure this increasing population.

Both the 2011 British and 2010 US censuses replicated the methods used in 2000/01 in spite of substantial further diversification in the ethnic/racial composition of their populations arising from migration, individuals' changing patterns of identification, and natural population change. This chapter focuses on the England and Wales Census because the count of mixed persons in Scotland and Northern Ireland has been relatively small and captured by an open response field (as opposed to tick boxes) in the 2001 and 2011 censuses. After a historical review of census development, we discuss what census categories may obscure, as well as reveal, about the British population.

The Evolution of the "Mixed" Category in the England and Wales 2001 Census

From the beginning of the 2001 Census Development Programme in 1994-95, there was unanimous support for including a "Mixed" category, primarily based on the recognition that this was a sizable and growing group: 230,000 persons had indicated that they were "mixed" in the two open response options in the 1991 Census.[14] However, unlike the US, there was no "mixed-race" movement in the UK that lobbied the census agencies for the change: the impetus came from users of census data in local and national government. Even in the US the mixed-race movement was not solely a grassroots movement amongst the mixed-race population but was strongly influenced by class, with many of those driving the movement possessing elite educational and professional qualifications.[15] The question tested in the 1999 Census Rehearsal was the one finally accepted for the 2001 Census with "Mixed" being captured by the four "cultural background" subgroups of "White and Black Caribbean," "White and Black African," "White and Asian," and a free-text "Any other Mixed background." Indeed, this test was the only formal assessment of these "Mixed" options.

The overarching term used—"Mixed" (which, in turn, has spawned the descriptor "mixedness")—neatly side-stepped debates about the existing nomenclature, like "mixed race," "mixed parentage," "dual heritage," "multiple heritage," "mixed origins," and others, all of which have gained some acceptance in different arenas. While frequently treated as synonyms, the terms reference different concepts (race, parentage, heritage, and origins) and some ("mixed parentage" and "dual heritage") suggest a background of just two groups. "Mixed race" is the preferred term amongst survey samples of young people and the general population who are themselves "mixed."[16]

Although the Census has used the "Mixed" label, the framework that encompassed the mixed categories was based on "race" in all but name (notably, the emphasis on color in the racialized "pan-ethnicities' of "White," "Mixed," "Asian or Asian British," "Black or Black British," and "Chinese or other ethnic group"). The three predesignated "mixed" cultural background categories are also suggestive of a "mixed *race*" conceptual base in that they all combine the term "White" with broad groupings like "Asian," in contradistinction to mixed ethnic identifiers utilizing the cultural background options, such as "White British and Indian."

Other national census agencies that have sought to capture the "mixed race" population have, similarly, eschewed difficult choices about the category label(s) by multiticking. The 2000 US Census used the instruction "Mark one or more races to indicate what this person considers himself/herself to be" (15 separate tick boxes—including four with free-text fields—being listed in the "race" question). Canada's 2001 and 2006 census questions (unlabeled) invited respondents to "Mark more than one or specify, if applicable" from 12 listed options, including one free text field. Those who marked more than one were described in tabular data as "multiple visible minorities." Where a generic label is used, it is frequently "mixed."[17]

The 2001 Census "Mixed" Options: Issues of Validity and Reliability

Based simply on *face validity*—the extent to which the mixed categories appear to be measuring what they were intended to measure—a number of critical observations can be made (and see Roth 2010 on Hispanics in the US). Firstly, the categories primarily privilege wider societal interpretations of "mixed race," that is, mixtures of "White" and *one* of the minority groups ("Black Caribbean," "Black African," and "Asian"). In accordance with this perspective, there is no mixed minority option (such as "Black and Asian"); such individuals have recourse only to a residual (write-in) "Any other Mixed background" category (see Mahtani and Moreno 2011; Mahtani et al., this volume). This has led some to argue that "the four choices offered for "Mixed" do not reflect the multiple sources that define people's mixed identity,"[18] (Finney and Simpson 2009, p. 36), which may encompass ethnic or country origins, religion, and nationality or national identity, and the possibility of multiple allegiances across these.

The rationale, then, in devising these "mixes" lay in the utilization of both the broad *section* labels and *cultural background* options used in the census question (see figure 10.1 for the England and Wales question),[19] though the "White" and "Asian" groups are reduced to single, undifferentiated categories. Such overarching labels provide a point of access to the longer-term historical processes that have influenced and shaped the nature of ethnic relations, including Britain's colonial projects in the Indian subcontinent, Africa, and the Caribbean; migration; discrimination based primarily on color; and the structural disadvantages that

WHAT IS YOUR ETHNIC GROUP?

A. White	D. Black or Black British
□ British	□ Caribbean
□ Irish	□ African
□ Any other White background,	□ Any other Black background,
please write in _____	please write in _____
B. Mixed	E. Chinese or other ethnic group
□ White and Black Caribbean	□ Chinese
□ White and Black African	□ Any other,
□ White and Asian	please write in _____
□ Any other Mixed background,	
please write in _____	
C. Asian or Asian British	
□ Indian	
□ Pakistani	
□ Bangladeshi	
□ Any other Asian background,	
please write in _____	

Figure 10.1. Ethnic Group Question Asked in England and Wales, 2001

derive from such broader processes. Census categorization, therefore, has to strike a balance between the myriad unique ways in which individuals may choose to identify in ethnic terms and the use of category labels that have meaning at the *population* level. Such categories have to build on a broad conceptual base and utilize a set of labels that are acceptable to respondents without burdening them with an overly long list of response options, which can increase the risk of nonresponse.

A second critical observation on the content of the "Mixed" options is the naming of two groups in each category and the use of a duplex (or double) write-in box. These point to an understanding of "mixedness" in terms of dual heritage (or mixed parentage) rather than more complex "mixedness," incorporating, for example, those children who have parent(s) who themselves are "mixed". As with the use of broad labels like "Asian," this approach is also likely to be reductionist with respect to the capture of a complex phenomenon like "mixedness," involving a trade-off between practicality and complexity (and its potential for respondent misunderstandings). If a critical mass of those identifying as "mixed" are, indeed, in the 'more than two groups' category, then this form of categorization may need rethinking.

Clearly, this trade-off is crucial in deciding the content of the classification. The primary purpose of the census is to provide data that is of utility for central government and other statutory public authorities rather than research findings of interest to social researchers. The intent of the census question is to obtain a top-of-head response to what a person considers themselves to be, in terms of an immediate measure of "mixedness" grounded in broader societal understandings of the concept of "mixed race." By contrast, an approach based on a person's ancestry (defining mixedness operationally) would capture a person's ethnicity in terms of their forebears rather than what they consider themselves to be. Data of the kind produced by the ethnic origin/ancestry questions asked in US and Canadian censuses produces a substantially higher count of multiple reporting than "mixedness" in population group questions and measures a different domain. Yet a middle way may be available through multiticking, enabling respondents to select more than two of the current categories if this was important to their "mixed" identity.

Finally, the use and prioritization of labels within the categories merits critical comment. The term "Asian" was used in the classification, both in the "Mixed" and "Asian or Asian British" sections, for the first time in the decennial census. The unguarded introduction of this term raises concerns about data quality as it is variously interpreted by the public as referring to people who have origins in the Indian subcontinent *and* continental Asia. Those who are mixes of White and East Asian (e.g., Chinese, Japanese) or Southeast Asian (e.g., Filipino, Malaysian, Vietnamese) origins may have ticked "White and Asian" *or* the open response "Any other Mixed background." Indeed, the countries of birth of the "White and Asian" group were heterogeneous, including 5 percent in the Far East. Further, while cultural background categories were privileged for the mixed "White and Black Caribbean" and mixed "White and Black African" options, those of Indian, Pakistani, and Bangladeshi background were subsumed under the "Asian" label, bringing into question the sustainability of this option as a "*cultural* background" category, and conflating race and ethnicity. Finally, the privileging of "White" as the coidentity—the first named group—may, for some, have triggered associations with White hegemonic culture and the asymmetry of race relations.

While the ONS has indicated that "the categories were based on the written descriptions collected in the 1991 Census,"[20] this needs to be questioned as the modus operandi for deciding new categorization. Indeed, the ONS Longitudinal Study shows that less than half of those identifying with one of the 2001 "mixed" groups used the free-text opportunities to identify themselves as mixed in 1991, and only a third in the case of the "White and Asian" group.[21] Given these low proportions and the relatively rapid increase in the size of the "mixed" group in the succeeding decade, the use of these 1991 write-in answers to decide the composition of the 2001 "mixed" categories was, perhaps, unsatisfactory.

After the 2001 Census, some of the foregoing critical observations based on face validity have led census users (central and local government and statutory and third-sector organizations) to redesign the "mixed" options.[22] For example, 12 additional codes were added by the Department for Children, Schools, and Families for "Mixed/Dual Background" for optional use in the annual school census. These extended categories were to meet the need for more finely granulated categorization, mainly to identify underperformance amongst several groups, which would otherwise have been masked by the broader categories.

With respect to the reliability of the 2001 Census "mixed" categories, we have virtually no data at all. Unlike the Great Britain 1991 Census ethnic group question and the US 2000 Census "race" question, no census validation survey was undertaken following the England and Wales 2001 Census. Consequently, there is no systematic data on test/retest reproducibility of the census ethnic categories. Those studies that have attempted to measure consistency in reporting the "mixed" groups in administrative data suggest greater instability than in the White British category.

Trying to Capture "Mixedness" in an Era of Superdiversity

The initial experiment of attempting to capture "mixedness" in the 2001 Census yielded a very substantial body of findings on this hitherto largely unmeasured group. Census classifications were also used in a huge variety of ethnically coded administrative collections by central and local government and in a large number of government surveys.

For England and Wales, the 2011 Census contained an almost identical "mixed" category set as the one used in the 2001 Census. The *section* label (see figure 10.1, above) was changed from "Mixed" to "Mixed/multiple ethnic groups" and the final open response option to "Any other Mixed/multiple ethnic background." While an ONS consultation found that the term "mixed" was acceptable to most data users, some argued that it could be perceived as derogatory, resulting in the renaming of the label.[23] While the three predesignated "mixed" options remain the same, "Asian" has been redefined by the relocation of "Chinese" from the "Chinese or other ethnic group" set it occupied in 2001 to the "Asian/Asian British" set in the 2011 England and Wales Census. Although a new "Arab" category has been added to the 2011 classification, there is no commensurate "White and Arab" mixed option. Findings from the 2011 Census are likely to provide the key source of ethnic data for governmental purposes until the early 2020s.

The Transformation in Ethnic Diversity

The addition of "multiple" to the "mixed" label in the 2011 Census provides a key to one of the most important demographic changes in Britain over the last two decades: an unprecedented increase from the

1990s in the ethnic diversity of the country. This has been driven by immigration (table 10.1), increased population mixing and interethnic union formation, and an increasing complexity in ethnic identification, frequently at the interface of race, ethnicity, nationality/national identity, and religion.[24] Large and abstract categories like Indian and African (so-called fictive unities) now compete with those that reflect our individuality and frequent multiple allegiances, such as "Ukrainian," "Mexican," "Gabon/French," "Arabic/Algerian," and "Punjabi Sikh."

The census ethnicity classification in its present form is no longer able to capture this level of diversity. Recently, for example, Vertovec concluded that census categories "do not begin to convey the extent and modes of diversity existing within the population today."[25] Hollinger talks of a "diversification of diversity,"[26] Baumann of "communities within communities, as well as cultures across communities,"[27] and Vertovec coined the term "super-diversity"[28] to describe this dynamic interplay of country of origin, ethnicity, languages, religion, regional and local identities, nationality, cultural values, migration channels, legal status, and the processes and practices associated with transnationalism.

Such a level of ethno-cultural diversity could, potentially, create hundreds of discrete categories for data collection. However, it is important to remind ourselves that some identities are more salient than others in measuring and tracking discrimination and disadvantage. For example, little importance in this context has been accorded to mixes *within* the five main pan-ethnicities. Moreover, not all dimensions of identity are legally recognized equality strands or bases of discrimination. Some sense can be made of this complexity through cross-tabulating person-level information in the census across multiple dimensions: in the 2011 Census language and national identity were added to ethnic group, religion, and country of birth. More attention needs to focus on the kinds of data we need and it would be premature to dismiss the Census.

However, there are challenges. Migration data reveals the emergence of substantial new communities (such as Poles, Filipinos, and Somalis). When subsequent generations are included, some of these communities may in fact be substantially larger. The lack of an obvious location in the Census may become conspicuous as some of these groups continue to increase in numbers. Population mixing between these groups

Table 10.1. Estimated Population Resident in the UK by Overseas-Born Country of Birth: Fifty Most Common Countries of Birth, July 2010–June 2011 and Position in 2004

	2010/11		2004
Country/rank 2009/10	Estimate	CI+/-	Estimate
1. India	694	36	502
2. Poland	587	33	95
3. Pakistan	442	29	281
4. Republic of Ireland	407	28	452
5. Germany	295	24	275
6. South Africa	234	21	178
7. Bangladesh	232	21	225
8. USA	188	19	145
9. Nigeria	174	18	91
10. Jamaica	150	17	136
11. France	130	16	95
12. Kenya	130	16	143
13. Italy	130	16	114
14. China	130	16	64
15. Sri Lanka	129	15	71
16. Philippines	124	14	62
17. Zimbabwe	121	15	94
18. Australia	115	15	112
19. Somalia	112	15	76
20. Lithuania	107	14	22
21. Romania	87	13	14
22. Ghana	86	13	76
23. Portugal	84	13	68
24. Canada	81	12	76
25. Turkey	76	12	61
26. Iran	74	12	62
27. Hong Kong	73	12	86
28. Iraq	68	11	50
29. Spain	67	11	51
30. Malaysia	62	11	51

Table 10.1. (continued)

| | 2010/11 | | 2004 |
Country/rank 2009/10	Estimate	CI+/-	Estimate
31. New Zealand	62	11	52
32. Netherlands	60	11	42
33. Slovakia	54	10	*
34. Latvia	53	10	*
35. Bulgaria	52	10	*
36. Afghanistan	50	10	*
37. Cyprus (EU)	50	10	74
38. Uganda	50	10	62
39. Brazil	50	10	28
40. Hungary	42	9	14
41. Nepal	41	9	*
42. Singapore	40	9	38
43. Russia	39	9	25
44. Japan	39	9	34
45. Mauritius	38	9	32
46. Tanzania	35	8	34
47. Greece	34	8	33
48. Zambia	34	8	31
49. Thailand	33	8	23
50. Czech Republic	30	8	*

* Not in ranking: These were countries not in the top 60 most common countries of birth in 2004, that is, those with an estimate of 14,000-plus. Source: Population by country of birth and nationality from the Annual Population Survey/Labour Force Survey (LFS), published by ONS, February 23, 2012. Accessed at www.ons.gov.uk/ons/.../population-by-country-of-birth-and-national on May 28, 2012.

and with the White British majority and other established communities is likely to take place at varying paces and in complex ways, reflecting such factors as the size of the groups, their geographical patterns of residence, and cultural attitudes to interethnic union formation. This mixing will produce a level of heterogeneity in the mixed population that is unprecedented and difficult to force into conventional census "mixed" categories.

In addition to interethnic friendships and hybrid cultural forms in urban areas,[29] the rate of interethnic union formation and offspring born to such partnerships will be influenced by changing attitudes to such unions. There is evidence, for example, that such unions may be becoming more accepted amongst second-generation Asians. One might also expect to see an increase in such union formation in areas of high ethnic diversity where no one group predominates, including those between people of disparate ethnic minority backgrounds. The fact that the most common interethnic marriages were between White and mixed-race people (26 percent) and the next between White and "Other ethnic groups" (15 percent) points to the potential for diversity in their offspring.

Finally, increasing diversity may arise from changing ethnic identifications. Some terms may be brought into wider usage as self-descriptors through processes of official recognition.[30] The availability of officially recognized "mixed" identities may, in itself, have catalyzed usage and, in much the same way, "Arab" may increase in salience as a self-identity following its introduction in the 2011 Census. Given the increasing recognition of—and value attached to—diversity in policy contexts, more people may choose to identify in their own unique ways when opportunities are present, as in the free-text fields offered in ethnic monitoring.

What Unprompted "Open Response" Survey Data Tells Us about the "Mixed" Group

Nearly all ethnicity data collection in service-provider and research settings has been based on the 2001 Census ethnicity classification. Therefore, the strategies that have been used to capture the growing complexity of the "mixed" population are limited. Our own interest has focused in particular on the availability of unprompted "open response" survey data for the "mixed" group, which may be an essential component of "superdiversity" and a population that could embrace multiple allegiances and identities. It might be argued that—where the goal is the accurate portrayal of identity and the capture of its multifariousness—such data best provides a point of access to superdiversity in that it is unconstrained by observer- or researcher-defined categories and the need to prioritize government-mandated groups.

A question on unprompted ethnicity was asked in our recent study of the racial identifications of 326 young (aged 18–25) "mixed race" people in further/higher education institutions.[31] The first question on the survey asked respondents to describe their race/ethnicity in their own words (an open response question). Such spontaneous descriptions are valid on their own terms. In support of the findings of the 2001 Census Development Programme focus groups and tests, the substantial majority of our respondents gave a *description* rather than a generic term only (like "mixed" or "mixed race"). These descriptions varied substantially in length, some combining just a couple of terms (e.g., "Mixed White/ Chinese") and some more extensive involving multiple identities (like "My father is fully British while my mother is ethnic Chinese & comes from Hong Kong. I have fair hair and only slightly Chinese looks. I am always mistaken for full Caucasian. I only speak English but have been brought up in largely Asian influences").

Overall, 60 percent of respondents named two groups and 20 percent three or more groups. A quarter (24 percent) used the term "half" (e.g., "half Japanese," "half English") and a small number fractionalized their identities in more complex ways (e.g. "quarter English," "quarter Irish," "quarter Spanish," "quarter Filipina"). Significant numbers—over a fifth in each case—included the national identity terms "English" and "British" in their responses.

What is distinctive about these unprompted open responses is their heterogeneity and frequent complexity, some combining racial/pan-ethnic terms like "Black," "White," and "Asian" with ethnic/national origin terms such as "English," "Somali," and "Polish" in the same description (for example, "My mother is English (white) and my father is Sri Lankan (Asian). I was born and brought up in Wales, which is what I consider my nationality to be (Welsh)"). While some respondents used

Census terms ("White British") and other expressions that included color terms like "black" and "white," only 14 (4 percent) explicitly referred to skin color in their descriptions, e.g. "My father is white Irish and my mother is mixed black Antiguan and white British. I call myself mixed race even though my skin is white."[32]

The fact that one-fifth of respondents named three or more groups challenges the "two group" format of the England and Wales 2001 and 2011 Census "mixed" categories, as does the frequent incorporation of national-identity terms in the descriptions respondents gave (as in "English, Welsh, Swiss, Kiwi, Indian, Singaporean. I am of mixed parentage—this is a good thing"). Clearly, it could be argued that this sample of young respondents attending university or college might be more knowledgeable about their heritage and more inclined to declare its full complexity. However, an analysis of 78 unprompted self-descriptions—the words used by mainly young "mixed race" people opportunistically interviewed in public (street) venues to describe themselves—yield similar findings.[33] In this "street" survey, the majority of respondents (65.4 percent) used two terms (e.g. "German/Guinea African") but 16.7 percent used three or more terms (e.g., "English/Greek/Jamaican"). Eight respondents (10.3 percent) used a generic term (e.g., "Mixed") and six (7.7 percent) a single group (like "Black African"). Again, the sheer complexity of terms, including bicultural labels, a "mixed" description as *one* of the named groups, and even regional identities (e.g., "Egyptian plus Jewish/Salford plus Jewish") characterize the set.

Another study had 130 verbatim descriptions (81.3 percent of those who selected "Other Mixed") given in a survey of over 9,500 young people (mainly 11–16) in Newham (a highly diverse London borough). These were individuals who eschewed the predesignated "mixed" category (thus a residual group), and who provided a write-in response to the "Other Mixed" category.[34] This data is interesting in that it provides information on the heterogeneous "Other Mixed" category, our knowledge of which was limited from the 2001 Census findings (in which no ethnic data was available for almost three-fifths of those who selected this category in England and Wales).

Many of the descriptions given by these Newham young people would be difficult to locate in the Census "mixed" categorization (e.g., "African and Russian," "Bolivian and Filipino," and "Mexican,

Bangladeshi"). Indeed, 78 percent named a *specific* country/nationality in their descriptions (e.g., "Portuguese," "Congolese," "Lebanese"). Twenty-five percent incorporated the national identity "British" in their descriptions (e.g., "British/Mauritian," "British/Yugoslav/Turkish"), 5 percent the term "English," and 4 percent "Irish." Again, a significant proportion in this residual category (11 percent) named three or more groups. Clearly, these young people more strongly reflect superdiversity than would an older cohort, suggesting that mixes based on categories such as those in the Census that have historical (including colonial) links with Britain may be of diminishing efficacy as a way of capturing mixed self-descriptions for young persons in areas of enormous cultural diversity. In such areas local authorities and other policy makers may need to consider the use of extended ethnic codes to capture meaningful "mixed" data.

What Is the Scale of Concealed Heterogeneity?

The scale of concealed heterogeneity in official "mixed" categorization in the country as a whole is difficult to answer as we cannot unpack the three closed Census "mixed" categories ('White and Black Caribbean," "White and Black African," and "White and Asian"), except through cross-tabulation by country of birth or national identity (where it is asked in surveys). The "Other Mixed" category is likely to be the most heterogeneous category and the one that perhaps best reflects the processes of globalization and migration. However, nearly all findings report it as an undifferentiated count—as did ONS in standard tables—and therefore of limited analytical value. This perhaps would not matter if the category count was relatively small. Indeed, in the 2001 Census only 155,688 people in England and Wales were enumerated as "Other Mixed," under a quarter (23.6 percent) of the "Mixed" population and the third largest "Mixed" group.

However, 2010 School Census data[35] (reflecting a young population) shows a very different picture. Amongst primary school pupils, the "Other Mixed" category was the *largest* group, accounting for 36.4 percent of 140,290 "Mixed" pupils, as it was, too, amongst secondary school pupils (35.2 percent of the 113,380 "Mixed" pupils). In 12 local authorities the proportion of "Mixed" primary school pupils in the

"Other Mixed" category exceeded 50 percent, including five London boroughs, and, indeed was over 40 percent in many others and also in major provincial cities as well as a few suburban areas. This is perhaps not surprising given that the highest rates of total international migration were recorded in London, the region with the highest non-UK born population. Also, the school data are for cohorts of young "mixed" people, reflecting relatively recent demographic changes.

In some of these boroughs there appears to be a marked age cohort effect, possibly pointing to the increasing impact of superdiversity. This does appear to be a new phase of migration to Britain, much more diverse and global in its composition and including countries not associated with Britain's colonial projects. However, it does not amount to a break from the country's colonial past: in 2009/10 the ten most common countries of birth in the UK included India, Pakistan, Republic of Ireland, Bangladesh, Nigeria, and Jamaica. A plausible reason for the utilization of "Other Mixed" is that people with heritages from highly diverse country origins simply do not see the relevance for them or their children of a set of racialized descriptors—"Black Caribbean," "Black African," and "Asian"—so closely aligned with Britain's colonial history. If, as the "mixed race" population continues to increase, the numbers in the "Other Mixed" category rise disproportionately, the utility of the Census "Mixed" categories for routine reporting purposes will diminish and in some London boroughs may have little advantage over a generic closed "Mixed" option.

Are Alternatives to Census Categorization Better at Capturing the Diverse "Mixed/Multiple" Population?

If the open response data are representative of the wider mixed population, then between one in five and one in six of the young mixed-race population have three or more constituent groups in their "mixedness" and between 30–40 percent choose to incorporate a national identity (such as "British" or "English") in their descriptions. Amongst the younger (teenage) cohort, almost four of every five in the "Other Mixed" group utilize a *specific* country or nationality in their descriptions. Hitherto, we have juxtaposed two *modus operandi* for collecting "mixed race" data: categorization as used in the 2001 and 2011 Censuses and unprompted open-response questions. While people do utilize the set of four Census "Mixed" categories to describe themselves, their choices are clearly restricted by the categories listed on the form. The four Census categories may also prompt people to identify more specifically than they otherwise might, ticking, say, "White and Black African" rather than simply declaring as "mixed." All census categorization involves some simplification of an individual's ethnic choices and it could be argued that the current categorization is fine-grained enough to produce meaningful data but not too diverse and fragmented in its coverage to be untabulatable or too unstable at the subgroup level. Open response, on the other hand, yields descriptions, which have high validity as they are unconstrained by a framework of response options. However, they lack utility for grouping people at a population level simply because the myriad different descriptions do not offer any easy route to aggregation into a smaller set of categories needed for policy analysis.

What are the classificationary options? Morning (see this volume) identifies three ways of capturing the mixed or multiple population in a cross-national survey of the 2000 Census Round (beyond open response): checking off more than one category; a generic mixed-ethnicity response option (like "Mixed," "Mestizo," and "Coloured"), and the specifying of one or more exact combinations of interest. Thus, to obtain more detail on the mixed-race population, we can either develop a more elaborate set of category options—a solution that, of course, may result in a poor response rate, due to complexity—or utilize multiticking (a strategy adopted in the US, Canada, and New Zealand censuses).

Our research on the sample of "mixed race" higher/further education students in Britain established the feasibility of using an extended classification (table 10.2) that captures many mixes concealed in the census categorization (such as a breakdown of "Asian" into "Indian," "Pakistani," and "Bangladeshi," the addition of "Chinese," "Other East or SE Asian," and "Arab" in those mixes involving "White," and the use of a "mixed minority" category).[36] While this classification would need testing in general population samples before it could be used in other settings (such as government social and general purpose surveys),

Table 10.2. Responses to 2001 Extended Classification for the "Mixed" Group[a]

Classification	Count
I. Black Caribbean and White	96
2. Black African and White	36
3. Other Black (please write in:_____)[b] and White	5
4. Indian and White	25
5. Pakistani and White	7
6. Bangladeshi and White	I
7. Chinese and White	I4
8. Other East or SE Asian (please write in:_____)[c] and White	2I
9. Arab (or Middle Eastern or North African) and White	24
10. A mix of two groups other than White (e.g., "Black and Chinese"): please write in:_____ [d]	I3
II. Any other mix: please write in:_____ [e]	75
I2. A single racial/ethnic group only: please write in:_____ [f]	9

Notes: [a] Mapping to 2001 Census categories: White and Black Caribbean (1); White and Black African (2); White and Asian (4,5,6); any other Mixed background (3, 7, 8, 9, 10, 11).
[b] Examples: "Native South American Indian"; "Asian."
[c] Examples: "Japanese"; "Filipino"; "Indonesian"; "Malaysian"; "Vietnamese."
[d] Examples: "South American and Mauritian"; "other mixed"; "Pakistani and Arab"; "Black and Venezuelan"; "Black and SE Asian."
[e] Examples: "Black, White, and Asian"; "White and Asian Caribbean"; "Half Indian, quarter Russian, quarter Dutch"; "Black Caribbean, Mauritian, and European White-English and Spanish"; "Indian and Hispanic"; "Black, White, and Chinese"; "Bengali Mauritian."
[f] This category was included for those with a mixed heritage—as captured in other questions on respondents' racial/ethnic identity—who wished to identify with a single group, e.g. "Black."
Source: Aspinall and Song 2013, main study sample (n=326).

it points to one solution where the unpacking of the complexity and diverse composition of the "mixed" group is needed.[37]

Arguably, a more elegant solution would be multiticking, since it can accommodate a much more extensive range of mixes than the specification of exact combinations (and does not lengthen the ethnicity classification). This option was tested in our research but respondents found it difficult to complete and did not satisfactorily enable them to describe their ethnic or racial identity.[38] Perhaps surprisingly, the information content (what the response tells us about the composition of the "mixedness") yielded by multiticking was poor. These findings which indicate that multiticking is not currently a recommended option for the UK were submitted to ONS (in England and Wales) and the General Register Office for Scotland and neither census agency decided to utilize this approach for the 2011 censuses after a further synthesis of the evidence.[39]

Post 2010 census evaluations in the US also raise concerns about the utility of this method.[40] Although multiticking yielded illuminating results from the viewpoint of sociologists and others interested in the phenomenon of "mixed race," for government purposes the low test/retest reproducibility findings produce data that performs poorly as a predictor of risks. Low reproducibility or inherent instability reduces the validity of comparisons across time, different geographies, and different administrative collections and introduces differential data quality into tabulations that include both multiple race and single race groups.

A final option would be to *add* conceptually to the measurement of ethnicity in UK decennial censuses and government social and general purpose surveys by including a question on a person's ancestry or ethnic origin, as have the censuses in the US and Canada. While such questions do not provide a measure of "mixed race" or "mixedness" at a population group level (yielding very substantially higher estimates of multiple reporting), they do give a measure of ethnic diversity. Such questions focus on country or national origins. The operationally defined, origins-based content of the question—asking about a person's ancestors or forbears rather than what they consider themselves to be— makes the question an unattractive substitute for one on ethnic or population group, yet valuable as a supplementary question on "community of descent."[41] The ONS has prioritized self-ascribed identity rather than a more mechanistic or prescriptive definition of ethnicity based on family origins. However, if the Newham data reported by Jones[42] on the "Other Mixed" group—with its very strong focus on country/national origins—points the way ahead, then this approach would have some advantage as an additional measure.

While our research did not include a census-type ancestry question, it did test a question developed by Berthoud that asks the respondent for the ethnic origins of his/her mother's family and father's family (using the 1991 Census ethnic group classification).[43] This question performed best of all the data collection instruments tested with respect to what it told us about the complexity and diversity of "mixedness." However, as with census ancestry questions, it too provided an *operational* definition of ethnic group rather than one based on ethnic identity and for that reason was removed in the 2001 Census Development Programme.

Conclusions

Multiethnic states such as Britain face various challenges in the classification and enumeration of ethnic minority populations in the future due to two main demographic changes.[44] First, in the new global migration, many of the new migrant groups have no link historically or culturally to Britain's colonial past, but comprise what Kymlicka calls "polyethnic minorities."[45] Second, a significant growth in mixed partnerships and people, and their increasingly diverse modes of identification, poses key questions about the validity and reliability of official classifications. Understandings of "race" and the significance of ethnic and racial difference are not only changeable across time, but are also sensitive to specific contexts and localities. Understandings of "race" and "mixed race" are moving targets, and thus there is always a potential disjuncture between ordinary understandings and practices "on the ground," and official measures of such complex phenomena.

Given the recent and continuing scale of international migration to Britain—resulting in an unprecedented level of ethno-cultural heterogeneity that has been termed "superdiversity"—our conventional census ethnic categorization, with its strong association with Britain's colonial past, may prove less satisfactory in enumerating the ethnic composition of the population. We do not have research findings on the "Other Mixed" group but it has been shown that districts that are ethnically heterogeneous—that have high ethnic diversity and where no one group predominates—encourage population mixing and interethnic union formation.[46] Amongst cohorts of young people the "Other Mixed" group has emerged as the largest amongst the four census "Mixed" categories, accounting for over half the population in the "Mixed" group in some areas. Open response data has shown that "mixedness" amongst this age group cannot satisfactorily be captured by *dual* heritage descriptors and that expressions of it are becoming increasingly tailored to a person's individual experiences, including the use of country or national origins rather than racialized pan-ethnicities like "Black," "White," and "Asian."

Furthermore, analysts must continue to address the interpretation of the ethnic and racial choices made on official forms. Such choices do not necessarily straightforwardly correspond with lived experiences;[47] nor do they tell us about the relative salience of ethnic and racial identifications in the lives of young mixed race people in Britain and elsewhere. However, the value of "mixed" categorization in the Census lies not just in providing a count of this population but in the very rich body of contextual information collected in the Census, including that on the demography and socioeconomic position of individuals and, consequently, also household and family members.

Where there is a need for data on the ethnic diversity of the population, new forms of data collection are needed. At a population group level, multiticking probably offers the best opportunity, in spite of concerns about data quality and response stability (further testing of which is needed to improve capture). However, "origins-based 'groupness'" may best be captured by an ancestry or ethnic origins question of the type that has been asked in the US and Canadian censuses.

NOTES

1. Aspinall Song (2013)., *Mixed Race Identities.*
2. Nagel (1994), "Constructing Ethnicity."Song (2003), *Choosing Ethnic Identity;* Cornell and Hartmann (2007), *Ethnicity and Race.*
3. Burton et al. (2010), "Measuring Ethnicity: Challenges and Opportunities for Survey Research."
4. Aspinall (2009), "Does the British State's Categorization of 'Mixed Race' Meet Public Policy Needs?"; Song (2012), "Making Sense of Mixture: States and the Classification of 'Mixed' People,"
5. Vertovec (2007b), *New Complexities of Cohesion in Britain: Super-diversity, Transnationalism and Civil-integration.*

6. Kibreab (1999) 'People, Place, Identity and Displacement."
7. Waldinger and Fitzgerald (2004), "Transnationalism in Question"; Favell (2008), *Eurostars and Eurocities: Free Movement and Mobility in an Integrating Europe;* Song (2003), *Choosing Ethnic Identity;* Levitt and Waters, eds. (2002), *The Changing Face of Home.*
8. Caglar, (1997), "Hyphenated Identities and the Limits of 'Culture,'" 169.
9. *Office for National Statistics. "Population by Country of Birth and Nationality from the Annual Population Survey/Labour Force Survey," published February 23, 2012. Accessed at* www.ons.gov.uk/ons/.../population-by-country-of-birth-and-national.
10. Song (2009), "Is Intermarriage a Good Indicator of Integration?"
11. UK Census (2011), http://www.ons.gov.uk/ons/guide-method/census/2011/index.html; Aspinall (2010), "Concepts, Terminology and Classifications for the 'Mixed' Ethnic or Racial Group in the UK"; Bradford (2006), *Who Are the "Mixed" Ethnic Group?*
12. Aspinall (2009b), "Does the British State's Categorisation of 'Mixed Race' Meet Public Policy Needs?"
13. Rees (2008), "What Happens when International Migrants Settle? Projections of Ethnic Groups in United Kingdom Regions."
14. Aspinall (1995), *The Development of an Ethnic Group Question for the 2001 Census.* Peter Aspinall was the ONS National Convenor for the ethnic group question in the 2001 Census Development Programme during 2005–2009.
15. Small (2001), "Colour, Culture and Class: Interrogating Interracial Marriage and People of Mixed Racial Descent in the USA"; DaCosta (2007), *Making Multiracials.*
16. Aspinall, Song, and Hashem (2008), "The Ethnic Options of 'Mixed Race' People in Britain: Full Research Report" (ESRC Research Grant RES-000-23-1507). Retrieved from http://www.esrcsocietytoday.ac.uk/ESRCInfoCentre/ (see "Awards and Outputs"); Aspinall and Song (2013), *Mixed Race Identities.*
17. Morning (2008), "Ethnic Classification in Global Perspective: A Cross-National Survey of the 2000 Census Round."
18. Finney and Simpson (2009), *"Sleepwalking to Segregation"? Challenging Myths about Race and Migration,* 36.
19. As a point of comparison, the 1991 census's "ethnic group" question contained nine categories: "White," "Black-Caribbean," "Black-African," "Black-Other, *please describe,*" "Indian," "Pakistani," "Bangladeshi," "Chinese," and 'Any other ethnic group, *please describe.*" The question instruction stated, "If the person is descended from more than one ethnic or racial group, please tick the group to which the person considers he/she belongs, or tick the 'Any other ethnic group' box and describe the person's ancestry in the space provided."
20. Bradford (2006), *Who Are the "Mixed" Ethnic Group?*

21. Platt, Simpson, and Akinwale (2005), "Stability and Change in Ethnic Groups in England and Wales."
22. Aspinall (2009b), "Does the British State's Categorisation of 'Mixed Race' Meet Public Policy Needs?"
23. The change also reflected a shift in the conceptual basis of the question from *cultural background* to *ethnic group or background*. The reasons for the change were not made explicit. Although the 2001 question asked respondents to indicate their "cultural background," the categories listed are countries or regions of family origin.
24. King-O'Riain (2007), "Counting on the Celtic Tiger: Adding Ethnic Census Categories in the Republic of Ireland."
25. Vertovec (2007b), *New Complexities of Cohesion, 7.*
26. Hollinger (1995), *Postethnic America: Beyond Multiculturalism.*
27. Baumann (1996), *Contesting Culture: Discourses of Identity in Multi-ethnic London, 10.*
28. Vertovec (2007b), *New Complexities of Cohesion.*
29. Back (1995), *New Ethnicities.*
30. Peterson (1987), "Politics and the Measurement of Ethnicity."
31. Aspinall and Song (2013), *Mixed Race Identities.*
32. Song and Hashem (2010), "What Does 'White' Mean? Interpreting the Choice of 'Rrace' by Mixed Race Young People in Britain."
33. Lincoln (2008), *Mix-d: UK. A Look at Mixed-Race Identities.*
34. Jones (2006), *Somewhere to Go? Something to Do? London Borough of Newham Young People's Survey.*
35. Department for Education. *Schools, Pupils and Their Characteristics, January 2010. Maintained Primary and Secondary Schools–Number of Pupils by Ethnic Group.* Retrieved from https://www.gov.uk/government/publications/schools-pupils-and-their-characteristics-january-2010.
36. Aspinall (2010), "Concepts, Terminology and Classifications"; Aspinall and Song (2013), *Mixed Race Identities.*
37. Song and Aspinall (2012), "Is Racial Mismatch a Problem for Young Mixed Race Young People in Britain?"
38. Aspinall, Song, and Hashem (2008), "The Ethnic Options of 'Mixed rRce' People."
39. Office for National Statistics (2008), "*Recommended Questions for the 2009 Census Rehearsal and 2011 Census*"; Scottish Government and General Register Office for Scotland (2008), Scotland's New Official Ethnicity Classification.
40. Bentley et al. (2003), *Census Quality Survey to Evaluate Responses to the Census 2000 Question on Race: An Introduction to the Data. Census 2000 Evaluation B.3.*
41. Hollinger (1995), *Postethnic America.*
42. Jones (2006), *Somewhere to Go?*
43. Berthoud (1998), "Defining Ethnic Groups: Origin or Identity?"

44. Aspinall (2009), "The Future of Ethnicity Classifications"; Song (2012), 'Making Sense of Mixture."

45. Kymlicka (1995), *Multicultural Citizenship.*

46. Feng et al. (2010), "Neighbourhood Ethnic Mix and the Formation of Mixed-Ethnic Unions in Britain."

47. Song (2010), "Is There a Mixed Race Group in Britain?"

11

Exporting the Mixed-Race Nation

Mixed-Race Identities in the Canadian Context

MINELLE MAHTANI, DANI KWAN-LAFOND, AND LEANNE TAYLOR

The whole world's mixing. There's nothing you can do about it. In about three hundred years, there's not going to be any more white people or black people. Everyone's just going to be beige. And I don't care. I'm already beige. We're all going to become some sort of hybrid between Chinese and Indian. They're the two largest populations in the world. And since we're going to mix anyway, why not start mixing now? Ladies, take some chances, sleep around a bit. If you see that comedian that you really want to have sex with, I say go for it! And while we're at it, maybe we should start mixing races now that would never normally mix, just to see what we'll get, like hooking up a Jamaican with an Italian. They could have little Pastafarians. I'm Indian, I can hook up with a Jew, and have little Hinjews. Get a guy from the Philippines with a girl from Holland—Hollapinos. Girl from Cuba with a guy from Iceland—little Icecubes. A French and a Greek—Freek. A German and a Newfie—little Goofies. It's gonna happen. We might as well help it along.
Russell Peters, *Call Me Russell*

Russell Peters is a Canadian comedian of South Asian descent who has built his career by exporting his brand of race-based humor internationally. In his stand-up routines, no ethnicity remains unscathed. He routinely rakes over the coals almost every racialized minority group. Peters has not only achieved national fame, but also global notoriety and great financial success. It is estimated that his net worth is over 20 million dollars Canadian. Peters has clearly struck a chord with audiences. Why has his racial-based humor resonated so strongly around the world?

We might begin by suggesting that racial jokes are a complicated pleasure. They can serve to reinforce racial prejudices and stereotypes, while also producing sites of creative subversion.[1] It is not our intention, however, to read into the merits and pitfalls of racially based humor, or ask if Peters adopts a transgressive stance that encourages the acceptance of ethnic pluralism. Rather, we are more interested in understanding how Peters' prediction of a new global mixed-race era holds particular currency. Through his bold and cheeky commentary on multiraciality, Peters reminds us that racial jokes can often serve as a barometer of social integration. They reflect attitudes and values of the zeitgeist and the racialized cultural geographies where one lives.

Critics and commentators alike have suggested that Russell Peters has been inspired by his experience of growing up in a multicultural country.[2] Peters has said, in reference to being raised in a racially diverse immigration suburb west of Toronto, that "growing up in Brampton, there were a lot of new immigrants. . . . There was a mixed bag of people, so I would learn a lot about everybody."[3] Others have further suggested that Peters, through his identification as a South Asian–Canadian, acts as a racial bridge: "as cultural hybrids, [comedy is used] to bridge a sensitive gap between the disparate worlds they inhabit."[4]

Peters has been commodified as a model of multicultural success. His agent markets him as a "naturally funny person with a multicultural outlook."[5] He has been deemed an ambassador for a multicultural Canada. Tourism Toronto officially named him the city's global ambassador in 2007[6] and one commentator went so far as to state that "Peters just may be the most charismatic ambassador for Canadian multiculturalism since Pierre Elliott Trudeau."[7]

How has Peters been positioned as an ambassador for multiculturalism? Scholars have argued that Canadian multicultural policy, which has served as a framework for national discourse on the construction of Canadian society, produces hyphenated identities (like Iranian-Canadian or Portuguese-Canadian), effectively positioning people who do not identify as British or French as outside of a Canadian identity through the use of the distancing hyphen.[8] Peters' riff on his predictions for a hybridized multiracial future is, of course, both superficial and sexist. But how does Peters' own hyphenated South Asian–Canadian identity inform his musings on the future of global mixing?

In this chapter, we interrogate the relationship between mixed-race identities and Canadian multiculturalism. We begin by briefly summarizing the history of the Canadian state-sponsored multiculturalism project. We also provide some general facts and figures about racial mixing in Canada before offering examples of the ways that some mixed-race Canadians understand multiculturalism as an ideology, policy, and demographic reality. More specifically, we suggest that mixed racialized identities can be superficially celebrated as living proof of the success of multiculturalism and in turn, a supposedly inclusive Canada. Yet, at the same time, mixed-race people continue to be racialized into categories of non-Whiteness and positioned outside of the nation-state. Mixed-race people play a crucial role because of the way they are positioned as key stakeholders in the success of multicultural policy.

Facts and Figures about Racial Mixing in Canada

Before delving into a discussion of the ethno-racial demographic realities of Canada, it is imperative to remind the reader that mixing between racial groups *in Canada* is not new. As Elam has emphasized in her critique of contemporary analyses of multiraciality emanating from the US context: "people of mixed descent are not a recent phenomenon: they have existed in often distinct, self-identified communities since the colonial era."[9] Elam has emphasized that it is important to ask new questions about the conceptualization of mixed-race identity in the current context. She suggests asking not why are there more mixed people now, but rather to question why it is that we *see* more people as mixed race now.[10] We find the work of DaCosta, who suggests the need to historically understand the contemporary vogue of racial miscegenation in part as a successful market invention, compelling.[11] As Mahtani and Moreno make clear, both popular and academic discussions of multiraciality have tended to disregard the experiences of non-White mixed-race people, "reflecting the common societal perception that the term 'mixed race' is synonymous with a black and white 'mix.'"[12] Canada as a nation-state provides a different context for a critical discussion of multiraciality between racialized immigrant groups because of the way that mixture is acknowledged in Canada through the category of "Métis" identity.[13] Arising out of two cultures most often designated as Euro-Canadian and Indigenous, the Métis are seen as the "children of the fur trade and the marriages between Amerindian women and the voyageurs."[14] The Métis comprise a population over 30,000 in Canada and yet remain underresearched and discussed in the current critical mixed-race literature.[15] What this backdrop does, then, is demonstrate that mixed race, as a category of identity, is legally embedded in Canada and yet this population remains largely invisible as a contemporary mixed group. As Culjak reminds us, it has largely been the Métis population who possess a distinctive culture that validates the complex racial identities of "mixed bloods" who develop a unified sense of ethnic consciousness toward the late 18th and early 19th centuries.[16] We believe it is important to briefly gesture to this population before we move on to critically explore multiculturalism in the lives of some self-identified mixed-race Canadians.

We provide a brief synopsis of Canada's demographic racial realities to set the stage for our discussion. We outline Canada's particular racial history, and hint at the ways this context has informed policy development. Canada's racist history is not fully unearthed in some policy circles, and that Canada continues to be represented as a country relatively free of racism, says something about the liberal image of the nation Canada seeks to export.

Canada has relied on immigrants since the 1800s, but since the 1960s, when major changes were made to Canadian immigration policies, the countries of origin of new Canadians have shifted from mostly European to mostly non-European countries. The Canadian immigration trends we refer to are also evident in other British Commonwealth countries; for example, Australian immigration policies prioritized European settlement, while non-European immigration was almost completely halted until the 1960s (see Perkins, this volume). Taylor, James, and Saul point out that for most of the 20th century, "Canada set out to control 'who' was able to become a 'Canadian.'"[17] In 1908, the Canadian immigration minister declared that "the Conservative Party stands for white Canada,"[18] and as Jansen has noted, "Up until the end of the second world war, Canada's immigration policy tended to be based purely on ascribed characteristics of prospective immigrants, in particular race and national origin."[19] Razack has also pointed out that immigration in Canada has upheld a particular racial social order in Canada, as it has been based on a "two-tiered structure of citizenship."[20]

Canada's image as a tolerant and welcoming place for immigrants— a view many Canadians uphold, and a reputation Canada holds internationally—must be understood as a superficial depiction. We caution that this image serves to downplay significant socioeconomic inequalities that racialized groups face in Canada. For example, in early-20-century Canada, immigration was restricted and denied to Chinese, Japanese, and South Asian people. In 1885, Canada implemented measures to protect a White settler nation, implementing a "head tax" against the Chinese. Japanese immigrants were also restricted entrance in 1920 (allowing only 150 per year) until World War II, when they were banned entry for more than two years as enemy aliens.[21] Japanese Canadians endured internment in prisoner of war camps, and were suspected of being spies based solely on their Japanese heritage. South Asian immigration to Canada endured similar restrictions in the early 20th century, having to endure "continuous voyage legislation" which required them to pay between $25 and $200 upon arrival to Canada.[22]

Not only were Chinese, Japanese, and South Asians in Canada controlled and excluded by the Canadian state, but so too were Africans, who have lived in Canada since 1628.[23] Africans or Blacks in Canada were routinely excluded because of what was seen as a sense of "benevolence," which decided that Africans were "unassimilable." In the words of the then Deputy Minister of Immigration expressed on January 14, 1955:

> It is from experience, generally speaking, that coloured people in the present state of the white man's thinking are not a tangible asset . . . . They do not assimilate readily and pretty much vegetate to a low standard of living . . . many cannot adapt themselves to our [cold] climatic conditions. To enter into an agreement which would have the effects of increasing coloured immigration to this country would be an act of misguided generosity since it would not have the effect of bringing about a worthwhile solution to the problem of coloured people and would quite likely intensify our own social and economic problems.[24]

This racist reasoning effectively dismisses the long history of African settlement in Canada.[25] Today, Canada is home to many more immigrants belonging to "visible minority" groups as defined by the Employment Equity Act.[26] The most recent census data on ethnocultural diversity in Canada noted several important trends:

- From 2001 (the previous census) to 2006, Canada's visible minority population increased by 27 percent (to over five million people, or 16.2 percent of the population). The growth of visible minority populations is five times the growth rate of the total population.
- In 2006, 75 percent of immigrants to Canada were visible minorities.
- The three largest visible minority groups in 2006 are (in order): South Asian, Chinese, and Black.
- Ninety-six percent of visible minorities in Canada live in metropolitan areas, compared to 68 percent of the total population.
- In 2006, 30 percent of visible minorities were born in Canada.[27]

In 1996, in order to more accurately provide data on racial minorities, the Canadian Census included an option that allowed individuals to indicate belonging to one or more group.[28] The driving force behind this census change was different from that in the US, which was influenced by multiracial activists' calls for multiracial representation.[29] Thompson points out that in Canada, "the enumeration of mixed-race people in 1996 made multicultural sense, aligning well with the (re)con ceptualized ideal of a Canadian multiculturalism that acknowledged and endorsed racial diversity" as a "positive value."[30] Because Canadians have generally been uncomfortable with questions about race, framing the census in a way that "endorsed racial diversity" and thus could be seen as "an issue of social justice and equality made it possible for the multicultural nation-building project to be re-imagined in multiracial terms."[31] As Song points out, multiethnic states face ongoing challenges of how to enumerate mixed populations, and this is complicated by the fact that there is little consensus on whether mixed people constitute a coherent group, or a racially disadvantaged group. Song goes on to point to the future challenge of enumerating the families or offspring of mixed-race individuals.[32]

Statistics Canada predicts that, by 2017, one in five Canadians will be a visible minority.[33] Mixed unions (marriages or common-law relationships between a visible minority and a nonvisible minority, or between visible minorities from different ethnocultural backgrounds) are also on the rise: in 2006, mixed unions made up 3.9 percent of Canadian couples, up from 3.1 percent in 2001, and 2.6 percent in 1991,[34] and many of these multiracial couples live in diverse cities like Toronto, Montreal and Vancouver. Mixed unions take place among a relatively youthful and highly educated population; the 2006 census data showed that the highest number of mixed unions occurred between individuals between the 15–34 age bracket. More people in mixed unions possessed a university degree (35 percent) compared to 21 percent of people in nonmixed pairings. Spouses and partners in mixed unions also displayed higher than average labor market participation rates, and a higher median family income.[35] There were also gender differences in the make-up of mixed unions in Canada. Arab, West Asian, Black, and South Asian men were all more likely than the women from their communities to partner or marry outside their group. Similarly, Filipino, Korean, Southeast Asian, Japanese, Chinese, and Latin American women were more likely than the men in their groups to be in mixed unions.[36] However, as Song argues, "there are various methodological and theoretical difficulties in establishing the link between intermarriage and integration, both of which are notoriously difficult to define, as there are multiple ways in which these concepts are theorized and operationalized."[37]

Multicultural Policy in Canada

Canada is envisioned as a multicultural society both inside and outside of the country. Abu-Laban and Gabriel emphasize that Canada is seen around the world as a place where multiculturalism exists[38] and Kymlicka explains that multiculturalism is understood as a "well-established practice, not just a rhetoric—and Canadian formulations are often studied as prototypes."[39] Enshrined in the constitution and embedded within government policies, Canada has had a multicultural policy framework in place since 1971, providing an unprecedented legislative context for the celebration of diversity and encouraging interaction between and among a variety of ethnic groups. At the same time, Canada has also been defined as an immigration nation, identifying immigrants as crucial assets in nation-building.

Prior to the institutionalization of official multiculturalism in 1971, Canada was described as a "bilingual and bicultural" nation, consisting of "two founding nations": the English and the French. One key difference between Canada and other Commonwealth countries is bilingualism and French-English relations. In Canada, a large French-speaking population (residing primarily in the province of Québec) has long played a key role in national politics. The Québecois and other Francophone groups in Canada see themselves as a distinct language and cultural minority, and this framework has been a key feature of national politics since European settlement began in Canada. As Nugent argues, the 1971 multiculturalism policy was partly a response to a large and increasingly important movement of immigrant groups who rejected the cultural dualism that the 1969 Royal Commission on Bilingualism and Biculturalism had put forth as a model.[40] Not only did the introduction of "bilingual and bicultural" policy bring the tensions between French and English into the public sphere for debate, but it also ignored Aboriginal Canadians as a founding people. As a number of critics have expressed, "many Anglo-Canadians are happy to employ multiculturalism in order to relegate Québec and First Nations to 'equal' (rather than 'special') status with other non-English cultural groups."[41] Many French Canadians, especially those in Québec, regarded official multiculturalism as a move to create a Canadian culture that absorbed Québec into the totality of the nation, as just one of many ethnic or cultural groups.[42] First Nations groups were similarly concerned that multiculturalism offered no recognition of official Indigenous status, and that it served only to reinforce the dominant status of English Canada. Mackey agrees with Handler that "multiculturalism implicitly constructs the idea of a core English-Canadian culture,"[43] and her book discusses how Aboriginal Canadians are "necessary players in nationalist myths: they are the colourful recipients of benevolence, the necessary 'others' who reflect back white Canada's self-image of tolerance."[44] As Kymlicka points out, the language of "visible minority," which was inherited alongside the shift to multiculturalism in the 1970s, does not include Aboriginal people, and this complicates attempts to address ongoing racism, discrimination and social inequality that so profoundly affect Aboriginal communities. He also notes that "multicultural" programs, even the most well-established ones, do not include Aboriginal people or communities, and that programs for First Nations, Aboriginal, Métis, or other Indigenous people are not considered "multicultural" programs.[45] First Nations groups and the Québecois have each made continuous efforts since the 1970s to distance themselves from official multiculturalism, and debates about the relationships of French Canadians' and First Nations Canadians' relationships to multiculturalism are ongoing.

Scholars like Fleras and Elliot, Kobayashi, and Bannerji insist that multicultural policy in Canada translates poorly into social justice for racialized minorities.[46] It is acknowledged that the promotion of Canada as a model of diversity and tolerance is incongruous with continuing inequality, discrimination, and differential outcomes for ethnic and racial minorities.[47] As Levine-Rasky and others point out,[48] there are tensions between the official act as enshrined in the constitution, which promotes liberal democratic values such as equality and fairness, and the persistence of discrimination, intolerance, and racism in Canada. This context is saturated with democratic discourses of racism.[49] It assumed that citizens in a democratic society are bound to principles of goodness, fairness, and equality. This influences discourses on multiraciality because "democratic racism permits people to maintain racist beliefs and behaviors while appearing to hold a positive notion of democratic values."[50]

Canadian multiculturalism as a policy and as a vernacular practice shapes Canadian institutions, identities, and everyday life. It is envisioned as a central feature of policy and planning at all levels of government.[51] Kymlicka insists that Canadians are unique because they have incorporated the accommodation of diversity into national identities and values, and that "Canadians view immigrants and demographic diversity as key parts of their own Canadian identity."[52] But definitions and descriptions of multiculturalism remain vague. Walcott uses "everyday multiculturalism" (also called "popular multiculturalism") to refer to the day-to-day interactions that take place in cities like Toronto, where people engage in the crossing of cultural barriers, participate in cultural translation, and remake themselves in relation to the other people and institutions in their lives.[53] Wood and Gilbert refer to three different notions of multiculturalism in Canada: government policy, social reality, and political ideology.[54] Following from Wood and Gilbert, how might we begin to understand how multiculturalism—as a policy, practice, ideology, and way of being in Canada—informs the experiences of some mixed-race Canadians?

Some argue that mixed-race people present a conundrum for multicultural policy because they are positioned as "ethnic" by the rules of multicultural policy, and at the same time, considered to be of English and/or French origin by virtue of their own mixed backgrounds.[55] We suggest in this chapter that mixed racialized identities are celebrated as living proof of the success of multiculturalism and Canada's respect for diversity and inclusion. However, such discourses often racialize mixed-race people into categories of non-Whiteness and position them outside of the nation-state.[56] It is notable that multicultural policy documents are peppered with the use of the term "ethnicity," encouraging Canadians to retain their ethnic identity within the boundaries of the nation-state, but the term "race" is noticeably omitted. This is markedly different from Mexico (see Sue, this volume) where race is used as a national marker. In Canada, this tendency has the effect of perpetuating colorblindness, making it more difficult to address racism. While some have read the multicultural policy's tendency to assert binary, hyphenated identities as liberating, we argue that it can also work to subsume expression of identities in complex ways.

The 2001 "Elijah case" provides a pertinent example of the way that mixed race has been addressed nationally in the courts.[57] This was the first case where the Supreme Court of Canada ruled whether race and racializing processes should be taken into account when determining custody for a child with parents from different racial backgrounds. The Supreme Court of Canada decided that, in determining the health and emotional wellbeing of Elijah (a mixed-race child), the racial difficulties he might potentially encounter were relevant to his case. In the end, Elijah remained with his mother as the main custodial parent, but the argument was made that Elijah, as a Black/White mixed child, would be perceived as Black. Questions were raised about the abilities of both sides of his family to appreciate and understand the daily realities that Elijah would face as a Black child. It was further suggested that because Elijah's father was African American, it would be easier for him to grow up in the United States, because there was a larger Black population there. As Walcott has pointed out, there has been little space in Canada "for imagining Blackness as Canadian,"[58] whereas in the US, despite a history of racism and ongoing racial inequality, one can be seen as both Black and American.

While there are some similarities between Canada and its neighbor the US in terms of demographics, large trends in immigration, and other language and cultural similarities, there are some key differences. Wayde Compton, a Canadian mixed-race poet and author, illustrates some of the differences he sees between Canadian and American understandings of race, in particular racial identity, Blackness, and mixed race. He describes the multiracial context in the US in this way:

> I think, oddly enough, that Americans have rendered the mixed-race conundrum easier, by virtue of their old traditions of extreme racist vigilance and the "one drop" rule. Because of that old system, even today it is hard to get African-Americans to accept the notion that anybody is "mixed-race." To them, everybody even remotely black is black, and any protest against that idea is greeted with suspicion and confusion.

In the Canadian context, Compton suggests that things are more pragmatic. He writes:

> Instead we tend to allow whites to define what is and isn't black, and white Canadians do so according to the colour metaphor, which they can't seem to see is a metaphor—to them, unless you are literally black-skinned (and who is?), you are not black, and what's worse is they have no word for what you are, and are likely to simply tell you "race doesn't matter," which, if you allow it, will leave you absolutely powerless and abject. That's white Canadian liberalism.[59]

Multiculturalism, as both vernacular and as ideology inform Compton's comments. As Taylor, James, and Saul suggest, racial identity is constructed, and necessarily informed by a social context of racism and racialization processes that identifies some people as "Other," regardless of their age.[60] Elijah's case provides an example of one of these instances; his White Canadian mother insisted on identifying Elijah as mixed race, while his father identified him as Black. It led the court to question: Can a person be both mixed race and Black at the same time? Such an identification reminds us yet again of the complexity of racial identities, further reiterating that there is no consensus regarding how family, courts, and larger society understand and locate mixed-race people.

In the next section, we suggest that mixed-race people are employed as emblematic of multicultural success in Canada. To make this claim, we cite from one of our author's current research projects, drawing from three of her interview excerpts.

Speaking Out: Mixed-Race Experiences and Canadian Multiculturalism

In interviews with self-identified mixed-race men in Toronto, Kwan-Lafond found that participants spoke about the ways that they felt Canadian multiculturalism shaped their lives.[61] Many of the participants noted that multicultural programming (cultural festivals and events) promoted wholesome, inclusive messages about social unity, inclusiveness, and diversity, while at the same time masking the realities of racism, inequality, and social distance that persist in Canada. Our first excerpt from Kwan-Lafond's interviews suggests that some mixed-race people believe that multiculturalism fails to address racism and racialized hierarchies. Multiculturalism continues to be viewed with skepticism by some mixed-race individuals, as Mahtani found in her own interviews with self-identified multiracial women more than ten years ago.[62] In Kwan-Lafond's interviews, Santo, a self-identified mixed Italian and Jamaican man in his twenties, emphasized that Canadians can partake in cultural celebrations without actually creating social bonds with the people from the cultures they are consuming. For Santos, this creates a genuine conflict:

> The whole multicultural thing can get cheesy, you know, like people who think they're all worldly because they like sushi, or 'cause they go to festivals and listen to African music, but they don't actually have any Black friends. That annoys me.

Santo's comments hint at the notion that in Canada, to be "worldly" is to be superficially savvy about non-White cultures through the commodification of the "other" including food, clothing, music, and other cultural goods that can be consumed on the multicultural market. As bell hooks has written, commodity culture "perpetuates the idea that there is pleasure to be found in the acknowledgement and enjoyment of racial difference."[63] However, these kinds of commodified multicultural practices often occur in the absence of meaningful social interactions with members of racialized groups, and therefore such efforts do not help to combat racism or cultural prejudice, but instead reinforce the maintenance of the status quo. They certainly cannot be touted as antiracist, despite the positive effects that partaking in culture as food, dress, or music may have on those who are not members of that culture. As hooks discusses, contact with the "other" as an intervention into racism is an "unrealized political possibility."[64] Santo implies that many Canadians believe that their contact with "other" cultures constitutes a progressive, and even antiracist, move. Multiculturalism as an ideology plays a subtle role in ensuring that marginalized groups are sometimes supportive and even enamored with the commodification of "otherness," insofar as it seems to offer recognition of their cultural group or other marginalized groups. However, as hooks reminds us, the "other" is usually presented in very recognizable forms, often derived from White Western narratives, and they do not facilitate critical analyses of the other in their representations.[65]

Santo's critique of multiculturalism is not remarkably different from the critiques leveled from individuals from non–mixed-race groups who have also insisted that multiculturalism allows for the superficial celebration of the three F's—fun, food, and festivals—harking back to the early 1970s "red boots" era of multicultural policy, during which the Canadian government funded various ethnic spectacles in an effort to encourage multicultural celebratory expressions.[66] Santos's comments about the commodification of otherness do, however, hold particular significance for mixed-race individuals who are further upheld as "symbols" of progress and racial/ethnic tolerance.

Speaking specifically to the way that mixed-race people are exploited in multicultural advertising, Manuel, who is Chinese and White (Italian/Dutch), explains how multiracial faces send a message about social harmony that is akin to war propaganda, in his view, because it presents an image of society that is in conflict with the ongoing challenges of social inequality:

> I've noticed that they use mixed faces in ads all the time, and sometimes I'll even see a mixed couple on a car ad or something. I think it's good. It makes it more normal . . . but sometimes it can remind me of like, war propaganda. You know like, big posters that say "everything is fine," "look, we're all living in harmony." But it's not true. I think we have to remember that it's still the media—everything looks perfect, but it's not real.

Manuel's critical observation that advertising capitalizes upon standardized images of what popular culture has come to see as mixed is powerful to us. His suggestion that such representations are akin to wartime propaganda is particularly potent. Some scholars have indicated that war propaganda has been utilized to ensure the diffusion of a deliberate, purposeful, and one-way message that serves the hegemonic status quo, rather than challenging it.[67] Manuel's musings about media images of a multicultural and multiracial world as unreal demonstrate that the manufactured and outward public face of Canadian multiculturalism may well be at odds with his social reality.

Manuel's views are similar to the perspective of other mixed-race Canadians, some of whom express their disconnection with Canadian multiculturalism. Karina Vernon, a participant in Nakagawa's documentary *Between: Living in the Hyphen* (2005) who identifies as Black, South Asian, Russian, and German, similarly questions multicultural ideology in the context of her multiracial experiences in Canada. As she explains, being placed in the realm of "other" (whether through feeling put on display or being asked questions such as "where are you from") "revokes [her] Canadianness." She adds, "I think that multiculturalism was never really designed to imagine me." Such perspectives offer a critique of multiculturalism in Canada that ultimately cannot and does not account for the experiences of particular racialized individuals.

Canada advertises itself internationally as a multicultural nation, and Toronto has worked to position itself as a quintessential global city. In an internet search of Toronto, tourism ads appear to focus heavily on the so-called cultural programming the city offers throughout the year. Caribana, the largest Caribbean-style cultural festival in North America, attracting over one million visitors annually, is often highlighted, along with proclamations encouraging tourists to visit one of Toronto's many ethnic neighborhoods (e.g., Chinatown, Little Italy, or Greektown). Participants in Kwan-Lafond's interviews took note of the incongruities between popular advertising images of multiraciality in the city and their racialized experiences. While Toronto is represented as diverse, and while we do not fault the outstanding social and cultural programs the city does offer, the reality is that wealth and privilege still falls largely along color lines, and social integration in the city is not a given.

What this brief excerpt from Manuel's interview encourages us to do is more critically consider the ways that some multiracial people believe they are uniquely situated to observe these incongruities. In Mahtani's research with mixed-race women in Canada, she found that some self-identified mixed-race women see themselves as occupying a space at the threshold of the margin, providing a perspective from which to consider the complexities of difference.[68] However, we are wary of the romanticization of multiraciality, which assumes that all mixed-race people read their identities as unique racialized subjects who, by merely identifying as mixed, offer up a special perspective on race.[69]

In our final excerpt from Kwan-Lafond's interviews, we reflect upon the thoughts and perceptions of Damien, a multiracial participant of Trinidadian (Indian) and White (Irish) descent, who comments on the rural and urban divide of racial diversity in Canada:

> Canada isn't really multicultural outside Toronto. . . . [In Toronto] even though everyone thinks they're so accepting, racism still completely exists. It's just nicer or something here, like people won't look at you as hard, but you know they're judging you the minute you walk into a store.

Damien's observations illustrate the subtle and multiple ways racism and multiculturalism are articulated through an understanding of Toronto as a "nice," and, it might be assumed, benevolent city. His use of the adjective "nice" to describe his perception of Toronto's urban geography is worthy of further investigation. Damien may be inadvertently gesturing to Toronto's nickname, "Toronto the Good," which derives from its history as a bastion of 19th-century Victorian morality. In contemporary parlance, the nickname is often employed to ironically refer to the city as either "less than great" or puritanical. Moving from the scale of the city to the scale of the nation, we are reminded of the work of Sherene Razack, who explores the ongoing presence of the imperialist narrative within discourses of nationalism, communicated through Canada's international reputation as a benevolent and lawful peacekeeper.[70] Damien encourages us to recognize the persistence of racism in Toronto despite the city's highly vaunted racial diversity, as if the latter prevents the presence of the former. Damien suggests that the perception of ubiquitous racial heterogeneity in Toronto does not mean that racialized individuals are subject to less scrutiny when it comes to storeowners making stereotypical assumptions about them as potential shoplifters. Multiculturalism as a legal, political, and social entity has served to support a model of white liberal tolerance through a vocabulary of good intentions. At the same time, however, it continues to underpin a complicit politics that does not fully address ongoing patterns of racism.

We include this excerpt with Damien because for some of Kwan-Lafond's interviewees, multiculturalism was rarely discussed without an accompanying conversation about the persistent reality of racism in their day-to-day lives. Interviewees seem to be generally supportive of increased diversity and policies that aim to advance multicultural policy, but they are frustrated with the continuing evidence of covert, subtle, and structural forms of racism in Canada. It is clear that not much has changed over time: more than ten years ago, Mahtani emphasized in her study of mixed-race women that "multicultural policy, where ethnic identities are celebrated as a backdrop for Canadian identity, often ensures that forms of institutionalized racism are rendered invisible."[71] Clearly, Canadian multiculturalism falls short in terms of perceived antiracist gains for some participants in both Mahtani's research then, and Kwan-Lafond's research now.

Towards a Critical Mixed-Race Politics in Canada

To conclude, we return to the Statistics Canada data cited earlier in the chapter. In light of our discussion of mixed-race identity in the

Canadian context, how might we more critically read Statistics Canada's assertion that mixed unions between visible and nonvisible minorities have significantly increased, leading to their prediction that by 2017, one in five Canadians will be a visible minority? In a Statistics Canada report on mixed unions, Milan and Hamm declare:

> Mixed unions can be seen as 'an engine of social change' by fostering positive attitudes toward visible minority groups, and by linking the social and family networks of the two partners.[72]

This comment suggests that we are moving toward a post-race state of change expedited through multiracial unions. Others have taken on the 2017 prediction as evidence of an emergent racially harmonious future and have even used it to predict coming social and economic possibilities in our increasingly diverse context. For example, in a working paper for a series entitled Research on Immigration and Integration in the Metropolis (RIIM), Pendakur draws on Statistics Canada's 2017 report and writes:

> We may hope that as the diversity of Canadian society grows, our sense of differentness diminishes, and the visibility of ethnic minorities disappears.[73]

We encourage readers to interpret these commentaries suspiciously. As self-identified mixed-race Canadians ourselves, we do not share in what we read as the authors' naive hope that ethnic minorities will become less visible, nor do we wish for a sense of differentness (whatever that may mean) to ebb. As Kwan-Lafond's interviews highlight, racialized and multiracial individuals experience a range of contradictions and challenges in Canada, despite its diversifying population and multicultural policy. Moreover, we recognize that intermarriage itself may not be the best indicator of integration, nor does it, as Song suggests, "ensure wholesale social acceptance."[74] Song cautions against such perceptions of intermixing as becoming the "you have made it litmus test," reminding us that "just as marriage into a White mainstream family does not guarantee a warm welcome and social acceptance, the experiences of 'mixed-race' offspring may be highly variable, with some experiencing their mixedness in predominantly positive ways, while others may perceive prejudice and various barriers because of their mixed ancestry."[75] Further, the preponderance of racial discrimination and exclusion in contexts such as Brazil (a society marked by a long history of racial and cultural mixing) supports the argument that racial intermarriage and mixed-race children do not challenge racism.[76]

However, Milan and Hamm and Pendakur are not alone in framing multiracial unions (including their offspring) and the disappearance of ethnic difference as something to which we should aspire. We return to the comedic spiel of Russell Peters discussed earlier in this chapter, where he asserts that "everyone's just going to be beige" and that "we're going to mix anyway," portending a color-blind mixed-race global future that will supposedly lead us to a universal racial way of being. The Statistics Canada study, Pendakur's report, and Peter's comedy intimate a movement toward, and desire for, racial sameness. These ideals animate the broader Canadian racial imagination.

We have argued in this chapter that mixed-race bodies are employed as living proof of racial progress in Canada, and are often used to propel simplistic mixed-race mythologies forward. While we are witnessing an increase in the panoply of representations of mixed-race identity in Canada,[77] it is important not to assume that these images are used solely to counter racism. Rather, images and ideas of mixed race can be galvanized and appropriated by various ideological camps in order to support their own arguments and agendas.[78] The types of privileges that are sought and gained through discourses of mixture reveal that Canadian racism is not the overt ugly beast that it is often thought to be. Forms of racism are taking on more nuanced and complex shapes in Canada. Social justice efforts that are meant to challenge oppression must account for the ways in which new privileges are fostered, nurtured, and sustained through an enduring politics of difference.

The interviews from Kwan-Lafond's research point us in an important direction—they illuminate the myriad ways that Canadian multiculturalism informs the lived experiences of some mixed-race individuals. For Santo, Manuel, and Damien, being mixed race is, in part, informed by the nation's preoccupation with commodifying and consuming particular differences through festivals, food, and fun; presenting itself as a "land of tolerance" through racial/ethnic propaganda; or assuming that urban and diverse contexts like Toronto are especially welcoming and free of bias. We are reminded to be vigilant to stealth-like neoliberal discourses of colorblindness ("we are all the same").[79] We further caution against the prevailing tendency to proclaim mixed race as an antiracist category of identity in and of itself, but rather to include within any critical conversation about multiraciality an attempt to complicate the privileges and premature celebration that tend to become attached to mixed-race issues and people.

We also think it is crucial to ask what is, in fact, actually unique about the perspective of mixed-race men in Kwan-Lafond's study in relation to larger Canadian and, ultimately, global questions and perspectives of racial mixture and racialization. Overall, the interviews not only reflect their experiences of multiculturalism but also point to their complex and shifting relationship with the nation-state. We offer some final comments on the Canadian context and in light of the focus of this edited collection. Giving attention to mixed people's experiences and perceptions in different national contexts allows us to question how laws, policies, and societal norms inform the perceptions and actions of communities, institutions, and individuals. Kwan-Lafond's interviews help us think about broader understandings of Canadian identity against which mixed race gets understood. The stories we shared here point to the different ways mixed-race people position themselves against exported readings of Canada as multicultural and tolerant.

The interviews further encourage us to ask how mixed-race Canadians negotiate and express their identities in ways that might wed them to the nation. What gets emphasized? What gets left out? Despite Canada's attempts to export an image of Canada as diverse, multicultural, and multiracial, claiming a mixed-race identity in Canada does not necessarily bring one closer to a sense of Canadianness, as might be the case in contexts like Mexico and Brazil where increasing expressions of mixed-race identity reflect national racial sentiments and are often privileged and asserted as a way of reaffirming a national identity such as "Mexicanness" or "Brazilness."[80] As stories of mixed-race people in Canada suggest, there is a disconnect between how individuals might identify individually and how they feel race and mixed race are constructed, commodified, and used on national and global levels. Multiculturalism still upholds hyphenated ideas of cultural and ethnic belonging—to identify as racially mixed is more difficult (even if it is privileged and celebrated nationally) because the discourse of multiculturalism does not allow for very fluid racial distinctions. Instead, there are clear markers of ethnicity and culture, which, while significant, are often essentialized.

The racial-identity expectations among Canadians may also play a role in mixed-race people's experiences. As Song and Aspinall explain in their study of racial perceptions of mixed-race young people in Britain, mixed-race people who did not expect their identifications to be validated and who did not associate their encounters with and identifications by others as racial prejudice tended to view their experiences as positive.[81] In this context, the more some mixed-race interviewees held high expectations and cared about outward validation of their identities, the more they felt misrecognized. Similarly, in Canada we question how particular expectations around multiculturalism as a quintessential Canadian value impact mixed race interactions and perceptions of their racialized selves. As Song and Aspinall suggest, it may well be that "a growing public recognition of mixed people . . . may not necessarily or automatically correspond with an enhanced set of individual ethnic options."[82]

Kwan-Lafond's interviewees offer an opportunity to clarify the difference between mixed-race individuals' experiences and perceptions of race, and other racialized individuals' (those individuals who do not identify as mixed race) experiences and perceptions. Phenotype plays a vital role here, but it is only one of many variables that influence mixed-race experiences. Some mixed-race Canadians may well be seen as members of a racialized minority group, whereas other mixed-race Canadians may be perceived as White. This difference may influence some mixed-race Canadians' perceptions, beliefs, and understandings of both race and racism. Racialized people who do not identify as mixed race also may experience a variety of forms of racial oppression, regardless of how they identify. Rockquemore, Brunsma, and Delgado recommend that researchers rethink the use of the term "race" in their analyses and instead distinguish between racial identity (an individual's self-understanding), racial identification (how others understand and categorize an individual), and racial category (what racial identities are available and chosen in a specific context), paying particular attention to the overlaps and discontinuities between the three.[83]

Lastly, we return to the work of Michele Elam who, as we suggested earlier, reminds us that racial mixture is nothing new.[84] What Kwan-Lafond's interviews illustrate is that while multiracial individuals may offer us valuable insights on the validity and utility of multiculturalism as a political, social, and cultural reality, we must also resist envisioning this critique as symbolic of multiracial newness or in ways that detract us from the importance of contributing to broader racial struggles and antiracist endeavors on a global scale. By asking how mixed bodies are taken up, ignored, commodified, constructed, celebrated, exploited, and deployed as neoliberal figures, we hope future analyses will move beyond seeing mixture as novel and instead ask how a more critical excavation of Canadian mixed-race identities might open up a radically different antiracist intellectual landscape.

NOTES

1. Francis, *Creative Subversions: Whiteness and Indigeneity in the National Imaginary*; Hirji, "Somebody Going to Get Hurt Real Bad: The Race-Based Comedy of Russell Peters."
2. Hirji, ibid.
3. Peters in Hirji, ibid., 578.
4. Lawrence in Hirji, ibid.
5. Hirji, ibid., 572.
6. Bonoguore, "Funnyman Peters to Talk Up Toronto."
7. Von Baeyer, "King of Multi-Culti," 56. Trudeau is the prime minister of Canada who oversaw the inauguration of a national multicultural policy.
8. Mahtani, "Interrogating the Hyphen-Nation: Canadian Multicultural Policy and 'Mixed Race' Identities."
9. Elam, *The Souls of Mixed Folk: Race, Politics and Aesthetics in the New Millennium*, 6.
10. Ibid.
11. DaCosta, *Making Multiracials: State, Family and Market in the Redrawing of the Color Line*.
12. Mahtani and Moreno, "Same Difference: Towards a More Unified Discourse in 'Mixed Race' Theory," 71.
13. Teillet, *The Métis of the Northwest: Towards A Definition of a Rights-Bearing Community for a Mobile People*.
14. Ibid.

15. Although see Mawani, *Colonial Proximities: Crossracial Encounters and Juridicial Truths in British Columbia, 1871–1921* ; Culjak, "Searching for a Place in Between: The Autobiographies of Three Canadian Metis Women"; Augustus, *Mixed Race, Legal Space: A Comparative History of Mixed-Ancestry Native Legal Identity in Canada, the U.S., and Australia, 1850–1950.*

16. Culjak, ibid.

17. Taylor, James, and Saul, "Who Belongs: Exploring Race and Racialization in Canada."

18. James, *Seeing Ourselves: Exploring Race, Ethnicity and Culture*, 243.

19. Jansen, "Problems and Issues in Post-war Immigration to Canada and Their Effects on Origins and Characteristics of Immigrants," 19.

20. Razack, *Dark Threats and White Knights: The Somalia Affair, Peacekeeping and the New Imperialism*, 4.

21. Taylor, James, and Saul, "Who Belongs: Exploring Race and Racialization in Canada."

22. Kelley and Trebilcock, *The Making of the Mosaic: A History of Canadian Immigration.*

23. Taylor, James, and Saul, "Who Belongs: Exploring Race and Racialization in Canada."

24. Calliste, "Race, Gender and Canadian Immigration Policy: Blacks from the Caribbean, 1900–1932," 136.

25. James, *Seeing Ourselves: Exploring Race, Ethnicity and Culture.*

26. More specifically, the term "visible minority" is defined by the *Employment Equity Act* (1986, 1995) as "persons, other than aboriginal peoples, who are non-Caucasian in race and non-white in colour." It is interesting to note that, in 2007, the United Nations Committee for the Elimination of Racial Discrimination criticized Canada's use of the term "visible minority" as discriminatory. The UN Committee argued that its usage violates the International Convention on the Elimination of All Forms of Racial Discrimination, which holds that any distinctions based on race, national or ethnic origin, or descent are discriminatory (http://www.cbc.ca/news/canada/story/2007/03/08/canada-minorities.html). Canada was asked to "reflect further" on its use of the term, and in 2011, it responded with a 74-page report examining the history of "visible minorities" over the years. The report argued that the term is "specific to the administration of the Employment Equity Act" and declared that Canada has no intentions of changing its usage of the term (http://www2.macleans.ca/tag/tom-flanagan/).

27. Statistics Canada, "Canada's Ethnocultural Mosaic."

28. This information was requested under the category "Population group." Response categories in the population group question on the Census included 11 mark-in circles and one write-in space. Respondents were asked "Is this person:" and instructed to mark more than one of the following response categories, or to specify another group, if applicable:

- White
- Chinese
- South Asian (e.g., East Indian, Pakistani, Sri Lankan, etc.)
- Black
- Filipino
- Latin American
- Southeast Asian (e.g., Vietnamese, Cambodian, Malaysian, Laotian, etc.)
- Arab
- West Asian (e.g., Iranian, Afghan, etc.)
- Korean
- Japanese
- Other—Specify

Respondents were informed that the collected information would be used to support programs that promote equal opportunity for everyone to share in the social, cultural, and economic life of Canada. In 2006, the Census Guide added the following instructions: "Population group should not be confused with citizenship or nationality," and "For persons who belong to more than one population group, mark all the circles that apply. Do not report 'bi-racial' or 'mixed' in the box provided" (Statistics Canada).

29. DaCosta, *Making Multiracials: State, Family and Market in the Redrawing of the Color Line.*
30. Thompson, "Making (Mixed-)Race: Census Politics and the Emergence of Multiracial Multiculturalism in the United States, Great Britain and Canada," 12–13.
31. Ibid., 13.
32. Song, "Is Intermarriage a Good Indicator of Integration?"
33. Bélanger and Caron Malenfant, "Ethnocultural Diversity in Canada: Prospects for 2017."
34. Statistics Canada, "Canada's Ethnocultural Mosaic."
35. Milan, Maheux, and Chui, "A Portrait of Couples in Mixed Unions."
36. Ibid.
37. Song, "Is Intermarriage a Good Indicator of Integration?", 333.
38. Abu-Laban and Gabriel, *Selling Diversity: Immigration, Multiculturalism, Employment Equity, and Globalization.*
39. Kymlicka, *Multicultural Odysseys: Navigating the New International Politics of Diversity*, 107.
40. Nugent, "Demography, National Myths, and Political Origins: Perceiving Official Multiculturalism in Québec."
41. Wood and Gilbert, "Multiculturalism in Canada: Accidental Discourse, Alternative Vision, Urban Practice."
42. Handler, *Nationalism and the Politics of Culture in Québec*, 125–26.
43. Mackey, *The House of Difference: Cultural Politics and National Identity in Canada*, 15.
44. Ibid.

45. Kymlicka, *Multicultural Citizenship: A Liberal Theory of Minority Rights.*
46. Fleras and Elliot, *Multiculturalism in Canada: The Challenge of Diversity;* Kobayashi, "Multiculturalism: Representing a Canadian Institution"; Bannerji, *The Dark Side of the Nation: Essays on Multiculturalism, Nationalism and Gender.*
47. Biles, Ibrahim, and Tolley, "Does Canada Have a Multicultural Future?"
48. Levine-Rasky, "Discontinuities of Multiculturalism"; Bannerji, *The Dark Side of the Nation: Essays on Multiculturalism, Nationalism and Gender.*
49. Henry and Tator, *The Colour of Democracy: Racism in Canadian Society.*
50. Dei, "Speaking Race: Silence, Salience, and the Politics of Anti-racist Scholarship."
51. Wood and Gilbert, "Multiculturalism in Canada: Accidental Discourse, Alternative Vision, Urban Practice."
52. Kymlicka, *Multicultural Citizenship: A Liberal Theory of Minority Rights,* 7.
53. Walcott, "What is the Future of Multiculturalism? Ask the Experts."
54. Wood and Gilbert, "Multiculturalism in Canada: Accidental Discourse, Alternative Vision, Urban Practice."
55. Mahtani, "Interrogating the Hyphen-Nation: Canadian Multicultural Policy and 'Mixed Race' Identities."
56. See Kwan-Lafond, "*Mixed Race Men in Canada: Identities, Masculinities and Multiculturalism*"; Mahtani, "Interrogating the Hyphen-Nation: Canadian Multicultural Policy and 'Mixed Race' Identities."
57. Edwards vs. Van de Perre.
58. Walcott, *Black Like Who? Writing Black Canada,* 48.
59. Wilkinson and Stouck, "The Epic Moment: An Interview with Wayde Compton."
60. Taylor, James, and Saul, "Who Belongs: Exploring Race and Racialization in Canada."
61. Kwan-Lafond, "*Mixed Race Men in Canada: Identities, Masculinities and Multiculturalism.*"
62. Mahtani, "Interrogating the Hyphen-Nation: Canadian Multicultural Policy and 'Mixed Race' Identities."
63. hooks, *Black Looks: Race and Representation,* 21.
64. Ibid.
65. Ibid.
66. See Mahtani, "Interrogating the Hyphen-Nation: Canadian Multicultural Policy and 'Mixed Race' Identities"; Mackey, *The House of Difference: Cultural Politics and National Identity in Canada;* Fleras and Elliott, *Multiculturalism in Canada: The Challenge of Diversity.*
67. Snow, *Information War: American Propaganda, Free Speech and Opinion Control since 9/11.*
68. Mahtani, "Mixed Metaphors: Situating Mixed Race Identity."
69. See McNeil, *Sex and Race in the Black Atlantic.*

70. Razack, *Dark Threats and White Knights: The Somalia Affair, Peacekeeping and the New Imperialism.*
71. Mahtani, "Interrogating the Hyphen-Nation: Canadian Multicultural Policy and 'Mixed Race' Identities," 475.
72. Milan and Hamm, "Mixed Unions," 2.
73. Pendakur, "Visible Minorities in Canada's Workplaces: A Perspective on the 2017 Projection," 2.
74. Song, "Is Intermarriage a Good Indicator of Integration?", 343.
75. Ibid., 341.
76. See Daniel and Lee, this volume.
77. See McNeil, *Sex and Race in the Black Atlantic;* DeRango-Adem and Thompson, *Other Tongues: Mixed-Race Women Speak Out;* Hill, *Black Berry, Sweet Juice;* Taylor, *Re-imagining Mixed Race: Explorations of Multiracial Discourse in Canada;* Mahtani, "Mixed Metaphors: Situating Mixed Race Identity."
78. Taylor, *Re-imagining Mixed Race: Explorations of Multiracial Discourse in Canada.*
79. See Roberts and Mahtani, "Neoliberalizing Race, Racing Neoliberalism: Representations of Immigration in the Globe and Mail."
80. See Sue, this volume; Daniel and Lee ,this volume.
81. Song and Aspinall, "Is Racial Mismatch a Problem for Young 'Mixed Race' People in Britain? The Findings of Qualitative Research."
82. Ibid., 21.
83. Rockquemore, Brunsma, and Delgado, "Racing to Theory or Retheorizing Race? Understanding the Struggle to Build a Multiracial Identity Theory."
84. Elam, *The Souls of Mixed Folk: Race, Politics and Aesthetics in the New Millennium.*

Global Mixed Race

A Conclusion

REBECCA C. KING-O'RIAIN

If the popular media in the United States was a gauge of the actual state of things, one would think that mixed race issues were relatively new and demographically widespread[1]—and there would be some truth to the widely presumed novelty of this demographic trend with 4.8 million people (or one in twelve marriages in 2012) reporting that they were interracial in the US.[2] However, others are quick to note that interracial relationships and mixed people are hardly new at all,[3] as we have seen in many of the historically informed chapters in *Global Mixed Race*. What is new, perhaps, is the formal enumeration of people as "mixed" and the increasing ability and desire to identify as such. While much of the research on people of mixed descent has been written about the US and UK, we were not convinced that these experiences were the same the world over. As Mark Christian (2000) tells us, it is important to

> understand each multiracial experience in its own right . . . assess how this interlocking international history has impacted on multiracial communities (p. 104) *and* analyze the links and similarities of international multiracial experiences (p. 112; italics added by author).

It is precisely these links as both enabled and shaped by globalization that we are analyzing here. While mixing is often seen as a solution to racial and social progress and increasing tolerance of difference, we were skeptical that increasing identification as mixed does not herald the end of race, and more importantly, racism. *Global Mixed Race* illustrates that there are many varied approaches and experiences of mixing.

Some are only loosely related to American notions of race. Even in nations that were historically tolerant of race mixing such as Mexico, Kazakhstan, and Trinidad and Tobago, there are still limits to identifying as mixed, no collective mixed identity, and persistent group and state boundaries.

So why discuss mixing and globalization now? We believe that in the current global, postcolonial, late-modern moment, there are increasingly people who identify themselves as being of two or more salient backgrounds. In a world that is highly racialized and where unitary and exclusive racial categories are widespread, such claims to mixing can deeply challenge existing ideas about race and other unitary social criteria used to divide people into groups. Yet, such claims to mixed identities are often denied and people are then forced to choose one, and only one, identity.

If anything, increasing international abilities to express multiple descent identification, both formally on the censuses and more informally elsewhere, has shown us that the debate about the efficacy of race is still alive and well. For some, the blurring of race labels may mean the concomitant blurring of social boundaries and a precursor to a colorblind time when race won't matter. For others, we have achieved harmony and to mention race or other social boundaries works to reinforce the idea that social divisions exist, impacting how we treat one another, and should be illegal. For example, in the United States, some have used recent state legislation in Arizona (House Bill 2281) to censor and attempt to ban the teaching of critical race theory and ethnic studies. The assumptions behind this move illustrate the deep disconnect between the scientific status of race as a created concept that has no biological basis and the social reality of the common ideas and practices of race.[4] If anything, the evidence presented in *Global Mixed Race* shows that the common ideas and practices of race, ethnicity, and nation, while possibly philosophically and logically illusory, still have a very real impact on the lives of mixed-descent people.

Research that examines only the logical foundations of race and refuses to take seriously the real-life implications of race[5] ignores the lived reality of what many or most people think of as racial or cultural characteristics. As with many hate crimes, if you are the target like Rabbi Jonathan Sandler and his two sons, Aryeh and Gavriel, who were killed in March 2012 in France, the attackers, or gun-wielding bigots, didn't stop to ask 'what are you?' but instead chose to shoot first and ask biologically determinist questions later.[6] Obviously, while some of the authors here assert that race is a social construction, racism continues to persist and have life-changing consequences for individuals in these nations.

Why *Global Mixed Race*?

So why call this book *Global Mixed Race*? Particularly post-1990, a significant literature has been dedicated to trying to define the relationship between race and mixed race.[7] Throughout this book we used the terms "people of mixed descent" and "mixed" to describe people who identify as coming from two or more discrete backgrounds. Sometimes they identify this background as being racial, linked to ideas of physical appearance, phenotype, skin color, and visibility in society, and sometimes as ancestry. Sometimes it is nationality, ethnicity, language, or culture that is used to identify this background. Scholars working on topics around the world have critiqued the idea of race mixture in a wide range of societies and from a variety of perspectives.[8] In the United States, the idea of mixed race is critically explored by Rainier Spencer, who asserts that the idea of mixed race at times ironically works to reify the concept of race—that you need race to be real in order to mix it and parse it into bits that can be mixed. He argues that this assumes an undisputed Black and White. In many other parts of the world, such as Kazakhstan, there does not seem to be a prior assumption that there is a unitary Black and unitary White, and so mixedness does not become the basis for an identity or identity politics.[9]

Steven Ropp points out that some scholars use the label of "people of mixed descent" to highlight the socially constructed nature of race.[10] That is, people of mixed descent are deemed to provide embodied proof that races are social conventions, because people have always mixed and still existed as bodily human beings despite scientific and social taboos against mixing. However, such arguments do not help us understand the ways that the mixing of race is organized and contested in different places at different times. It is this vital task of comparative and grounded analysis that this volume has undertaken. One response to the complex issues surrounding the concept of race has been to treat the use of the word "race" suspiciously and to consider in more detail the complex and complicit relationship between imperialism, colonialism, globalization, hybridity, and diasporic theory with multiraciality.[11] Naomi Zack has argued philosophically for a stance that is anti-race—that we should not use the category or concept of race or mixed race in our thinking or speech.[12] But is that possible? Does it reflect the everyday lived experiences of mixed people? More recently, Suki Ali has argued for a post-race position and approach to mixed race, arguing the dubious origins of the term "race" as a precursor to "mixed race."[13] Alana Lentin and Gavan Titley critique this idea. They write, "The 'post' in post-race sidesteps the fact that, for advocates of post-racialism, it is racelessness (Goldberg 2002), which is actually being invoked. To be post something is at least to acknowledge its past significance. However, the central conviction of post-racialism is the denial of the salience of race in the lived experience of the racialized."[14]

Even with hopeful post-racial thinking, there is still a persistent identification in many countries with being mixed and there are other places, as the chapters on Kazakhstan and Trinidad and Tobago show us, where discussions of mixing don't always revolve around understandings of race, but rather other factors such as nationality, religion, and language. This is because the conditions and recognition of mixing are different throughout the world. For example, some legal changes—such as the end of the ban on mixed marriages in 1967 in the US, the end of apartheid in 1994 in South Africa, or the implementation of affirmative action in the US to counter centuries of state and institutional discrimination against Blacks—led thousands of people who had lived their lives as monoracial Whites to "become" multiracial to apply for perceived economic benefits or access to education. Affirmative action already existed in many nations before the US put it into effect for African Americans beginning in 1961. What is more, many other nations have begun affirmative action programs due to the spread of global ideas of race from the US as can be seen now in Brazil, a nation that touts itself as a multiracial melting pot. Similar cases can be found for Whites who suddenly claimed Maori ancestry in New Zealand or are pushed into identifying into particular categories in Canada in order to gain reparations. There are also cases of "mixed-race chic"[15] where people identify with being multiracial not for apparent gain, but because of a symbolic coolness that they feel will accompany it. Finally, for some, mixedness may be optional, such as in Trinidad and Tobago[16] or in other places not captured in this book, as an identity that is not significant to them at all.

Global Conclusions

After reading the chapters in this book, what have we learned?

1. Rethinking Identity Categories

It is clear that many people are in the process of rethinking social identity categories (both their content and their form). By comparing this process in different contexts, we see that *identity declaration* and *identity differentiation and categorization* are linked and that they may operate globally to transfer, cross-pollinate, or cancel each other out.[17] *Identity declaration* (what people say they think they are) and *identity differentiation* (what other people say they are) are processes shaped by larger national narratives (or lack thereof) about mixing. If there is a clash between the two processes, this might matter because the social action taken based on that interaction of attributing meaning to language, religion, or ethnicity is marked by external signals like skin color, hair texture, and accent. This means that mixed people are not just mislabeled or shaped but have agency to use outsiders' views of them to take action. For example, in Mexico, White Veracruzanos can assert Whiteness by saying "others say I am White" while being seen to maintain humility about that skin color privilege and at the same time not compromise their Mexicanness.[18] They can therefore claim to have "Spanish in me," but not to be Spanish, but rather authentically Mexican, which is by definition something new and fundamentally mixed. Brown Veracruzanos, because they are not light-skinned, are able to say they are Mexican and don't have the privilege to make that claim to Whiteness, but they still can distance themselves from Africaness and indigeneity. They have more freedom to identify as Europeans because they can't reap the benefits of looking White. Both groups clearly draw on the national Mexican ideology in forming their own identities.

It is clear from the preceding chapters that there is no one global mixed-race collective experience. In fact, the US, while the backdrop for much of the discussion around mixed-race issues, is clearly only one model of many and perhaps not the most common model across the world. We can see how mixed experiences are varied not only across nations, but at different levels of social analysis as well such as the nation-state (Canada, Mexico, Brazil), governmentality (Kazakhstan), national identity (Zambia), transnationality (US and Okinawa), and categorization (UK and—per chapter 1—globally).

2. Roles of States

It is clear that states and their concomitant national narratives shape the experiences of those who define themselves as mixed. However, global forces and flows of migration, transnationalism, and increased techno-logical communication also shape people's identities, mediating belong-ing across multiple locations and nation states. By asking how the state acts upon people of mixed descent, we hope to add to studies of how states classify and monitor diversity or even superdiversity where there is no one mixed collective identity emerging (unlike the US).[19]

For example, Maureen Perkins (Australia) and Rhoda Reddock (Trinidad and Tobago) in this volume point out that superdiversity may in fact not go far enough to be used as a tool to understand mix-ing on a global level, but at the same time suggest that mixed people under globalization may be able to more easily identify as cosmopoli-tan world citizens because of their diverse social experiences. While some mixed people may come to believe they hold cosmopolitan iden-tities oriented to global perspectives, not all are upper-middle class as much of the literature on globalization assumes. For example, Welty in this volume shows us that many mixed people in Okinawa were distinctively not middle class and were not the quintessential mobile elites. However, this did not curtail their ability to have ties and search for cues to identity, family, and belonging back and forth across the Pacific Ocean in Okinawa, the US, and Japan. In this sense, trans-national mixed Okinawans, and others like them, may be emblem-atic of, and key to understanding, the process of globalization and cosmopolitanism.

Both globalization and the continuing roles of nation-states affect the mixed population in each place considered here. This is clear when Morning in this volume examines many state racial and ethnic classification schemes side by side to find there is a diverse range of how and why mixed-race people are categorized or caught between categories. In the UK also, Aspinall and Song found that there is a proliferation of identity assertions, which are not captured well by the census. Yet, states continue to strive to capture these identity assertions in aggregate as a way to gauge success in reaching political and economic equality. While they are globally linked, they are all also uniquely local and linked to local issues of access to power, historical legacies, and self-images that mixed people may have of themselves. As Wendy Roth tells us, there may even be many systems of racial classification and stratification in people's minds about "how race works."[20]

Of course, it is worth remembering that globalization means different things in different places. In Kazakhstan, "internationalism," an opening up to global forces, harkens back to a past history of diversification and building of the "peoples' friendship" republic. Modernity in Kazakhstan, unlike other countries, has not meant internationalization but has given rise to an increase in Kazakh national pride and preferences for Kazakh-speaking peoples.

MULTICULTURALISM AND THE STATE

Globalization for mixed people in New Zealand and Kazakhstan does not mean multicultural internationalization but instead a quest for authenticity through identity politics, possibly influenced by civil rights movements in other parts of the world. Farida Fozdar reminds us that in New Zealand Maori groups identify mixed people as authentically Maori because of blood connection. New Zealand is more color conscious and the state is officially bicultural, unlike Australia. Maori rights in New Zealand are linked to racial heritage and Maori tribes accept mixed children as Maori because of that blood connection; therefore, globalization has meant a need for authenticity amongst the indigenous population there.

Minelle Mahtani, Dani Kwan-Lafond, and Leanne Taylor argue that in Canada, mixed people are skeptical of the nation-state's "food and festivals" celebratory approach, which emerged in the 1970s to support state multiculturalism. This had long-lasting legacies for all people of color in Canada. State structures encourage mixed people in Canada to strategically essentialize their identity as ethnic minorities in part to further serve as proof that the Canadian model of multiculturalism is a success.

Even nation-states like Canada and Australia, or often idealized "mixed" nations, like Trinidad and Tobago and Mexico, that profess to be formally multiracial still struggle to truly incorporate those minority groups, like the Métis and aboriginal, who are not of finite social categories but transcend and blur the very boundaries by which they are measured.

Canada has enshrined in its constitution that it is a multicultural nation. Like Australia, the state emphasizes that it supports a multicultural project, but when you scratch the surface, that may not be the case.[21] In Canada and Australia, the formal discourse and state discourse may hide deep inequalities and exclusions, in turn disadvantaging mixed people. The mixed experience in Canada is held up as living proof of the success of multiculturalism and a supposedly inclusive Canada. At the same time, mixed people are also racialized as non-White and positioned outside of the nation-state. In this sense, mixed people are positioned as stakeholders in the success of national multicultural projects by being the bridges that connect across cultural groups (and now nations). But as mixed people clearly state, they are not always bridges to be tread upon.[22]

In Zambia, despite rhetoric of "One Zambia, One Nation," most folks still define Zambianness by ethnicity. In Mexico, being authentically Mexican is based on color. In Germany, while there is no term for mixed race or intermarriage and there are no official statistics, this does not mean that mixing doesn't exist. The state decries the fallacy of racial terms and yet is still deeply ethnically and linguistically German, with citizenship determined still through the rule of *jus sanguinis*. As Paul Spickard and Miriam Nandi state, "race did not go away, it was recoded as culture"; most Germans perceive Muslims, Africans, and Asians as not German even if they are citizens and taxpayers born in Germany. This is further racialized by the distinction made in Germany of what constitutes your mix. If you are of German background mixed with Irish, Polish, or Austrian (read White), you are more eligible to be socially accepted as "German" than if you are part Turkish, African, or Asian.

There is ample evidence in *Global Mixed Race* that physical appearance matters in many, but not all, places around the world. We are not all becoming a polyglot of ethnic ambiguity of the sort used to sell Benetton shirts and the color line is not disappearing. Mixed-race bodies, then, are not just a "pigment of the imagination"[23] in art, literature, and film, but instead are popular commodified images used by global capital to sell both products and ideas of cosmopolitanism, multiculturalism, and globality.[24] In effect, one thing that mixed people around the world may have in common is their continued encounter with mixed racism and exoticization in global marketing and popular culture.

3. What Is Global about All This?

Globalization and the experiences of mixed people are intimately tied together. Exploitation of labor, the historical legacy of colonization, military occupation, the movement of people and goods, transnational trading, globalized work and business, and capitalism all work to color the lived experiences of mixed people. Does this mean that globalization makes mixing more frequent? Does globalization make mixing more prominent in public discourse and therefore more accepted? Will other social characteristics take the place of race and nation to divide and make differences between us? Or will we all become homogeneously mixed and these social differences won't matter anymore?

Even if we look at the countries where mixing has long taken place (Mexico, Brazil, and Trinidad and Tobago), there are other differences that arise (color and class) that continue to create salient differences between people. Not all people (e.g., *douglas* in Trinidad and Tobago) have an equal chance to identify as mixed. In these instances, there is no homogeneous collective mixed identity. Clearly a multiracial national narrative and structure is no guarantee of racial harmony and belonging. Even being colonized by the same forces (e.g., the UK) does not mean that the mixed experiences are similar. The experience of being mixed in Trinidad and Tobago is very different from that of Zambia, Australia, or Canada.

GLOBAL TRENDS

There are also global trends that influence most if not all of the places studied in *Global Mixed Race*. The flow of global ideas about race and ethnicity has increased the possibility and promoted the spread of mixed identification. Affirmative action programs in Brazil are directly linked to US notions of race imported and localized within a Brazilian racial formation that links individuals, through institutions of higher education, to official state notions of race. Maori in New Zealand have adopted American-style identity politics, localizing around Maoriness rather than universalizing it because they need strategically to essentialize or play a game of "monoracial prescriptiveness"[25] to gain access to resources. Fozdar argues that due to the impact of globalization the need for authenticity is increased.

This is possibly also in play in Canada, where government and the public push mixed-race people to be "of color" when it serves the state's purposes while at the same time the state does not recognize or provide reparations for Indigenous or First Nations groups such as the Métis. Morning shows us that many censuses around the world coalesce around certain patterns through the sharing of ideas about race and ethnicity. The UK Census, for example, takes its ideas for categorization partly from other parts of the world, and others follow their lead.

4. Limits on the Liminal Space

The experience of being caught between two socially recognized categories—being put under pressure to choose one, or being thought of as suspect or less than "authentic" because one is not purely one thing or the other—is common across many groups of mixed people. Interestingly, we can see this in places where mixing is understood as the norm and there are no racial census categories such as in Mexico, where White Veracruzanos try not to flaunt their Whiteness for fear of not being Mexican enough. We can also see it in Kazakhstan, where there is a distinct lack of racial discourse in the post-Soviet era and yet people are forced to choose one "nationality" (what most Americans and Northwest Europeans would call "ethnicity") on their passports. The liminal space of asserting and living out hybrid identities is still a challenge in most parts of the world. However, the basis for those identities is different in different places. In Japan and Germany in the post–World War II era, pure or homogeneous and assumed uniform ancestry still seems to inform discussions of who is of the nation in terms of citizenship and belonging, even while there is denial of racial inequalities. Often, too, these liminal spaces are gendered, and it is women particularly who are caught between the boundaries, doing boundary work, or left to defend boundaries that may in fact bind them culturally and socially. Even in contexts where mixedness is fundamental to national ideologies, colorism is often an important factor for mixed identities—in Mexico, for example, where access to full membership in the nation is different for dark-skinned than for light-skinned *mestizos.*.

Likewise, it is around the issue of the legal status of mixed people that states often become key racializing, gendering deciders as to who can love whom, who is considered to constitute a family, and who can be legitimately recognized as such.[26] In Okinawa, if parents were not legally married or their marriage was not recognized by the US, the mixed children were, by default, Japanese citizens. Some mixed Okinawans had US citizenship because they were claimed by American fathers and therefore recognized by the American state, but they couldn't get Japanese citizenship precisely because their fathers were American and not Japanese. Still others were not registered in family shrines in Japan and were therefore stateless. This means that one could live one's whole life in Okinawa but still not be legitimately Okinawan, and one could speak English but not be legitimately American either. In these examples, it is clear that state racialization controls rights through the recognition of who legitimately belongs to whom based on a complex intertwining of language, culture, race, body, state racialization, and gendering, embedded in notions of family.

In Zambia, state immigration restrictions by the UK were tied to notions of what constituted a family across racial, cultural, and national boundaries defined so that "Eurafricans" could not (until 1980) be British because of their mixed backgrounds. In this sense, although many scholars of globalization would have us believe that ideas and people fly around the world unimpeded, nation-states are still significant barriers for some mixed people, as they often come to shape, and in some cases strongly regulate, such people's ability to belong. As we saw in chapters

1 and 10, the official and lived racial realities of mixed people are shaped by racial identification processes within the nation-state. Official versus individual definitions influence each other. Census categories shape the way people identify, but they also have to reflect racial reality or the categories are useless because people don't use them. There can, of course, as we saw in the case of Kazakhstan, be a mismatch between official and experienced identity. In effect, states may have to respond to growing mixed communities as they place pressure on them to reflect the reality of the cultural and racial landscape.[27]

While mixed populations in a range of nations have unique trajectories and local social, political, and economic contexts, we do gain by comparing them with other places to see how they are similar and different, how they affect each other, and how they are affected by globalization. For example, the comparisons in *Global Mixed Race* tell us that the world is clearly shaped by colonial (gendered and racialized) histories, but in the end, there are similar trends in the ways that people caught between social categories come to recognize hybridity, and not all of them are linked to race. In Kazakhstan, for example, we see that language, culture, and nationality are far more important than what Americans might call "race" or attention to physical appearance, ancestry, and color. Yet with increasing contact with Western culture and ideas, the idea of race is increasingly used in Kazakhstan. So is race more important in Western contexts? It may well be.

Unlike Kazakhstan, in the case of Brazil we find that attention to skin color and notions of colorism (lightness being better than darkness) still prevails, even within a national ideology that valorizes multiraciality, so in this case at least, hierarchies of color and mixing are not mutually exclusive. Therefore, while local contexts and histories matter, there are similarities across the world in terms of mixed race. The role of the state, whether in Kazakhstan regarding passports, or in Mexico embedded not through state categorization but through a national ideology of mixing in the "Mestizo State,"[28] seems to be a factor that can't be ignored.

Alongside globalization is the idea that nations are becoming more formally mixed. Australia and Canada, and to some extent the UK, see themselves as multicultural states. Germany and Japan are ideologically single-race states. In Mexico, Brazil, and Trinidad and Tobago, it is not just multiculturalism but also multiraciality that is a strong part of the national ideology. Yet, as our chapters show, even in those formally multiracial states, not everyone has equal access to membership.

5. A New Globalized Colonialism?

As Rhoda Reddock says in her chapter on Trinidad and Tobago, in many places "pure races are elsewhere and mixing is what happens locally." Under globalization, there is a tie to past colonization that pushes mixing down into local as well as global culture, and oftentimes this process means that states in developed nations use recognition and racialization to determine rights.[29] Juliette Milner-Thorton shows us that Eurafricans in Zambia were not recognized by the British state because of rules of hypodescent (unlike Brazil) in order to deny citizenship and rights to mixed progeny of White British men and elite African women.

In this process, the state purposefully racialized the mixed progeny as "not British" because their parents were not legally married or did not have the money to register their marriage, thus denying their children paternity and therefore UK citizenship until the 1980s. Many years later in Okinawa, Welty shows us that mixed people were left legally literally betwixt and between two nation-states (Japan and the US) as well as alienated from local (Okinawan) cultures because of their inability in some cases to prove paternity—when the proof was literally written on their faces. In Zambia, mixed people were not absorbed into the native population but instead tried to claim whiteness, they were, in Milner-Thorton's words "contained to empire and denied admission to the metropole." As a past strategy of colonization, we could ask: Has this morphed under globalization into a continued strategy to attempt to contain difference to the margins of the world and perhaps preserve the global metropole for pure or privileged persons?

6. Mixed People as Symbols

One trend that does seem to be common the world over is that mixed people have often been made into symbols of various sorts.[30] In many places, mixed people symbolically represent "national unity." In Trinidad and Tobago, *douglas*[31] are held up as the key to harmonious society (bridges), but there is no actual social coalescing of *douglas* into a buffer group because Indianness is exclusive and can't be mixed; Blackness, on the other hand, is absorbent and inclusive—you can be African and mixed at the same time. In Brazil, mixed people have been a key symbol in the narratives of racial democracy and have been seen as the multicultural and multiracial future. In Kazakhstan, the emergence of mixed people was seen as the beginning of the "friendship of the peoples' republic." In these examples, mixed people are seen as positive symbols of progress and multicultural understanding. There are deep untested assumptions about who mixed people are, how they identify, and how assimilation or cultural change works. One thing is clear: while some mixed people may be bridges, many are not.

In Zambia, Eurafrican faces (unlike those of mixed people in Kazakhstan or Mexico) primarily symbolized conquest and were a sore reminder of the country's colonized past, not the harbinger of a multiracial, multicultural future. In Okinawa, multiracial people were stereotypically seen as "love children" born of illegitimate (perhaps even illicit) sexual relations and reminders of war and occupation both by Japan and the US. Clearly, mixed people in these places were treated differently from the unmixed people around them, but they did not all have the same differences.

It is possible that multiraciality under some circumstances and in some contexts could be a vehicle for imagining and achieving collaboration in a social order where racial differences have limited or at least considerably less significance in the distribution of wealth (Daniel and Lee, this volume). Yet more often than not in this book we see that some mixed bodies are constant reminders of a not-so-long-ago colonial or military occupation and represent the stigma and face of war, which is very different from being mixed in Kazakhstan (where "mixing is the future") or in Mexico (where "everyone is mixed"). Even racialization—which reaches across national borders such as in the experiences of mixed Okinawan—must be authenticated via language as well as ancestry.

The symbolic presence of mixed people allows some around them to practice democratic racism, that is, to recognize mixed people but maintain racist beliefs and behavior. This democratic racism may be a version of plastic multiculturalism in which other people see themselves as cosmopolitan because they recognize the multiplicity of cultures in mixed people in superficial ways. However, they don't recognize that this is because they have the power to appropriate culture from others and generalize and normalize it into their own experiences. Their encounter with mixed people is a kind of mixed-race tourism, even voyeurism. Societies might be better off if they moved from appropriating mixed people as symbols of progress to actually equalizing the power to speak and normalizing difference while being mindful that mixed people have often been used by conservatives and progressives alike to further political claims to colorblindness and multiculturalism.

HIERARCHY REMAINS

In our comparisons around the world, it is clear that the position of mixed people within societies and nation-states still varies along racial and ethnic continuums, though few remain within a binary racial system.[32] Even within a mixed-race middle there are continuing hierarchies of acceptance and privilege. The chapters here illustrate that the presence of mixed people, even over long historical periods, does not indicate a declining significance of social boundaries, including racial ones. In fact, the position of mixed people may be more than ever determined by state processes of racialization such as racial categorization on national censuses. Mixed people are not always a precursor or corollary to multiculturalism, as seen in Canada and Australia.

And yet, our lived experiences tell us that while there may not yet be a community of globally mixed people, there are certainly the beginnings of a commonality of experience (often exclusionary from both of the communities of descent) that spans the globe with increasing efficiency and speed. This does not mean that mixed people somehow inherit superhuman powers to undo the meanings of race or to bridge communities in times of strife. Blurring and blending race or ethnicity or nationality may mean that a hybrid space is developing, but it is clear that this space is not always as transgressive of identity concepts as we would like it to be.

7. Meanings of Mixedness

On the other hand, mixing may be so prevalent as to be seen to lose its uniqueness and perhaps its social importance. In many of the chapters here, we encounter people who are so mixed they don't know "what they are." For example, intermarriage is seen positively as the main mechanism for merging Soviet nations into a single Soviet people. Ethnicity is seen increasingly as a biological or genetic unit and a potential cause of warfare, even genocide. Kazakhstan, in this context, is lauded as a showcase of ethnic harmony because of its high rates of intermarriage and a Soviet-style "friendship of the peoples."

In Australia, we learn that there is a "multiplicity of hyphenations" with no one dominant group being mixed with the mainstream population. However, mixed people still feel that they must choose between parents, between official versus subjectively experienced identities, and between identities consistent with historical legacy versus more modern, transnational contemporary identities. This creates in both Kazakhstan and Australia a sense that there is no collective mixed identity.

This may give rise to the idea of *flexible racialization*, where meanings are made and attributed around differences such as color, class, culture, ethnicity, and ancestry as a form of racializing the social. This would expand Michael Omi and Howard Winant's ideas of racialization and racial projects across the globe.[33] Things like phenotype or color may not be read socially the same everywhere and also may not be experienced the same everywhere.

After touring the world, if only partially through the chapters here in *Global Mixed Race*, we can see that class, colonial history, gender, ethnicity, and place can still mediate race in very specific and local ways while still being strongly shaped by global forces, which are bringing people of different backgrounds together with greater frequency. While some would predict that this "rainbow of races" globalized world would mean increased understanding, we see that this may or may not be the case depending upon where in the world you are. Although mixed identification is more socially acceptable and recognized than ever before, it is a long way from the panacea of racial and ethnic harmony as it is often portrayed. But it is a place to start.

NOTES

1. Squires, *Dispatches from the Color Line*.
2. Wang, "The Rise of Intermarriage Rates, Characteristics Vary by Race and Gender."
3. Elam, *Souls of Mixed Folk*.
4. Alcoff, "In Arizona: Censoring Questions About Race."
5. Banton, "*The Colour Line and the Colour Scale in the Twentieth Century*."
6. Vos Iz Neias? "Toulouse—A Look at the Victims of French Attacks."
7. Cornell and Hartmann, *Ethnicity and Race*; Root, *Multiracial Experience*; Spickard and Daniel, *Racial Thinking*; Ifekwunigwe, *Mixed Race Studies*; Lipsitz, *Possessive Investment in Whiteness*; Winters and DeBose, *New Faces in a Changing America*.
8. DaCosta, *Making Multiracials*; Daniel, *Race and Multiraciality*; Stoler, *Carnal Knowledge*.
9. Spencer, *Spurious Issues*; Premdas, *Identity, Ethnicity and Culture in the Caribbean*.
10. Ropp, "Do Multiracial Subjects Really Challenge Race?: Mixed-Race Asians in the United States and the Caribbean."
11. See Gilroy, "Race Ends Here," for more on this type of argument.
12. Zack, *Race and Mixed Race*; Zack, *American Mixed Race*.
13. Ali, *Mixed-Race, Post-Race*.
14. Lentin and Titley, *The Crisis of Multiculturalism*, 79.
15. Spencer, "Mixed-Race Chic."
16. Parker and Song, *Rethinking "Mixed Race."*
17. For another view on this see Rockquemore, Brunsma, and Delgado, "Racing to Theory or Retheorizing Race? Understanding the Struggle to Build a Multiracial Identity Theory," or more recently, Song and Aspinall, "Is Racial Mismatch a Problem for Young 'Mixed Race' Young People in Britain?"
18. Bettez, *But Don't Call Me White*.
19. Vertovec, "Super-diversity and Its Implications"; Morning, *The Nature of Race: How Scientists Think and Teach about Human Difference*.
20. Roth, *Race Migrations*.
21. Mahtani and Moreno, "Same Difference: Towards a More Unified Discourse in 'Mixed Race' theory."
22. McNeil, *Sex and Race in the Black Atlantic: Mulatto Devils and Multiracial Messiahs*; McNeil, "'Mixture is a Neoliberal Good': Mixed-Race Metaphors and Post-Racial Masks."
23. Edwards, Ganguly, and Lo, "*Pigments of the Imagination: Theorising, Performing and Historicising Mixed Race*."
24. Matthews, "*Eurasian Persuasions: Mixed Race, Performativity and Cosmopolitanism*."
25. Song, "*Making Sense of 'Mixture': States and the Classification of 'Mixed' People*."

26. Ibrahim, *Troubling the Family*.

27. Song, "*Making Sense of 'Mixture': States and the Classification of 'Mixed' People*."

28. Lund, *Mestizo State: Reading Race in Modern Mexico*.

29. King-O'Riain, "*Racialization, Recognition and Rights*"; Mahtani, *Mixed Race Cartographies*.

30. Mahtani, "What's In a Name?"; McNeill, "'Mixture is a Neoliberal Good': Mixed-Race Metaphors and Post-Racial Masks."

31. This refers to mixed-race people in Trinidad and Tobago.

32. England, "Mixed and Multiracial in Trinidad and Honduras: Rethinking Mixed-Race Identities in Latin America and the Caribbean."

33. Omi and Winant, *Racial Formation in the United States*.

Abadan-Unat, Nermin. 2011. *Turks in Europe: From Guest Worker to Transnational Citizen*. New York: Berghahn.

ABC. 2010. "Aboriginal Woman 'Not Dark Enough' for Advocacy Job." Australian Broadcasting Corporation, http://www.abc.net.au/news/stories/2010/11/04/3056815. htm (accessed May 10, 2012).

Abdulah, Norma. 1987. *Trinidad and Tobago 1985: A Demographic Analysis*, St. Augustine: ISER.

"Abertas inscrições para o V Seminário Sobre a Identidade Mestiça." 2012. http://www. nacaomestica.org/.

Abu-Laban, Yasmeen, and Christina Gabriel. 2002. *Selling Diversity: Immigration, Multiculturalism, Employment Equity, and Globalization*. Toronto: University of Toronto Press.

Adams, Michael. 2007. *Unlikely Utopia: The Surprising Triumph of Canadian Pluralism*. Toronto: Viking.

Adorno, Sérgio. 1999. "Racial Discrimination and Criminal Justice in São Paulo." In Reichmann, Rebecca (ed). *Race Relations in Contemporary Brazil: From Indifference to Equality*. University Park: Pennsylvania State University Press.

Alcoff, Linda Martin. 2012. "In Arizona: Censoring Questions About Race." *New York Times*. http://opinionator.blogs.nytimes.com/2012/04/01/ in-arizona-censoring-questions-about-race/.

Ali, Suki. 2003. *Mixed-Race, Post-Race: Gender, New Ethnicities and Cultural Practices*. Oxford: Berg.

Alves, Jerson César Leão. 2007. E-mail to G. Reginald Daniel, October 9/10.

Ammon, Ulrich, Hans Bickel, Jakob Ebner, et al. 2004. *Variantenwörterbuch des Deutschen: Die Standardsprache in Österreich, der Schweiz und Deutschland sowie in Liechtenstein, Luxemburg, Ostbelgien und Südtirol*. Berlin: Walter de Gruyter.

Anderson, Warwick, 2002. *The Cultivation of Whiteness: Science, Health and Racial Destiny in Australia*. Melbourne: Melbourne University Press.

Andrews, George Reid. 1991. *Blacks and White in São Paulo, Brazil, 1888–1988*. Madison: University of Wisconsin Press.

Appadurai, Arjun. 1996. *Modernity At Large: Cultural Dimensions of Globalization*. Minneapolis: University of Minnesota Press.

Appiah, Kwame Anthony. 1992. *In My Father's House: Africa in the Philosophy of Culture*. London: Oxford University Press.

———. 1994. "Identity, Authenticity, Survival: Multicultural Societies and Social Reproduction." In Gutman, Amy (ed.). *Multiculturalism: Examining the Politics of Recognition*. Princeton, NJ: Princeton University Press.

———. 2005. *The Ethics of Identity*. Princeton NJ: Princeton University Press.

Armstrong, Bruce. 1989. "Racialisation and Nationalist Ideology: The Japanese Case." *International Sociology* 4 (3): 329–43.

Asato Eiko. 2003. "Okinawan Indentity and Resistance to Militarization and Maldevelopment." In Hein, Laura, and Mark Selden (eds.). *Islands of Discontent: Okinawan Responses to Japanese and American Power*. Lanham, MD: Rowman & Littlefield.

Aspinall, Peter J. 1995. "The Development of an Ethnic Group Question for the 2001 Census: The Findings of a Consultation Exercise with Members of the OPCS 2001 Census Working Subgroup." London: SE Institute of Public Health, United Medical and Dental Schools.

———. 2009a. "'Mixed Race', 'Mixed Origins' or What? Generic Terminology for the Multiple Racial/Ethnic Group Population." *Anthropology Today* 25 (2): 3–8.

———. 2009b. "Does the British State's Categorisation of 'Mixed Race' Meet Public Policy Needs?" *Social Policy & Society* 9 (1): 55–69.

———. 2009c. "The Future of Ethnicity Classifications." *Journal of Ethnic and Migration Studies* 35 (9): 1417–35.

———. 2010. "Concepts, Terminology and Classifications for the 'Mixed' Ethnic or Racial Group in the UK." *Journal of Epidemiology and Community Health* 64 (6): 557–60.

Aspinall, Peter J., Miri Song, and Ferhana Hashem. 2008. "The Ethnic Options of 'Mixed Race' people in Britain: Full Research Report" (ESRC Research Grant RES-000-23-1507). http://www.esrcsocietytoday.ac.uk/ESRCInfoCentre/ (see: Awards and Outputs).

Aspinall, Peter J., and Miri Song. 2013. *Mixed Race Identities*. London: Palgrave Macmillan.

Astor, Michael. 2004. "Brazil Tries Quotas to Get Racial Equality." *Los Angeles Times*, February 29: A3.

Attwood, Bain, and John Arnold (eds.). 1992. *Power, Knowledge and Aborigines*. Bundora, Victoria: La Trobe University Press.

Augustus, Camie. Forthcoming. *Mixed Race, Legal Space: A Comparative History of Mixed-Ancestry Native Legal Identity in Canada, the U.S., and Australia, 1850–1950*. PhD dissertation, University of Saskatchewan.

Austin-Broos, Diane. 1994. "Race/Class: Jamaica's Discourse of Heritable Identity." *New West Indian Guide/Nieuwe West-Indische Gids* 68 (3/4).

Awatere, Donna. 1984. *Maori Sovereignty*. Auckland: Broadsheet Magazine Ltd.

Back, Les. 1995. *New Ethnicities*. London: UCL Press.

Bade, Klaus J. 1994. *Auslander, Aussiedler, Asyl: Eine Bestandsaufnahme*. München: C.H. Beck.

Bade, Klaus J., and Jochen Oltmer (eds.). 2003. *Aussiedler: deutsche Einwanderer aus Osteuropa*. Göttingen: V&R Unipress.

Bailey, Stanley R. 2002. "The Race Construct and Public Opinion: Understanding Brazilian Beliefs about Racial Inequality and Their Determinants." *American Journal of Sociology*, 108 (2): 406–39.

———. 2009. *Legacies of Race: Identities, Attitudes, and Politics in Brazil*. Stanford, CA: Stanford University Press.

Bannerji, Himani. 2000. *The Dark Side of the Nation: Essays on Multiculturalism, Nationalism and Gender*. Toronto: Canadian Scholar's Press.

Banton, Michael. 2012. "The Colour Line and the Colour Scale in the Twentieth Century." *Ethnic and Racial Studies* 35 (7): 1109–31.

Barbassa, Juliana. 2011. "Brazil Launches Program to End Extreme Poverty." *Boston Globe*. http://www.boston.com/business/articles/2011/06/02/brazil_launches_program_to_end_extreme_poverty/.

Barbieri, William A., Jr. 1998. *Ethics of Citizenship: Immigration and Group Rights in Germany*. Durham, NC: Duke University Press.

Barnard, F. M. 1965. *Herder's Social and Political Thought: From Enlightenment to Nationalism*. Oxford: Clarendon Press.

———. 2003. *Herder on Nationality, Humanity, and History*. Montreal: McGill-Queen's University Press.

Barnes, Taylor. 2011. "For the First Time, Blacks Outnumber Whites in Brazil." *Miami Herald*. http://www.miamiherald.com/2011/05/23/v-fullstory/2231323/for-the-first-time-Blacks-outnumber.html#ixzz1Vjw8qUwa.

Bartholomew, John C. 1982. *World Atlas*. 12th ed. Edinburgh: John Bartholomew and Son.

Baumann, Gerd. 1996. *Contesting Culture: Discourses of Identity in Multi-ethnic London*. Cambridge: Cambridge University Press.

Bawer, Bruce. 2006. *While Europe Slept: How Radical Islam is Destroying the West from Within*. New York: Broadway Books.

Bayly, C. A. 1999. "The British and Indigenous Peoples, 1760–1860: Power, Perception and Identity." In Daunton, Martin, and Rick Halpern (eds.). *Empire and Others: British Encounters with Indigenous Peoples, 1600–1850*. London: UCL Press.

Beck, Ulrich. 2002. "The Cosmopolitan Perspective: Sociology in the Second Age of Modernity." In Vertovec, Steven, and Robin Cohen (eds.). *Conceiving Cosmopolitanism*. Oxford: Oxford University Press.

Bélanger, Alain, and Éric Caron Malenfant. 2005. "Ethnocultural Diversity in Canada: Prospects for 2017." *Canadian Social Trends*, Statistics Canada. Catalogue no. 11-008:18–22.

Bellich, James. 1986. *The New Zealand Wars and the Victorian Interpretation of Racial Conflict*. Auckland: Auckland University Press.

Bentley, Michael, Tracy Mattingly, Christine Hough, and Claudette Bennett. 2003. *Census Quality Survey to Evaluate Responses to the Census 2000 Question on Race: An Introduction to the Data. Census 2000 Evaluation B.3.* Washington, DC: US Census Bureau.

Berger, Peter, and Thomas Luckmann. 1967. *The Social Construction of Reality: A Treatise in the Sociology of Knowledge.* New York: Anchor Books/Doubleday.

Berthoud, Richard. 1998. "Defining Ethnic Groups: Origin or Identity?" *Patterns of Prejudice* 32 (2): 53–63.

Bettez, Silvia Cristina. 2011. *But Don't Call Me White: Mixed Race Women Exposing Nuances of Priviledge and Oppression Politics.* Boston: Sense Publishers.

Bhabha, Homi. 1994. *The Location of Culture.* London: Routledge.

———. 1996. "Cultures In Between." In Hall, Stuart, and Paul Du Gay (eds.). *Questions of Cultural Identity.* London: Sage Publications.

Biles, John, Erin Tolley, and Humera Ibrahim. 2005. "Does Canada Have a Multicultural Future?" *Canadian Diversity* 4 (1): 23–28.

Blickle, Peter. 2002. *Heimat: A Critical Theory of the German Idea of Homeland.* Rochester, NY: Camden House.

Blum, Alain, and C. Gousseff. 1996. "Statistiques Ethniques et Nationales dans l'Empire Russe et en URSS." In Rallu, J. L., and Y. Courbage (eds.). *Démographie et Ethnicité.* Paris: INED.

Blumenfeld, Warren J., Khyati Y. Joshi, and Ellen E. Fairchild (eds.). 2009. *Investigating Religious Oppression in the United States.* Rotterdam: Sense Publishers.

Blunt, Alison. 2005. *Domicile and Diaspora: Anglo-Indian Women and the Spatial Politics of Home.* Oxford: Blackwell.

Boladeras, Jean. 2007. "The Desolate Loneliness of Racial Passing." In Perkins, Maureen (ed.). *Visibly Different: Face, Place and Race in Australia.* Bern: Peter Lang.

Bonilla-Silva, Eduardo. 2006. *Racism Without Racists: Color-blind Racism and the Persistence of Racial Inequality in the United States.* Lanham, MD: Rowman & Littlefield.

Bonnet, Alistair. 1998. "How the British Working Class Became White: The Symbolic (Re)formation of Racialized Capitalism." *Journal of Historical Sociology* 11 (3): 322.

Bonoguore, Tenille. 2008. "Funnyman Peters to Talk up Toronto." *Globe and Mail,* May 16, 2008: A15.

Bourdieu, Pierre, and Loïc Wacquant. 1991. "On the Cunning of Imperialist Reason." *Theory, Culture, and Society* 16 (1): 41–58.

Bozic-Vrbancic, Senka. 2005. "After All, I Am Partly Maori, Partly Dalmatian, but First of All I Am a New Zealander." *Ethnography* 6 (4): 517–42.

Brace, C. Loring. 2005. *"Race" Is a Four-Letter Word: The Genesis of a Concept.* New York: Oxford.

Bradford, Ben. 2006. *Who Are the "Mixed" Ethnic Group?* London: ONS.

"Brasília–DF. Comissão Geral para Debater o Estatuto da Igualdade Racial." Nação-mestiça. http://www.nacaomestica.org/.

Brathwaithe, E. Kamau. 1974. *Contradictory Omens: Cultural Diversity and Integration in the Caribbean*. Kingston: Savacou.

Braithwaite, Lloyd. 1957. "Sociology and Demographic Research in the British Caribbean." *Social and Economic Studies* 6 (4): 83–116.

Braithwaite, Lloyd. 1970 [1953]. *Social Stratification in Trinidad*. Kingston: Institute for Social and Economic Research, University of the West Indies at Mona.

Braun, Robert, and Ruud Koopmans. 2010. "The Diffusion of Ethnic Violence in Germany. The Role of Social Similarity." *European Sociological Review* 26 (1): 111–23.

Brelsford, W. V. 1965. *Generation of Men: The European Pioneers of Northern Rhodesia*. Salisbury: Stuart Manning.

Brereton, Bridget. 1979. *Race Relations in Colonial Trinidad: 1870–1900*. Cambridge: Cambridge University Press.

———. 1981. *A History of Modern Trinidad: 1783–1962, Kingston, London and Port of Spain*. London: Heinemann.

Briscoe, Mattie H. 1956. "A Study of Eight Foreign-Born Children of Mixed Parentage Who Have Been Adopted by Negro Couples in the U.S." MA thesis, Atlanta University School of Education.

Brodkin, Karen. 1998. *How Jews Became White Folks and What That Says About Race in America*. New Brunswick, NJ: Rutgers University Press.

Bromlei, Iu. V. 1973. *Etnos I etnografiia*. Moscow: Nauka.

Broome, Richard. 2010. *Aboriginal Australians: A History Since 1788*. 4th ed. Sydney: Allen & Unwin.

Broomfield, Sidney Spencer. 1931. *Kachalola or the Mighty Hunter*. New York: William Morrow.

Brown, Cindy (alias). 2009. Interview with Lily Anne Yumi Welty, Kadena, Okinawa, July 7.

Brubaker, Rogers. 1992. *Citizenship and Nationhood in France and Germany*. Cambridge, MA: Harvard University Press.

———. 1996. *Nationalism Reframed: Nationhood and the National Question in the New Europe*. Cambridge: Cambridge University Press.

Brunsma, David L. (ed.). 2006. *Mixed Messages: Multiracial Identities in the "Color-Blind" Era*. Boulder, CO: Lynne Rienner Publishers.

Bryan, Patrick. 1996. "The Creolization of the Chinese Community in Jamaica." In Reddock, Rhoda (ed.). *Ethnic Minorities in Caribbean Society*. Kingston: ISER.

Buchanan, Patrick J. 2002. *The Death of the West: How Dying Populations and Immigrant Invasions Imperil Our Country and Civilization*. New York: Thomas Dunne Books/St. Martin's Press.

Burdick, John. 1992. "The Myth of Racial Democracy." *North American Congress on Latin America Report on the Americas* 25 (4): 40–42.

———. 1998. "The Lost Constituency of Brazil's Black Movement." *Latin American Perspectives* 25 (1): 136–55.

Burton, Jonathon, et al. 2010. "Measuring Ethnicity: Challenges and Opportunities for Survey Research." *Ethnic and Racial Studies* 33 (8): 1332–49.

Byron, Jessica. 2000. "The Impact of Globalization on the Caribbean." In Benn, Denis, and Kenneth Hall (eds.). *Globalisation: A Calculus of Inequality: Perspectives from the South*. Kingston: Ian Randle.

Cabezas, Amalia. L. 2009. *Economies of Desire: Sex and Tourism in Cuba and the Dominican Republic*. Philadelphia: Temple University Press.

Caglar, Ayse S. 1997. "Hyphenated Identities and the Limits of 'Culture.'" In Modood, Tariq, and Pnina Werbner (eds.). *The Politics of Multiculturalism in the New Europe: Racism, Identity and Community*. London: Zed Books.

Calliste, Agnes. 1994. "Race, Gender and Canadian Immigration Policy: Blacks From the Caribbean, 1900–1932." *Journal of Canadian Studies* 28 (4): 131–47.

Callister, Paul. 2008. "Skin Colour: Does It Matter in New Zealand?" *Policy Quarterly* 4 (1): 18–25.

Callister, Paul, Robert Didham, and Anna Kivi. 2009. "Who Are we? The Conceptualisation and Expression of Ethnicity." *Official Statistics Research Series 4*. http://www.statisphere.govt.nz/official-statistics-research/series/vol-4.htm (accessed May 18, 2012).

Caplan, Lionel. 2001. *Children of Colonialism: Anglo-Indians in a Postcolonial World*. Oxford: Berg.

Castles, Stephen, and Alastair Davidson. 2000. *Citizenship and Migration: Globalization and the Politics of Belonging*. Houndsmills: Macmillan.

Catuogo, Claudio. 2010. "Boatengs Käfig." *Süddeutsche Zeitung*, June 23, 2010. http://www.sueddeutsche.de/sport/wm-kevin-prince-boateng-boatengs-kaefig-1.963868.

Childs, Erica Chito. 2009. *Fade to Black: Interracial Images in Popular Culture*. Lanham, MD: Rowman & Littlefield.

Chin, Rita. 2007. *The Guest Worker Question in Postwar Germany*. Cambridge: Cambridge University Press.

———. 2009. "Guest Worker Migration and the Unexpected Return of Race." In Chin et al., *After the Nazi Racial State: Difference and Democracy in Germany and Europe*. Ann Arbor: University of Michigan Press.

Chin, Rita, Heide Fehrenbach, Geoff Eley, and Atina Grossmann (eds.). 2009. *After the Nazi Racial State: Difference and Democracy in Germany and Europe*. Ann Arbor: University of Michigan Press.

Ching, Leo T. S. 2001. *Becoming "Japanese": Colonial Taiwan and the Politics of Identity Formation*. Berkeley: University of California Press.

Choo, Christine. 2004. "Chinese-Indigenous Australian Connections in Regional Western Australia." In Wilding, Raelene, and Farida Tilbury (eds.). *A Changing People: Diverse Contributions to the State of Western Australia*. Perth, Western Australia: Department of Premier and Cabinet, Office of Multicultural Affairs.

Choo, Christine, Antoinette Carrier, Clarissa Choo, and Simon Choo. 2007. "Being Eurasian." In Perkins, Maureen (ed.). *Visibly Different: Face, Place and Race in Australia*. Bern: Peter Lang.

Christian, Mark. 2000. *Multiracial Identity: An International Perspective*. London/New York: Macmillian/St. Martin's Press.

Christy, Alan S. 1993. "The Making of Imperial Subjects in Okinawa." *Positions* 1 (3): 607–39.

CIA. 2012. "Australian People." Central Intelligence Agency Handbook. http://www.theodora.com/wfbcurrent/australia/australia_people.html (accessed May 13, 2012).

Clark, Maureen. 2001. "*Unmasking Mudrooroo*." *Kunapipi: Journal of Postcolonial Writing* XXIII (2): 48–62.

CNN Wire Staff. 2012. "George Zimmerman Charged, Hearing Expected Thursday." http://edition.cnn.com/2012/04/11/justice/florida-teen-shooting/index.html.

Cohen, Robin. 2001a. "The Diaspora of a Diaspora: The Case of the Caribbean." In Goulbourne, Harry (ed). *Race and Ethnicity: Critical Concepts in Sociology.* Volume II. London: Routledge.

———. 2001b. "Fuzzy Frontiers of Identity: The British Case." In Goulbourne, Harry (ed). *Race and Ethnicity: Critical Concepts in Sociology.* Volume II. London: Routledge.

Collins, Patricia Hill. 2005. *Black Sexual Politics: African Americans, Gender and the New Racism.* New York: Routledge.

"Coloque de volta MESTIÇO no censo do IBGE." Naçãomestiça. http://www.nacaomestica.org/.

Conceição, Fernando. 2004. "As cotas contra o apocalipse." Folha de São Paulo, Caderno Mais, June 27, 2004.

Constable, Nicole. 2005. *Cross-Border Marriages: Gender and Mobility in Transnational Asia.* Philadelphia: University of Pennslyvania Press.

Coon, Carleton. 1939. *The Races of Europe.* New York: Macmillan.

Coon, Carleton, Stanley M. Garn, and Joseph B. Birdsell. 1950. *Races: A Study of the Problems of Race Formation in Man.* Springfield, IL: Charles C. Thomas.

Cornell, Stephen, and Douglas Hartman. 2007. *Ethnicity and Race: Making Identities in a Changing World.* Thousand Oaks, CA: Pine Forge Press.

Costa, Emilia Viotti da. 1985. *The Brazilian Empire: Myths and Histories.* Chicago: University of Chicago Press.

Cottrol, Robert J. 2013. *The Long Lingering Shadow: Slavery, Race, and Law in the American Hemisphere.* Athens and London: University of Georgia Press.

Cox, David. 1987. *Migration and Welfare: An Australian Perspective.* Sydney: Prentice-Hall.

Cox, Lindsay. 1993. *Kotahitanga: The Search for Maori Political Unity.* Auckland: Oxford University Press.

Cox, Oliver. 1970. *Caste, Class, and Race: A Study in Social Dynamics.* New York: Monthly Review Press.

Culjak, Toni. 2001. "Searching for a Place in Between: The Autobiographies of Three Canadian Metis Women." *American Review of Canadian Studies* 31 (1/2): 137–57.

DaCosta, Kimberly. 2007. *Making Multiracials: State, Family and Market in the Redrawing of the Color Line.* Stanford, CA: Stanford University Press.

Daniel, G. Reginald. 2002. *More than Black? Multiracial Identity and the New Racial Order.* Philadelphia: Temple University Press.

———. 2006. *Race and Multiraciality in Brazil and the United States: Converging Paths?* University Park: Pennsylvania State University Press.

———. 2012. *Machado de Assis: Multiraciality and the Brazilian Novelist.* University Park: Pennsylvania State University Press.

Darroch, Michael, and Gordon Darroch. 2010. "Commentary: Losing our Census." *Canadian Journal of Communication* 35: 609–17.

Davis, F. James. 1991. *Who Is Black? On Nation's Definition.* University Park: Pennsylvania State University Press.

DeBonis, Steven. 1995. *Children of the Enemy: Oral Histories of Vietnamese Amerasians and Their Mothers.* Jefferson, NC: McFarland.

Degler, Carl N. 1971. *Neither Black nor White: Slavery and Race Relations in Brazil and the United States.* Madison: University of Wisconsin Press.

Dei, George. 2007. "Speaking Race: Silence, Salience, and the Politics of Anti-Racist Scholarship." In Hier, Sean P., and B. Singh Bolaria (eds.). *Race and Racism in 21st Century Canada, Continuity, Complexity, and Change.* Peterborough, ON: Broadview Press.

Deloria, Philip. 1998. *Playing Indian.* New Haven, CT: Yale University Press.

Demograficheskii ezhegodnik Kazakhstana. Statisticheskii sbornik. 2008. Astana, Kazakhstan.

DeRango-Adem, Adebe, and Andrea Thompson (eds.). 2011. *Other Tongues: Mixed-Race Women Speak Out.* Toronto: Inanna.

Deutschlandstiftung Integration. 2010. *Sarrazin: Eine deutsche Debatte.* München: Piper.

DIAC. 2010. "Fact Sheet 2." Australia Department of Immigration and Citizenship. http://www.immi.gov.au/media/fact-sheets/02key.htm (accessed March 13, 2012).

DeWitt, Mike, and Adam Stepan, 2007. "Brazil in Black and White." http://www.pbs.org/wnet/wideangle/shows/brazil2/.

Dineen-Wimberly, Ingrid. 2009. "Mixed-Race Leadership in African America: The Regalia of Race and National Identity in the U.S., 1862–1916." PhD dissertation, Department of History, University of California Santa Barbara,.

Diptee, Audra. 2000. "Indian Men, Afro-Creole Women: 'Casting' Doubt on Interracial Sexual Relationships between the Indo and Afro Communities of the Late Nineteenth Century Caribbean." *Immigrants and Minorities* 19 (3): 1–24.

Doortmont, Michel. 2005. *The Pen-Pictures of Modern Africans and African Celebrities by Charles Francis Hutchinson: A Collective Biography of Elite Society in The Gold Coast Colony,* Leiden: Brill.

Dotson, F., and L. Dotson. 1963. "Indians and Coloureds in Rhodesia and Nyasaland." *Race* 5 (1): 61–75.

Dougla: A Celebration of Trinidad and Tobago, November/December 2009.

Douglass, Lisa. 1992. *The Power of Sentiment: Love, Hierarchy and the Jamaican Family Elite.* Boulder, CO: Westview Press.

Douillet, Catherine M. 2005. "A Contradictory Callaloo: Ethnic Divisions and Mixing in Trinidad." PhD thesis, Graduate College, University of Iowa.

Dower, John W. 1999. *Embracing Defeat: Japan in the Wake of World War Two*. New York: W.W. Norton.

Drössler, Stefan. 2007. Liner notes to *Nathan der Weise* (orig. München: Filmhaus Bavaria, 1922). Directed by Manfred Noa; written by Hans Kyser; based on the stage play by Ephraim Lessing. Edition Filmmuseum. 2d ed. http://www.edition-filmmuseum.com/product_info.php/language/en/info/p26_Nathan-der-Weise.html (retrieved April 16, 2011).

Dummett, Ann, and Andrew Nicol. 1990. *Subjects, Citizens, Aliens and Others: Nationality and Immigration Law*. London: Weidenfeld and Nicolson.

Durie, Mason. 1998. *Te Mana, Te Kawanatanga: The Politics of Maori Self-Determination*. Auckland: Oxford University Press.

Dutt, Kuntala Lahiri. 1990. *In Search of a Homeland: Anglo-Indians and McCluskiegunge*. Calcutta: Minerva Associates.

Duvall, Ted (alias). 2009. Interview with Lily Anne Yumi Welty, Ginowan, Okinawa, September 21.

Dzidzienyo, Anani. 1979. "The Position of Blacks in Brazilian and Cuban Society." *Minority Group Rights Reports, 7*. London: Minority Rights Group.

Eberhardt, Piotr. 2003. *Ethnic Groups and Population Changes in Twentieth-Century Central-Eastern Europe: History, Data, and Analysis*. Armonk, NY, and London: M.E. Sharpe.

Edgar, Adrienne. 2007. "Marriage, Modernity and the 'Friendship of Nations': Interethnic Intimacy in Postwar Soviet Central Asia in Comparative Perspective." *Central Asian Survey* 26 (4) :581–600.

Edwards, Penny, Debjani Ganguly, and Jacqueline Lo. 2007. "Pigments of the Imagination: Theorising, Performing and Historicising Mixed Race." *Journal of Intercultural Studies* 28 (1): 1–13.

Elam, Michele. 2011. *The Souls of Mixed Folk: Race, Politics and Aesthetics in the New Millennium*. Palo Alto, CA: Stanford University Press.

Ellinghaus, Katherine. 2006. *Taking Assimilation to Heart: Marriages of White Women and Indigenous Men in the United States and Australia, 1887–1937*. Lincoln: University of Nebraska Press.

England, Sarah. 2010. "Mixed and Multiracial in Trinidad and Honduras: Re-thinking Mixed-Race Identities in Latin American and the Caribbean." *Ethnic and Racial Studies* 33 (2): 195–213.

Enloe, Cynthia. 2000. *Bananas, Beaches and Bases: Making Feminist Sense of International Politics*. Los Angeles: University of California Press.

Erickson, Rebecca J. 1995. "The Importance of Authenticity for Self and Society." *Symbolic Interaction* 18 :121–44.

Etnodemograficheskii Ezhegodnik Kazakhstana: Statisticheskii Sbornik. 2006. Almaty, Kazakhstan.

Fanon, Franz. 2008. *Black Skin, White Masks*. New York: Grove Press.

Favell, Adrian. 2008. *Eurostars and Eurocities: Free Movement and Mobility in an Integrating Europe*. Oxford: Blackwell.

Feng, Zhiqiang, Paul Boyle, Maarten van Hamm, and Gillian Raab. 2010. "Neighbourhood Ethnic Mix and the Formation of Mixed-Ethnic unions in Britain." In Stillwell, John, and Maarten van Ham (eds.). *Ethnicity and Integration*. Dordrecht: Springer.

Ferguson, James. 1999. *Expectations of Modernity: Myths and Meanings of Urban Life on the Zambian Copperbelt*. Berkeley: University of California Press.

Fernández, Patricia, Juan Enrique García, and Diana Esther Ávila. 2002. "Estimaciones de la Población Indígena en México." In *La Situación Demográfica de México*. México D.F.: CONAPO.

Fichte, Johann Gottlieb. 2008 [807]. *Addresses to the German Nation*. Translated by Gregory Moore. Cambridge: Cambridge University Press.

Fierman, William. 2006. "Language and Education in Post-Soviet Kazakhstan: Kazakh-Medium instruction in Urban Schools." *Russian Review* 65: 98–116.

Fija Bairon and Patrick Heinrich. 2007. "'Wanne Uchinanchu—I Am Okinawan': Japan, the U.S. and Okinawa's Endangered Languages." *Asia Pacific Journal* (Japan Focus). http://japanfocus.org/-Fija-Bairon/2586 (accessed July 14, 2009).

Fine, Gary Alan. "Crafting Authenticity: The Validation of Identity in Self-Taught Art." *Theory and Society* 32: 153–80.

Finney, Nisa, and Ludi Simpson. 2009. *"Sleepwalking to Segregation"? Challenging Myths about Race and Migration*. Bristol: Policy Press.

Fish, Robert. 2002. "The Heiress and the Love Children: Sawada Miki and the Elizabeth Saunders Home for Mixed-Blood Orphans in Postwar Japan." PhD dissertation, Department of History, University of Hawai'i at Manoa..

Fleras, Augie, and Jean Leonard Elliot. 1992. *Multiculturalism in Canada: The Challenge of Diversity*. Toronto: Nelson Canada.

Flint, John. 1974. *Cecil Rhodes*. Boston: Little, Brown.

Flores, René, and Edward E. Telles. 2012. "Social Stratification in Mexico: Disentangling Color, Ethnicity, and Race." *American Sociological Review* 77 (3): 486–94.

Fontaine, Pierre-Michel. 1981. "Transnational Relations and Racial Mobilization: Emerging Black Movements." In Stack, John F. (ed.). *Ethnic Identities in a Transnational World*. Westport, CT: Greenwood Press.

Ford Foundation. 2011. http://www.fordfoundation.org/regions/brazil.

Ford, Margot. 2009. *In Your Face: A Case Study in Post-Multicultural Australia*. Darwin: Charles Darwin University Press.

Forrest, James, and Kevin Dunn. 2006. "'Core' Culture Hegemony and Multiculturalism: Perceptions of the Privileged Position of Australians with British Backgrounds." *Ethnicities* 6 (2): 203–30.

Forte, Maximilian C. 2011. "Carib Identity, Racial Politics, and the Problem of Belonging." http://indigenousreview.blogspot.com/2011/05/carib-identity-racial-politics-problem.html, accessed on December 28, 2011.

Foster, Mira. Forthcoming. "Successful Immigrants? The Stories of Polish Immigrants in Germany." In Spickard, Paul R. (ed.). *Multiple Identities: Migrants, Ethnicity, and Membership*. Bloomington: Indiana University Press.

Fozdar, Farida. 2011a. "Constructing Australian Citizenship as Christian: Or How to Exclude Muslims from the National Imagining." In Lobo, Michele, and Fethi Mansouri (eds.). *Migration, Citizenship and Intercultural Relations*. Burlington: Ashgate.

Fozdar, Farida. 2011b. "The Choir Boy and the Mad Monk: Christianity, Islam, Australia's Political Landscape and Prospects for Multiculturalism." *Journal of Intercultural Studies* 32 (6): 621–36.

Francis, Margot. 2011. *Creative Subversions: Whiteness and Indigeneity in the National Imaginary*. Vancouver: University of British Columbia Press.

Franco, Nádia. 2012. "Dilma sanciona Lei de Cotas e veta apenas artigo que criava mecanismo de Seleção." *Terra*, August 29, 2012. http://noticias.terra.com.br/brasil/noticias/0,,OI6113370-EI306,00-Dilma+sanciona+Lei+de+Cotas+e+veta+apenas+artigo+que+criava+mecanismo+de+selecao.html

Freyre, Gilberto. 1963a. *The Mansions and the Shanties*. Translated by Harriet de Onís. New York: Alfred A. Knopf.

———. 1963b. *The Masters and the Slaves*. Translated by Harriet de Onís. New York: Alfred A. Knopf.

———. 1970. *Order and Progress*. Translated and edited by Rod W. Horton. New York: Alfred A. Knopf.

Friesen, Abraham. 2006. *In Defense of Privilege: Russian Mennonites and the State Before and During World War I*. Winnipeg: Kindred Productions.

Fry, Peter. 2000. "Politics, Nationality, and the Meaning of Race." *Daedalus* 129 (2): 83–118.

Fry, Peter, and Yvonne Maggie. 2007. "Política Social de Alto Risco." In Fry, Peter, and Yvonne Maggie Marcos, Chor Maio, Simone Monteiro, and Ricardo Ventura Santos. *Divisões Perigosas: Políticas Raciais no Brasil Contemporâneo*. Rio de Janeiro: Civilização Brasileira.

Fukuchi Hiroaki. 1980. *Okinawa no konketsuji to haha tachi (Okinawa's mixed bloods and their mothers)*. Naha: Aoi Umi Shuppansha.

Fulbeck, Kip. 2006. *Part Asian, 100% Hapa*. San Francisco: Chronicle Books.

Galdino, Daniela, and Larissa Santos Pereira. 2003. "Acesso à Universidade: Condições de Produção de um Discurso Facioso." In Bernardino, Joaze, and Daniela Galdino. *Levando Raça a Sério: Ação Afirmativa e Universidade*. Rio de Janeiro: P&A Editora.

Ganter, Regina. 2006. *Mixed Relations: Asian-Aboriginal Contact in North Australia*. Crawley, Perth: University of Western Australia Press.

Garcea, Joseph. 2009. "Postulations on the Fragmentary Effects of Multiculturalism in Canada." *Canadian Ethnic Studies* 40 (1): 141–60.

García Díaz, Bernardo. 2002. "La Migración Cubana a Veracruz 1870–1910." In Vilaboy García Díaz, Bernardo and Sergio Guerra (eds.). *La Habana/Veracruz, Veracruz/La Habana: Las Dos Orillas*. Xalapa: Universidad Veracuzana.

Gardiner, Greg, and Eleanor Bourke. 2000. "Indigenous Populations, 'Mixed' Discourses and Identities." *People and Place* 8 (3): 43–52.

Gelfand, M. 1961. *Northern Rhodesia in the Days of Charter*. Oxford: Oxford University Press.

Ghosh, Bimal (ed.). 2000. *Return Migration: Journey of Hope or Despair*. Geneva: International Organization of Migration.

Gilroy, Paul. 1998. "Race Ends Here." *Ethnic and Racial Studies*. 21 (5): 838–47.

———. 2000. *Between Camps: Nations, Culture and the Allure of Race*. London: Allen Lane.

Glissant, Edouard. 1981. *Le Discours Antillais*. Paris: Editions de Seuil.

Gobineau, Arthur comte de. 1999 [1853–55]. *The Inequality of Human Races*. Translated by Adrian Collins. New York: Howard Fertig.

Göktürk, Deniz, David Gramling, and Anton Kaes (eds.), 2007. *Germany in Transit: Nation and Migration, 1955–2005*. Berkeley: University of California Press.

Golash-Boza, Tanya. "Does Whitening Happen? Distinguishing between Race and Color Labels in an African-Descended Community in Peru." *Social Problems* 57: 138–56.

Goldani, Ana Maria. 1999. "Racial Inequality in the Lives of Brazilian Women." In Reichmann, Rebecca (ed.). *Race Relations in Contemporary Brazil: From Indifference to Equality*. University Park: Pennsylvania State University Press.

Goldberg, David Theo. 2002. *The Racial State*. Oxford: Wiley.

Goldschmidt, Henry, and Elizabeth McAlister (eds.). 2004. *Race, Nation, and Religion in the Americas*. New York: Oxford.

Gomes, Nilma Lino, and Aracy Alves Martins. 2004. *Afirmando Direitos: Acesso e Permanêcia de Jovens na Universidade*. Belo Horizonte: Autêntica.

Gonzalez Navarro, Moisés. 1970. "Mestizaje in Mexico During the National Period." In Morner, Magnus (ed). *Race and Class in Latin America*. New York: Columbia University Press.

Goodhart, David. 2008. "Has Multiculturalism Had Its Day?" *Literary Review of Canada* 16 (3): 3–4.

Goodyear, Rosemary. 2009. "The Differences within, Diversity in Age Structure between and within Ethnic Groups." Statistics New Zealand. www.stats.govt.nz/.../population/census.../the-differences-within.ashx (accessed March 1, 2012).

Goot, Murray, and Ian Watson. 2005. "Immigration, Multiculturalism and National Identity." In Wilson, Shaun, Gabrielle Meagher, Rachel Gibson, David Denemark, and Mark Western (eds.). *Australian Social Attitudes*. Sydney: University of New South Wales Press.

Graham, Lloyd B. 1958. *The Adoption of Children from Japan by American Families 1952–1958*. Dissertation, Department of Social Work, University of Toronto.

Grant, Madison. 1916. *The Passing of the Great Race, or The Racial Basis of European History*. New York: Scribner's.

———. 1925. *Der Untergang der großen Rasse: Die Rassen als Grundlage der Geschichte Europas*. Translated by Rudolf Polland. München: Lehmanns.

Grazian, David. 2003. *Blue Chicago: The Search for Authenticity in Urban Blues Clubs*. Chicago: University of Chicago.

Gregor, Neil. 2010. Review of Rita Chin, Heide Fehrenbach, Geoff Eley, and Atina Grossmann, eds., *After the Nazi Racial State: Difference and Democracy in Germany and Europe. American Historical Review* (December): 1548–49.

Grieco, Elizabeth M., and Rachel C. Cassidy. 2001. "Overview of Race and Hispanic Origin."Washington, DC: U.S. Department of Commerce.

Gross, Ariela J. 2007. "'Of Portuguese Origin': Litigating Identity and Citizenship Among the Little Races in Nineteenth-Century America." *Law and History Review* 25 (3): 467–512.

Guimarães, Antonio Sérgio Alfredo. 1999. "Measures to Combat Discrimination and Racial Inequality in Brazil." In Reichmann, Rebecca (ed.). *Race Relations in Contemporary Brazil: From Indifference to Equality.* University Park: Pennsylvania State University Press.

———. 2003. "Ações Afirmativas para a População Negra nas Universidades Brasileiras." In Emerson dos Santos, Renato, and Fátima Lobato (eds). *Ações Afirmativas: Políticas Públicas Contra as Desigualdades Raciais.* Rio de Janeiro: DP&A Editora.

Haebich, Anna. 2010. *Broken Circles: Fragmenting Indigenous Families 1800–2000.* Fremantle, WA: Fremantle Arts Centre Press.

Hage, Ghassan. 1998. *White Nation: Fantasies of White supremacy in a multicultural society.* Annandale, NSW: Pluto Press.

———. 2003. *Against Paranoid Nationalism: Searching for Hope in a Shrinking Society.* Sydney: Pluto Press.

Hall, Catherine. 1999. "William Knibb and the New Constitution of the New Black Subject." In Daunton, Martin, and Rick Halpern (eds.). *Empire and Others: British Encounters with Indigenous Peoples, 1600–1850.* London: UCL Press.

Hall, Kevin. 2002. "Brazil Program Will Set Aside Jobs for Blacks: Government Plans to   Address Inequities" *Detroit Free Press, June* 21, 2002. http://www.freep.com/news/nw/nbrazil11_20011001/.

Hanchard, Michael George. 1994. *Orpheus and Power: The Movimento Negro of Rio de Janeiro and São Paulo, Brazil, 1945–1988.* Princeton, NJ: Princeton University Press.

Handler, Richard. 1988. *Nationalism and the Politics of Culture in Québec.* Madison: University of Wisconsin Press.

Haraksingh, Kusha. 1992. "Caste in Trinidad and in India." Guest lecture to Introduction to Sociology I, University of the West Indies, St. Augustine.

Harewood, Jack. 1975. "The Population of Trinidad and Tobago." Port of Spain: CICRED Series.

Haritaworn, Jin. 2009. "Caucasian and Thai Make a Good Mix." *European Journal of Cultural Studies* 12 (1):59–78.

Harris, Angela P. 2009. "Introduction: Economies of Color." In Glenn, Evelyn Nakano (ed.). *Shades of Difference: Why Skin Color Matters.* Stanford, CA: Stanford University Press.

Harris, David R., and Jeremiah Joseph Sim. 2002. "Who Is Multiracial? Assessing the Complexity of Lived Race." *American Sociological Review 67*: 614–27.

Harris, Marvin. 1964. *Patters of Race in the Americas.* New York: Walker.

Hasenbalg, Carlos. 1985. "Race and Socioeconomic Inequalities in Brazil." In Fontaine, Pierre-Michel (ed.). *Race, Class and Power in Brazil.* Los Angeles: UCLA Center for African American Studies.

Henry, Frances, and Carol Tator. 2006. *The Colour of Democracy: Racism in Canadian Society, 3d ed.* Toronto: ITP Nelson.

Hensler, Benjamin. 2007. "Nao vale a pena (Not Worth the Trouble?): Afro-Brazilian Workers and Brazilian Anti-Discrimination Law." *Hastings International and Comparative Law Review* 30 (3): 267–346.

Herbert, Eugenia. 2002. *Twilight on the Zambezi: Late Colonialism in Central Africa.* Basingstoke: Palgrave Macmillan.

Hernández Cuevas, Marco Polo. 2004. *African Mexicans and the Discourse on Modern Nation.* Dallas: University Press of America.

———. 2005. *África en el Carnaval Mexicano.* México D.F.: Plaza y Valdes Editores.

Hernández, Tanya Katerí. 2012. *Racial Subordination in Latin America: The Role of the State, Customary Law, and the New Civil Rights Response.* New York: Cambridge University Press.

Herrera Lima, Fernando. 2001. "Transnational Families: Institutions of Transnational Social Space." In Pries, Ludger (ed.). *New Transnational Social Spaces: International Migration and Transnational Companies in the Early Twenty-first Century.* New York: Routledge.

Higman, Barry. 2006. "The Chinese in Trinidad: 1806–1838." In Look Lai, Walton (ed.). *Essays on the Chinese Diaspora in the Caribbean.* St. Augustine: self-published.

Hill, Lawrence. 2001. *Black Berry, Sweet Juice.* Toronto: Harper Collins.

Hirji, Faiza. 2009. "Somebody Going to Get Hurt Real Bad: The Race-Based Comedy of Russell Peters." *Canadian Journal of Communication* 34: 567–86.

Hirsch, Francine. 2005. *Empire of Nations: Ethnographic Knowledge and the Making of the Soviet Union.* Ithaca, NY: Cornell University Press.

Hollinger, David A. 1995. *Postethnic America: Beyond Multiculturalism.* New York: Basic Books.

———. 1998. "National Culture and Communities of Descent." *Reviews in American History* 26 (1): 312–28.

Holloway, Steven R., Richard Wright, and Mark Ellis. 2012. "Constructing Multiraciality in U.S. Families and Neighborhoods." In Edwards, Rosalind, Suki Ali, Chamion Cabellero, and Miri Song (eds.). *International Perspectives on Racial and Ethnic Mixedness and Mixing.* Abingdon, Oxon.: Routledge.

hooks, bell. 1992. *Black Looks: Race and Representation.* Cambridge, MA: South End Press.

———. 1995. *Yearning: Race, Gender, and Cultural Politics.* Boston: South End Press.

———. 2002. "Racial Quotas for a Racial Democracy." *NACLA Report on the Americas* 38 (4): 20–25.

Htun, Mala. 2004. "From 'Racial Democracy' to Affirmative Action: Changing State Policy on Race in Brazil." *Latin American Research Review* 39 (1): 60–89.

Hugel-Marshall, Ika. 2008. *Invisible Woman: Growing Up Black in Germany.* Oxford: Peter Lang.

Huntington, Samuel P. 1996. *The Clash of Civilizations and the Remaking of World Order.* New York: Simon & Schuster.

——. 2004. *Who Are We? The Challenges to America's National Identity.* New York: Simon & Schuster.

Hutton, Christopher M. 2005. *Race and the Third Reich: Linguistics, Racial Anthropology and Genetics in the Dialectic of Volk.* Cambridge: Polity.

Hyaman, Mari. 2012. "Brazilian Supreme Court Approves Racial Quotas in Univesity." April 29, 2012. http://latindispatch.com/2012/04/29/brazilian-supreme-court-approves-racial-quotas-in-university/.

Ibrahim, Habiba. 2012. *Troubling the Family: The Promise of Personhood and the Rise of Multracialism.* Minneapolis: University of Minnesota Press.

Ifekwunigwe, Jayne O. 2004. *Mixed Race Studies: A Reader.* London: Routledge.

Igenhorst, Heinz. 1997. *Die Russlanddeutschen: Aussiedler zwischen Tradition und Moderne.* Frankfurt-am-Main: Campus.

Instituto Brasileiro de Geografía e Estadísticas (IBGE). 2000. *Censo Demográfico 2000. Características Gerais da População. Resultados da Amostra. Tabelas de Resultados.* Rio de Janeiro: Fundação IBGE.

Jakupov, Jumabai. 2009. *Shala Kazakh: Proshloe, Nastoiashchee, Budushchee.* Almaty, Kazakhstan.

James, Carl E. 2003. *Seeing Ourselves: Exploring Race, Ethnicity and Culture.* 3d. ed. Toronto: Thompson Educational Publishing.

Jansen, C. J. 1981. "Problems and Issues in Post-war Immigration to Canada and their Effects on Origins and Characteristics of Immigrants." Paper presented at Meetings of the Canadian Population Society, Halifax: Dalhousie University.

Jeter, Jon. 2003. "Affirmative Action Debate Forces Brazil to Take Look in the Mirror." *Washington Post,* June 16, 2003.

Jacobs, Margaret. 2005. "Maternal Colonialism: White Women and Indigenous Child Removal in the American West and Australia, 1880–1940." *Western Historical Quarterly* 36: 453–76.

Johnson, Akemi. 2004. "Island Haafu, Tokyo Haafu: Learning English at the AmerAsian School in Okinawa." Senior honors thesis, Brown University.

Johnston, Marc P., and Kevin L. Nadal. 2010. "Multiracial Microaggressions: Exposing Monoracism." In Sue, Derald Wing (ed.). *Microaggressions and Marginality: Manifestation, Dynamics, and Impact.* Hoboken, NJ: John Wiley & Sons.

Jones, Gail, and Veronica Brady. 1997. Interview with Veronica Brady. *Journal of Australian Studies* 54/55: 143–45.

Jones, Jan. 2006. *Somewhere to Go? Something to Do? London Borough of Newham Young People's Survey.* Northampton, UK: Mattersoffact.

Joppke, Christian. 2004. "The Retreat of Multiculturalism in the Liberal State: Theory and Policy." *British Journal of Sociology* 55 (2): 237–57.

Jordon, D. Winthrop. 2013. "Historical Origins of the One-Drop Rule in the United States." Edited by Paul Spickard. *Journal of Critical Mixed Race Studies* 1 (1).

Jupp, James. 2007. *From White Australia to Woomera: The Story of Australian Immigration.* Port Melbourne, Victoria: Cambridge University Press.

Jupp, James, and John Nieuwenhuysen (eds.). 2007. *Social Cohesion in Australia.* Port Melbourne, Victoria: Cambridge University Press.

Kamel, Ali. 2006. *Não Somos Racistas: Uma Reação Aos Que Querem Nos Transformar Numa Nação Bicolor. 2a impressão.* Rio de Janeiro: Editora Nova Fronteira.

Kamizato, Elizabeth (alias). 2007. Interview with Lily Anne Yumi Welty, Osaka, December 23.

Katz, Ilan. 2012. "Mixed Race across Time and Place: An International Perspective." In Edwards, Rosalind, Suki Ali, Chamion Cabellero, and Miri Song (eds.). *International Perspectives on Racial and Ethnic Mixedness and Mixing.* Abingdon, Oxon.: Routledge.

Katzew, Ilona. 2004. *Casta Painting: Images of Race in Eighteenth-Century Mexico.* New Haven, CT: Yale University Press.

Keane, A. H. 1901. *Ethnology.* Cambridge: Cambridge University Press.

Kelley, Ninette, and Michael Trebilcock. 1998. *The Making of the Mosaic: A History of Canadian Immigration.* Toronto: University of Toronto Press.

Kempadoo, Kamala. 1999. *Sun, Sex and Gold: Tourism and Sex Work in the Caribbean.* Lanham, MD: Rowman & Littlefield.

Kerr, George H. 2000. *Okinawa: The History of an Island People.* Revised ed. Boston: Tuttle.

Khalid, Adeeb. 2007. *Islam after Communism: Religion and Politics in Central Asia.* Berkeley: University of California Press.

Khan, Aisha. 1993. "What Is a Spanish:? Ambiguity and 'Mixed' identity in Trinidad." In Yelvington, Kevin (ed.) *Trinidad Ethnicity.* Knoxville: The University of Tennessee Press.

Khanna, Nikki. 2010. "'If You're Half Black, You're Just Black': Reflected Appraisals and the Persistence of the One-Drop Rule." *Sociological Quarterly* 51 (1): 96–121.

Khoo, Siew-Ean. 2010. "Generational Change in Ethnic Composition and Inter-ethnic Marriage: Implications for Australian "Multiculturalism in the 21st Century." Draft for presentation at "A New Era in Australian Multiculturalism?" workshop, Melbourne, November 19–20.

Kibreab, Gaim. 1999. 'People, Place, Identity and Displacement." *Journal of Refugee Studies* 12 (4): 384–429.

Kich, George Kitahara. 1996. "In the Margins of Sex and Race: Difference, Marginality, and Flexibility." In Root, Maria P. P. (ed.). *The Multiracial Experience: Racial Borders as the New Frontier.* Newbury Park, CA: Sage.

Kidd, Rosalind. 1997. *The Way We Civilise: Aboriginal Affairs—the Untold Story.* Brisbane: University of Queensland Press.

Kim, Bok-Lim C. 1977. "Asian Wives of U.S. Servicemen: Women in Shadows." *Amerasia Journal* 4 (1): 91–115.

Kina, Saeko (alias). 2009. Interview with Lily Anne Yumi Welty, Chatan, Okinawa, October 19.

King, Michael. 1988. *Being Pakeha: An Encounter with New Zealand and the Maori Renaissance*. Auckland: Hodder & Stoughton.

King, Rebecca C. 2000. "Racialization, Recognition and Rights: Lumping and Splitting Multiracial Asian Americans and the 2000 Census." *Journal of Asian American Studies* 3 (2): 191–217.

King, Russell. 2000. "Generalizations from the History of Return Migration." In Ghosh, Bimal (ed.). *Return Migration: Journey of Hope or Despair*. Geneva: International Organization for Migration.

King-O'Riain, Rebecca C. 2000. "Racialization, Recognition and Rights: Lumping and Splitting Multiracial Asian Americans and the 2000 Census" [as Rebecca C. King]. *Journal of Asian American Studies* 3 (2): 191–217.

———. 2006. *Pure Beauty: Judging Race in Japanese American Beauty Pageants*. Minneapolis: University of Minnesota Press.

———. 2007. "Counting on the Celtic Tiger: Adding Ethnic Census Categories in the Republic of Ireland." *Ethnicities* 7 (4): 516–42.

———. Working paper. "Globalization, Emotional Ties and Digital Technology: Skyping and the Intimate Transnational Practices of International Families and Couples."

Kirk-Greene, Anthony. 1979. "Introduction." In Allen, Charles (ed).. *In Tales from the Dark Continent*. New York: St. Martin's Press.

Kissane, Karen. 2010. "Case against Bolt to Test Racial Identity, Free-Speech Limits." theage.com.au. September 30, 2010. http://www.theage.com.au/action/printArticle?id=1956248 (accessed March 18, 2012).

Klein, Herbert S. 1972. "Nineteenth-Century Brazil." In Cohen, David W., and Jack P. Greene (eds.). *Neither Slave nor Free: The Freemen of African Descent in the Slave Societies of the New World*. Baltimore: Johns Hopkins University Press.

Klekowski von Koppenfels, Amanda. 2003. "Aussiedler Migration to Germany: Questioning the Importance of Citizenship for Integration." Paper prepared for Alumni Conference, Common Global Responsibility, Washington, DC. November 6–9.

Knight, Alan. 1990. "Racism, Revolution, and Indigenismo: Mexico, 1910–1940." In Graham, Richard (ed). *The Idea of Race in Latin America, 1870–1940*. Austin: University of Texas Press.

Kobayashi, Audrey. 1993. "Multiculturalism: Representing a Canadian Institution." In Duncan, James S., and David Ley (eds.). *Place/Culture/Representation*. London: Routledge.

Kohn, Hans. 1967. *Prelude to Nation-States: The French and German Experience, 1789–1815*. Princeton, NJ: D. Van Nostrand.

Kozeki, Keiko 1967. *Nihonjin Keiko: Aru konketsu shōjo no shuki* [*Japanese Keiko: The Memoirs of a Multiracial Girl*]. Tokyo: Bunka Hōsō Shuppanbu.

Krauss, W. W. 1941. "Race Crossing in Hawaii: A Summary of Six Years of Research." *Journal of Heredity* 32: 371–78.

Kuczynski, R. R. 1953. *Demographic Survey of the British Colonial Empire, Volume 3.* Oxford: Oxford University Press.

Kukutai, Tahu. 2008. "Ethnic Self-Prioritisation of Dual and Multi-ethnic Youth in New Zealand." Statistics New Zealand. www.stats.govt.nz/.../ethnic-self-prioritisation-dual-multi-ethnic-youth-nz.ashx (accessed March 1, 2012).

Kwan-Lafond, Danielle. 2009. *Mixed Race Men in Canada: Identities, Masculinities and Multiculturalism.* Master's thesis, Ontario Institute for Studies in Education, University of Toronto.

———. 2011. "Racialized Masculinities in Canada." In Laker, Jason (ed.). *Canadian Perspectives on Men and Masculinities.* Oxford: Oxford University Press.

Kymlicka, Will. 1995. *Multicultural Citizenship.* Oxford: Oxford University Press.

———. 2007. *Multicultural Odysseys; Navigating the New International Politics of Diversity.* New York: Oxford University Press.

———. 2010. *Multicultural Citizenship: A Liberal Theory of Minority Rights.* New York: Oxford University Press.

La Ferla, Ruth. 2003. "Generation E.A.: Ethnically Ambiguous." *New York Times,* December 28. http://www.nytimes.com/2003/12/28/style/generation-ea-ethnically-ambiguous.html?pagewanted=all&src=pm.

Laidlaw, Zoe. 2005. *Colonial Connections 1815–45: Patronage, the Information Revolution and Colonial Government.* Manchester: Manchester University Press.

Lake, Marilyn, and Henry Reynolds. 2008. *Drawing the Global Colour Line: White Men's Countries and the Question of Racial Equality.* Melbourne: Melbourne University Press.

Laruelle, Marlene. 2008. "The Concept of Ethnogenesis in Central Asia: Its Political Context and Institutional Mediators, 1940–1950. " *Kritika* 9 (1): 169–88.

Lawrence, Lee. 2006. "South Asian Stand-Up Comedy." *Wall Street Journal Asia,* December 15, 2006: W12.

Lee, Christopher Joon-Hai. 2009. "'A Generous Dream to Realize': The Making of the Anglo-African Community of Nyasaland 1929–1940." In Adhikari, Mohamed (ed.). *Burdened by Race: Coloured Identities in Southern Africa.* Cape Town: University of Cape Town Press.

Lee, Jennifer Wenshya, and Yvonne M. Hébert. 2006. "The Meaning of Being Canadian: A Comparison Between Youth of Immigrant and Non-Immigrant Origins." *Canadian Journal of Education* 29 (2): 497–520.

Lentin, Alana and Titley, Gavan. 2011. *The Crisis of Multiculturalism: Racism in a Neo-Liberal Age.* London: Zed Books.

Lesser, Jeffrey H. 1991. "Are African-Americans African or American?: Brazilian Immigration Policy in the 1920s." *Review of Latin American Studies,* 4 (1): 115–37.

———. 1999. *Negotiating National Identity: Immigrants, Minorities, and the Struggle for Ethnicity in Brazil.* Durham, NC: Duke University Press.

Levine-Rasky, Cynthia. 2006. "Discontinuities of Multiculturalism." *Canadian Ethnic Studies* 3: 87–104.

Levitt, Peggy, and Mary Waters (eds.). 2002. *The Changing Face of Home*. Cambridge, MA: Harvard University Press.

Lie, John. 2004. *Multi-ethnic Japan*. Cambridge, MA: Harvard University Press.

Lincoln, Bradley. 2008. *Mix-d: UK. A Look at Mixed-Race Identities*. Manchester: Multiple Heritage Project/Ahmed Iqbal Ullah Education Trust.

Lipsitz, George. 2006. *The Possessive Investment in Whiteness: How White People Profit from Identity Politics*. Philadelphia: Temple University Press.

Local Government Association. 2008. *Where Have Recent In-Migrants Gone?* London: Local Government Association.

Lockwood, W. B. 1976. *An Informal History of the German Language, With Chapters on Dutch and Afrikaans, Frisian, and Yiddish*. 2d ed. London: Deutsch.

Lomnitz, Claudio. 1992. *Exits from the Labyrinth: Culture and Ideology in the Mexican National Space*. Berkeley: University of California Press.

Long, Edward. 1774. The *History of Jamaica*. London: T. Lownudes.

Look Lai. Walton. 2006. "The Trinidad Experience." In Walton Look Lai (ed.). *Essays on the Chinese Diaspora in the Caribbean*. St. Augustine: Self-published.

Lovell-Webster, Peggy. 1987. "The Myth of Racial Equality: A Study of Race and Mortality in Northeast Brazil." *Latinamericanist* (May): 1–6.

Lovell-Webster, Peggy, and Jeffery Dwyer. 1988. "The Cost of Not Being White in Brazil." *Sociology and Social Research* 72 (2): 136–38.

Loveman, Mara. 2009. "The Race to Progress: Census-Taking and Nation-Making in Brazil 1870–1920." *Hispanic American Historical Review* 89 (3): 435–70.

Lund, Joshua. 2012. *Mestizo State: Reading Race in Modern Mexico*. Minneapolis: University of Minnesota Press.

Luke, Carmen, and Allan Luke. 1999. *Theorizing Interracial Families and Hybrid Identity: An Australian Perspective*. Educational Theory 49 (2): 223–49.

Mackey, Eva. 2002. *The House of Difference: Cultural Politics and National Identity in Canada*. Toronto: University of Toronto Press.

Mahtani, Minelle. 2002a. "Interrogating the Hyphen-Nation: Canadian Muticultural Policy and 'Mixed Race' Identities." *Social Identities* 8 (1): 67–90.

———. 2002b. "What's In a Name?" *Ethnicities* 2 (4): 469–490.

———. 2005. "Mixed Metaphors: Situating Mixed Race Identity." In Lee, Jo-Ann and John Lutz (eds.). *Situating "Race" and Racisms in Space, Time and Theory*. Montreal: McGill-Queen's University Press.

———. Forthcoming. *Mixed Race Cartographies: Resisting the Romanticization of Multiraciality in Canada*. Vancouver: UBC Press.

Mahtani, Minelle, and April Moreno. 2001. "Same Difference: Towards a More Unified Discourse in 'Mixed Race' Theory.'" In Parker, David, and Miri Song, *Rethinking "Mixed Race"*. London: Pluto Press.

Mandaza, I. 1997. *Race, Colour and Class in Southern Africa: A Study of the Coloured Question in the Context of an Analysis of the Colonial and White Racial Ideology, and*

African Nationalism in Twentieth Century Zimbabwe, Zambia and Malawi. Harare: Sapes Books.

Mandel, Ruth. 2008. *Cosmopolitan Anxieties: Turkish Challenges to Citizenship and Belonging in Germany.* Durham, NC: Duke University Press.

Marchetti, Gina. 1994. *Romance and the "Yellow Peril:" Race, Sex and Discursive Strategies in Hollywood Fiction.* Berkeley: University of California Press.

Marger, Martin N. 1991. *Race and Ethnic Relations: American and Global Perspectives.* Belmont, CA: Wadsworth.

Margolis, Mac. 2003. "Brazil's Racial Revolution: Affirmative Action Has Finally Come of Age, And Latin America's Most Diverse Society May Change in Ways Few Had Ever Imagined." *Newsweek International.* 3 (11): 46.

Marques, Luciana. 2011. "Um em cada dez brasileiros é extremamente pobre: Governo estabelece renda familiar per capita de 70 reais por mês como piso abaixo do qual cidadão já se encontra em situação de miséria." Veja, April 3, 2011. http://veja.abril. com.br/noticia/brasil/governo-define-valor-de-70-reais-para-extrema-pobreza.

Martin, Terry. 2000. "Modernization or Neotraditionalism? Ascribed Nationality and Soviet Primordialism." In Fitzpatrick, Sheila, (ed.). *Stalinism: New Directions.* New York andLondon: Routledge.

———. 2001. *The Affirmative Action Empire: Nations and Nationalism in the Soviet Union, 1923–1939.* Ithaca, NY: Cornell University Press.

Martins, Sérgio da Silva, Carlos Alberto Medeiros, and Elisa Larkin Nascimento. 2004. "Paving Paradise: The Road from 'Racial Democracy' to Affirmative Action in Brazil." *Journal of Black Studies* 34 (6): 787–816.

Marx, Anthony W. 1998. *Making Race and Nation: A Comparison of South Africa, the United States, and Brazil.* Cambridge: Cambridge University Press.

Mason, Phillip. 1958. *The Birth of a Dilemma.* Oxford: Oxford University Press.

Matsushita, Shizuko. 1951. "Konketsuji wo sodatete" (*Raising Multiracials*). *Fujinkoron* 37 (12): 76–78. December 1951.

Matthews, Julie. 2007. "Eurasian Persuasions: Mixed Race, Performativity and Cosmpolitanism." *Journal of Intercultural Studies* 28 (1): 41–54.

Mawani, Renisa. 2009. *Colonial Proximities: Crossracial Encounters and Juridicial Truths in British Columbia, 1871–1921.* Vancouver: University of British Columbia Press.

McClelland, Keith, and Sonya Rose. 2006. "Citizenship and Empire, 1867–1928." In Hall, Catherine, and Sonya Rose (eds.). *At Home with the Empire: Metropolitan Culture and the Imperial World.* Cambridge: Cambridge University Press.

McNeil, Daniel. 2010. *Sex and Race in the Black Atlantic: Mulatto Devils and Multiracial Messiahs.* London: Routledge.

———. 2012. "'Mixture is a Neoliberal Good': Mixed-Race Metaphors and Post-Racial Masks." *Dark Matter* 9, 11. http://ww.darkmatter.101.org/site.

"Mestiçofobia É Racismo." http://www.nacaomestica.org/.

"Mestizo Identity Elimination Public Policies and Color, Race, Ethnicity Classificatory Systems" http://www.nacaomestica.org/.

Milan, Anne, and Brian Hamm. 2004. "Mixed Unions." *Canadian Social Trends*, Statistics Canada Catalogue no. 11-008-XPE: 2–6.

Milan, Anne, Hélene Maheux, and Tina Chui. 2010. "A Portrait of Couples in Mixed Unions." *Canadian Social Trends*. Statistics Canada: Catalogue No. 11-008-X.

Miller, Daniel. 1994. *Modernity—An Ethnographic Approach: Dualism and Mass Consumption in Trinidad*. Oxford: Berg.

Miller, Marilyn. 2004. *The Rise and Fall of the Cosmic Race: The Cult of Mestizaje in Latin America*. Austin: University of Texas Press.

Miller-Idriss, Cynthia. 2009. *Blood and Culture: Youth, Right-Wing Extremism, and National Belonging in Contemporary Germany*. Durham, NC: Duke University Press.

Milner-Thornton, Juliette. 2007. "A Feather Bed Dictionary: Colonialism and Sexuality." *History Compass Journal* 5: 1111–35.

———. 2009. "Absent White Fathers: Coloured Identity in Zambia." In Adhikari, Mohamed (ed.). *Burdened by Race: Coloured Identities in Southern Africa*. Cape Town: Cape Town University Press.

———. 2011. *The Long Shadow of the British Empire: The Ongoing Legacies of Race and Class*. New York: Palgrave Macmillan.

Moore, Dennison. 1995. *Origins and Development of Racial Ideology in Trinidad: The Black View of the East Indian*. Tunapuna, Trinidad and Tobago: Chakra.

Moreno Navarro, Isidoro. 1973. *Los Cuadros del Mestizaje Americano: Estudio Antropológico del Mestizaje*. Madrid: Ediciones Jose Porrua Turanzas.

Moreton-Robinson, Aileen. 2006. "Whiteness Matters." *Australian Feminist Studies* 21 (50): 245–56.

Morimoto, Rosa (alias). 2009. Interviews with Lily Anne Yumi Welty, Ginowan, Okinawa, June 27; Kadena, Okinawa, September 27.

Morning, Ann. 2000. "Who Is Multiracial? Definitions and Decisions." *Sociological Imagination* 37 (4) : 209–29.

———. 2003. "New Faces, Old Faces: Counting the Multiracial Population Past and Present." In DeBose, Herman, and Loretta Winters (eds.). *New Faces in a Changing America: Multiracial Identity in the 21st Century*. Thousand Oaks, CA: Sage.

———. 2008. "Ethnic Classification in Global Perspective: A Cross-National Survey of the 2000 Census Round." *Population Research and Policy Review* 27 (2) :239–72.

———. 2011. *The Nature of Race: How Scientists Think and Teach about Human Difference*. Berkeley: University of California Press.

Münz, Rainer. 2003. "Ethnic Germans in Central and Eastern Europe and Their Return to Germany." In Münz, Rainer, and Rainer Ohlinger (eds.). *Diasporas and Ethnic Migrants: Germany, Israel and Russia in Comparative Perspective*. New York: Routledge.

Murphy-Shigematsu, Stephen. 2001. "Multiethnic Lives and Monoethnic Myths: American-Japanese Amerasians in Japan." In Williams-León, Teresa, and Cynthia L. Nakashima (eds.). *The Sum of Our Parts: Mixed Heritage Asian Americans*. Philadelphia: Temple University Press.

Murphy-Shigematsu, Stephen. 2002. *Amerajian no kodomotachi: shirarezaru mainoriti mondai [Amerasian Children: Understanding the Minority Problem]*. Translated by Sakai Sumiko. Tokyo: Shueisha Shinsho.

Muzondidya, James. 2001. "Sitting on the Fence or Walking a Tightrope? A Political History of the Coloured Community in Zimbabwe, 1945–1980." PhD thesis, University of Cape Town.

———. 2005. *Walking a Tightrope: Towards a Social History of the Coloured Community of Zimbabwe*. Trenton, NJ: Africa World Press.

———. 2009. "Race, Ethnicity and the Politics of Positioning: The Making of Coloured Identity in Colonial Zimbabwe 1890–1980." In Adhikari, Mohamed. *Burdened by Race: Coloured Identities in Southern Africa*. Cape Town: University of Cape Town Press.

Nagel, Joanne. 1994. "Constructing Ethnicity." *Social Problems* 41 (1): 152–76.

Nakashima, Cynthia. 1992. "The Invisible Monster: Creation and Denial of Mixed-Race People." In Root, Maria (ed.). *Racially Mixed People in America*. Thousand Oaks, CA: Sage.

Nascimento, Abdias do. 1979. *Mixture or Massacre? Essays on the Genocide of a Black People*. Translated by Elisa Larkin Nascimento. Buffalo: Puerto Rican Studies and Research Center, State University of New York at Buffalo.

Nazzari, Muriel. 1996. "Concubinage in Colonial Brazil: The Inequalities of Race, Class, and Gender." *Journal of the Family* 21 (2): 107–24.

Neves, Francisco. "Two Brazils." Brazzil, May 1, 2002. http://www.brazzil.com/content/view/2562/68/.

Nobles, Melissa. 2000. *Shades of Citizenship: Race and the Census in Modern Politics*. Stanford, CA: Stanford University Press.

Nogueira, Oracy. 1985 [1954]. "Preconceito Racial de Marca e Preconceito Racial de Origem (Sugestão de um Quadro de Refêrencia para a Interpretação do Material sobre Relações Raciais no Brasil)." In Nogueira, Oracy (ed.). *Tanto Preto Quanto Branco: Estudo de Relações Raciais*. São Paulo: T.A. Queiroz.

Noiri, Naomi. 2007. "Two Worlds: The Amerasian and the Okinawan." *Social Processes in Hawai'i* 42: 211–30.

Norington, Brad. 2010. "Free World Must Hold Firm on Cultural Identity in Battle Against Terrorism, John Howard Warns." *Australian*, September 29, 2010: 201.

Nugent, Amy. 2006. "Demography, National Myths, and Political Origins: Perceiving Official Multiculturalism in Québec." *Canadian Ethnic Studies* 38 (3): 21–36.

O'Donnell, Renate Bridenthal, and Nancy Reagin (eds.). 2005. *The Heimat Abroad: The Boundaries of Germanness*. Ann Arbor: University of Michigan Press.

Oehmke, Philipp. 2010. "Boah, Bruder, da ist Bierhoff dran" *Der Spiegel* 28. http://www.spiegel.de/spiegel/print/d-71558830.html.

Office of Management and Budget. 1997. "Revisions to the Standards for the Classification of Federal Data on Race and Ethnicity." In *Federal Register*. Washington, DC: OMB.

Office for National Statistics. 2008. "Recommended Questions for the 2009 Census Rehearsal and 2011 Census." London: ONS.

Okazawa-Rey, Margo. 1997. "Amerasian Children in GI Town: A Legacy of U.S. Militarism in South Korea." *Asian Journal of Women's Studies* 3 (1): 71–102.

Okpewho, Isodore. 1999. In Davies, Carole Boyce, and Ali A. Mazuri (eds.). *The African Diaspora: African Origins and New World Identities.* Bloomington: Indiana University Press.

Oliveira, Mariana. 2009. "Estatuto da Igualdade Racial divide movimento negro." G1.Globo.Com. 14.8.2009 http://g1.globo.com/Noticias/Brasil/0,,MUL1301785-5598,00-ESTATUTO+DA+IGUALDADE+RACIAL+DIVIDE+MOVIMENTO+N EGRO.html.

Omi, Michael, and Howard Winant. 1993. "On the Theoretical Concept of Race." In McCarthy, Cameron, and Warren Crichlow (eds.). *Race, Identity and Representation in Education.* New York: Routledge.

———. 1994. *Racial Formation in the United States: From the 1960s to the 1990s.* 2d ed. New York: Routledge.

Osava, Mario. 2005. "Rights—Brazil: Blacks Demand Adoption of Promised Measures." Inter-Press Service News Agency, November 16, 2005. http://www.ipsnews. net/news.asp?idnews=31051/.

Oshiro, Masayasu.1985. *Konketsuji: Okinawa kara no kokuhatsu kokuseki no nai seishun [Mixed Blood: Indicted Youth without Nationality from Okinawa].* Tokyo: Kokusai Johosha.

Owen, June. 2002. *Mixed Matches: Interracial Marriage in Australia.* Sydney: University of New South Wales Press.

Padilla, Mark B. et. al. 2008. *Love and Globalization: Transformations of Intimacy in the Contemporary World.* Vanderbilt, TN: Vanderbilt University Press.

Paisley, Fiona. 2004. "Discoveries Made in the Archives." In Macintyre, Stuart (ed.). *The Historian's Conscience: Australian Historians on the Ethics of History.* Melbourne: Melbourne University Press.

Paixão, Marcelo. 2004. "Waiting for the Sun: Account of the (Precarious) Social Situation of the African Descendant Population in Contemporary Brazil." *Journal of Black Studies* 34 (6): 743–65.

Paradies, Yin. 2006. "Beyond Black and White: Essentialism, Hybridity and Indigeneity." *Journal of Sociology* 42 (4): 355–67.

Park, Robert E. 1928. "Human Migration and the Marginal Man." *American Journal of Sociology* 33 (6): 88193.

Parker, David, and Miri Song (eds.). 2001. *Rethinking "Mixed Race."* London: Pluto Press.

Pastoureau, Michel. 2008. *Noir: Histoire d'une couleur.* Paris: Éditions du Seuil.

Pendakur, Krishna. 2005. "Visible Minorities in Canada's Workplaces: A Perspective on the 2017 Projection." *Vancouver Centre for Excellence* no. 05-11.

Perkins, Maureen. 2004. "Australian Mixed Race." *European Journal of Cultural Studies* 7 (2): 177–99.

——— (ed.). 2007. *Visibly Different: Face, Place and Race in Australia.* Bern: Peter Lang.

Peters, Russell. 2010. *Call Me Russell.* Toronto: DoubleDay Canada.

Peterson, Richard A., and N. Anand. 2004. "The Production of Culture Perspective." *Annual Review of Sociology* 30: 31–34.

Peterson, William. 1987. "Politics and the Measurement of Ethnicity." In Alonso, William, and Paul Starr (eds.). *The Politics of Numbers.* New York: Russell Sage.

Pierson, Donald. 1967. *Negroes in Brazil: A Study of Race Contact at Bahia.* Carbondale: Southern Illinois University Press.

Piggott, Gareth. 2006. "Simpson's Diversity Indices by Ward 1991 and 2001." DMAG Briefing 2006/2. London: Greater London Authority.

Piza, Edith, and Fúlvia Rosemberg. 1999. "Color in the Brazilian Census." *In Reichmann, Rebecca (ed.). Race Relations in Contemporary Brazil: From Indifference to Equality.* University Park: Pennsylvania State University Press.

Platt, Lucinda, Ludi Simpson, and Bola Akinwale. 2005. "Stability and Change in Ethnic Groups in England and Wales." *Population Trends* 121: 35–46.

Platts, John T. 1884. *A Dictionary of Urdu, Classical Hindi, and English.* London: W. H. Allen & Co.

Povinelli, Elizabeth. 2000. *The Cunning of Recognition: Indigenous Alterities and the Making of Australian Multiculturalism.* Durham, NC: Duke University Press.

Premdas, R. 1998. *Identity, ethnicity and culture in the Caribbean,* St Augustine, Trinidad: The University of the West Indies/St Augustine, School of Continuing Studies.

Puri, Shalini. 1997. "Race, Rape, and Representation: Indo-Caribbean Women and Cultural Nationalism." *Cultural Critique* 36 (spring).

Puri, Shalini. 2004. *The Caribbean Postcolonial Social Equality, Post-Nationalism and Cultural Hybridity.* New York: Palgrave.

Putnam, Robert. 2007. "E Pluribus Unum: Diversity and Community in the Twenty-first Century. 2006 Johan Skytte Prize Lecture. *Scandinavian Political Studies.* 30 (2): 37–174.

Pybus, Cassandra. 2001. *A Touch of the Tar: African Settlers in Colonial Australia and the Implications for Issues of Aboriginality.* London Papers in Australian Studies: No. 3. London: Menzies Centre for Australian Studies.

———. 2006. *Black Founders: The Unknown Story of Australia's First Black Settlers. Sydney:* University of New South Wales Press.

———. 2011. "'Tense and Tender ties': Reflections on Lives Recovered from the Intimate Frontier of Empire and Slavery." *Life Writing* 8 (1): 5–17.

Qadeer, Mohammed, and Sandeep Kumar. 2005. "Toronto's Ethnic Enclaves: Sites of Segregation or Communities of Choice?" http://ceris.metropolis.net/events/seminars/2005/May/Sandeep1.pdf (Accessed December 16, 2010).

Queiroz, Delcele Mascarenhas. 2003. "A Negro, Seu Acesso ao Ensino Superior e as Ações Afirmativas" In Bernardino, Joaze, and Daniela Galdino (eds.). *Levando a Raça a Sério: Ação Afirmativa e Universidade.* Rio de Janeiro: DP&A Editora.

"Racial Quotas in Brazil Require Browns Identify Themselves as Negro." 2012. http://nacaomestica.org/blog4/?p=5603.

"Racism against Multiracials in Brazil." 2006. http://www.nacaomestica.org/racism_against_mestizos.htm.

Rallu, Jean-Louis, Victor Piché, and Patrick Simon. 2004. "Démographie et Ethnicité: Une Relation Ambiguë." In Caselli, Graziella, Jacques Vallin, and Guillaume Wunsch (eds.). *Démographie: Analyse et Synthèse*. Paris: Institut National d'Etudes Démographiques.

Rana, Junaid. 2011. *Terrifying Muslims: Race and Labor in the South Asian Diaspora*. Durham, NC: Duke University Press.

Razack, Sherene. 2004. *Dark Threats and White Knights: The Somalia Affair, Peacekeeping and the New Imperialism*. Toronto: University of Toronto Press.

Reddock, Rhoda. 1994. "Douglarization and the Politics of Gender Relations in Contemporary Trinidad and Tobago: A Preliminary Analysis." *Contemporary Issues in Social Sciences*, 1 (1): 98-127.

———. 1998. "The Indentureship Experience: Indian Women in Trinidad and Tobago 1945-1917." In Jain, Shobhita, and Rhoda Reddock (eds.). *Women Plantation Workers: International Experiences 1845-1917*. Oxford: Berg.

———. 1999. "Jahaji Bhai:The Emergence of a Dougla Poetics in Trinidad and Tobago." *Identities: Global Studies in Culture and Power*, 5(4): 569-601.

———. 2007. "We are Becoming Each Other: Africans and South Asians in Trinidad and Tobago." Closing plenary address, Diasporic Counterpoint: Africans, Asians and The Americas conference, Northwestern University.

Rees, Phil. 2007. "Ethnic Population Projections: Review and Illustration of Issues." Paper presented to Cathie Marsh Centre for Census and Survey Research. http://www.ccsr.ac.uk/events/segint/workshops/documents/PhilReesEthnicPopulation-ProjectionsCCSRWorkshop.pdf.

Regis, Ferne Louanne. 2011. "The Dougla in Trinidad's Consciousness." *History in Action* 1, 2 (1).

Reichmann, Rebecca. 1995. "Brazil's Denial of Race." *North American Congress on Latin America Report on the Americas* (28) 6: 35-42.

Republic of Zambia Statistics. 2000. "Population Composition and Size" (ch 3) In *Housing and Population Main Zambia Census Report, Vol. 10*.

Reynolds, Henry. 2005. *Nowhere People: How International Race Thinking Shaped Australia's Identity*. Ringwood: Penguin.

Ripley, William Z. 1899. *The Races of Europe*. New York: Appleton.

Risério, Antonio. 2007. *A Utopia Brasileira e Os Movimentos Negros*. São Paulo: Editora 34 Ltda.

Roberson, James E. 2003. "Uchinâ Pop: Place and Identity in Contemporary Okinawan Popular Music." In Hein, Laura and Mark Selden (eds.). *Islands of Discontent: Okinawan Responses to Japanese and American Power*. Lanham, MD: Rowman & Littlefield.

Roberts, David, and Minelle Mahtani. 2010. "Neoliberalizing Race, Racing Neoliberalism: Representations of Immigration in the Globe and Mail." *Antipode* 42 (2): 248-57.

Rochetti, Ricardo. 2004. "Not as Easy as Black and White: The Implications of the University of Rio de Janeiro's Quota-Based Admissions Policy on Affirmative

Action." *Vanderbilt Journal of Transnational Law* 37.1423, November 2004. http://
web.lexis-nexis.com/universe/document?_m=5eb66ec1eb9aff3afe64e92c41a1df
60_docnum=3&wchp=dGLbVlb-zSkVb&_md5=0571753367a1a6b0fa45e7841eee1
b9b/.

Rock, David, and Stefan Wolff (eds.). 2002. *Coming Home to Germany? The Integration
of Ethnic Germans from Central and Eastern Europe in the Federal Republic.* New
York: Berghahn.

Rockquemore, Kerry Ann, and David L. Brunsma. 2007. *Beyond Black: Biracial Identity in America.* Lanham, MD: Rowman & Littlefield.

Rockquemore, Kerry Ann, David L. Brunsma, and Daniel Delgado. 2009. "Racing to
Theory or Retheorizing Race? Understanding the Struggle to Build a Multiracial
Identity Theory." *Journal of Social Issues* 65 (1): 13–34.

Rodriguez, Lynette. 2007. "But Who Are You Really?" In Maureen Perkins (ed., *Visibly
Different: Face, Place and Race in Australia.* Bern: Peter Lang.

Roediger, David. 1991. *The Wages of Whiteness.* London: Verso.

Rohter, Larry. 2003. "Racial Quotas in Brazil Touch Off Fierce Debate," *New York
Times*, April 5, 2003. http://www.nytimes.com/2003/04/05/international/
Americas/05BRAZ.html/.

Roll, Heike. 2003. "Young Ethnic German Immigrants from the Former Soviet Union:
German Language Proficiency and Its Impact on Integration." In Münz, Rainer, and
Rainer Ohlinger (eds.). *Diasporas and Ethnic Migrants: Germany, Israel and Russia
in Comparative Perspective.* New York: Routledge.

Roman, Meredith. 2005. "Another Kind of Freedom: The Soviet Experiment with Antiracism and Its Image as a Raceless Society, 1928–1936." PhD dissertation, Michigan
State University.

Root, Maria P. P. (ed.). 1996. *The Multiracial Experience: Racial Borders as the New
Frontier.* Newbury Park, CA: Sage.

Ropp, Steven Masami. 1997. "Do Multiracial Subjects Really Challenge Race?: Mixed-
Race Asians in the United States and the Caribbean." *Amerasia Journal* 23 (1): 1–16.

———. 2002. "The Nikkei Negotiation of Minority/Majority Dynamics in Peru and
the U.S." In Hirabayashi, Lane Ryo, Akemi Kikumura-Yano, and James Hirabayashi
(eds.). *New Worlds, New Lives: Globalization and People of Japanese Descent in the
Americas and from Latin America in Japan.* Palo Alto, CA: Stanford University
Press.

Roth, Wendy. 2010. "Racial Mismatch: The Divergence between Form and Function in
Data for Monitoring Racial Discrimination of Hispanics." *Social Science Quarterly*
91 (5): 1288–311.

———. 2012. *Race Migrations: Latinos and the Cultural Transformation of Race.* Stanford, CA: Stanford University Press.

Russell, Lynette. 2002. *A Little Bird Told Me.* Sydney: Allen & Unwin.

Russell-Wood, Anthony John R. 1972. "Colonial Brazil." In Cohen, David. W., and Jack
P. Greene *Neither Slave nor Free: The Freemen of African Descent in the Slave Societies of the New World.* Baltimore, MD: Johns Hopkins University Press.

———. 1982. *The Black Man in Slavery and Freedom in Colonial Brazil*. London: Palgrave Macmillan.

Saada, Emmanuelle. 2002. "Race and Sociological Reason in the Republic: Inquiries on the Métis in the French Empire (1908–37)." *International Sociology* 17 (3, September): 361–91.

Sampson, Richard. 1956. *They Came to Northern Rhodesia*. Lusaka: Government Printer.

Sanders, Ruth H. 2010. *German: Biography of a Language*. New York: Oxford University Press.

Sansone, Livio. 2003. *Blackness Without Ethnicity: Constructing Race in Brazil*. New York: Palgrave Macmillan.

Santos, Sales Augusto dos. 2003. "Ação Afirmativa e Mérito Individual." In Santos, Renato Emerson dos, and Fátima Lobato (eds.). *Ações Afirmativas: Políticas Contra as Desigualdades Raciais*. Rio de Janeiro: DP&A Editora.

Sarrazin, Thilo. 2010. *Deutschland schafft sich ab [Germany Abolishes Itself]*. München: DVA.

Sawada, Miki. 1980. *Haha to ko no kizuna : Erizabesu sandāsu hōmu no sanjūnen [The Bond between a Mother and Child: Thirty Years of the Elizabeth Saunders Home]*. Kyoto: PHP Kenkyujo.

Schäfer-Wünsche, Elisabeth. 2005. "On Becoming German: Politics of Membership in Germany." In Spickard, Paul (ed.). *Race and Nation: Ethnic Systems in the Modern World*. New York: Routledge.

Schwarz, Patrick (ed.). 2010. *Die Sarrazin Debatte: Eine Provokation—und die Antworten*. Hamburg: Edel.

Schwartzman, Luisa Farah. 2008. "Who Are the Blacks." *Cahiers de la Recherche sur l'Éducation et les Savoirs* 7 (October): 27–48.

———. 2009. "Seeing Like Citizens: Unofficial Understandings of Official Racial Categories in a Brazilian University." *Journal of Latin American Studies* 41 (2): 221–50.

Scottish Government and General Register Office for Scotland. 2008. *Scotland's New Official Ethnicity Classification*. Edinburgh: GRO(S).

Segal, Daniel. 1993 "'Race' and 'Colour' in Pre-Independence Trinidad and Tobago." In Yelvington, Kevin (ed.). *Trinidad Ethnicity*. Knoxville: University of Tennesee Press.

Senocak, Zafer. 2000. *Atlas of a Tropical Germany*. Translated by Leslie A. Adelson. Lincoln: University of Nebraska Press.

Serlis, Julia Katherine. 2004. "Islands and Autochthons: Coloureds, Space and Belonging in Rhodesia and Zimbabwe (Part 1)." *Journal of Social Archaeology* 4: 405–26.

Sheffer, Gabriel. 2006. *Diaspora Politics at Home and Abroad*. Cambridge: Cambridge University Press.

Silva, Nelson do Valle. 1985. "Updating the Cost of Not Being White in Brazil." In Fontaine, Pierre-Michel (ed.). *Race, Class, and Power in Brazil*. Los Angeles: UCLA Center for African American Studies.

Silva, Nelson do Valle, and Carlos A. Hasenbalg. 1999. "Race and Educational Opportunity in Brazil." In Reichmann, Rebecca (ed.). *Race Relations in Contemporary*

Brazil: From Indifference to Equality. University Park: Pennsylvania State University Press.

Simon, David J., James R. Pletcher, and Brian V. Seigel. 2008. *Historical Dictionary of Zambia.* 3d ed. Lanham, MD: Scarecrow Press.

Simpson, Anthony. 2003. *"Half-London" in Zambia: Contested Identities in a Catholic Mission School.* Edinburgh: Edinburgh University Press.

Sinha, Mrinalini. 1995. *Colonial Masculinity: The "Manly Englishman" and the "Effeminate Bengali" in the Late Nineteenth Century.* Manchester: Manchester University Press.

Siss, Ahyas. 2003. *Afro-Brasileiros, Cotas, e Ação Afirmativa: Razões Históricas.* Rio de Janeiro: Quartet Editora.

Skidmore, Thomas A. 1974. *Black into White: Race and Nationality in Brazilian Thought.* New York: Oxford University Press.

———. 1992–93. "Race Relations in Brazil." *Camões Center Quarterly* 4 (3–4): 49–57.

Skrbis, Zlatko. 2008. "Transnational Families: Theorising Migration, Emotions, and Belonging." *Journal of Intercultural Studies* 29 (3): 231–46.

Slezkine, Yuri. 1994. "The USSR as a Communal Apartment, or How a Socialist State Promoted Ethnic Particularism." *Slavic Review* 53: 414–52.

Small, Stephen. 2001. "Colour, Culture and Class: Interrogating Interracial Marriage and People of Mixed Racial Descent in the USA." In Parker, David, and Miri Song (eds.). *Rethinking "Mixed Race."* London: Pluto Press.

Smithers, Gregory. 2009. *Science, Sexuality, and Race in the United States and Australia, 1780s–1890s.* New York: Routledge.

Snelson, Peter D. 1974. *Educational Development in Northern Rhodesia 1883–1945.* Ndola: National Education Department.

Snow, Nancy. 2003. *Information War: American Propaganda, Free Speech and Opinion Control Since 9/11.* Toronto: Hushion House.

Song, Miri. 2003. *Choosing Ethnic Identity.* Cambridge: Polity Press.

———. 2009. "Is Intermarriage a Good Indicator of Integration?" *Journal of Ethnic and Migration Studies* 35 (2): 331–48.

———. 2010. "Is There a Mixed Race Group in Britain?" *Critical Social Policy* 30 (3): 337–58.

———. 2012. "Making Sense of Mixture: States and the Classification of 'Mixed' People." *Ethnic and Racial Studies* 35 (4): 565–73.

Song, Miri, and Peter Aspinall. 2012. "Is Racial Mismatch a Problem for Young 'Mixed Race' People in Britain? The Findings of Qualitative Research." *Ethnicities.* Published online February 17, 2012. DOI: 10.1177/1468796811434912.

Song, Miri, and Ferhana Hashem. 2010. "What Does 'White' Mean? Interpreting the Choice of 'Race' by Mixed Race Young People in Britain." *Sociological Perspectives* 53 (2): 287–92.

Spencer, Rainier. 2006. *Challenging Multiracial Identity.* Boulder, CO, and London: Lynne Rienner.

———. 2009. "Mixed-Race Chic." *Chronicle of Higher Education.* http://chronicle.com/article/Mixed-Race-Chic/44266/.

——. 2011. *Reproducing Race: The Paradox of Generation Mix*. Boulder, CO: Lynne Rienner.

Spickard, Paul R. 1989. *Mixed Blood: Intermarriage and Ethnic Identity in Twentieth Century America*. Madison: University of Wisconsin Press.

——. 2004. "Illogic of American Racial Categories." In Ifekwungiwe, Jayne O. (ed.). *Mixed Race Studies: A Reader*. London: Routledge.

——. 2007. *Almost All Aliens: Immigration, Race, and Colonialism in American History and Identity*. New York: Routledge.

——. 2010. *Japanese Americans: The Formation and Transformation of an Ethnic Group*. Revised ed. New Brunswick, NJ: Rutgers University Press.

Spickard, Paul R., Rowena Fong, and Patricia L. Ewalt. 1995. "Undermining the Very Basis of Racism—Its Categories." *Social Work*, 40.5: 581–84.

Spickard, Paul R., and Daniel G. Reginald. 2004. *Racial Thinking In The United States: Uncompleted Independence*. South Bend, Indiana: University of Notre Dame Press.

Spoonley, Paul. 1993. *Racism and Ethnicity*. Auckland: Oxford University Press.

Squires, Catherine R. 2007. *Dispatches from the Color Line: The Press and Multiracial America*. New York: SUNY Press.

Stalin, I. V. 1936. "Marxism and the National Question." In *Marxism and the National and Colonial Question*. London: Lawrence and Wishart.

Statistics Canada. 2006. "Canada's Ethnocultural Mosaic." *Statistics Canada*, Catalogue No. 97-562-X.

St. Bernard, Godfrey. 1999. "Ethnicity and Attitudes Towards Inter-Racial Marriages in Multiracial Society: The Case of Trinidad and Tobago." In Premdas, Ralph (ed.). *Identity, Ethnicity and Culture in the Caribbean*. St. Augustine: School of Continuing Studies, UWI.

Stepan, Nancy Leys. 1991. *The Hour of Eugenics: Race, Gender and Nation in Latin America*. Ithaca, NY: Cornell University Press.

Stern, Alexandra Minna. 2003. "From Mestizophilia to Biotypology: Racialization and Science in Mexico, 1920–1960." In Appelbaum, Nancy, Anne Macpherson, and Karin Alejandra Rosemblatt (eds.). *Race and Nation in Modern Latin America*. Chapel Hill: University of North Carolina Press.

Stoler, Ann Laura. 1997. "Sexual Affronts and Racial Frontiers: European identities and the cultural politics of exclusion in colonial Southeast Asia." In Cooper, Frederick, and Ann Laura Stoler (eds.). *Tensions of Empire: Colonial Cultures in a Bourgeois World*. Berkeley: University of California Press.

——. 2002. *Carnal Knowledge and Imperial Power: Race and the Intimate in Colonial Rule*. Berkeley: University of California Press.

——. 2009. *Along the Archival Grain: Epistemic Anxieties and Colonial Common Sense*. Princeton, NJ: Princeton University Press.

Stopford, Annie. 2007. "Mothering Children of African Descent: Hopes, Fears and Strategies of White Birth Mothers." *Journal of Pan African Studies* 2 (1): 62–76.

Stratton, Jon. 1998. *Race Daze: Australia in Identity Crisis*. Annandale, NSW: Pluto Press.

Stratton, Jon, and Ien Ang. 1998. "Multicultural Imagined Communities: Cultural Difference and National Identity in Australia and the USA." In Bennet, David (ed.). *Multicultural States: Rethinking Difference and Identity*. London: Routledge.

Stuckert, Robert P. 1976. "'Race' Mixture: The Black Ancestry of White Americans." In Hammond, Peter B. (ed.). *Physical Anthropology and Archaeology: Introductory Readings*. New York: Macmillan.

Sturdevant, Saundra Pollock, and Brenda Stoltzfus. 1992. *Let the Good Times Roll: Prostitution and the U.S. Military in Asia*. New York: New Press.

Sue, Christina. 2009. "An Assessment of the Latin Americanization Thesis." *Ethnic and Racial Studies* 32: 1058–70.

———. 2010. "Racial Ideologies, Racial-Group Boundaries, and Racial Identity in Veracruz, Mexico." *Latin American and Caribbean Ethnic Studies* 5: 273–99.

Suny, Ronald Grigor. 1993. *The Revenge of the Past: Nationalism, Revolution, and the Collapse of the Soviet Union*. Stanford, CA: Stanford University Press.

Susokolov, A. A. 1987. *Mezhnatsional'nye braki v SSSR*. Moscow.

Sussman, Nan. 2000. "The Dynamic Nature of Cultural Identity throughout Cultural Transitions: Why Home Is Not So Sweet." *Personality and Social Psychology Review* 4 : 355–73.

Suzuki, Marika. 2003. "Empowering Minority Youth in Japan: The Challenge of the AmerAsian School in Okinawa." MA thesis, Stanford University.

Szerszynski, Bronislaw, and John Urry. 2006. "Visuality, Mobility and the Sosmopolitan: Inhabiting the World from Afar." *British Journal of Sociology* 57 (1): 11–131.

Taylor, Charles. 1992. *Multiculturalism and "The Politics of Recognition."* Princeton, NJ: Princeton University Press.

Taylor, Leanne. 2008. "Looking North: Exploring Multiracial Experiences in Canadian Context." In Renn, Kristen A., and Paul Shang (eds.). *Biracial and Multiracial College Students: Theory, Research, and Best Practices in Student Affairs*. Jossey-Bass: New Directions for Student Services series. 123: 83-91.

———. 2009. *Re-imagining Mixed Race: Explorations of Multiracial Discourse in Canada*. PhD dissertation, Department of Education, York University.

Taylor, Leanne, Carl E. James, and Roger Saul. 2007. "Who Belongs: Exploring Race and Racialization in Canada." In Johnson, Genevieve Fuji, and Randy Enomoto (eds.). *Race, Racialization and Antiracism in Canada and Beyond*. Toronto: University of Toronto Press.

Teillet, Jean. 2008. *The Métis of the Northwest: Towards A Definition of a Rights-Bearing Community for a Mobile People*. Master'ss of Law thesis, University of Toronto.

Telles, Edward E. 2004. *Race in Another America: The Significance of Skin Color in Brazil*. Princeton, New Jersey, NJ: Princeton University Press.

Telles, Edward E., and Christina Sue. 2009. "Race Mixture: Boundary Crossing in Comparative Perspective." *Annual Review of Sociology* 35: 129–46.

Thomas, Derrick. 2005. "I Am Canadian." *Canadian Social Trends*, 11-008. Ottawa: Statistics Canada.

Thompson, Debra. 2011. "Making (Mixed-)Race: Census Politics and the Emergence of Multiracial Multiculturalism in the United States, Great Britain and Canada." *Ethnic and Racial Studies* 35 8: 1409–26.

Thompson, Victor. 2006. "A New Take on an Old Idea: Do We Need Multiracial Studies?" *Du Bois Review* 3 (2): 437–47.

Tilbury, Farida. 2007. "The Retreat from Multiculturalism: The Australian Wxperience." Pluralism, Inclusion and Citizenship. 3rd Global Conference, Interdisciplinary.net, Salzburg. November 2007. http://www.inter-disciplinary.net/ati/diversity/pluralism/pl3/Tilburyper cent20paper.pdf (accessed March 9, 2012).

———. 2000a. "'What's in a Name?': Wadjula Self-Labelling and the Process of Reconciliation." *Culture, Law and Colonialism 1* (2): 73–88.

———. 2000b. "'Some of my Best Friends are Maori but...': Cross-Ethnic Friendships, Ethnic Identity and Attitudes to Race Relations in New Zealand." PhD Tthesis, Department of Sociology and Social Policy, Victoria University of Wellington.

Tilley, Virginia Q. 2005. "Mestizaje and the 'Ethnicization' of Race in Latin America." In Spickard, Paul (ed.). *Race and Nation: Race and Nation: Ethnic Systems in the Modern World.*. New York and London: Routledge.

Tishkov, V. A. 2003. *Rekviem po etnosu. Issledovaniia po sotsial'noi i kul'turnoi antropologii.* Moscow: Nauka.

Tizard, Barbara, and Ann Phoenix. 2002. *Black, White or Mixed Race?: Race and Racisms in the Lives of Young People of Mixed Parentage.* New York: Routledge.

Tomlinson, John. 1999. *Globalization and Culture.* Chicago: University of Chicago Press.

Topilin, A. V. 1995. "Mezhnatsional'nye sem'i i migratsiia: voprosy vzaimovlianiia," *Sotsiologiia natsional'nykh otnosheniia "Sotsis"* 7.

Trinidad and Tobago Central Statistical Office. 2011. Population and Housing Census. http://www.cso.gov.tt/sites/default/files/content/images/census/TRINIDAD%20AND%20TOBAGO%202011%20Demographic%20Report.pdf.

Trinidad Registrar-General's Department. 1948. Census of the Colony of Trinidad and Tobago: April 9, 1946 (West Indian Census 1946).

Troen, S. Ilan, and Klaus J. Bade (eds.). 1994. *Returning Home: Immigration and Absorption into Their Homelands of Germans and Jews from the Former Soviet Union.* Beer Sheva, Israel: Hubert H. Humphrey Institute for Social Ecology, Ben Gurion University of the Negev.

Tsolidis, Georgina. 1993. "Re-envisioning Multiculturalism within a Feminist Framework." *Journal of Intercultural Studies* 14: 1–13.

Tsuda, Takeyuki. 2004. "No Place to Call Home: Japanese Brazilians Discover They Are Foreigners in the Country of Their Ancestors." *Natural History* 113 (3): 50–55.

Twine, France Winddance. 1997. *Racism in a Racial Democracy: The Maintenance of White Supremacy in Brazil.* New Brunswick, NJ: Rutgers University Press.

Uberoi, Varun. 2009. "Multiculturalism and the Canadian Charter of Rights and Freedoms." *Political Studies* 57: 805–27.

Udo-Ekpo, Lawrence T. 1999. *The Africans in Australia: Expectations and Shattered Dreams*. Henley Beach, SA: Seaview Press.

UK Census. 2011. http://www.ons.gov.uk/ons/guide-method/census/2011/index.html.

Urías Horcasitas, Beatriz. 2007. *Historias Secretas del Racismo en México, 1920-1950*. México D.F.: Tusquets Editores México.

US Census Bureau. 1918. "Negro Population 1790-1915." Washington, DC: Government Printing Office.

Valverde, Kieu-Linh Caroline. 1992. "From Dust to Gold: The Vietnamese Amerasian Experience." In Root, Maria P. P. (ed.). *Racially Mixed People in America*. Newbury Park, CA: Sage.

Van Imhoff, Evert, and Gijs Beets. 2004. "A Demographic History of the Indo-Dutch Population, 1930-2001." *Journal of Population Research* 21 (1): 47–72.

Vasconcelos, José. 1925. *La Raza Cósmica*. Baltimore: John Hopkins University Press.

Vaughn, Bobby.2001. "Race and Nation: A Study of Blackness in Mexico." Thesis, Department of Anthropology, Stanford University.

Vertovec, Steve. 2007a. "Super-diversity and Its Implications." *Ethnic and Racial Studies* 29 (6): 1024–54.

———. 2007b. *New Complexities of Cohesion in Britain. Super-diversity, Transnationalism and Civil-Integration*. London: Commission on Integration and Cohesion.

Villardi, Raquel. 2004. "Acesso à Universiadade por Meio de Ações Afirmativas: Estudo da Situação dos Estudantes com Matrícula em 2003 e 2004 (Junho)." UERJ (Universidadedo Estado do Rio de Janeiro) Report.

Villarreal, Andrés. 2010. "Stratification by Skin Color in Contemporary Mexico." *American Sociological Review* 75: 652–78.

Vos Iz Neias? 2012. "Toulouse—A Look at the Victims of French Attacks." http://www.vosizneias.com/103180/2012/03/19/toulouse-a-look-at-the-victims-of-french-attacks.

Von Baeyer, Jakob. 2007. "King of Multi-Culti." *Maclean's Magazine*, June 17, 2007: 56–57. http://www.macleans.ca/culture/entertainment/article.jsp?content=20070618_106213_106213

Von Koppenfels, Amanda Klekowski. "*Aussiedler* Migration to Germany: Questioning the Importance of Citizenship for Integration." Paper prepared for the Alumni Conference, "Common Global Responsibility." Working Group 4: Migration Issues. Washington, DC, November 6–9, 2003.

Walcott, Rinaldo. 2003a. "What Is the Future of multiculturalism? Ask the Experts." http://aries.oise.utoronto.ca/experts/october2003/rwalcott300.mov (Aaccessed 2 December 2, 2010).

———. 2003b. *Black Like Who? Writing Black Canada*. 2d rev. ed. Toronto: Insomniac Press.

Waldinger, Roger, and Fitzgerald, David. 2004. "Transnationalism in Question." *American Journal of Sociology*, 109 (5): 1177–95.

Walker, Ranginui. 1987. *Nga Tau Tohetohe: Years of Anger*. Auckland: Penguin.

———. 1990. *Ka Whawhai Tonu Matou: Struggle Without End.* Auckland: Penguin.

———. 1995. *"Maori Sovereignty."* In Melbourne, Hineani (ed.). *Maori Sovereignty: The Maori Perspective.* Auckland: Hodder Moa Beckett.

Wang, Wendy. 2012. "The Rise of Intermarriage Rates, Characteristics Vary by Race and Gender." Pew Research Center. http://www.pewsocialtrends.org/2012/02/16/the-rise-of-intermarriage/.

Ward, Colleen. 2006. "Acculturation, Identity and Adaptation in Dual Heritage Adolescents." *International Journal of Intercultural Relations* 30 (2): 243–59.

Waters, Mary. 1990. *Ethnic Options: Choosing Identities in America.* Berkeley: University of California Press.

Weber, Max. 1978. *Economy and Society.* Berkeley: University of California Press.

Weitz, Eric D. 2002. "Racial Politics without the Concept of Race: Reevaluating Soviet Ethnic and National Purges." *Slavic Review* 61 (1): 1–29.

Wells, Diane E. 2000. "'Between the Difference': Trinidadian Women's Collective Action." Doctoral dissertation, New York University.

Wetherall, William. 2007. "Japan's Nationality Law: A Primer and Guide to Other articles." http://members.jcom.home.ne.jp/yosha/yr/nationality/Nationality_primer.html (accessed January 14, 2011).

Whitehead, Neil. 2005. "Black Read as Red: Ethnic Transgression and Hybridity in Northeastern South America and the Caribbean." In Restall, Matthew (ed.). *African-Native Relations in Colonial Latin America.* Albuquerque: University of Albuquerque/New Mexico Press.

Whitten, Norman E., and Arlene Torres. 1998. *Blackness in Latin American and the Caribbean: Eastern South America and the Caribbean.* Bloomington: Indiana University Press.

Wilkinson, Myler, and David Stouck. 2002. "The Epic Moment: An Interview with Wayde Compton." *West Coast Line* 36.2 (38): 130–45. http://www.westcoastline.ca/sample_texts/compton_int.pdf.

Williams-León, Teresa K. 1989. "International Amerasians: Third Culture Afroasian and Eurasian Americans in Japan." MA thesis, Department of Asian American Studies, University of California at Los Angeles.

———. 1991. "Marriage between Japanese Women and U.S. Servicemen since World War II." *Amerasia Journal* 17 (1): 135–54.

Williams-León, Teresa K., and Cynthia L. Nakashima (eds.). 2001. *The Sum of Our Parts: Mixed Heritage Asian Americans.* Philadelphia: Temple University Press.

Wilson, Terry P. 1992. "Blood Quantum: Native American Mixed Bloods." In Root, Maria P. P. (ed.). *Racially Mixed People in America.* Newbury Park, CA: Sage.

Wilson, William Julius. 1980. *The Declining Significance of Race.* Chicago: University of Chicago Press.

Windle, Joel. 2008. "The Racialisation of African Youth in Australia." *Social Identities: Journal for the Study of Race, Nation and Culture* 14 (5): 553–66.

Winters, Loretta I., and Herman L. DeBose. 2002. *New Faces in a Changing America: Multiracial Identity in the 21st Century.* Newbury Park, CA: Sage.

Wood, Charles H., and José Alberto Magno de Carvalho. 1998. *The Demography of Inequality in Brazil*. New York: Cambridge University Press.

Wood, Patricia K., and Liette Gilbert. 2005. "Multiculturalism in Canada: Accidental Discourse, Alternative Vision, Urban Practice." *International Journal of Urban and Regional Research* 29 (3): 679–91.

Woollacott, Angela. 2006. *Gender and Empire*. Basingstoke: Palgrave Macmillan.

Yokota, Ryan Masaaki. 2013. "Okinawan Nationalism(s): From Independence to Autonomy, and from Diasporic Nationalism to Indigenousness." PhD dissertation, Department of History, University of Chicago.

Yonetani, Julia. 2003. "Future 'Assets,' but at What Price? The Okinawa Initiative Debate." In Hein, Laura, and Mark Selden (eds.). *Islands of Discontent: Okinawan Responses to Japanese and American Power*. Lanham, MD: Rowman & Littlefield.

Young, Robert. 1996. *Colonial Desire: Hybridity in Theory, Culture, and Race*. Oxford and New York: Routledge.

Yuh, Ji-Yeon. 2002. *Beyond the Shadow of Camptown: Korean Military Brides in America*. New York: New York University Press.

Zack, Naomi. 1994. *Race and Mixed Race*. Philadelphia: Temple University Press.

———. 1995. *American Mixed Race: The Culture of Microdiversity*. Lanham, MD: Rowman & Littlefield.

PETER J. ASPINALL is Reader in Population Health, University of Kent. His publications include around sixty journal articles on ethnicity terminology and classifications, ethnic identity, and ethnicity and health, in journals such as *Journal of Epidemiology & Community Health, Social Policy and Society,* and *Anthropology Today,* and a forthcoming book (with Miri Song), *Mixed Race Identities.*

G. REGINALD DANIEL is Professor of Sociology at the University of California, Santa Barbara. He has numerous publications that explore this topic, including the books *More Than Black? Multiracial Identity and the New Racial Order* (2002), *Race and Multiraciality in Brazil and the United States: Converging Paths?* (2006), and *Machado de Assis: Multiracial Identity and the Brazilian Novelist* (2012). In 2012, Daniel received the Loving Prize at the Fifth Annual Mixed Roots Film and Literary Festival in Los Angeles.

ADRIENNE L. EDGAR is Associate Professor of Modern Russian and Central Asian History at the University of California, Santa Barbara. After receiving her PhD from the University of California, Berkeley in 1999, she spent one year at Harvard University on a postdoctoral fellowship before taking up her current position. Edgar is the author of *Tribal Nation: The Making of Soviet Turkmenistan* (2004) and a number of articles on ethnicity, nationality, and gender in Soviet Central Asia.

FARIDA FOZDAR is Professor in Anthropology and Sociology at the University of Western Australia. She completed her PhD in New Zealand in 2000, and after holding a position at Murdoch University she took up an Australian Research Council Future Fellowship at UWA in 2011, exploring national, transnational, and postnational identities. She is the coauthor of *Race and Ethnic Relations* (2008).

REBECCA C. KING-O'RIAIN is Senior Lecturer at the National University of Ireland Maynooth. She has published articles in *Ethnicities, Sociology Compass, Journal of Asian American Studies,* and *Amerasia Journal.* Her book *Pure Beauty* (2006) examines the use of blood-quantum rules in Japanese American beauty pageants and she is currently working on a manuscript on *The Globalization of Love: Love in Mixed Couples and Families on Skype.*

DANI KWAN-LAFOND is a PhD student in sociology at York University in Toronto. She is also a social worker and the cofounder of two registered Canadian charities who works with marginalized and at-risk youth, new Canadians, and children with social or behavioral challenges. She is also the recipient of the 2011 Vanier Canada Graduate Scholarship, one of the most prestigious doctoral scholarships in Canada.

ANDREW MICHAEL LEE received his master's degree in social and political thought from York University in 2007. He went on to obtain a second master's degree in sociology from the University of California, Santa Barbara, in 2009. Before graduate school, Andrew worked for several years as both an urban and rural educator in the US as well as abroad.

MINELLE MAHTANI is Associate Professor in the Department of Human Geography and the Program in Journalism at University of Toronto Scarborough. She is the winner of the 2012 Glenda Laws Award from the Association of American Geographers. She is a former television journalist with CBC TV news and is outgoing President of the Association for Canadian Studies. She identifies as a woman of mixed race of Indian and Iranian descent.

JULIETTE BRIDGETTE MILNER-THORNTON is Adjunct Research Fellow in the School of Humanities, Griffith University, Queensland, Australia. She is the author of *The Long Shadow of the British Empire* (2012) and has published several chapters and journal articles on the subject. She holds a PhD from Griffith University and identifies as an African Australian woman of mixed British, Italian, Lithuanian Jewish, Zambian, and Zulu descent.

ANN MORNING is Associate Professor of Sociology at New York University and a faculty affiliate of New York University Abu Dhabi. Her doctoral thesis was a corecipient of the American Sociological Association's 2005 Dissertation Award and was published in book form in 2011 as *The Nature of Race: How Scientists Think and Teach about Human Difference*. Morning was the recipient of a 2008–2009 Fulbright research award to visit the University of Milan-Bicocca, and she has consulted on racial statistics for the European Commission in Brussels and the US Census Bureau. She holds her PhD in sociology from Princeton University.

MIRIAM NANDI is Assistant Professor of English and Margarete von Wrangell Fellow at the University of Freiburg, Germany. She holds a PhD in English from the University of Freiburg, and attended the School of Criticism and Theory at Cornell University in 2005. She is the author of two books, *M/Other India/s: The Role and Representation of Social Injustice in Indian-English and Vernacular Indian Fiction* (2007) and *Gayatri Spivak: An Intercultural Introduction* (2009).

MAUREEN PERKINS is a Fellow of the Royal Historical Society and teaches History and Anthropology at Curtin University, Western Australia. She is the author of *Visions of the Future* (1996) and *The Reform of Time* (2001) and the editor of *Visibly Different* (2007) and *Locating Life Stories: Beyond East-West Binaries in (Auto)Biographical Studies* (2012). She also coedits a Peter Lang series, Studies in Asia-Pacific "Mixed Race."

RHODA REDDOCK is Professor of Gender, Social Change, and Development and Deputy Principal of the University of the West Indies

(UWI), St. Augustine Campus in Trinidad and Tobago. Her books include *Women, Labour and Politics in Trinidad and Tobago (1995)*, a CHOICE Outstanding Academic Book for 1995; *Caribbean Sociology: Introductory Readings* (2000); and more recently, *Sex, Power and Taboo* (2009). She is an Associate Editor of the *Journal of Latin American* and *Caribbean Ethnic Studies*.

STEPHEN SMALL is Associate Professor of African American Studies at the University of California, Berkeley, and Extraordinary Professor of History at the University of Amsterdam. He is the coauthor of *New Perspectives on Slavery and Colonialism in the Caribbean* (2012).

MIRI SONG is Professor of Sociology at the University of Kent. Her books include *Helping Out: Children's Labor in Ethnic Businesses* (1999), *Choosing Ethnic Identity* (2003), and the forthcoming *Mixed Race Identities* (with Peter Aspinall). She is currently working on a Leverhume Trust–funded project on mixed-race people and the intergenerational transmission of identities and practices.

PAUL SPICKARD is Professor of History and Affiliate Professor of Black Studies, Asian American Studies, East Asian Studies, Religious Studies, and the Center for Middle Eastern Studies at the University of California, Santa Barbara. He is author or editor of sixteen books and seventy-odd articles on race, migration, and related topics in the United States, the Pacific, Northeast Asia, and Europe, including *Multiple Identities* (2013), *Almost All Aliens* (2007), *Race and Nation* (2005), and *Mixed Blood* (1989).

CHRISTINA A. SUE is Assistant Professor of Sociology at the University of Colorado, Boulder. Her research focuses on race, ethnicity, and immigration, with a regional emphasis on the United States and Latin America. Her work has been published in the *American Journal of Sociology*, the *Annual Review of Sociology*, and *Ethnic and Racial Studies*, and she is author of *Land of the Cosmic Race* (2013).

LEANNE TAYLOR is Assistant Professor in the Faculty of Education at Brock University, Canada. Her research and publications address multiracial identity, social justice and equity education, and the experiences of marginalized and "at risk" youth in secondary and postsecondary schools.

SAULE K. UALIYEVA is Senior Lecturer of Sociology in the Department of Philosophy and Human Problems at D. Sericbaev East-Kazakhstan State Technical University. She received her PhD in Historical Sciences in Kazakhstan. Ualiyeva is the author of *Family-Marriage Relations of Population in Kazakhstan on Border Centuries (2012)* and coauthor of *Reproductive Aims of East Kazakhstan Women (2006).*

LILY ANNE YUMI WELTY is currently a Ford Foundation Fellow and a visiting scholar at the UCLA Asian American Studies Center. She grew up in Oxnard, California, speaking Japanese and English in a mixed-race household and now holds a PhD in history from the University of California, Santa Barbara.